Studies Series in International Financial, Economic, and Technology Law
(Vol 6 2003–2004: Successor to the Yearbook of
International Financial and Economic Law)

GLOBAL FINANCIAL SECTOR DEVELOPMENT

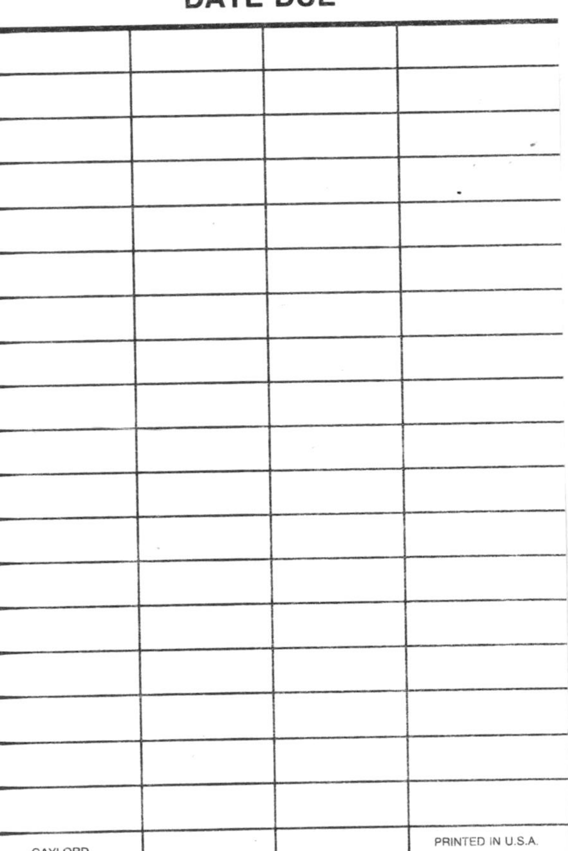

Studies in International Financial, Economic, and Technology Law

Global Financial Sector Development

General Editors

Joseph J. Norton and Christos Hadjiemmanuil

BIICL
British Institute of International and Comparative Law
www.biicl.org
The SMU Dedman School of Law
www.law.smu.edu
The London Forum for International Economic Law and Development
www.lforum.org

Published and Distributed by
The British Institute of International and Comparative Law
Charles Clore House, 17 Russell Square, London WC1B 5JP
www.biicl.org

Published and distributed by
The British Institute of International and Comparative Law

British Library Cataloguing in Publication Data
A catalogue record of this book is available from the British Library

ISBN 0–903067–94–3
ISSN 1748–2763

Typeset by Cambrian Typesetters
Camberley, Surrey
Printed in Great Britain by Biddles Ltd
King's Lynn

TABLE OF CONTENTS

SPONSORING ORGANIZATIONS

The SMU Dedman School of Law

The SMU Dedman Law School (founded in 1917), began distinguishing itself, over sixty ago, when the late Dean Storey established the first 'Legal Center' in the US. The Law School has an international alumni base of over 2000 in 65 countries, many of whom are now at the highest levels of government, legal practice and business in their respective countries; has a library rich in international and comparative legal resources; has a faculty, over half of which are actively involved in international studies; has a curriculum long-known for its strengths in business, commercial, taxation and international law and in dispute resolution; has a well-functioning visiting scholar and SJD program designed to promote postgraduate international legal scholarship; has a program for the regular visits of distinguished law professors from around the world; has the most comprehensive array of student-edited and faculty supervised international publications of any law school (ie, with *The International Lawyer*, *Law and Business Review of the Americas*, this *Studies* series and a book series on IEDL); has two active, student international moot dispute resolution programs; has a high quality summer program at University College, Oxford; has academic institutional links that can offer students a semester abroad or postgraduate legal studies abroad; has one of the most developed and longstanding LLM programs for international students; has Faculty regularly studying and lecturing abroad and being involved with law reform efforts world-wide; hosts, on a regular basis, high-level international conferences, research seminars, roundtables and distinguished lecture series; supports international institutes and foreign study programs involving faculty, students and external experts, that promote academic programs and studies concerning cutting-edge commercial, financial, information technology law and law reform issues, conducts, on a regular basis, co-sponsored international conferences in Europe, Africa, Asia and Latin America; and is based in a local community containing a highly sophisticated legal profession, one of the largest arrays of multinational firms in the country, one of the major high tech bases, and one of the major international airports and transportation networks in the country. The Law School is a constituent institution of the London Forum.

The British Institute for International and Comparative Law (BIICL)

BIICL is an academic institution established in 1895 specializing in all aspects of international law. One of its distinctive features is its genuinely international membership and approach. Membership is worldwide and open to all without restrictions on nationality. The Institute is best suited to bring together judges and practitioners, academic lawyers and civil servants and to provide both authoritative legal analysis and practical experience. The Institute has, in addition to its other international and comparative law interests, a particular interest in legal issues involving global financial regulatory and transactions matters. Recent leaders of the Institute have included Lord Denning; the late Professor Kenneth R Simmonds; Lady Fox, QC; and Professor Mads Andenas; Professor Gillian Triggs is the current Director of the Institute. The British Institute publishes legal research in a variety of forms to meet the various needs of its members and the wider legal community. It publishes the *International and Comparative Law Quarterly*—one of the leading journals in its field, the *ICLQ* is published four times a year—a fortnightly *Bulletin of Legal Developments*; and a strong backlist of books, whilst continuing to publish new titles on a wide variety of subjects, including financial law, International Economic Development Law (IEDL), human rights, environmental law and the law of war. In addition, the Institute maintains active research centres/programmes in investment treaty law, WTO, dispute resolution, data protection, tort law, company law, competition law, and French law. During the course of a given year, BIICL conducts more than 150 high-quality lectures, conferences, seminars, discussion groups and works shops. BIICL is also a constituent member of the London Forum for International Economic Law and Development.

THE ASIAN INSTITUTE OF INTERNATIONAL FINANCIAL LAW (AIIFL)

The Asian Institute of International Financial Law (AIIFL), established in the University of Hong Kong Faculty of Law in 1999, is becoming a leading Asian academic centre in international financial law.

The University of Hong Kong was established in 1911, and the Department of Law, in 1969, with four teachers and forty students. On 1 July 1984, the Faculty of Law was formed, comprising the Department of Law and the Department of Professional Legal Education. The Department of Law has responsibility for the Bachelor of Laws (LLB) and undergraduate mixed degree programmes. The Department of Professional Legal Education teaches the Postgraduate Certificate in Laws (PCLL), a one-year course of more practice-oriented instruction. Both departments contribute to postgraduate coursework programmes including a variety of LLM and Postgraduate Diploma programmes. The Faculty of Law also offers the research degrees of MPhil, PhD and SJD. At present, the Faculty has about 50 staff and roughly 1,300 students.

Corporate and financial law has been one of the Faculty's key areas for a number of years. To support development of this area, HKU awarded the Faculty a Distinguished Visiting Professor post, which was taken up in

1999–2000 by Professor Joseph J Norton, Sir John Lubbock Professor of Banking Law at the University of London and James L Walsh Distinguished Faculty Fellow in Financial Institutions Law and Professor of Law at Southern Methodist University. During his tenure at HKU, Professor Norton assisted in the establishment of both AIIFL and the LLM in Corporate and Financial Law (LLM(CFL)) Programme. Professor Norton and Mr. Say Goo became the founding Directors of AIIFL in July 1999. Mr. Charles Booth was appointed Director of AIIFL in December 2000.

AIIFL serves as the umbrella for the research and academic activities of its Fellows (drawn from the Faculty of Law and HKU generally) and its Honorary and Visiting Fellows (academics and professionals from outside HKU). The research areas of AIIFL Fellows cover many aspects of the ongoing reform of corporate and financial law throughout the region, with a continuing focus in the areas of financial institutions and markets, WTO/corporate and commercial law, and corporate insolvency and restructuring. Our Fellows have continued to lead in cutting edge WTO-related corporate and financial law research, supported through a seed grant from the University of Hong Kong Foundation for Educational Development and Research, and a generous endowment from the University. The endowment has enabled the Faculty of Law to establish the University-wide East Asian International Economic Law and Policy (EAIEL) Programme, with which AIIFL works closely. Reflecting upon the Faculty's successes in the area of international economic law, the WTO selected HKU to serve as the partner for its annual Asia-Pacific Regional Trade Policy Course in December 2003.

In addition to close collaboration with the EAIEL Programme, AIIFL and the LLM (CFL) Programme work together closely, reflecting the interrelationship between teaching and research in corporate and financial law. The LLM (CFL) Programme currently has over 40 students from around the world and offers approximately 10 courses each year, with the Paul Hastings Visiting Professorship in Corporate & Financial Law supporting teaching in the Programme. AIIFL is a constituent institution of the London Forum.

The Mandela Institute

The Law School at the University of the Witwatersrand (Wits) launched the Mandela Institute in 2000, to honour the contribution of Mr Mandela to the transformation of South Africa. The calibre of the Law School's Graduates has led to many describing the School as South Africa's premier law school.

As a centre of excellence, the Mandela Institute undertakes research, develops policy and offers advanced teaching in global law—that is to say those areas of law that connect South Africa, and the developing world, to the global world economy. Subjects taught include competition law, intellectual property law, banking law, company law, telecommunications law, the development of appropriate regulatory regimes, and international arbitration.

The Mandela Institute is working to create an enhanced legal framework and skills base as a contribution to the wider goal of economic growth. To this end, it has established formal links with the London Forum and has appointed Professor Norton to its board. The Mandela Institute was represented at the first general meeting hosted by the London Forum in 2003 and will host a seminar in South Africa in collaboration with the London Forum and the Asian Institute of International Financial Law in August 2004. As a further illustration of the collaboration between the institutions, Professor Itzikowitz has taught in the Emerging Markets and Legal Aspects of International Finance courses at Queen Mary College and Professor Norton and Associate Professor Arner of the Asian Financial Institute have taught in the Banking and Financial Markets Masters course offered under the aegis of the Mandela Institute.

The Mandela Institute comprises professors and research fellows in the School of Law, specifically recruited to endow the Institute with lawyers of the highest standing. To enhance further its expertise, a number of endowed Chairs and research fellowships have, or are being established.

Alumni and committed supporters of the Law School include President of the Constitutional Court, Justice Arthur Chaskalson; Justice Richard Goldstone, Chancellor of the University of the Witwatersrand, former Justice of the Constitutional Court and former prosecutor of the United Nations War Tribunals of the former Yugoslavia and Rwanda and Mr Len Berkowitz former legal adviser to the Governor of the Bank of England, now consultant to Freshfields.

The Mandela Institute has been involved in a number of law reform projects in sub-Saharan Africa and attracts many students from other parts of the African continent. The Mandela Institute seeks to educate a new generation of skilled South African and African commercial lawyers—black and white. The Mandela Institute is a constituent institution of the London Forum.

London Forum for International Economic Law and Development

The London Forum was established in the Autumn of 2001 for the primary purpose of providing a vehicle for the global promotion of developing country scholarship by developing country scholars in the IEDL area. The primary activities venue is London and its primary administrative base is at the SMU Dedman School of Law in Dallas, Texas. This being said, it was and is intended that the Forum operates, on a global basis, as an 'umbrella' vehicle supporting, but relying on a group of Constituent Institutions and Collaborating Institutions. The Constituent Institutions, which will also provide activities venues, comprise the following:

- SMU Dedman School of Law and its Law Institute of the Americas and Institute of International Financial Commercial and Technology Law;
- International Financial Law Unit of the Centre for Commercial Law Studies, Queen Mary, University of London;
- British Institute of International and Commercial Law;
- Mandela Institute of Wits University (Johannesburg);
- Asian Institute of International Financial Law of the University of Hong Kong; and
- René-Jean Dupuy Center for Law and Development (Bibliothéque Alexandria)

Selection of Collaborating Institutions members are made by the General Meeting of the Constituent Parties. At the Constituent Parties Meeting in May 2005, five institutions were voted as Collaborating Institutions; Shanghai University of Finance and Economics (SUFE), the Law Faculty of the External University of Columbia (Bogotá), the Law Faculty of the Catholic University of Brasilia, the Islamic Law Program at Harvard University, and the University of the West Indies Law Faculty and Business School. In addition, authorization was given Prof Norton and Dr Shams to undertake discussion with institutions in Singapore, Latin America, Indonesia, Africa and the United States, and to report back to the Constituent Parties.

The Forum is dedicated to the legacy of the late Dr Ibrahim Shihata, long-standing General Counsel of the World Bank and one of the leading scholars and policymakers in international economic law and development in the twentieth century. Dr Shihata was a steadfast advocate of the role of law and legal institutions in international economic relations and institutions and of the value of interconnecting IFIs and the Academy in meaningful forms of collaboration.

The London Forum is committed to the mission of pooling, fostering and developing specialized scholarship in the area of international economic development law as it relates to Developing Countries, by providing a range of coordinated venues based in London and at the other Constituent and Collaborating Institutions, for meaningful research, debate and capacity-building as well as for academic, curricular and programme development and publication opportunities accessible to young and promising scholars and policy-makers from the Developing World. The forum also undertakes specific capacity-building training programmes.

SMU Institute of International Financial, Commercial and Technology law

The Institute was established within Southern Methodist University, Dallas, Texas, in 1982 (originally the SMU Institute of International Banking and

Finance) and based at the SMU Dedman School of Law, the Institute serves as an interdisciplinary forum for research, publications, conferences and research seminars in the international finance area, with input from SMU's Law School, Political Science and Economic Departments and the Edwin L Cox School of Business. The Institute conducts several major international conferences, is actively involved in economic law reform projects in relation to emerging economies. Finally, the Institute regularly produces books and other scholarly articles and papers.

SMU International Law Review Association

The Association comprises more than 50 students of the School of law of the Southern Methodist University who assist with the editorial work involved in the publication of this series, *The International Lawyer, Law and Business Review of the Americas*.

EDITORIAL AND SUBMISSION POLICIES

This *Studies Series* is a refereed, annual publication produced jointly by the British Institute of International and Comparative Law and the Southern Methodist University Dedman School of Law and its Institute of International Finance, Commercial and Technology Law in cooperation with the London Forum for International Economic Law and Development, the Asian Institute of International Finance (AIIFL), University of Hong Kong and the Mandela Institute, Wits University, Johannesburg. The *Study Series* relies on the guidance of a distinguished Advisory Board, on the ongoing editorial cooperation of a Board of Editors and on the editorial staff of the SMU International Law Review Association.

The *Study Series* addresses selective legal, financial and economic issues in the area of international financial law, covering both public and private law dimensions and encompassing national, regional and international perspectives. Each year the volume will center around a coherent topic. The next (2005) volume (vol No 7) which is already in the editorial process, will center around comparative corporate governance issues post-Enron. The following (vol No 8) to come out will address Islamic finance issues.

COMMENTARY

CONFRONTING FINANCIAL SECTOR PROBLEMS: A PERSPECTIVE FROM AFRICA*

ADESEGUN A AKIN-OLUGBADE**

CHAPTER OUTLINE

I. INTRODUCTION: THE IMPORTANCE OF FINANCIAL SECTOR DEVELOPMENT FOR REDUCING POVERTY

Thirteen years ago, as part of my SJD Thesis, I examined how four banks had to devise innovative structures to circumvent national banking laws which created barriers to region-wide banking in anglophone and francophone West African Countries. As in-house lawyer in the African Development Bank Group, I have been involved in and closely followed the liquidation of two banking institutions with extensive banking networks in Africa, namely, the former BCCI and the Meridien BIAO. The African Development Bank Group lost deposits that it held in the BCCI, and the Bank was a shareholder of Meridien BIAO. The topic of this regional seminar is therefore of keen interest.

* Keynote Luncheon Speech by Adesegun A Akin-Olugbade, at the *Regional Seminar on Comparative Experiences in Confronting Banking Sector Problems in the Sub-Saharan Africa Region* held on 14–15 Oct 2003 in Cape Town, South Africa. The author acknowledges the assistance provided by Mr Seward Cooper, Mr Michael Mahmoud, and Mr Duncan Kiara in preparing this keynote speech. The author also expresses his appreciation to Ernesto Aguirre and his colleagues of the Global Bank Insolvency Initiative for the kind gesture of inviting a development bank lawyer, from the most disadvantaged region in the world, to have lunch in Cape Town with such a distinguished group.
** General Counsel, African Development Bank, Tunis SJD (Harvard).

The overarching vision of the African Development Bank Group[1] highlights development and poverty reduction in Africa as its 'primordial challenge'. The financial sector has a direct role in the promotion of development and the reduction of poverty. As such, the Bank has to be increasingly involved in supporting financial sector development on the continent.

My topic is about how to confront financial sector problems in Africa. Introducing the IMF's assessment of the key issues concerning the design and application of orderly and effective insolvency procedures, my colleague, François Gianviti, general counsel of the IMF, stated: 'reform in this area can play a major role in strengthening a country's economic and financial system'. Indeed, as theoretical and empirical research has shown, economic growth requires the mobilization of long-term savings, which can then be channelled into productive investment. The financial sector's contribution to development and poverty reduction comes through various channels. First, the financial sector provides the facilities and instruments for mobilizing savings and allocating them to consumption and investment purposes. Secondly, a well-developed financial system enhances the effectiveness of macroeconomic policies to promote price stability, which is conducive to development and high economic performance. Thirdly, the financial sector is the main channel through which countries enter the mainstream of globalization and reap benefits via increased trade, capital flows, and access to technological know-how. Fourthly, as provider of financial services that are used as inputs in other productive sectors, the financial sector helps to economize services that are used as inputs in other productive sectors. The financial sector further helps to economize on the cost of transactions and enables economic agents to pool, price, and exchange, risks, thereby increasing the efficiency of use of resources, and the rate of growth. Fifthly, the financial sector has the ability to contribute directly to poverty reduction through intermediaries, such as Microfinance Institutions (MFIs) and the informal financial sector, that provide savings and credit facilities to the Micro, Small and Medium Enterprises (MSMEs), the poor, and the disadvantaged in the rural sector.

I will first give a brief outline of the historical development of the financial markets in Africa and the recent reforms in this sector, as they occurred in many African countries. These reforms and the problems that were and still are connected with them shall be discussed in a next step. In a final section, I will then make some suggestions about how these problems can be confronted and what a future strategy for the African financial sector should look like.

[1] The African Development Bank Group is made up of the African Development Bank (ADB), the African Development Fund (ADF) and the Nigeria Trust Fund (NTF).

As would be expected, given my professional background and experience, the proposed future strategy will emphasize the role of law and legal structures, as well as the contribution that international institutions like the African Development Bank Group should make in this regard.

II. FINANCIAL SECTOR PROBLEMS IN AFRICA

Let me now begin by briefly illustrating the core difficulties that face financial institutions and markets in Africa.

A. Historical Development of the Financial Sector in Africa

In the last century, in the period from independence to about the late 1980s, many African countries, in common with other developing countries, regarded the financial sector as a conduit for financing government deficits, and as an instrument for directing credit to 'priority' sectors of the economy, often at controlled and subsidized interest rates. At the same time, financial institutions were created in the public sector, and some private financial institutions were nationalized to enable government to 'promote development'. These institutions were likely to be driven by political rather than economic objectives, which led to a misallocation of credit, and a concomitant high proportion of non-performing loans. For instance, before Malawi began to reform its financial sector, there were only two banks in operation, namely the National Bank of Malawi and the Commercial Bank of Malawi, both State-owned. Preferential lending rates were granted for agriculture, and banks were required to direct 50 per cent of their credit to the sector. Other loans tended to be concentrated in a few conglomerates, which also accounted for most of the deposits. These features of the financial sector were not unique to Malawi. Overall, the financial systems in Africa developed all the hallmarks of financial repression, including widespread government dominance in ownership, management and procedures of financial institutions, corruption, directed credits, negative real interest rates, and poor investment decisions. Additionally, many African countries suffered from deficient financial infrastructure including weak supervisory and regulatory frameworks, the absence of clearly defined and enforceable property and contractual rights, and lack of human intellectual capacity. As a result, the financial sector failed to become a dynamic instrument of development.

Most governments' perception of the role of the financial sector in development began to change in the light of various crises in the financial sector that occurred as a result of these policies. Efforts to resolve these crises have been accompanied by very high costs, like in Mauritania, where five banks were recapitalized at a cost of 15 per cent of GDP, or in Nigeria and Kenya, where several banks also became severely financially distressed.

B. Reforms in the Financial Sector

African countries thus started to adopt more market-oriented policies gradually, and initiate reforms of their financial systems to ensure efficient implementation of their former policies. A common element underlying all the reform programs has been the adoption of a market-based approach that includes financial liberalization. The reforms were largely conceived within the framework of structural adjustment programs supported by the IMF and the World Bank that were generally devised and proposed by the staffs of the IFIs and lacked national ownership. Initially, the emphasis of the reforms was on restoring macroeconomic stability, principally by reducing fiscal deficits and their financing by the banking system. These reforms were gradually expanded to include granting central banks more autonomy in the conduct of monetary policy, liberalizing interest rates, and gradually eliminating administrative allocation of credits. Other elements of the reforms implemented in the more recent past have comprised the introduction of indirect monetary policy instruments, restructuring and recapitalization of weak and insolvent banks, and improving infrastructures, including bank supervision and accounting and auditing practices.

C. Evaluation of the Reforms

On the one hand, these reforms have led to a perceptible reduction of financial repression and African countries have also made substantial progress in the area of monetary policy operations, and in liberalizing the external sector. Prudential lending and capital adequacy guidelines have been introduced, banks re-capitalized and restructured, non-bank financial institutions and stock markets established in many countries, and some progress made in strengthening banking supervision and adopting prudential regulations. On the other hand, most countries in Africa have, despite reforms, not advanced in the degree of financial intermediation. Some of the most important causes of the slow uptake of the reforms are:

- *Failure to Increase Saving Rates and to Mobilize Savings*

The financial sector reforms failed to substantially increase the level of domestic savings. For instance, the ratio of savings to GDP in Malawi was reported to be at a mere 0.7 per cent of GDP in 1998.[2] The same rate in

[2] See Rosalind Mowatt *Prospects for Financial Sector Reform in the Context of Regional Integration in* SADC 22 (2001), available at <http://www.acp-eu-trade.org/documents/ 108_mowatt_prospects.pdf>.

Mozambique stood at 1.7 per cent.[3] The average rate of gross domestic savings in Africa declined from 27.1 per cent of GDP during 1975–84 to 17.4 per cent during 1996–2000. Although a number of African countries deepened their financial markets by establishing stock markets during the 1990s, these markets remain generally small in size, with very few listed companies and low market capitalization. They are also characterized by high transaction costs, low liquidity, inadequate or inappropriate market regulations, and lack of or inadequate transparency.

- *Failure to Address the Access to Financial Services by the Informal Sector*

The reforms have also failed to address how to significantly improve the access of the economically active poor, women, micro-entrepreneurs and small enterprises, to credit and other financial services facilities. This gap was partly filled by the informal sector, which has responded positively to the financial services needs of the poor, such as savings mobilization and credit and money transfer that exist especially in the rural areas. In Nigeria, for example, the informal sector is reputed to control as much as 70 per cent of the Nigerian Economy. However, most informal financial institutions generally have a limited capital base and little access to borrower funds. Their operations are generally limited to specific localities and communities, are short-term in nature, and consumption-oriented. Their linkages with the formal sector also remain weak, and the financial flows between the formal and informal markets continue to be negligible. Even among informal financial institutions, there are few or no direct linkages. The vast needs of micro and small enterprises remain unmet, as they draw on informal lenders who tend to be either expensive or too small and unreliable as a source of finance. Furthermore, the existence of such institutions reflects high costs of monitoring and high associated risks of lending faced by the formal banking sector.

- *Financial Sector Leakages, Capital Flight and Corrupt Practices*

Financial sector deregulation and liberalization, without proper or adequate institutional safeguards, have encouraged capital flight. The president of the Institute of Chartered Accountants of Nigeria (ICAN), at a recent meeting with H.E. President Olusegun Obasanjo, disclosed that Nigerians currently lodge a huge US$170 billion in foreign banks, and that 62 Nigerians had abandoned over GBP100 million in a London bank. Fortunately, their names were not disclosed, or we would have had our e-mail systems jammed by unsolicited proposals from alleged relatives offering fantastic financial rewards. Although the objective of the disclosure was

[3] ibid at 24.

to illustrate that Nigerians have more than enough resources in foreign banks to cancel the country's external debts (estimated to be between US$25–30 billion), the information is also indicative of the lack of confidence by Nigerians in the country's financial system.

III. CONCLUSION: HOW TO CONFRONT FINANCIAL SECTOR PROBLEMS IN AFRICA

The past experiences of the financial sector in Africa may provide some useful guidance for drafting a future strategy to improve this sector and to confront the existing problems that were just briefly pointed out. In designing this strategy, we have taken cognizance of the advice from Joseph E Stiglitz, Winner of the Nobel Prize in Economics, that: 'Financial Sector Deregulation and the excessive reliance on capital adequacy standards has been misguided and destabilizing: what is required is a broader, less ideological approach to regulation, adapted to the capacities and circumstances of each country.'[4]

Distinguished readers:

- A well-functioning financial system is an ongoing process and its development requires a long-term view and commitment by country authorities and their development partners;
- A stable and sound macro-economy, including price stability and sustainable domestic and external debt situation, is important for establishing an environment conducive to investment. Financial sector reforms must, therefore, be preceded by a comprehensive assessment of the fragility of the financial system and measures to address weaknesses in this regard;
- Country ownership of the program, which can be defined as joint identification of program goals, consensus within the government leadership, up-front actions to demonstrate conviction, and broad outreach regarding reform goals within the body politic, is an essential precondition for the successful implementation of the reforms and must be explicitly promoted. Financial sector reforms will not be effective unless all constituent bodies, ie governments, central banks, other local stakeholders and international development partners are brought on board and buy into the reforms;
- Financial sector reform is not sustainable unless it is comprehensive and penetrates down to the institutional level, and only if technical assistance components are a part of the reform package;
- Good governance, including the rule of law, ability to enforce contracts,

[4] Joseph E Stiglitz, Globalization and its Discontents 238 (2003).

good public sector management, the fight against corruption and an efficient, independent, impartial judiciary are essential for promoting efficient financial systems;
- Emphasis must be put on introducing competition and appropriate infrastructure, especially effective prudential regulations; and
- Informal financial institutions could be made to serve efficiently a larger section of the population which has little access to formal financial intermediaries.

The future strategy needs to address four interrelated 'gaps' or inadequacies of past reforms.

First, there is the 'financial intermediation' gap, emanating from the fact that the financial systems in many African countries are still narrow and shallow, as well as fragile and vulnerable, and the financial environment is not quite stable. In the absence of corrective measures, this often leads to financial disintermediation.[5]

Secondly, there is the 'development' gap in that the system lacks the institutions and instruments necessary to promote an increase in savings, especially mobilized financial saving, and meet the needs for long-term investment finance. Most African countries remain vulnerable to price and supply shocks due to the restricted focus on a few core sectors. Kenya, for example, which has a broad range of successful enterprises in the agricultural, industrial and tertiary sectors, is an exception, rather than the norm.

Thirdly, there is the 'poverty reduction' gap in that the needs for financial services by Micro, Small and Medium Enterprises (MSMEs), the poor, and the disadvantaged, especially in the rural areas, remain largely unmet. Renowned Peruvian economist Hernando de Soto offers one model that could help developing countries overcome the poverty reduction gap. De Soto's guiding principle is the idea of 'animating' dead capital.[6] According to De Soto the problem in developing countries is not that they lack wealth, but that they lack the institutional framework to recognize and trade capital. De Soto calls wealth in these countries 'dead capital', meaning that its real value cannot be unlocked by the poor because it is not recognized by a formal legal system and thus can only be traded or sold within a narrow, informal community. To illustrate his approach, De Soto for instance describes how it took his researchers 32 months to get legal approval from 11 agencies to open a manufacturing facility in Peru and contrasts this situ-

[5] In my Doctorate Thesis, I examined how four banking institutions had to devise innovative structures to circumvent national banking laws which created barriers to region-wide banking in francophone and anglophone West African Countries.

[6] Hernando De Soto, The Mystery of Capital: Why Capitalism Triumphs in the West and Fails Everywhere Else (2000).

ation with the fact that the same task took merely three hours in Tampa, Florida. An important step toward reform would thus be to reduce legal barriers that keep entrepreneurs 'extralegal', or outside of a country's formal economic system.

Fourthly, an 'implementation' gap arises, which is principally due to a lack of adequate human and technical capacity. The implementation and enforcement of reforms has been greatly compromised by the lack of adequate human intellectual capital within the enforcement authorities (central banks and in some instances the capital markets regulators), and payments systems remain weak. The situation has been compounded by the absence of political will at the national, sub-regional and regional levels.

A comprehensive strategy needs to be designed to fill all these gaps. Hence, it is important to strengthen the legal, regulatory and prudential systems as well as to develop monitoring systems that provide early warning of potential banking problems. Furthermore, mechanisms for the restructuring and recapitalization of weak banks and other non-bank financial institutions have to be developed, as it is the goal of the Global Bank Insolvency Initiative. Besides, it will be crucial to develop appropriate securities markets and financial institutions regulations to safeguard their viability and to promote the regional harmonization of banking and prudential criteria as well as establishing regional supervisory mechanisms. A model in the latter respect might be the banking commissions (Commissions Bancaire) that were established by the Member States of the CFA monetary unions in West Africa (BCEAO) and Central Africa (BEAC).

The African Development Bank has provided financing for reforms of the financial sector in African countries, and has been designated the lead institution for promoting the financial sector under the New Partnership for Africa's Development (NEPAD). The African Development Bank's Board of Directors recently adopted a new Financial Sector Development Policy, and the Bank's private sector development strategy increasingly emphasizes the provision of medium- and long-term lines of credit to banks and other financial intermediaries in its African Member States to finance SMEs. The African Development Bank will also cooperate with other regional institutions, notably the African Union (AU) and the United Nations Economic Commission for Africa (ECA) in strengthening financial sector reforms in Africa. In this regard, we welcome, in particular, the African Union's objective of establishing an African Central Bank.[7] We also welcome and provide support to other regional initiatives such as OHADA and the African Law Institute. The African Development Bank recently provided a grant of US$1 million to the Common Court of Justice and Arbitration (CCJA) of

[7] Treaty Establishing the African Union, Art 19 (The Financial Institutions).

OHADA to strengthen this institution established under the OHADA Treaty. The Bank, within the context of NEPAD, is finalizing a study on how to strengthen corporate governance in Africa.

The Global Bank Insolvency Initiative will be an important milestone on the roadmap to the improvement of the financial sector in Africa. The African Development Bank wishes the initiative the best of success.

ARTICLES—GENERAL

LEGAL DEVELOPMENT COOPERATION: CONDITIONS, PRINCIPLES, AND METHODS

CLAES SANDGREN

CHAPTER OUTLINE

This chapter is an attempt to paint a broad picture of legal development cooperation by emphasizing the particular requirements of legal assistance, its principles, and methods. This means that a considerable number of general, policy, and technical issues related to legal development cooperation are left aside.

I. BACKGROUND, DEVELOPMENT AND THEORY

A. *Background*

For the past two decades a very large number of countries in the South and in Eastern Europe have been undergoing a transformation. One-party States are becoming democracies and controlled economies are changing into market economies.[1] Assets held in collective ownership—whether State or other kinds of societal ownership—are being privatized. Many economies that formerly had high inflation rates are being stabilized. Closed economies are opening to the surrounding world and becoming internationalized. There is also a form of 'modernization' of many cultures; this modernity affects the values, lifestyle, and even identity of many people. This is a process that not only embraces countries in transition in the former Communist world, but also a number of countries in Africa, Asia, and Latin America which have suffered from economic stagnation and/or political totalitarianism. The process opens these countries' legal systems to far-reaching demands for reform.[2]

1. *Conclusions for legal development cooperation*

In countries in transition, it is the issue of a transformation that requires judicial reform on a broad front. For countries in the process of liberalization, eg India and some countries in Latin America, they are largely concerned with deregulation[3] and repromulgation of the body of laws governing the market economy. The legal system is influenced by this transformation and creates a basis for it, but can also be a means of keeping a tight rein on its negative effects. This also implies that the law will come into focus for a donor more clearly than in the past.

B. *Developments*

1. *Previous developments*

Judicial issues are not completely new in the context of development cooperation. The so-called Law & Development Movement, which had its beginning in the USA, was very popular in the 1960s, but only achieved limited results. The movement, which was based on a 'modernisation

[1] Janine S Hiller and Snjezana Puselj Drezga, *Progress and Challenges of Privatization: The Croatian Experience*, 17 U PA J INT'L ECON L 383, 383–4 (1996).

[2] See, eg Joseph J Norton FINANCIAL SECTOR REFORM IN EMERGING MARKETS (BIICL 2000).

[3] Barry R Weingast *The Economic Role of Political Institutions: Market-Preserving Federalism and Economic Development*, 11 JL ECON & ORG 1, 1–2 (1995).

theory' popular at the time, had an evolutionary approach to development, namely that it occurred (and ought to occur) in a chain of given steps which result in the same values and institutions as in the West. It also had ethnocentric features, that is, familiarity with and respect for the culture of the rule of law, and assumed that the social context in recipient countries was imperfect. In the third world, however, there was a widespread scepticism of the values and judicial models which were characteristic of legal development cooperation at the time. The movement thus passed into a twilight phase, which did not prevent many developing countries from cautiously trying to reform their legal systems on the basis of their own conditions and with some inspiration from industrialised countries. Though inputs for legal development cooperation have thus been in a backwater for some time, there was an upswing during the latter part of the 1980s and that continued to accelerate throughout the 1990s.[4]

2. *Legal development cooperation today*

Legal development cooperation continues to grow today, even if it is from a relatively low level. Vietnam is one example of these rapid developments. The United Nations Development Programme (UNDP) existed first (1992) and was soon followed by Sweden and France. Apparently, Vietnam now has 30 donors in the field of legal development cooperation, which implies that the country may be over-financed. In general, most donors and lenders are increasing their activities in the judicial sector. The World Bank[5] and UNDP, as well as the Inter-American Development Bank (IDB) and Asian Development Bank (AsDB), are very active and the International Monetary Fund (IMF) consistently maintains the need for judicial reforms. In the past, judicial projects were financed through grants, but in recent years an increasing number of countries have taken loans from international financial institutions for broad judicial programmes. Policy work is also underway in several places, eg in the United Kingdom's Department for International Development (DFID) and UNDP, even if the thinking is not nearly as sophisticated as policy development in the mature development cooperation sectors.

3. *Legal development cooperation in Eastern Europe*

Significant inputs are being made in Eastern Europe by the European Bank for Reconstruction and Development (EBRD), the European Union (EU),

[4] Matthew M Getter *Yugoslavia and the European Economic Community: Is a Merger Feasible?* 11 UPAJIBL 789 (1990).

[5] See Judicial Reform Program, *available at* <http://www4.worldbank.org/legal/leglr/> (last visited March 2003).

the World Bank and others. Here, legal development cooperation is closely related to EU expansion, since it requires far-reaching judicial reforms in the countries in transition which are now applying for membership. Recently, there has been an increase in consciousness of the sector 'justice and home affairs' and the major problems that can arise in the negotiations. Candidate countries have increasingly been forced to devise strategies for a reformation of the entire judicial sector. In other countries in transition, including Russia, and post-conflict countries, like the former Yugoslavia, the need also exists for judicial reform for which knowledge and resources are lacking.

4. *Conclusions for legal development cooperation*

Developments uniformly indicate a continued expansion of legal development cooperation. Thus, it is apposite for a donor to closely follow the rapid developments that are underway, and to systematically make use of the experiences that have been gained and the development of competence that is undertaken.

C. *Why Legal Development Cooperation?*

1. *The importance of the institutions*

Socio-economic research has shown how important institutions are for both economic growth and for poor and other vulnerable groups. One category of institutions is the judicial in a broad sense which includes both State and private organizations and the judicial framework Characteristic of the market economy are the institutions—regulations and organs that are taken for granted in the West—which control the activities of the actors on the market.

2. *The importance of the costs of transactions*

The cost of transactions is typically large in a developing country and, as a consequence, companies are reluctant to invest or to embark on risky transactions including long-term commitments. This restricts economic growth and necessitates a reliable and efficient judiciary, since it can reduce these costs.

3. *Globalization*

Globalization has many dimensions.[6] Here, it is natural to point out that a

[6] STANLEY, ARONOWITZ , HEATHER GAUTNEY, AND CLYDE W. BARROW. IMPLICATING EMPIRE:

country can use the law as an instrument to embrace the opportunities that globalization offers, eg to participate in international trade and attract investments. It can also counteract its negative effects. Not least, many of the losses of suzerainty of weaker States that may follow in the wake of globalization can be offset through agreements on the global plane, eg control of financial activity and organized crime. Human rights are also included in this pattern as an integrated part of trade treaties.

4. *'Modern Development Cooperation'*

Development cooperation that regards its task as creating *preconditions* for growth has good reasons to give priority to legal development cooperation. This can lead to an increased exchange of resources and development processes within many social sectors. A well-functioning judicial system also improves the outlook for development cooperation and for other efforts being made in many sectors.

5. *Perspective*

(a) *The concept of development.* Already, the concept of 'development' implies that a society has a minimal rule of law.[7] If people are arbitrarily imprisoned, if 'justice' can be bought, if the spread of crime is unchecked, if agreements are not honoured, or if sentences are not enforced, serious problems abound in society. The quality of a system of justice in a society consequently has a value of its own and it has a place in the concept of development.

(b) Poverty. Human rights and freedoms are of great importance for the poorest of the poor. Such an approach emphasises the individual's own capabilities and counteracts the reduction of the poor to victims or clients. It is also the poorest who are most affected by high crime rates. Projects that include education on rights, legal aid, mechanisms of appeal, crime

Globalization and Resistance in the 21st Century World Order (New York: Basic Books 2003); Neil Brenner, State/Space: A Reader (Blackwell Oxford 2003); Will Hutton, A Declaration of Interdependence: Why America Should Join the World (1st American edn, WW Norton, New York 2003); Jan Nederveen Pieterse, Globalization and Culture: Global Melange (Rowman & Littlefield, Lanham 2004); George Ritzer, The Globalization of Nothing (Pine Forge Press 2004). See also Heba Shams *Law in the Context of Gloablization: A Framework of Analysis*, 35 Int'l Law 1589–1626 (2001).

[7] Boniface Ahunwan, Globalization and Corporate Governance in Developing Countries: A Micro Analysis of Global Corporate Interconnection between Developing African Countries and Developed Countries. Series on International Law and Development (Transnational Publishers 2003); World Bank, Legal Vice Presidency. 'The World Bank Legal Review: Law and Justice for Development' (Kluwer Law International Washington, DC, The Hague; New York; World Bank 2003).

prevention, etc have a clear poverty profile. The judicial framework can also help the poor to organize themselves, eg in water-user co-operatives and similar types of organizations. A poverty approach also has positive effects on gender equality.

(c) *Human Rights*. Human rights are to an increasing degree a general starting point for development cooperation. Such a human rights perspective assumes that a system of justice exists which can guarantee respect for these rights, ie regulations governing rights and institutions which ensure that the rights can have substance and form the basis of the growth of a 'culture of human rights'.[8] The judicial system is particularly important for the poor, as they do not have recourse to other means of asserting their rights. Similarly, the judicial system, eg laws on procurement and transparency, can contribute to combating corruption; and laws, which entail a liberalization of the economy, can remove the grounds for certain forms of corruption.

(d) *Equality*. Sexually related violence ought to be dealt with in a judicial way, like rape and other assault, trade in women, prostitution, child marriage, female circumcision etc. Equality in the woman's economic position can also be reinforced via the judiciary, particularly through counteracting discrimination in the workplace and strengthening her right to own property, including rights of inheritance. Constitutional reforms can reinforce women's position in political life.

(e) *Environment*. Legislation to protect the environment has with time come to be a central feature of inputs to safeguard the environment.[9] It is not only concerned with ecological protection in a narrow sense—protection against pollution of air, water etc—but also the legislation that regulates agriculture, industry, and other environmentally sensitive commercial activities.

[8] KENNETH W HUNTER AND TIMOTHY C MACK, INTERNATIONAL RIGHTS AND RESPONSIBILITIES FOR THE FUTURE (Praeger 1996); ROBERT G PATMAN, UNIVERSAL HUMAN RIGHTS? (St Martin's Press, New York 2000); JOSEPH WRONKA, HUMAN RIGHTS AND SOCIAL POLICY IN THE 21ST CENTURY: A HISTORY OF THE IDEA OF HUMAN RIGHTS AND COMPARISON OF THE UNITED NATIONS UNIVERSAL DECLARATION OF HUMAN RIGHTS WITH UNITED STATES FEDERAL AND STATE CONSTITUTION.

[9] Elisabeth Mann Borgese et al, *Marine Issues: From a Scientific, Political and Legal Perspective* (KLUWER LAW INTERNATIONAL The Hague; New York 2002). Damien Geradin *The Liberalization of Electricity and Natural Gas in the European Union,* EUROPEAN MONOGRAPHS 27 (Kluwer Law International The Hague; London; Boston: 2001). Law of the Sea Institute Conference (29th Denpasar Indonesia 1995). Sustainable Development and Preservation of the Oceans: The Challenges of Unclos and Agenda 21. (Law of the Sea Institute, William S Richardson School of Law, University of Hawaii, 1997). Peter H Sand, Transnational Environmental Law: Lessons in Global Change. International Environmental Law and Policy Series; Vol 53 (Kluwer Law International, The Hague; Boston, 1999).

6. *Conclusions for legal development cooperation*

Judicial reform facilitates reforms in many sectors. In numerous cases, it is a prerequisite for better use of resources. Legal development cooperation can contribute to such judicial reform. It can also strengthen the judicial system in a country, which can be a great support for all those who seek to assert their rights, not least, those without property, minorities, and others who cannot maintain their rights in any other way.

D. *The Law, Democracy, and Economy*

1. *The law and democracy*

The law and democracy are related. Politics and the judiciary are thus not two separate spheres. Judicial reforms are political—human rights,[10] for instance, offer the individual greater safeguards against the State and in this way limit its powers. On the other hand, judicial reforms often are reliant on political reforms—independence for the courts, for example, requires adopting a political stance.

2. *The law and the economy*

Functioning markets and the rule of law also impact on one another in various ways. Judicial reforms are largely economic reforms. In many cases bankruptcy legislation, for instance, leads to the restructuring of (State) companies. Conversely, a number of judicial reforms require economic reforms, eg privatization, while at the same time privatization of State enterprises requires a well-functioning legal system. A close correspondence between judicial reforms and economic policies must exist. The law can play an important role for economic developments, at least if the Government has sound economic policies.

3. *Conclusions for legal development cooperation*

The three spheres of politics, economy, and law are closely related. Judicial

[10] Christina Biebesheimer, Francisco Mejâia, and Inter-American Development Bank. Justice Beyond Our Borders: Judicial Reforms for Latin America and the Caribbean. Washington, DC; distributed by the Johns Hopkins University Press for the Inter-American Development Bank 2000, Peter J Burnell *Democracy Assistance: International Cooperation for Democratization* [Democratization Studies, London; Portland, OR: F Cass, 2000. Ibrahim FI Shihata, Sabine Schlemmer-Schulte, and Keyong Dong. Liber Amicorum Ibrahim FI Shihata: International Finance and Development Law The Hague [The Netherlands]; (Kluwer Law International, Boston, 2001). Peter H Solomon, *Courts and Transition in Russia: The Challenge of Judicial Reform* (Westview Press, Boulder, Co 2000).

reforms that do not harmonize with political and economic reforms lose a degree of efficacy. Those who design legal development cooperation must keep an eye on the judicial interplay with politics and the economy; otherwise, there is a risk that the inputs become inoperative. There are also reasons to direct inputs to areas where the law has particular significance for economic developments.[11] An example is the private sector in general and capital markets. Within the sphere of the rule of law, one can point out that the law is central to combating discrimination and corruption.

II. JUDICIAL FUNCTIONS AND LEGAL DEVELOPMENT COOPERATION

A. *Attitudes to the Law*

1. *Instrumental approach*

To a large degree, the law is a tool of those in power; that is, it is primarily the tool of the political powers. This is how it functions in all types of regimes. In totalitarian regimes, the law tends only to be regarded as such a 'tool', and the regime as per definition good.

2. *Intrinsic value and counterbalance*

In democracies, the law also has an intrinsic value and can even provide a counterbalance that limits the authority of those in power in favour of certain basic values. Human rights fulfil such a function irrespective of whether they are laid down in the Constitution or backed up by international agreements. This means that not even a popularly elected Parliament can legitimately take decisions exactly as they wish. Among other things, minorities have the law to protect them.

3. *The framework of the market economy*

Law can also fulfil a third function; namely, to be a framework for economic transactions. Its aim is primarily to reduce the costs of trans-

[11] Council of Europe. Evaluation of Legislation: Proceedings of the Council of Europe's Legal Cooperation and Assistance Activities (2000–1) (Council of Europe Publishing, Strasbourg: 2001). Information and Legal Cooperation Concerning 'Information Society Services': Convention Ets No 180 Opened for Signature in Moscow on 4 Oct 2001 and Explanatory Report. Legal Issues. Strasbourg [Croton-on-Hudson, NY: Council of Europe Pub; Manhattan Pub Co, distributor], 2001 Council of Europe. European Committee on Legal Cooperation., and Council of Europe.

actions in a market economy. In such cases, regulations are typically neutral in relation to the State's interests. In the first place, in cases where they negotiate on such issues, economic actors should agree on the content of the regulations with the addition of certain protective mechanisms.

4. *Conclusions for legal development cooperation*

In all the countries now leaving one party rule and planned economies, there is a need also to deal with the instrumental approach to the law which prevailed previously. For political reasons, it is a painful process for politicians and others. The culture of the rule of law is also a restriction in the sense that the instrumental view is so deeply rooted even among lawyers that they find it difficult to liberate themselves from it. Such an approach blocks both legal development cooperation which would like to promote reforms of the rule of law, and deregulation which robs the State and State enterprises of a favoured position in economic life.

B. *General Functions*

1. *Functions*

The law fulfils a number functions in all societies. One can broadly distinguish between the following functions, each of which is carried out by one or more institutions:

- Creating the law (done by law-makers and precedence-setting bodies);
- Conflict resolution (courts, arbitration councils, extra-judicial organs, direct negotiations);
- Control of the implementation of rules and agreements (police, public prosecutors, courts);
- Representatives of the parties (legal aid organizations, advocates, paralegals and other non-professional representatives);
- Execution (executive authorities, prison and correctional services, tax authorities);
- Checks on the system (ombudsmen, norm-testing organs, human rights organizations, media); and
- Morale formation (all).

2. *Conclusions for legal development cooperation*

This catalogue indicates that the legal system as a whole functions more or less well. The catalogue thereby also becomes a tool for analysis of legal support, both ex-ante and ex-post. It is a reminder that legal support should not routinely be chosen to top the list. If weaker parts of the system are found lower down on the list, this can be reason to direct attention to them, which is often important from a poverty perspective.[12]

C. *Functions of the Rule of Law and the Market Economy*

If one turns to the contents of legal support, one can differentiate between two main categories of inputs, namely, support to the rule of law (C.1) and inputs directed at the market (C.2).

1. *Rule of law inputs*

a. *Monitoring Function*

Support to the rule of law has the aim of strengthening the constitutional State ('rechtsstaat', 'rättsstat'). Not unusually, the attempt to create 'increased justice' is in some sense regarded as a monitoring function for inputs of this type. It is a diffuse concept, but is nevertheless important when evaluating inputs of this type, with the result that one should attempt to clarify the goal for the inputs as far as possible. There are, for instance, reasons to distinguish between formal and material justice, and between the rule *of* law (more or less, security of life and property) and rule *by* law (more or less, subjection to the law).[13] Of greatest operative value is perhaps the distinction between security of life and property, equality before the law, security before the law, and accessibility of the law.

b. *Functions*

(a) Rule of law, or security of life and property, is a concept that is used in the most varied contexts, including development cooperation. Thus, one ought to clarify what is entailed. Lawfulness, predictability, and perhaps other things, may be considered. One ought also to pose the question if it is only due process which is referred to, or whether the concept of the rule of law also entails a certain minimum material standard in the form of human rights.

[12] Project Group on Administrative Law. The Status of Public Officials in Europe: Recommendation No R (2000) 6. Legal Issues. Strasbourg Croton-on-Hudson, NY, USA: Council of Europe Pub; Manhattan Pub [distributors], 2000. Demo-Droit Programme, Themis (Project), and Council of Europe. The Training of Judges and Prosecutors: In Matters Relating to Their Professional Obligations and Ethics. Strasbourg Croton-on-Hudson, NY, USA: Council of Europe Pub; Manhattan Pub [distributor], 1997. Vincent Kronenberger, and TMC Asser Instituut. The European Union and the International Legal Order: Discord or Harmony? The Hague Norwell, MA: TMC Asser Press; Sold and distributed in North, Central, and South America by Kluwer Law International, 2001. Sevastik, Per Legal Assistance to Developing Countries: Swedish Perspectives on the Rule of Law. Dordrecht, Kluwer Law International, The Netherlands; Cambridge, MA: 1998.

[13] Themis (Project), Demo-Droit Programme, and Council of Europe. Judicial Control of Administrative Acts: Multilateral Seminar, Madrid, 13-15 Nov 1996. Strasbourg Croton-on-Hudson, NY, USA: Council of Europe Pub; Manhattan Pub [distributor], 1997.

(b) Equality before the law is often regarded as part of the rule of law, but it also has connections with the accessibility of the law. It requires equality before the law, non-discrimination, as well as equality between parties in conflict.

(c) Security before the law is directed at the individual's security. In contrast to security of life and property, security before the law is not pointedly directed against encroachment by the State. On the contrary, it demands action by the police and other State organs against crime, damage, transgressions, and the exercise of gratuitous violence on the part of the State, etc. Here, however, there is a link to human rights: the failure on the part of the State to move against serious crimes against an individual can be a violation of the rights of an individual.

(d) Accessibility of the law ('access to justice') is a prerequisite for giving substance to regulations about security of life and property, equality before the law, and security before the law. This includes reasonable costs, legal aid, clearly written and easily available laws, other legal sources and information material, rapid process, and physical access to courts and other judicial institutions.

All four functions have significance for the poor, perhaps particularly accessibility of the law. Examples in the area of rule of law inputs are constitutional reforms, criminal-political reforms, reinforcement of the courts, human rights, guarantees for freedom of expression, transparency, combating corruption, and legal aid.

2. *Market economy inputs*

a. *Functions*

(a) Definition of property. Regulations should offer comprehensive property security, including non-material rights, eg through safeguards against confiscation and the creation of a system for registering fixed property and businesses etc. Through this, conditions for land reform and for credit institutions are created, which in turn form the basis for investments.

(b) Exchange of rights. Contractual rights, rights of purchase, transport, public procurement and various other topics are included here.

(c) Entrance to and exit from the market. It encompasses the law of association, banking law, financial market law, credit legislation, bankruptcy law, fair/unfair competition law, etc.

(d) Compensation for damage. Regulations that define what is unlawful damage and that stipulate compensation to one who has suffered unlawful damage.

(e) The market structure and the actors' actions on the market. Here competitive legislation, disloyal competition and legal safeguards are meant (rental law, labour law, consumer safeguards, etc).

Examples in the area of market economy inputs are privatization of telephone, electricity, and other State enterprises (which usually involve serious losses for the State); the capital market and mortgage system; insolvency (debt recovery, bankruptcy, collection of claims); central parts of commercial law, among others those highlighted by the World Trade Organization (WTO); environmental protection and conflict resolution.[14] The areas mentioned here also require competent institutions to apply the regulations, like registration authorities, free competition bodies, boards of executors, courts and arbitration councils etc. For the poorest, regulations about the right to land and other property safeguards, credit and insurance, and protective legislation are of immediate relevance.

3. *Conclusions for Legal Development Cooperation*

Rule of law (7.1) and market economy (7.2) inputs have different directions and goals in principle, but they also interact: property safeguards, independent courts, security of life and property, equality before the law, and security before the law are characteristic of the rule of law, and at the same time are prerequisites for the development of the market economy. Predictability is a common denominator. In a corresponding way, market economy reforms contribute to a strong judicial State, eg in the form of increased public access and freedom of expression, and greater independence from the State. Not least important is that a constitutional State must be largely financed by taxes, which is why a sound economy is an advantage in a constitutional State.

III. THE JUDICIAL SECTOR AND LEGAL DEVELOPMENT COOPERATION

A. Delimiting and Defining

1. *Definition of Legal Development Cooperation*

One can work with a judicial *legal concept* or with a sociological one where the latter is broader than the former. Both have their place within legal

[14] Yong-Shik Lee *Safeguard Measures in World Trade: The Legal Analysis* (Kluwer Law International The Hague; London; New York, 2003); Joost Pauwelyn, Conflict of Norms in Public International Law: *How WTO Law Relates to Other Rules of International Law*, Cambridge Studies in International and Comparative Law, CUP Cambridge 2003; World Trade, Forum, *Role of the Judge in International Trade Regulation: Experience and Lessons for the* WTO, Ann Arbor: UNIV OF MICHIGAN PRESS, 2003.

development cooperation. This also concerns traditional law, since the poorest can to a limited extent gain advantages from the official law.

No judicial areas ought to be excluded from legal development cooperation even if certain of these areas can be more delicate or less meaningful than others. It should, however, be noted that human rights, corruption, administration, etc are transverse processes and, when dealing with them, they also belong to other 'spheres of development cooperation'.

Institutional delimitation is also not completely clear, nor does it need to be. The institutions which can be given space within legal development cooperation—alongside the judicial organs in a narrow sense—include the following:

- The public sector, including the central authorities, tax authorities, registration of property etc.;
- Parliament, the electoral commission;
- Civil society (non-governmental organizations, informal conflict-resolution organizations, chambers of commerce, auditing agencies, etc.); and
- The media.

It should be noted that the concept of the judicial sector as well as the rule of law can have extremely varied substance. The UN, for example, includes media and the military in the concept of the rule of law.

Nor is the relationship to *good governance* unambiguous. It is simplest to see legal development and good governance as two parallel processes that partly overlap, which is why some legal support can very well be regarded as support of good governance. Examples are inputs that aim at transparency, accountability, and combating corruption. Honesty and efficiency in an administration can be of particular importance for the poor.

Support to *human rights* can be included in legal development cooperation. It ought to be observed, however, that human rights are sometimes seen as a concept that is broader than the judicial sector. Support for human rights occurs in the most diverse projects and, in particular, references are perhaps made to human rights as support for a certain project. One ought to be clear about these conceptual differences when choosing terminology and designing inputs. If one talks about human rights projects it ought to be clear whether it is the project's goal that motivates the name—projects related to (the right to) health, education, etc can then be included—or whether it is the institutions themselves that are given support when it may be natural to draw boundaries at the human rights institutions in the strict sense.

2. *Conclusions for Legal Development Cooperation*

Legal development cooperation requires a clear understanding of the law and the phenomena related to it. It probably does not matter so much that many of the concepts, which have just been mentioned, are used in a different sense in various contexts. Nor is it a problem that legal support is not clearly defined, as long as it is based on a sound analysis.

B. The Sections of the Sector

Legal development cooperation can be allocated to all parts of the judicial sector. A brief review of these sections follows.

1. *Legal Sources*

Legal development cooperation is usually completely focused on the official, national body of law. Here, legislation is central, possibly including the requisite preparatory work for each law. Legal precedence (judiciary) and literature (doctrine) are also legal sources. In many areas the informal (traditional) law is of great significance, which is why planning of projects must also take the latter into account and perhaps also seek to build on the resource which it entails.

2. *Institutions*

There are a large number of 'institutions' in the judicial arena that can be encompassed by legal development cooperation:

- Legislators (ministries, committees, parliament etc.);
- The courts and other organs for conflict-resolution (formal and informal);
- Executive organs (board of executors, prisons and correctional services, tax authorities);
- Representatives (advocates, bankruptcy administrators, paralegals, public prosecutors);
- The police;
- 'Judicial authorities' (management of competition, registration of companies and non-material rights, property registration, consumer safeguards etc.);
- Legal aid institutions (State; private);
- Educational and research institutions;
- The legal profession as a whole (administrative jurists, company lawyers, etc.);
- Supervisory organs (Justice Ombudsman institutions, advocates, associations of advocates and other professional bodies, eg auditors, human rights organizations, public authorities, eg finance inspectorate, consumer associations, the media);

- Functionaries (personnel well-versed in the law, administrative officials, 'informal decision-makers' (village headmen and the like)); and
- 'Users' (the public seeking justice, parties in civil law conflicts, the accused, sentenced and imprisoned, victims of crimes and other plaintiffs, human rights organizations).

3. *Below structure*

(a) Buildings, material, Information Technology (IT) and other equipment;
(b) Collections of laws and sentences, literature and information systems;
(c) Administration and methods of work.

4. *Legal Culture*

The traditions, values, ways of thinking, methods, unwritten regulations, professional standards and ethics, etc that are features of the legal system and judiciary in a country are part of the judicial culture. One can also include the position of the legal system in society and the approach of the public and the powers that be on the system and the knowledge about it. Attention has increasingly focused on the legal culture and its significance. This factor is difficult to grasp, but important, as it can jeopardize many reforms. It is for this reason alone that an eye ought to be kept on it in legal development cooperation.

5. *Conclusions for Legal Development Cooperation*

The 'judicial sector' is broad and heterogeneous. Those sections of the sector to receive support are often selected in a routine-like way. Goals and perspectives for inputs ought to guide the selection to some extent, which can lead to a more appropriate choice of those parts of the sector on which inputs focus. Both a poverty perspective and an egalitarian perspective naturally focus on the users and perhaps lead to attention being paid to the knowledge and attitudes of the public.

C. *Judicial Pluralism*

1. *Judicial Normative Systems*

Several competitive and interactive normative systems should be taken into account in the framework of legal development cooperation:

- Domestic State law (formal law; official law, including transplanted 'modern law');
- Law, custom, judicial praxis;

- Internationally binding norms, particularly international agreements, eg WTO's regulations and EU law (formal law);
- Colonial law (usually with traces of local law);
- Religious law, eg sharia;
- Informal law (traditional law), usually in the form of local customs;
- Socialist law, including planned economies (more an approach than legislated in the South);
- Traditions of common law and civil law;
- Norms not prescribed by law: prestige, contacts, ethnic links, family ties; and
- 'Non-legal': more or less illegal methods, eg bribery, threats, violence (cf the controls exercised by the mafia).

2. *Traditional Law and the Relation Between Normative Systems*

Normative systems compete, interact, and affect one another. Official law and traditional law are rivals, but they also interplay with each other. Local customs and religious laws can be sources of justice for the official law, thereby giving legitimacy to both of these normative systems. The law is also continuously changing: normative systems develop,[15] and even traditional law is affected by modern influences and other impulses. Traditional African societies are more open, more inclined to change and more conflict-ridden than Westerners previously believed. Many 'chiefs' who judge according to traditional law wish to educate themselves in the official law. Here, a possibility emerges of utilizing traditional institutions to supply legal aid. It can, however, also be mentioned that traditional courts in many cases have not proved to be suitable for resolving one of the most common types of conflict, namely land conflicts.

Judicial pluralism not only depends on different normative systems but also relies on different values, traditions, and 'forms of rationality'[16] to contribute to pluralism. The same is true of the different organs that 'administrate' normative systems—international organs, official courts, private and alternative forms of conflict-resolution, religious leaders, local chiefs, etc.

[15] Carlos E Alchourrâon, Eugenio Bulygin, and Ernesto Garzâon Valdâes, *Normative Systems in Legal and Moral Theory: Festschrift for Carlos E. Alchourrâon and Eugenio Bulygin*, Duncker & Humblot, Berlin, 1997; Thomas M Franck, Fairness in International Law and Institutions. OXFORD NEW YORK: CLARENDON PRESS; OXFORD UNIVERSITY PRESS, 1995.

[16] Michel van de Kerchove, and François Ost, *Legal System between Order and Disorder*, OXFORD; NEW YORK: OXFORD UNIVERSITY PRESS, 1994; Antonio Anselmo Martino, *Expert Systems in Law*, North-Holland, Amsterdam, New York: 1992; Josep J Moreso, *Legal Indeterminacy and Constitutional Interpretation. Law and Philosophy Library*; V. 37. DORDRECHT; BOSTON: KLUWER ACADEMIC PUBLISHERS, 1998.

A particular range of problems exists regarding to competition between common law and civil law. Opinion is divided on the possibilities of merging both of these traditions, as in the EU, and how it should be implemented in that case.

3. *Conclusions for Legal Development Cooperation*

A donor can have reasons to take all normative systems and the relations between them into account. Judicial pluralism means that the formal (official law) ought not automatically to be given precedence before the informal, which may emphasize a bottom-up perspective and other 'alternative perspectives', eg minority rights, life-style and identity. An alternative perspective can also create awareness of judicial limitations. In certain 'judicial cultures' the official law is accorded little weight by comparison with family ties, ethnic links, prestige, contacts, and similar means of manipulating the law. At the same time, it is important not to be seduced by traditional and informal law. It can have repressive features and also be unserviceable to promote commerce and development.

D. *Civil Society*

1. *Developments*

Civil society has a large role to play in legal development cooperation. It can encompass non-governmental organizations, informal groups, and sometimes also the media. To be included in this context, it is desirable for an organization to be independent, transparent, and have democratic roots and a democratic way of working. Not infrequently, one must resign oneself to more modest demands; even in relatively developed countries in Eastern Europe, where civil society has remained weak.

2. *Judicial Organizations*

One can generally differentiate between two categories of non-governmental organizations in the field of legal development cooperation:

- Organizations that provide social services; in this case, primarily the organizations that offer or supply legal aid are of interest; and
- Opinion-forming organizations; here the issue may be to monitor respect for human rights in a more general way, influence the work of legislation and international setting of norms, prosecuting pilot cases, observing trials, spreading information (about constitutional rights or new legal cases) etc.

3. *Conclusions for Legal Development Cooperation*

Consideration of support to judicial organizations depends on several circumstances, eg what is permitted, the needs and resources (economic, competence etc). Support to the former (a, above) is usually more expensive than to the latter (b, above). Judicial access may, however, improve substantially, thanks to the former. Experience of the latter category of organization is good on the whole. There is usually no reason for donors to exclude support to civil society for the reason that bilateral legal cooperation is being undertaken with the country in question.

E. The State and the Private Sector

1. *The Relationship Between the State and the Private Sector*

Features of the relationship between the State and the private sector include both cooperation and rivalry. The State and civil society require, support, and keep checks on each other and in some cases they compete with each other. From the viewpoint of a private actor, the State may be both the problem and the solution.

Certain functions can only be undertaken by State institutions and should be performed without being affected by irrelevant considerations. To some extent such institutions are a prerequisite for the private sector. They provide guarantees for non-governmental organizations, against injustices for instance, and also—paradoxically enough—against unfair treatment by State institutions. The State is also a guarantor of certain private mechanisms, like the carrying out of arbitration and alternative conflict-resolution mechanisms. At the same time, in certain cases the State is the supervisor of non-governmental organizations like bar associations, as well as the opposite party, in policy issues and conflicts for instance. The State can function as financier, concession granter, and public prosecutor, sometimes in relation to one and the same organization.

Conversely, private organizations are a prerequisite for the State's way of functioning. They keep an eye on and influence the State, train State personnel, inform the public about the State's work, and carry out tasks on behalf of the State. Many tasks can be performed by both the State and private agencies (like education, legal aid, conflict resolution, information dissemination, influencing public opinion).

2. *The Informal Sector*

The informal sector is variegated (one can differentiate between illegal, non-registered and non-reported companies and transactions). The sector is problematic from the viewpoint of legal development cooperation. On the one hand, it often functions fairly well and is extensive, in many countries being 50–75 per cent of the economy. Legal development cooperation ought not to harm this sector, particularly as the poor work within it. On the other hand, it is a grey area with illegal aspects that can hardly be directly supported by a donor. High transaction costs inhibit the expansion of informal businesses and corruption flourishes in this grey area.

3. *Conclusions for Legal Development Cooperation*

Legal development cooperation ought to build on the insight that while certain functions can be carried out only by the State, others can only be done by civil society. In addition, private actors can give support to the State and vice versa. State measures can sometimes be the best way of facilitating the growth of non-governmental organizations. Legal development cooperation can achieve an increased degree of efficiency if donors utilize their opportunities to combine support to the State and the private sector. Donors may even sometimes have reason to talk of the violation of human rights while at the same time giving assistance to the very institutions of the State that are responsible for the violations.

The planning of legal support is sometimes done as if the informal sector did not exist. This is a pragmatic approach to the problem, but is debatable. The long-term goal ought to be to design a system of justice so that these enterprises become a part of the regular economy. It would lay the basis for the expansion of many small businesses, thanks to lower transaction costs and thereby give the State increased revenue from taxation. It would also reduce the opportunities for corruption.

IV. LEGAL DEVELOPMENT COOPERATION

A. *Special Requirements for Legal Development Cooperation*

1. *Central Powers*

The law and the central powers are closely linked. A system of justice is the responsibility of the State and judicial reforms are dependent on the support of those in power. They must be built on the central State institutions which make up the core of the judiciary, like courts, prosecutors, and the executive. If these conditions for support do not exist, development cooperation cannot build a functioning judiciary.

Judicial reforms may threaten the position of those in power, for example, because the party and the State are no longer synonymous and the State's power is restricted; new centres of power may arise that compete with the political powers; respect for minorities is enforced; critical reviews become possible, and the law, and thus the lawyer, each gain new roles.

2. *Demand*

Sometimes there is a lack of genuine demand for judicial reform, not only because it might lead to undesirable consequences for many of the interested parties, but also because old ways of thinking remain in post-communist societies. The aforementioned is relevant not only to politicians but also to businessmen who are used to a 'rent-seeking-culture', and to the legal profession which is at risk because its knowledge may become outdated. Many proponents of the profession may have 20–30 remaining years at their posts and may have good reason and opportunity to object. To the extent that re-schooling is impossible, dismissal may provide the only accessible route.

3. *Vulnerability*

Legal development cooperation projects are vulnerable not only because there may be a change for those who hold power. Unlike, for instance, the physical belowstructure, legal reforms can easily be obliterated or undermined. They are more vulnerable than many other projects also because the legislation to implement the reforms or the institutional build-up is often delayed, which is why nothing happens although a law is adopted or another measure has been taken with the help of development cooperation. Often the donor does not have a role to play in this part of the implementation nor has any insight into it.

4. *Point of Departure*

For other reasons, developing countries are often characterized by a lack of reliable information, poor communications, and a high cost of transactions. In addition, the judicial sector is often neglected and functions poorly as a result of other sectors having higher priority. It may be characterized by small resources and low educational levels. Institutions are often so rundown that one cannot build on them because the parties that should be involved are often too weak to be able to cooperate with them. The system is more or less corrupt and compromised, and people in general have no confidence in it.

5. *The Culture of Justice etc.*

The law is culturally and historically conditioned and great differences exist between different regions and countries. In many cases, the developing world has rudimentary systems of justice where informal law is central, while many East European countries can build upon a previous, often well developed, system. Clear differences also exist between East European countries, just as between developing countries in various regions. This is true of legal-cultural differences (approach to the law and the role of lawyers, systems, concepts, sources of jurisprudence, the study of legislation etc). Legal-cultural differences, like language problems and other factors, have shown themselves to lead to serious communication problems in the legal arena, even in cooperation with the East, though these countries are relatively well developed.

6. *Standards*

Judicial reform and thus legal development cooperation has certain given points of departure. These concern international agreements that set a standard for human rights as well as the entire body of commercial law (WTO, ASEAN, international treaties, praxis, codes, lex mercatoria etc) which must have a specific content to create the environment to promote trade and investment. For certain countries, a 'treaty' enforced by the international community exists, like the Dayton agreement for Bosnia and Hercegovina, or a more traditional form of peace accord, like in Central America. For presumptive members of the EU, the judicial content is also largely given—the system of justice must meet a 'West-European standard'[17] (cf Copenhagen criteria, acquis, etc). In addition, there are organs that keep an eye on whether the above-mentioned standards are achieved, which is why legal development cooperation must also pay attention to the institutional side. In the third world there are, however, strong forces that question the legitimacy of the donor community to assert these standards and other 'universal values', to the extent that they conflict with traditional values and lifestyles.

7. *The Process of Change*

When the law in the South is reformed, traditional laws may lose their functionality, without new ones becoming effective. Such a vacuum can only be avoided if judicial modernization is undertaken with great sensitivity to the role of the traditional judiciary. Legal development cooperation in Eastern Europe must also be designed to take into account that 'transitional law'

[17] Mauro Cappelletti, Monica Seccombe, and Joseph Weiler, *Integration through Law: Europe and the American Federal Experience,* W de Gruyter, Berlin; New York: 1985; Hans-W Micklitz, and Stephen Weatherill, *European Economic Law, Tempus Textbook Series on European Law and European Legal Cultures,* Ashgate/Dartmouth, Aldershot, Hants., England; Brookfield, Vt, USA 1997.

has particular features that in many ways are unknown to Western jurists. The process of change may create space for misuse since control mechanisms are not necessarily developed at the same pace as the transition. To make the choice of the speed and sequence for judicial reforms requires specialized knowledge.

8. *The Independence of Institutions*

Several judicial institutions enjoy an entrenched independence that has no equivalent in other social sectors. They are also more closely linked to national sovereignty than, for instance, the social sector or the belowstructure. The courts, the public prosecutor, and certain other institutions may be involved. They cannot simply be 'reformed' and thus advice and dialogue may need to occur in more restrained forms than currently.

9. *Formalization*

A formalization of the judicial system may have advantages, in the form of higher levels of knowledge, more uniform application of justice, etc. It is not unusual for village headmen and other practitioners of traditional law to desire to raise their level of knowledge by schooling themselves in 'modern law'. A formalization can, however, also contribute to the system becoming more expensive and more complex. This may lead to paralegals being pushed aside, with the result that accessibility for the poor deteriorates.

10. *The Resource Base*

The resource base in donor countries is more limited in the field of legal development cooperation than in most others. This is not only because the area is new, but also because many jurists do not have the relevant knowledge: their knowledge is limited about developing countries and they have not assimilated the experiences that have been gained in other areas of development cooperation. They also have limited knowledge of comparing the law and 'transitional justice' (transition from one system to another). They gladly yield to the temptation to teach about their domestic law and automatically recommend their own administrative and organizational solutions. Thus, the resource base may restrict what can be achieved in the short term. Increased cooperation of experts from several countries would be healthy.

11. *Conclusions for Legal Development Cooperation*

In the preceding, a number of circumstances peculiar to legal development cooperation are pointed out though some of these may also play a role in other areas in a less accentuated way. Taken together, these circumstances involve a number of restrictions that require detailed planning of legal development cooperation projects. A good quality risk and an interest analysis are required as part of the preparations, as are a clear and long-term vision and a preparedness to allocate resources.

B. Principles for Legal Development Cooperation

1. To Learn From Experience

Donors have hitherto acted pragmatically, as they did not have a theoretical and consistent model for legal development. The experiences mentioned above ought naturally to be taken into account. One ought to avoid an evolutionist, instrumental, and ethnocentric approach to the law. However, the conditions for legal development cooperation are now more favourable than in the past. Not only is there more knowledge about legal development cooperation, but conditions have also improved. In addition, there is a better understanding of the importance of the judiciary, as a result of the process of change which was mentioned at the beginning, and in many countries, eg in Latin America, there is now a stability which makes them better equipped for judicial reform.

2. National Resources

Many of the problems which are a feature of the legal systems in the South and in Eastern Europe are caused by a scarcity of resources and the evil circle this creates. It relates to corruption, lack of competent personnel, inefficient ways of working, drawn-out procedures, citizens' lack of trust in the system, inadequate access for the poor, bad premises, out-dated equipment, etc. In dialogue, a central task for donors should be to point out the necessity for the Government to allocate resources to the judicial system. If it does not, its commitment can be called into question. The forms for judicial reform may influence the Government in the correct direction. If it proceeds through a well-rooted process, this may improve the prospects for the Government to allocate the means required for a reformation.

3. System Approach (holistic view)

One of the few recognized principles for legal development cooperation is probably the need for a system approach. First, conditions in sectors other than the judicial affect the latter and the reverse. A weak school system, for example, has an impact, since illiterate people have difficulty in asserting their rights with the assistance of the legal system. The legal system can protect the media from interference while, at the same time, the media can combat corruption in the legal system.[18] Secondly, a system approach encapsulates demands on agreement between economic policies and judicial reforms as well as between political developments and judicial reforms. Both of these system approaches (which can be said to have an external perspective) in general agree with development cooperation trends to emphasize the general policy environment in partner countries and to adopt an integrated approach as a basis for cooperation.

Thirdly, in a system approach the various parts of the legal system hang together and must be taken into account—both regulations and institutions (internal perspective). Civil society should be accorded its rightful place and informal (traditional) law and informal institutions must be brought into the picture. Here, the elements that are more difficult to grasp can be found, like attitudes to the law and other parts of the culture of justice.

Fourthly, reforms should be implemented on the basis of well-founded priorities, in a sequence and with a speed that suits the conditions in the concrete case, for both the first mentioned (external) and the third (internal). A system approach entails that not everything needs to be done at one and the same time.

The demand for a holistic view is particularly apparent during structural reform of the legal system (see 14.9 below) and one ought to avoid introducing a very broad programme which lacks clear focus. If the judicial reformation is part of a sectoral reform, there is also a demand for a holistic view, though it may be less stressed, while many isolated inputs require a less ambitious framework.

4. *Developing Capacity*

In agreement with the need for a system approach, capacity development should be as much of a catch-word in the field of legal development cooperation as in most other sectors. The legal system as a whole ought to be purposefully organized, including the relations between and tasks of its institutions. Judicial institutions ought to be given the competence, tools, and other resources, organization and methods of work, [19] etc which are

[18] See UN Conference on Financing for Development available at <http://www.un.org/esa/ffd/> (the Monterrey Consensus and its new 'holistic' approach to development)

[19] Capacity Building for Environmental Law in the Asian & Pacific Region; V. Ii: Approaches and Resourc. Manila: Asian Development Bank, 2002; Najeeb M Al-Nauimi, and Richard Meese, *International Legal Issues Arising under the United Nations Decade of International Law,* The Hague; Boston Cambridge, MA, USA: MARTINUS NIJHOFF PUBLISHERS; Sold and distributed in the USA and Canada by Kluwer Law International, 1995; Law of the Sea Institute, Conference (29th: 1995: Denpasar Indonesia), et al. Sustainable Development and Preservation of the Oceans: The Challenges of Unclos and Agenda 21. Honolulu: Law of the Sea Institute, William S Richardson School of Law, University of Hawaii, 1997; World

required for them to be able to fulfil their role. In this context, capacity refers to all parts of the system, not only to the key organs, but also to institutions like those for education and further education. If such capacity is built up, not only the legal system as such is favoured, but it also contributes to the general attempt to strengthen governance of society.

5. *Long-term Perspective and Resources*

System changes require firm establishment, a long-term vision with corresponding programming, sustainability and resources, so that judicial reforms can be implemented. Smaller, isolated projects may be justified, but if possible, ought then to act as a stimulus to the system changes.

6. *Money or Ideas?*

The poorer the policy environment, the greater the reason to focus on the ideas. To the extent that development cooperation is utilizable, the reasons to do so are reinforced. Conditions at central level have small chance of influencing the recipients to a similar degree as legal development cooperation concerns the interests of the central powers. At the local level, conditionality may often be more effective. One should add that cooperation with the East should in principle be based on utilizing legal knowledge to build up capacity, so that funds for the legal area are not used to finance investments in, for example, belowstructure.

7. *Reform Process*

Experience indicates that the approach to judicial reform has considerable significance, sometimes as great as the material content of the reforms. It requires a broad process that involves the interested parties and includes education about the judicial reforms and spreading information on them. Such a process can create the clarity, predictability, and legitimacy required for the acceptance of the regulations and have the intended effects. It can also clarify which parties are most favoured by a certain input.

8. *Comparative Advantages*

A donor's comparative advantages may affect the choice of countries for legal development cooperation, the choice of areas of input, and the choice of methods. It may seem easier to specialize in certain types of inputs, for

Trade Organization. The WTO: Capacity Building and Development: A Proposal: WTO 2001.

example, the development of organizations in the ministry of justice or accessibility of the law; however, the disadvantages of such a selection procedure (cf 18.2 below) are tangible as long as they do not rest on a firm foundation, eg the standards for legal development cooperation (see 13.6 above).

9. *Choice of Approach and Ambitions*

It is desirable for a donor to have a clear understanding of the ambitions—and thereby the resources and the time perspective—which should form the basis for legal development cooperation in any concrete case. One can differentiate between support to structural reform, 'integrated inputs', and clearly limited inputs:

(a) If the object is to give support to a *structural reform* of the judicial sector, the ambition is set high. Resources and time horizons must be adapted to this, since it concerns contributing to a change of basic conditions, including the legal culture and other supports.
(b) If the object is to support judicial reform in a *sector,* the ambition is typically set lower. Judicial reform is here usually integrated in a more extensive reform, eg of the State administration, a social sector, the financial market or an industry. Judicial reform which is a part of structural adaptation can also be regarded as an integrated input. This type of integration can become an effective way of giving substance to development cooperation based on human rights.
(c) One can also conceive of *limited projects* of varying kinds, like seminars, field studies, individual legislative measures, buying literature, etc.

The choice of ambition and approach has consequences not only for the need for resources and the time perspective, but it also affects the risks and relevance of the inputs. Assessment of the relevance of the inputs and how they can be implemented becomes easier the lower down the ladder one goes and, correspondingly, the vulnerability and risks of the inputs are reduced. Methodologically, the same thing can be achieved by departing from a clear and well-defined problem of which the recipient is well-aware (bottom-up), after which the programme can be extended. Alternatively, one can take a holistic view from the beginning (top-down), but it is theoretically more satisfying but usually riskier.

10. *Prerequisites and Timing*

It is not only the needs of the recipient country and the donor's resources which ought to determine which level of ambition and approach is suitable. At least as important are the conditions and the timing. If the prerequisites for large reforming projects are missing, eg because the political will is not there, the ambitions must be adapted to this reality, irrespective of which urgent needs are apparent. Similarly, one must be cautious in delicate situations, even if the political will to reform is strong; in the legal area it is the rule rather than the exception that recipient capacity is weak.

11. Target Groups

Most legal development cooperation projects are probably of use to both the citizens in general and to certain individuals. A mortgage system, for instance, fosters general economic development, but is also of use to the agriculturist who can get credit. Freedom of the press can be of general use, eg if it counteracts corruption, at the same time as it can protect an individual whose rights are violated.

Sometimes it is said that inputs should start with the people or the individual. Yet it is not so easy to see in which way an *individual perspective* could lead to any assistance other than the development of institutions. If, for example, one strengthens the office of the public prosecutor or legal aid and reforms the rest of the system, one may reduce time spent awaiting trial to the advantage of the detainees.

An individual perspective may, however, serve as a reminder that institutions are simply means to strengthen an individual's abilities. If a poor person cannot utilize her/his rights because s/he cannot read, one ought to admit that her/his rights are not realized, rather than assert that s/he has not made use of the law. An individual perspective may also be a good tool of analysis. One can analyse which effects an input has on a certain category of individual and can also analyse the legal system by following an individual through the system, for example, a woman who has been raped or a citizen who has a claim or wants to establish a business. In this way, a poverty or an egalitarian perspective can hopefully make a greater impact in the planning of the project. An individual perspective can also be a starting point for cooperation based on human rights.

12. Conclusions for Legal Development Cooperation

Principles and methods for legal development cooperation must be adapted to the particular prerequisites of legal development cooperation (see 13 above). This means that the lack of resources in the sector must be taken into account, that a holistic view is required, and that the principles, which have been referred to in the preceding, must be upheld. Since legal development cooperation is relatively new and principles and methods less tested than is desirable, particular care has been devoted to the aspect of the principles.

C. *Transfer of Regulations?*

1. *Transfer of Regulations or Capacity*

A large number of legal development cooperation projects are made up of the transfer of legislation, judicial institutes, and institutions from the donor's national system. It is not beyond the bounds of possibility that such transfers may have positive effects, but the angle of approach is ethnocentric, with the result that attention is diverted from the context in the recipient country, like its traditions and legal culture, and the need for accepting the legislation. Particularly in countries where the law only has a small role to play as a means for controlling society, such transfers may have difficulty in becoming established. Alternatives that have already been mentioned include capacity development with the aim of strengthening the recipient country's capacity to analyse its needs, design its legislation and judicial institutes, and build institutions.

2. *Regulations and Institutions*

Building up capacity is both costly and requires time. As we saw, in certain respects there is an answer to the question of when is 'the law correct' (see 13.6). Then it is legitimate to participate in ensuring that such regulations and institutes are introduced, but only to the extent that the local context is taken into account. This includes the implementation of international agreements and certain generally accepted principles of the market economy, and the standards set by the EU.

3. *Models*

To the extent that regulations and institutes are transferred, there are reasons to prefer models that have shown themselves to work in different contexts. Examples are Unidroit's, UNCITRALS' and ICC's well-established work with models.[20] Similarly successful national codification can be

[20] Paul AU Ali, The Law of Secured Finance: An International Survey of Security Interests over Personal Property, Oxford; New York: OXFORD UNIVERSITY PRESS, 2002; Henri C Alvarez, David W Rivkin, and Neil Kaplan, Model Law Decisions: Cases Applying the Uncitral Model Law on International Commercial Arbitration (1985–2001). The Hague; New York: KLUWER LAW INTERNATIONAL, 2003; VK Bhatia, Christopher Candlin, and Maurizio Gotti, Legal Discourse in Multilingual and Multicultural Contexts: Arbitration Texts in Europe, LINGUISTIC INSIGHTS, V. 6. Bern; New York: P Lang, 2003; Campbell, Dennis, United Nations Commission on International Trade Law., and United Nations Commission on International Trade Law. Working Group VI (Security Interests). International Secured Transactions. Dobbs Ferry, NY: Oceana Publications, 2003; Ferrari, Franco, et al. The Draft Uncitral Digest and Beyond: Cases, Analysis and Unresolved Issues in the UN Sales Convention: Papers of the Pittsburgh Conference Organized by the Center for International Legal Education (Cile). London: Sweet & Maxwell, 2004.

employed, eg the Netherland's and Quebec's codifications which have been successfully used recently in Eastern European countries like Russia, and Latin American countries like Argentina. The AsDB has created a system for disseminating comparative legal material to be used in the work of judicial reform. To the degree that the legal development cooperation of a country encompasses transfers, it thus need not necessarily be concerned with certain, perhaps peculiar, regulations of this country. A different matter is that legal institutes of any country may provide impulses for judicial reform or that national 'experts' of the country are perhaps not familiar with the relevant regulations.

4. *Conclusions for Legal Development Cooperation*

The transfer of regulations and institutes are often linked to tremendous difficulties and are usually a less efficient form of development cooperation than building up capacity. To the extent that regulations and institutes are implanted, there are reasons to select models that have already shown themselves to work in different contexts.

D. *Legal Development Cooperation to 'Difficult Countries'?*

1. *'Difficult Countries'*

One of the main problems for legal development cooperation may be that those in power do not have a genuine interest in judicial reforms. A repressive structure, attitudes to the law, the effects of the communist heritage, corruption, organized crime and other factors may each play a role.

2. *Influence of Attitudes*

The dialogue may provide space for influencing attitudes. Even in the most difficult environments, it is usually possible to give support to forming public opinion and perhaps consensus, eg convincing the public of the value of judicial reforms or about humane criminal policies. This may occur in the form of support to non-governmental organizations and the private sector (bar council, commercial organizations, media that work for judicial reforms, etc). Such support can in any case give visibility and safeguards in authoritarian environments. At best, networks are created which have a multiplicatory effect.

3. *Education, Further Education, and Research, etc.*

The education of teachers of jurisprudence can be a way of proceeding, even in difficult countries. The development of curricula, didactics and literature can be added to the list. Similarly, the further education of practising lawyers may be promising as well as participation in regional conferences and similar events. For both of these categories of lawyers, an exchange with colleagues in other countries may be of great value. New knowledge and feelings of collegiality create self-confidence and can sow the seeds of renewal. Depending on the choice of subject matter, judicial research may be more sensitive, but usually it is recognized that there is a dearth of knowledge.

4. *A New Generation*

In nearly all 'difficult countries', there is a younger generation that is knowledgeable and inclined to seek change. There may be reasons to direct tailor-made inputs to this category, eg to contribute to making contacts in foreign countries which can function as a stimulus to their efforts.

5. *Conclusions for Legal Development Cooperation*

Not unusually there is good reason to refrain from legal development cooperation to regimes which are repressive or at least 'difficult'. If there are strong reasons nonetheless to make an input, great care must be devoted to designing it. Otherwise, there is a substantial risk that the input may legitimize undemocratic structures and produce meagre results.

E. *Legal Development Cooperation to Countries After Conflicts*

Increasing attention has been drawn to the fact that the law can not only play a role in preventing conflict. It is also an important instrument in 'post-conflict situations', eg Bosnia, Haiti, Cambodia, Kosovo, Serbia, Eastern Europe, East Timor, as well as South Africa and several other African countries.

1. *Reconciliation, Truth, and Legal Proceedings*

There are always reasons to attempt to bring clarity to what has happened. It is a psychosocial concern and may contribute to reconciliation. To bring war criminals to justice and demand other kinds of accountability is normally desirable, but in certain cases amnesty may be motivated (eg if a referendum has been held or 'both sides' are agreed on ignoring the past). Truth commissions do not exclude trials, since the latter typically encompass fewer people and take more time.

2. *Restitution and Compensation*

Normally, a well-functioning judicial system is required for restitution and compensation to be possible. It includes restitution of housing, land, other property, and of jobs and additional economic recompense in those cases where restitution is not possible. Compensation for non-payment of earnings and compensation for psychological suffering are also on the list.

3. *Protection of Minorities*

Many conflicts have an ethnic background, which is why effective safeguards of minority rights are a precondition for a sustainable peace. It is concerned with judicial safeguards from discrimination at all levels[21]—from the Constitution to local bye-laws—and in many areas, like protection against discrimination in the work place, at school, by the police, and the judicial system.

4. *Support to Returnees*

It should be a central part of a post-conflict policy to facilitate the situation for returning exiles, which not only requires strong support from the legal system in several respects which have already been mentioned, but also the right to get credit for time spent abroad when the rate of pay is set, a law to validate foreign examinations, and a law to get documents.

5. *Support to Civil Society*

Different phases in a country require different sorts of support to civil society. After a conflict, organizations that deliver social services of various kinds are needed, eg legal aid, but also organizations which build public opinion regarding issues like those mentioned in E.1–E.4. Support to civil society may, however, not take the place of inputs to State institutions, since a number of functions can only be undertaken by them.[22]

6. *Conclusions for Legal Development Cooperation*

After a conflict it is necessary to build up the legal system again, since a

[21] See United States Dept of Justice Civil Rights Division Federal Protections against National Origin Discrimination [Washington, DC?]: US Dept of Justice, Civil Rights Division, 2001; Protecciones Federales Contra La Discriminaciâon Por Origen Nacional [Washington, DC?]: Departamento de Justicia de los EE.UU, Divisiâon de Derechos Civiles, 2001.

[22] Martha Fineman, *The Autonomy Myth: A Theory of Dependency,* NEW YORK: NEW PRESS, 2004; Marc Morjâe Howard, *The Weakness of Civil Society in Post-Communist Europe,* Cambridge, UK; New York, NY: CAMBRIDGE UNIVERSITY PRESS, 2003; Petr Kopeckây, and Cas Mudde, *Uncivil Society?: Contentious Politics in Post-Communist Europe,* ROUTLEDGE STUDIES IN EXTREMISM AND DEMOCRACY; 1. London; New York: Routledge, 2003; Victor Segesvary *World State, Nation States, or Non-Centralized Institutions?: A Vision of the Future in Politics,* Lanham, MD: UNIVERSITY PRESS OF AMERICA, 2003.

number of urgent needs can only be met if there is a well-functioning system of justice. Thus it is desirable for an identification of needs to be made as soon as possible. What has been said here about 'post-conflict countries' is largely also applicable in countries that have been hit by natural disasters, even if the views put forward in 17.1 and 17.3 usually are assumed to have less relevance.

V. METHODS FOR LEGAL DEVELOPMENT COOPERATION

A. *Methods for Legal Development Cooperation*

1. *General*

It is apparent that there are a number of conditions that apply specially to legal development cooperation (see 13 above), but one can nevertheless assume that what is good methodology for development cooperation as a whole is good practice also for this form. For reasons touched on in the preceding, legal development cooperation may, however, be both more sensitive and more vulnerable than development cooperation in many other areas. Thus, particular care ought to be devoted to accountability, sustainability, building capacity, and similar factors.

2. *Accountability of the Recipient*

The accountability of the recipient (ownership) is central, since in many cases the institutions in the legal area are weak and there may be pockets of resistance to the desire to reform. The more ambitious the reforms (see 14.9 above), the greater the demand for accountability of the recipient. A factor that may affect accountability—and thus is one of its indicators—is the political will which can advantageously be manifested in a strategy for the sector. Other positive factors are the division of costs, loan financing, the strength of the partners in cooperation, problem and need orientation (which counteracts the control of what is on offer), and interactive ways of working which start with the recipient's problems. It is desirable for accountability to be based on a genuine partnership both between parties in development cooperation and between the Government of the partner country and those with interests in the projects. There may be a need for an analysis of interests to reveal the attitudes of key actors to the projects. In the case where the recipient is not prepared to shoulder responsibility, the idea should be set in the foreground and the volume of cooperation be restrained. This suggests that partners in cooperation, for instance the Ministry of Justice, may need to be strengthened and perhaps also that non-governmental organizations become involved.

3. *Sustainability*

A clear shouldering of responsibility makes for a good prognosis for sustainability. In addition, sustainability is furthered by a long-term perspective, mutual trust, capacity building, and integration of the work in the national budget. It should be observed that sustainability does not always need to be institutional, but can be supported by individuals who circulate in the 'judicial sector'. Many organizations may never become self-sustaining and often it is healthy for civil society to be restructured.

4. *Building Capacity*

It has been pointed out that building capacity may have many different aspects, but analytically, capacity is a key factor. It should be noted that one cannot casually build on existing judicial institutions, irrespective of how tempting this may be in a short-term perspective. Some parts of the legal system will be so compromised and in other ways run-down that one is paving the way for problems if one does not build up something new. Perhaps the Ministry of Justice is an exception; there is no alternative if one wants to deal with this central institution, for instance, because its analytical capacity must inevitably be strengthened. The legal area is well-suited to cooperation between partners ('twinning') or other forms of fraternal collaboration as a method of building up capacity, and is not limited to Eastern Europe, where the EU is working for such cooperation on a large scale in candidate countries.

5. *Planning, Follow-up and Evaluation*

Legal support often needs more careful planning and follow-up than other areas. A system approach (see 14.3 above) requires planning on the part of the donor so that it does not remain a reaction to isolated wishes on the part of the donor. Such planning requires good knowledge of the system in its entirety. If such knowledge cannot be gained, there may be reasons to limit the ambitions and perhaps to prefer a 'bottom-up' approach. In Eastern Europe, the situation may permit a freer view as a result of the Copenhagen criteria largely prescribing what should be done.

The goal for legal support can be based on functions, standards, and other aspects that have been touched on already, particularly those that permit operationalization and can be translated into indicators for measurement. A logical framework approach (so-called LFA) may be an excellent tool for the design of these projects. It is, however, not always so easy to define the precise goal and the target groups, or to assess the effects of the interventions at different levels. But the framework approach ought to be a useful method if one wants to find out what the result is at the end, since it requires a holistic view that also takes into account the circumstances beyond the legal system (see 14.3 above).

One ought to be open to the need for a complementary approach. It reveals itself in that inputs in this area—similarly to inputs in other difficult areas—are often changed during the course of the programme, with the result that the original goal becomes less relevant. Follow-up and evaluation may thus need to take place using a somewhat different yardstick than the original objectives. A process-oriented approach may then be required. One can also pay attention to the way the system functions rather than its results. This indicates that evaluations of inputs of this type ought to include the rationality of the inputs (relevance) and not remain with efficiency and goal achievement.

6. *Coordination*

As might be expected, coordination of legal support is far from perfect. Among other things, it is notoriously weak between ministries of justice in recipient countries. In Eastern Europe, coordination has broken down and the EU as the dominant actor has neglected other donors. Increased coordination and exchange of experiences is desirable. Experiences from other areas of development cooperation indicate that efficient coordination is simplified if a common programme for reform exists; the above-mentioned standards may fulfil such a function to some extent. Preferably there ought to be an institutional structure for coordination.

Does it cause damage if a recipient is given conflicting advice? This usually happens, but it is not inevitable, if the recipient has the capacity to evaluate all the advice and combine it in an insightful way as, for example, Vietnam appears to be trying to do. It remains to be seen if the hybrids of common and civil law that are now evolving have a future. Coordination ought preferably to include inputs made through non-governmental organizations, since they often go together with the inputs made between States.

7. *Dialogue*

A donor may have legitimate grounds for expressing critical views, especially if they are based on standards for human rights. Since a well-functioning legal system is a prerequisite for citizens to be able to assert their rights, it is legitimate for a donor not only to take up violations of human rights, but also anomalies in the system of justice. On the other hand, there may be faults in the central functions which is why criticism may touch on national sovereignty. This is a cogent argument for being tactful in the dialogue.

8. *Focus on Eastern Europe*

West-European countries' self-interest not only creates a good basis for cooperation with their neighbours, but also a 'pressure to offer supplies'. It is thus relevant whether the principle of division of costs can be maintained, so that the cooperation can become firmly established and safeguarded in the partner country. If a division of costs cannot be achieved—it may, for instance, be difficult in Russia, Latvia or Lithuania—the establishment should be safeguarded in another way. One example is a clearly articulated account by the partner country of its needs and priorities in the legal area. Not uncommonly, the donor side has sought this in vain. Causes are lack of competence on the part of the recipient and linguistic problems. It is also possible that one can reduce the demands moderately in those cases where projects relate directly to an EU requirement or alternately to very strong self-interests of the donor country. In the latter case, it is then desirable that the 'donor country interests' make their own contributions. In other cases one should design the cooperation to be more in line with the methodology that is traditionally applied in development cooperation with the South.[23] It should also be noted that there may be a great need in a certain sector, eg the judicial, but that there is a lack of projects, which is why the partner country may have good reason not to allocate means.

9. *Focus on Development Cooperation After Conflicts*

After a civil war or disaster it is often the public institutions that are incapable of taking responsibility. This may be an argument for rapid measures from the donor community and perhaps also for generous financing of running costs and other local expenses. At the same time, there may be a need to set up conditions for development cooperation, for example, to protect minorities or to adopt anti-corruption measures. The result may be strongly donor-controlled assistance with little opportunity for accountability by local politicians and authorities. This is a disadvantage for efficient development cooperation and undermines the democratic process. This dilemma requires the donor to go forward in stages, to involve local actors and to be flexible.

[23] Baker, Gideon, Civil Society and Democratic Theory: Alternative Voices. Routledge Innovations in Political Theory 9. London; New York: Routledge, 2002; Diamond, Larry Jay, and Marc F Plattner, Democracy after Communism. A Journal of Democracy Book. Baltimore, MD: Johns Hopkins University Press, 2002; FJM Feldbrugge, Law in Transition. Law in Eastern Europe; No. 52. The Hague; New York: M Nijhoff, 2002.

10. *Conclusions for Legal Development Cooperation*

The role of the development cooperation authorities in the field of legal development cooperation is demanding. Strategic planning, design of inputs, and follow-up are among the factors involved here and are difficult to assess and in other ways the inputs are risky. Probably the basis for decisions is in many cases poorer in this area than in many others. In addition, a holistic view is desirable at the same time as the level of knowledge remains rudimentary. Caution and methodical care are required. Legal support may be required in many 'factual areas'—eg environment, capital markets, belowstructure—which is why a donor must combine such professional knowledge with legal expertise.

B. *Need for the Development of Competence*

1. *Lack of Knowledge*

Development cooperation in the legal area takes place in a theoretical vacuum compared to many other areas. There is no established theoretical framework to form the basis for inputs. Not least, there is hardly any research on the legal system of societies in transition. It presumably needs an inter-disciplinary approach which combines traditional legal studies with judicial philosophy, legal anthropology and general theoretical development thinking. Similarly, studies are required of the conditions necessary to develop and support traditional law and its institutions and the opportunity to combine traditional and official law as well as their respective institutions. The methodology of development cooperation also needs to grow so that it can be adapted to the conditions in the legal area. This requires, inter alia, the systematic documentation and application of experiences.

2. *Conclusions for Legal Development Cooperation*

The vacuum that exists argues for things like a careful approach and flexibility in the area of development cooperation, projects that are not too large, careful planning and, sometimes, a bottom-up approach.

GLOBALIZATION OF FINANCIAL MARKETS: AN INTERNATIONAL PASSPORT FOR SECURITIES OFFERINGS?

DOUGLAS W ARNER*

CHAPTER OUTLINE

* BA (Drury), JD (SMU), LLM (London). Associate Professor and Deputy Director, Asian Institute of International Financial Law, Faculty of Law, The University of Hong Kong; Visiting Fellow, Centre for Commercial Law Studies, University of London; and Deputy Director, London Institute of International Banking, Finance and Development Law. The author would like to thank the following for their comments and assistance: Christopher D Olive, Jones Day Reavis & Pogue (Dallas); Matthew S Morgan, Allen & Overy (London); and Chantal Hébert, Baker & McKenzie (Hong Kong). Any errors, of course, lie with the author.

I. INTRODUCTION

International sales and trading of securities are nothing new. In fact, studies suggest that international securities activities existed at least from the initial formation of stock exchanges in Europe. Over the last twenty years, there has been an increasing interest in international securities, their issuance, trading and regulation.[1] This trend slowed somewhat with recent emerging markets financial crises around the world, but increased again to the end of 2000, with the highest volume of mergers activity in history and massive capital raising by technology (especially telecommunications companies), to drive the volume and value of international securities business to, in absolute terms, the highest level ever. As equity markets stalled in 2001 with the collapse of the internet bubble and terrorist attacks in the United States, new issues activity in international securities markets has become quiet, but not silent, with global issues still planned and discussion of related issues continuing.[2]

While securities markets have always encompassed international participants and sales, prior to the First World War, such activities were essentially unregulated. During the period from the First World War to the 1960s, international capital movements were tightly regulated and restricted through legislative efforts of individual countries. One purpose of the Bretton Woods system was in fact to prevent financial instability of the sort seen in the first half of the 20th century and this was the system with which Sir Joseph Gold was closely involved. Beginning in the 1960s, restrictions on capital movements began to be relaxed, with a resulting growth of international financial activities, culminating in the collapse of the Bretton Woods fixed exchange rate system in 1973. Sir Joseph was deeply involved in these developments and in attempting to secure international financial stability in the years following. Following the collapse of Bretton Woods, the remainder of the 1970s were characterised by petrodollar recycling, culminating in the emerging market debt crisis of the 1980s. Towards the end of Sir Joseph's career at the IMF, changes in the international financial markets began to intensify. As the move towards State dominance of indi-

[1] Harold James INTERNATIONAL MONETARY COOPERATION SINCE BRETTON WOODS (Washington DC 1996) at 12.

[2] T Major *Deutsche Bank aims to go ahead with US listing*, FINANCIAL TIMES WEEKEND (15/16 Sept 2001) (discussing planned listing of 'global shares' on the New York Stock Exchange on 3 Oct 2001).

vidual economies began to reach its limits, the world-wide trend towards privatization of State-owned companies and assets beginning in the 1980s in the United Kingdom under Margaret Thatcher led to interest **[in?]** and need for offerings of equity securities in multiple capital markets throughout the world,[3] creating the first 'global offerings', and highlighted the 'internationalisation' of financial markets. Nonetheless, most such activities have taken place in the context of individual domestic markets, with foreign participants (whether issuers, purchasers or dealers) forced to meet the individual national requirements of any given jurisdiction of interest, a situation not dissimilar to that originally envisioned under Bretton Woods, but now in a far different context.

As a result of the pressures of internationalization of financial markets, beginning with a number of regional experiments, steps have been taken toward the acceptance of foreign credentials for offerings and listings of securities on an equal basis with those of domestic participants, of which the European efforts to develop a single market for capital in the context first of the European Communities and now the European Union are the most advanced. For a variety of reasons, most of these efforts have not been entirely successful, often due to lack of synchronization of domestic legal systems with the increasingly open and internationalized character of international financial markets. As a result of increasing 'globalization' of financial markets in the 1990s, efforts are now being focused on the development of international standards applicable to securities markets, with the aim of harmonizing minimum standards and eventually to support mutual recognition based upon common standards, including for offerings and listings of securities. Sir Joseph would have realised that the old system was no longer appropriate and that new initiatives, preferably on an international basis, were needed in order to limit volatility in a rapidly changing financial landscape in order to prevent the sorts of economic disturbances common prior to the establishment of the IMF. While he probably would have preferred a more coherent, international and formal path, he would have recognized that this is not always possible and certainly would have been interested in progress. It is in this light and in light of the comments of Sir Joseph's son, Richard, representing the next generation of international legal practitioners, that this article is presented.

After describing the trends noted above in general terms, this article analyses the issue of whether, for the first time, international efforts may lead to the development of an agreed format for the content of an international offering/listing document acceptable in jurisdictions around the

[3] For development of this thesis, See Daniel Yergin and Joseph Stanislaw, THE COMMANDING HEIGHTS: THE BATTLE BETWEEN GOVERNMENT AND THE MARKETPLACE THAT IS REMAKING THE MODERN WORLD (New York 1998) esp 370–1.

world, ie a 'global prospectus' or 'international passport prospectus'. The growing importance and usefulness of such a mechanism is underscored by recent cross-border corporate mergers and acquisitions, proposed mergers and alliances between stock exchanges around the world, and the development of 'global shares', traded on multiple markets.

Following this introduction, section II of this chapter discusses briefly the historical development of international securities markets. The most significant developments in this respect are the development of the Euromarkets and initiatives seeking to encourage international listings through relaxation of domestic standards for foreign issuers. These initiatives however do not truly foreshadow the development of a single global offering document, but rather reflect the needs and requirements of internationalization of competition between markets for business opportunities represented by cross-border offerings and listings. Section III discusses the development of two significant regional initiatives supporting mutual recognition of securities offerings: the multi-jurisdictional disclosure system (MJDS) involving the US and Canada; and the securities Directives of the European Union (EU). These initiatives are the precursors to recent efforts to promote the creation of a single offering document for offering and listing securities around the world involving the efforts of the International Organization of Securities Commissions (IOSCO) and the International Accounting Standards Committee (IASC). Section IV discusses the content of the international standards as devised, both non-financial international listing requirements and financial and accounting harmonization and standards. Section V discusses the implementation process in the US, EU, and elsewhere. Section VI concludes with a short discussion of the implications of the development of a global prospectus for further globalization of financial markets.

This author concludes that these changes are driven by a search for high standards of regulation (necessary to encourage investor participation) and by the move toward creation of a single capital market in Europe to rival that in the US. It is suggested these trends will focus consolidation in other smaller markets (eg the various countries of east Asia), along with a move towards higher 'international' standards in markets in such jurisdictions around the world, if they are to maintain the interest of international investors. Nonetheless, even with an international passport for securities offerings and listings, domestic requirements will continue to address issues of enforcement and corporate governance.

II. DEVELOPMENT OF INTERNATIONAL SECURITIES MARKETS

In the 17th and 18th centuries, the international capital markets of Europe were dominated by Amsterdam, with some competition from Geneva and Genoa. Dutch investments centred on (in consecutive periods), first, its Empire and the Continent; Britain until the Anglo-Dutch Wars; then France and the United States until the occupation of Amsterdam during the Napoleonic Wars.[4] Throughout this period activities took place through a variety of instruments such as loans, bonds, annuities, and equity securities and involved sophisticated techniques such as short selling, puts, calls, and futures.[5] While loan contracts were in use, company law, including that governing equity securities, was quite undeveloped. The essential absence of any sort of regulation of securities markets or offering requirements in all likelihood exacerbated the frequency and severity of periodic panics and crashes.

In the 19th century, London became the leading centre for international financial activities, although Paris provided strong competition. By the beginning of the First World War, the London financial markets were involved in a breadth and depth of international financial transactions rivalling in sophistication and extent those of today.[6] In fact, measurements of the degree of financial integration in the world economy indicate that at the beginning of the 20th century, the world was more interconnected than at any subsequent time, including the 1990s.[7] Such developments were not limited to London, Paris and Amsterdam: records indicate that foreign issues and listings of both foreign bonds and other trading securities were relatively common in Frankfurt in the 19th century.[8]

While the link has not been made explicitly, it is probable that the development of standardized company law (including basic requirements for financial reporting) in Britain and the US encouraged the development of the markets.[9] Nonetheless, regulation of market activities and abuses remained largely governed by the common law in both England and the US, making redress often difficult.[10]

[4] See C Kindleberger, A FINANCIAL HISTORY OF WESTERN EUROPE (1993 2nd edn), 208–14.

[5] ibid at 210.

[6] See ibid at 214–20.

[7] James, above n 1, at 12.

[8] See Kindleberger, above n 4, at 223–4. According to figures produced by Böhme, there were nine such issues in the period 1801–20 from countries such as Austria (4), Holland (2), Italy (1), and Russia (1). In the period 1851–60, there were 80, including Austria (17), Hungary (3), France/Belgium (5), Holland (1), Italy (13), Spain (2), and the US (35). *Id* at 224 (citing Helmut Böhme, Frankfurt und Hamburg, Des Deutsches Reiches Silber und Goldloch und die Allerenglishste Stadt des Kontinents (Frankfurt 1968), at 156–61.

[9] See B Black *The Legal and Institutional Preconditions for Strong Securities Markets*, 48 UCLA L REV 781 (2001); B Cheffins *Does Law Matter? The Separation of Ownership and Control in the United Kingdom*, 30 J LEGAL STUD 459 (2001); L Bebchuk and M Roe, *A Theory of Path Dependence in Corporate Ownership and Governance*, 52 STAN L REV 127 (1999); J Coffee *The Future as History: The Prospects for Global Convergence in Corporate Governance and its Implications*, 93 NW U L REV 641 (1999).

[10] See generally ibid. In the US, 'blue sky' laws began to develop early in the 20th century. See J Macey and G Miller *Origin of the Blue Sky Laws* 70 TEX L REV 347 (1991).

While the First World War significantly reduced international securities activities, the Crash of 1929 and the Great Depression drastically reduced international securities activities outside of Europe and the US until the 1960s (centred during this period in New York, reflecting the United States' position as the world's banker). This drastic reduction in international financial activity reflected a conviction that the fundamental destabilization of the previous decades had stemmed from 'volatile and irresponsible flows of capital ("hot money")' and that the international financial system could only function effectively if such flows were curtailed.[11]

In the US, Congressional studies in the 1930s led to the conclusion that one of the causes of the market crash and the depression that followed was excessive speculative activities in the financial markets and market abuses that both encouraged such activities and prejudiced the proper operation of the markets.[12] As a result, the US enacted the first comprehensive legal regime for the regulation of securities activities, including issues, issuers, financial intermediaries and market participants, all based on the premise of full and fair disclosure of all material information.[13]

This period marked the beginning of a period of increasing regulation of financial institutions and markets in the developed world, primarily as a response to varied crises. Outside of the US, securities activities continued to be regulated through company law and individual exchange rules, although in many cases they continued to remain unregulated outside of traditional sources of remedies in the domestic legal system. As will be discussed in the following section, this trend towards increased regulation, especially in the US, combined with largely closed national financial markets, had an unintended consequence: the development of an international and unregulated capital market based, once again, in London.

A. *The Euromarkets*

A post-war market in dollar deposits and lending began in the late 1940s, when the new Chinese Communist Government began to place its dollar earnings with a Soviet bank in Paris (the Banque Commerciale pour l'Europe du Nord).[14] In 1957–8, European banks, primarily in London and Switzerland, began to deal more extensively in dollars.[15] The markets that developed, first in syndicated lending, then in bonds ('Eurobonds') in the 1960s, became known as the 'Eurodollar' markets. Rapidly, however, these

11 James, above n 1, at 32. See ibid at 87–92, 125.

12 See HR Rep No 85, 73rd Cong, 1st sess (1933).

13 See J Seligman THE TRANSFORMATION OF WALL STREET: A HISTORY OF THE SECURITIES AND EXCHANGE COMMISSION AND MODERN CORPORATE FINANCE (1982).

14 James, above n 1, at 179.

15 Kindleberger, above n 4, at 439.

markets expanded beyond dollars and beyond Europe, although they are still known as the Eurocurrency markets or the Euromarkets.[16] The Euromarkets developed as a truly international market, structured to avoid domestic regulatory restrictions and their success has stimulated internationalization of domestic markets and increasingly globalization of financial markets. While the Euromarkets, with their emphasis on syndicated loans and bond offerings, fall somewhat outside the scope of the analysis of this article, given its focus on the development of a single set of issuing and trading requirements for international equity offerings, they are nonetheless important as an illustration of the possibilities available in the development of global capital markets.

As noted, the Euromarkets sought to avoid domestic regulation and in fact grew partly as the result of such restrictions in the US The development of the Eurobond market was partly stimulated by the registration requirements of US securities regulation and partly by the Interest Equalization Tax (IET) imposed in the US in 1963 to reduce the borrowings of European countries in the US.[17] With the repeal of the IET and all other restrictions on capital movements out of the US in 1973, bonds began to be issued simultaneously in New York (through allowances by the Securities and Exchange Commission (SEC)) and European financial centres, and eventually in financial centres around the world such as Hong Kong, Singapore and Tokyo, thus marking the beginning of the first multi-jurisdictional offerings of securities, albeit debt securities.

The development of the Eurocurrency markets was stimulated further by the Oil Price Shocks of 1973 and 1979, following which international banks undertook to recycle the increased earnings of oil States, earned in dollars and deposited principally in London and Switzerland (so-called 'petrodollars').[18] While this process of recycling was successful following the first shock in 1973, it was less successful following the second shock in 1979 when combined with a global surplus of liquidity.[19] Until the Debt Crisis of the 1980s (which began with Mexico's default in 1982),[20] lending dominated over bonds in the Euromarkets, in the form of both bilateral term loans and multi-lender syndications. These sorts of transactions were and are typically documented through a loan and syndication agreement, both of which have assumed a relatively standardized form, changed only

[16] According to Kindleberger, a 'eurocurrency' is any currency borrowed and lent (whether through term loans, syndications or bonds) outside the country that uses the currency. ibid at 440. The market in fact travels around the world daily, shifting from market to market as the time zone advances, although London remains the hub.

[17] Kindleberger, above n 4, at 441; James, above n 1, at 179.

[18] See James, above n 1, at 309–46.

[19] See ibid at 347–408.

[20] See Yergin and Stanislaw, above n 3, at 130–3.

slightly to reflect the experiences of each new crisis.[21] While these markets are truly global and while the loans themselves are increasingly traded and exchanged in various forms, they are private law contractual instruments: unregulated and not traditionally considered securities. Further, they are structured intentionally to avoid domestic regulation, in preference for structures built largely on private English law.

During the resolution of the Debt Crisis throughout the 1980s, bonds began to take precedence as banks securitised rescheduled debt and sought to decrease their risk exposure and increase their margins through a preference for bonds.[22] Syndicated lending nonetheless remained significant.[23] Like loans, Eurobonds have developed standardized forms, in the form of trust indenture agreements and offering documents.[24] As well, Eurobonds remain essentially unregulated, and as with the Euromarkets generally, their structures developed to avoid regulation in domestic legal systems. Unlike loan agreements, which remain essentially contractual undertakings, bonds are traditional securities and therefore typically subject to domestic regulatory concern and therefore scrutiny. As a result, Eurobonds have traditionally not been listed in the US and instead have focused on exchanges such as London and Luxembourg with simple rules governing offer, sale and listing of international bonds. Further, over time, the Eurobond market has been specifically exempted from most regulation (though not all) in Europe, primarily in order to protect the position of London's financial markets and as a reflection of the institutional nature of the market and the consequent view that such players do not require the same level of protection as small investors: they are able to look after themselves. In order to encourage international offerings in the US, the US SEC has made special efforts to support access to the US market through the promulgation of Regulation S and, more specifically, Rule 144A, and their predecessors.[25]

As highlighted above, unlike domestic capital markets, the Euromarkets are essentially unregulated and unsupervised (although the financial standing of participants is carefully monitored, both by government agencies (in the case of financial institutions) and private ratings agencies such as

[21] See J Norton and C Olive *International Syndicated Lending: The Legal Context for Economic Development in Latin America* 21 NAFTA L Rev 21 (1996); R Cranston Principles of Banking Law (1997) ch 11; P Wood International Loans, Bonds and Securities Regulation (1995), chs 1–7.

[22] See R Buckley *A Tale of Two Crises: The Search for Enduring Reforms of the International Financial System*, 6 UCLA J Int'l L & Foreign Aff 2 (2001). See also, W Cline *International Debt Reexamined* (Washington DC 1995).

[23] See Norton and Olive, above n 21.

[24] See generally R Smith and I Walter, Global Banking (1997), ch 9; Wood, above n 21, chs 8–10 (discussing the standard content of trust indentures and bond offerings).

[25] For a discussion, see generally M Steinberg International Securities Law: A Contemporary and Comparative Analysis (1999) ch 4.

Standard & Poor's and Moody's). Participants (almost exclusively financial institutions, major international corporations, and sovereigns and their agencies) operate outside the traditional requirements of domestic securities markets, primarily because these sorts of participants are deemed capable of guarding their own interests and because the principal operating arenas for the Euromarkets fear loss of business and stature. Rather, arrangements are made through contracts (loan agreements, syndication and participation arrangements, and trust indenture agreements). Thus, while these markets are global in nature and the legal arrangements involved are quite standardised, they are also organic by nature, having grown up between and around domestic legal requirements.

B. Internationalization: Domestic Efforts to Encourage International Listings

As a result of the increasing awareness of firms, securities exchanges and governments of the advantages of securities markets for accessing capital (reflected at least partially in the successes of the Euromarkets), individual countries and securities exchanges have undertaken generally unilateral initiatives to encourage foreign listings on domestic exchanges and in domestic markets.[26] While some advances have been made in encouraging such activities, because each individual jurisdiction developed its own requirements, the expense and complexity remained have largely remained prohibitive.[27] Recent international consolidation of securities exchanges (discussed in the final section, below) are the most recent of these efforts.

During the 1980s, privatization of State-owned assets, including such companies as British Steel and British Telecommunications, required access to investors in markets outside of the home jurisdiction, essentially due to the massive amounts of securities required to be offered and sold. In such circumstances, the cost of compliance with the domestic offering requirements of multiple jurisdictions could be absorbed by the large value of the offering itself. With the success of multi-jurisdictional offerings in such circumstances, financial institutions and their legal advisors realised the possibilities for truly 'global offerings' by private companies, as well as privatizations throughout the world. States likewise saw the advantages that could be gained for their own markets and firms by encouraging market access by foreign firms. Finally, developments in investment theory (especially portfolio theory) and relaxations of restrictions on institutional investors encouraged such investors to seek to diversify their portfolios through the acquisition of foreign securities.

[26] See ibid, ch 1.

[27] See H Jackson and E Pan *Regulatory Competition in International Securities Markets: Evidence from Europe in 1999—Part I*, 56 Bus Law 653 (2001).

The result was the development of different mechanisms to allow foreign issuers to list and/or sell their securities to domestic investors, most importantly through the development of 'depository receipts' whereby securities listed on a foreign exchange could be traded on a domestic exchange, if certain requirements were met.[28] In addition to depository receipts, securities regulators and stock exchanges began to allow certain derivations from domestic requirements for foreign issuers.[29] The most important of these has been the minimal deviation of the US SEC from traditional home country requirements in the area of accounting standards, shelf-registration and short form registration Statements.[30]

The dangers of the increasing internationalization of financial markets, however, were graphically shown during the worldwide collapse of stock market values in October 1987. Following drastic falls and halts in trading on numerous exchanges (including the New York Stock Exchange (NYSE) and the Stock Exchange of Hong Kong), domestic regulators began to analyse the new risks, as well as the new opportunities, presented by internationalization. The result was not only a strengthening of domestic standards and systems in many cases, but also increased international dialogue not only among securities regulators but also among central bankers and treasury officials, especially from the major industrialised countries.

III. INTERNATIONALIZATION OF STANDARDS FOR SECURITIES OFFERINGS: REGIONAL INITIATIVES

Because of the difficulties of international financial cooperation and agreement on standards, regional efforts have been undertaken with increasing frequency since the late 1950s as an attempt at pragmatic solutions to the problems and needs of international financial markets.[31] Until the period following the world-wide market collapse of 1987, however, securities regulation was typically not considered significant enough to merit international cooperative efforts. On a regional basis, the most significant efforts to date are those involving, respectively, the United States and Canada, and the countries of Europe.

[28] See J Gonzalez and C Olive *Foreign Issuer Disclosure and Accounting Compliance in US Public Offerings and Securities Listings*, 1 NAFTA L REV 39 (1995).

[29] See Steinberg, above n 25, chs 1 and 4 (discussing domestic initiatives to encourage foreign listings and issues).

[30] See Gonzalez and Olive, above n 28. Regulation S also falls under this categorization to some extent, in that it relaxes extraterritorial application of US securities laws (but not of antifraud provisions). In reality, this only reflects a realisation that the rest of the world is in fact unlikely to adopt standards identical to those in the US and that actual application of such a principle of universal extraterritoriality was impracticable and politically disadvantageous in discussions with other sovereign States.

[31] See James, above n 1, at 467–89; Kindleberger, above n 4, at 436–50.

A. The US and Canada: The Multijurisdictional Disclosure System

The Multijurisdictional Disclosure System (MJDS) originally began life as a proposal of the US SEC to create a system for the facilitation of multinational securities offerings in the US, the U.K. and Canada.[32] According to the SEC, 'to provide context for public comment on internationalization', it presented 'two conceptual approaches' to facilitate multinational offerings: (i) the reciprocal approach and (ii) the common prospectus approach, and requested comment on a series of questions dealing with these approaches.[33] Under the reciprocal approach, each country would agree to accept a prospectus which was accepted in the issuer's domicile and which met certain minimum requirements.[34] Under the common prospectus approach, a common prospectus would be developed which would then be filed simultaneously with each country's respective securities regulatory authority.[35] Following comment on the original release, the SEC, the Ontario Securities Commission and the Commission des valeurs mobilières du Quebec proposed the MJDS between the US and Canada in 1989, reflecting a 'hybrid' between the reciprocal and the common prospectus approaches.[36] The UK was not included for a number of reasons,[37] including differences in registration, accounting and auditing requirements,[38] and potential illegality interposed with the UK's acceptance of the Single Europe Act in 1986.[39]

As adopted, the MJDS is not an international legal agreement, but rather parallel sets of domestic administrative rules. In the US, the SEC, a Federal administrative agency empowered with Congressionally delegated rule-making powers, promulgated one set of rules governing securities transactions covered by US Federal securities laws[40] which, if necessary under State law, could have been adopted by the various State securities regulatory

[32] US Securities and Exchange Commission (SEC) 'Facilitation of Multinational Securities Offerings,' Securities Act of 1933, Release No 33-6568, File No S7-9-85, 17 CFR Part 230, 1985 SEC LEXIS 2074, 28 Feb 1985.

[33] ibid, SEC Release No 33-6568, at 1. [34] ibid at 3. [35] ibid.

[36] See US SEC, 'Multijurisdictional Disclosure', RIN 3235-AC64, File No S7-19-89, Rel nos 33-6841, 34-27055, 39-2217, 17 CFR Parts 230, 239, 240, 249, 260, 269, 1989 SEC LEXIS 1377, 24 July 1989, at 4.

[37] See D Johnston and KD Rockwell, Canadian Securities Regulation (2nd edn 1998), at 319–20, esp n 99 and 102.

[38] See C Jordan *The Thrills and Spills of Free Riding: International Issues before the Ontario Securities Commission*, 23 CANOTE BUS L J 379 (1994), at 381.

[39] See, *eg*, J Lipsius *The 1996 Intergovernmental Conference*, 20 EUR L REV 235 (1995), at 237; J Kingston *External Relations of the European Community—External Capacity Versus Internal Competence*, 44 INT'L COMP L QUART 659 (1995), at 659.

[40] US SEC 'Multijurisdictional Disclosure and Modifications to the Current Registration and Reporting System for Canadian Issuers', Rel nos 33-6902, 34-29354, 39-2267, IC-18210, 17 CFR Parts 200, 201, 210, 229, 230, 239, 240, 249, 260, 269 (Parts 1 to 3), 1991 SEC Lexis 1217, 21 June 1991.

agencies in order to apply to offerings within each respective State. In Canada, the Canadian Securities Administration, a non-governmental association of provincial regulatory authorities,[41] agreed and published a 'national policy',[42] which was then implemented in each province through provincial legislation or statutorily delegated agency rule-making powers.

The Canadian MJDS permits public offerings of securities of US issuers that meet specified eligibility requirements to be made in Canada on the basis of disclosure documents prepared in accordance with US law, with certain additional Canadian disclosures. Canadian authorities accept documents reviewed by the SEC, but monitor materials filed under the MJDS to confirm compliance with its specific disclosure and filing requirements. Financial Statements must be reconciled to Canadian Generally Accepted Accounting Principles (GAAP) or to International Accounting Standards (IAS),[43] although this does not apply to offerings of debt or preferred shares rated by an approved rating agency.[44]

The US MJDS permits Canadian issuers meeting eligibility criteria to satisfy certain SEC registration and reporting requirements by providing disclosure documents prepared in accordance with the requirements of Canadian securities regulatory authorities. That document is filed with the SEC, along with a 'cover page, certain legends and various exhibits'.[45] Accounting standards may be in accordance with US or Canadian GAAP, but not IAS.

In practice, the MJDS has not fulfilled its potential. While it was intended to be a first step towards international harmonization,[46] in reality it has resulted only in increased harmonization of US and Canadian regulation, with the various Canadian authorities making most of the compromises.[47] It has however increased Canadian access to US markets and stimulated some interest on the part of US issuers in Canadian markets.[48]

B. European Securities Markets

While both the oldest stock exchange[49] and the world's most significant

[41] ie, a non-statutorily self-regulatory organization.

[42] Canadian Securities Administration, Multijurisdictional Disclosure System, National Policy No 45 (Can).

[43] ibid 3.10 (Reconciliation of Financial Statements).

[44] ibid. See also s 3.4 (Offerings of Debt or Preferred Shares Having an Approved Rating).

[45] Rel No 33-6902, above n 40.

[46] See ibid at 6: '[T]he MJDS is designed with the intention of mitigating on a broader scale the difficulties posed by multinational offerings. Thus, the Commission is continuing its work with securities regulators of other countries with a view toward extending the multijurisdictional disclosure system.'

[47] Johnston and Rockwell, above n 37, at 319–20. See Jordan, above n 38, at 381.

[48] Johnston and Rockwell, above n 37, at 320.

[49] Amsterdam Stock Exchange.

international financial centre[50] are located in Europe, widespread individual ownership of securities was not common during the twentieth century outside of the United Kingdom prior to the 1990s.[51] Several explanations have been advanced to explain this, including: the major economic dislocations resulting from two World Wars and other armed conflicts; exchange and capital market controls imposed by European governments; the predominance of bank lending over securities offerings in corporate finance; the relatively small number of listed companies in Continental Europe, each with only a minority of shares available in the open market; relatively high transaction costs; insufficient or non-existent transparency and liquidity in European securities markets; the absence of regulation affording investor protection; lack of public confidence in and understanding of securities markets; and popular aversion to the risks of securities investment.[52] The development of securities markets in Europe, however, has become an objective of national policy in most Member States of the European Union and today of the EU generally, due in large part to the privatization of many State-owned enterprises beginning in the 1980s.

A study of capital markets by the European Economic Community (EEC) in 1966 addressed impediments to the effective functioning of national markets and their availability to foreign borrowers. The Segré Report[53] (so-called after the chairman of the group of experts and the principal author, Claudio Segré) found that national markets in Europe discriminated in favour of domestic borrowers, especially national governments, as against foreign, primarily through regulations governing the investment of funds of savings banks and insurance, assistance for housing, etc. In addition, few European securities were listed on stock exchanges outside the domicile of the issuing company. As a result of practical governmental needs (combined with the forces of harmonization, access deregulation, and prudential re-regulation inherent in the process of opening developing the 'Maastricht' principal of free movement of capital), national securities regulation in Western Europe has begun to develop in recent years.[54] Prior to the 1990s, however, securities regulation in Western Europe had been virtually non-existent outside of the United Kingdom.[55] Although company law was well-developed across Western Europe, European stock exchanges have

[50] London.

[51] See Benn Steil, *et al*, THE EUROPEAN EQUITY MARKETS: THE STATE OF THE UNION AND AN AGENDA FOR THE MILLENNIUM (1996).

[52] Manning Gilbert Warren III *Global Harmonization of Securities Laws: The Achievements of the European Communities*, 31 HARV INT'L L J 185, 194 (1990) [hereinafter Global Harmonization].

[53] EEC, Commission, The Development of a European Capital Market (Brussels 1966) (Segré Report). See Kindleberger, above n 4, at 438–9.

[54] Global Harmonization, above n 52, at 194.

[55] ibid, at 194.

been historically self-regulating, with little or no direct oversight by national governments.[56] Moreover, European States have not historically mandated full disclosure systems for the distribution or trading of securities, nor have they prohibited insider trading or other market manipulative practices long prohibited by the United States.[57]

Most of the EU Member States only moved to develop broad-based equity markets from the late 1980s on. Further, the present State of EU financial services markets is still absent any comprehensive and consistent regulation and enforcement as in the US While the current EU system is complex, it is still not so complex as that of the US (though the EU system is designed as a comprehensive and coherent regulatory system).

The EU framework for investment services provides minimum standards for accounting and auditing standards, listings and stock exchange regulation, company law, market conduct regulation, and regulation of institutional investors. It should be borne in mind, however, that this framework is not complete: since its purpose is to ensure the harmonization of the laws of the Member States in so far as this is necessary for the achievement of a single market and to fill gaps relating to cross-border activities, it builds on the existing national systems of company and securities laws rather than trying to replace them by a complete new system. The purpose of this article is not to evaluate the specific provisions of the EU framework; however, a general appreciation of the key elements of the EU framework is necessary to understand the development of the European passport prospectus.

1. *The Creation of a Common Market in Investment Services*

The EU legislative framework for financial markets seems to be grounded in a concept that can be thought of as a search for equivalence among disparate regulatory and legal systems, while taking into account the continuing reality of separate and distinct national legal and regulatory regimes as the basis of any overall EU initiatives.[58] Initially, efforts focused on harmonization of rules across Member States; however, this proved impossible in many areas and in the 1980s, efforts moved to development

[56] ibid.

[57] When the Public Offers Prospectus Directive was proposed in 1981, only five members of the EU required prospectus disclosure to investors in public offerings of securities, namely: Belgium, France, Ireland, Luxembourg, and the United Kingdom. 1980–1981 EUR PARL DOC (COM No 893) (1980), OJ EUR COMM (No C 355) 39, explanatory memorandum, para 6 (1981). As of 1990, West Germany still imposed no prospectus upon issuers in connection with public offers of securities not listed on an exchange. Global Harmonization, above n 2, at 195 n 54.

[58] See B Steil et al Equity Trading IV: The ISD and the Regulation of European Market Structure in THE EUROPEAN EQUITY MARKETS: THE STATE OF THE UNION AND AN AGENDA FOR THE MILLENNIUM 113 (1996).

of mutual recognition based upon common minimum standards. These key principles were outlined in the Commission's 1985 White Paper[59] and enshrined in the 1986 Single Europe Act[60] implementing the common internal market on the basis of 'mutual recognition', based on common minimum standards applicable in all Member States through European Directives and implemented through domestic legislation. According to this methodology, all Member States agree to recognize the validity of one another's laws, regulations, and standards, thereby facilitating free trade in goods and services without the need for prior harmonization,[61] while limiting the scope for competition among rules by mandating Member State conformity with a 'floor' of essential minimum European requirements.[62] As such, investment services regulation in the EU seeks to avoid the problem of competitive deregulation and regulatory arbitrage that may undermine the legitimacy and efficiency of financial markets.[63]

As a general matter, the EU system of securities regulation rests on the EU company law Directives and accounting Directives. In turn, the basic framework for the EU securities regulatory regime is founded upon a series of Directives known as the stock exchange Directives[64] (enacted prior to the 1986 Single European Act, but subsequently amended to provide for mutual recognition) and now consolidated into a single Directive,[65] as well as Directives dealing with collective investment schemes (eg mutual funds),[66] unlisted prospectuses,[67] and insider dealing.[68]

The second level of EU investment services regulation deals with the establishment of a single market in financial services, based on the common minimum framework provided by the basic company law, accounting and securities Directives. This level centres principally around the Investment Services Directive (ISD) and the Capital Adequacy Directive (CAD). To put

[59] COMPLETING THE INTERNAL MARKET: WHITE PAPER FROM THE COMMISSION TO THE EUROPEAN COUNCIL (Milan, 28–29 June 1985).

[60] Single European Act (1986).

[61] See Steil, above n 58. This principle underlies the Second Banking Directive (2BCD) as well as the ISD. ibid.

[62] ibid, at 114. According to commentators, the Commission has recently followed the mutual recognition principle to a much greater extent than the harmonization principle. ibid, at 115; see also Global Harmonization, above n 52.

[63] See Global Harmonization, above n 52.

[64] The Stock Exchange Listing Directives include: the Admission Directive, the Listing Particulars Directive, the Interim Reports Directive and the Major Holding Directive.

[65] Directive 2001/34/EC of the European Parliament and of the Council of 28 May 2001 on the admission of securities to official stock exchange listing and on information to be published on those securities, OJ L 184 (2001) (the 'Consolidated Stock Exchange Directive').

[66] Council Directive 85/611/EEC of 20 Dec 1985 on the coordination of laws, regulations and administrative provisions relating to undertakings for collective investment in transferable securities (UCITS), OJ L 375 (1985).

[67] Public Offer Prospectus Directive, preamble at 8.

[68] Insider Dealing Directive.

this in a broader perspective, the single market is rooted in basic tenets of the Treaty of Rome respecting the free movement of capital, establishment and services, and is manifested in the various single 'passport' directives.[69] Under the concept of the 'single' passport, an EU firm authorized in one Member State (its 'home State') and wishing to operate in other Member States ('host States') will generally be able to choose to supply services through branches or to supply services on a cross-border basis without having a permanent physical presence in the host State.[70] The intended benefit of the passport is that it should increase competition by opening markets to a wider range of participants and by allowing firms to choose the most cost-effective means of supplying services to a particular market.[71]

Combined with the basic framework established in the company law and securities Directives and the capital standards of the CAD, the ISD was meant to establish the framework for a comprehensive European system of securities regulation.

2. *The Underlying Legal and Financial Belowstructure: Company Law*

Many areas traditionally considered in the US as matters of securities law rather than corporate law are covered under the company law framework in Europe and elsewhere. EU company law is based on the prohibition of discrimination within the EU based on the nationality of an entity organized within a Member State under Article 7 of the Treaty of Rome.[72] Companies organized under the laws of one Member State have the right to establish branches in other Member States.[73] Further, regulation for the protection of shareholders, employees, and creditors must be equivalent throughout the EU.[74] As a result of the political impossibility of achieving strict harmonization in this very diverse area,[75] the EU began to propose Directives which prescribed only basic, essential principles, with a requirement of mutual recognition among the Member States.[76]

[69] The passport directives in the financial services area include: (i) the First and Second Banking Coordination Directives (1BCD and 2BCD) (banking); (ii) the Investment Services Directive (ISD) (investment firms and securities markets); (iii) the UCITS Directive (collective investment schemes); (iv) the First, Second and Third Life Assurance Directives (life assurance); (v) the First, Second and Third Non-Life Insurance Directives (non-life insurance); and (vi) the proposed First Pension Funds Directive (pension funds).

[70] See *The EU Single Market in Financial Services*, BANK OF ENGLAND QUAR BULL 92 (Feb 1993).

[71] ibid.

[72] Treaty Establishing the European Economic Community, 25 Mar 1957, 298 UNTS 11, Art 7 (hereinafter, 'Treaty of Rome').

[73] ibid, Art 58.

[74] ibid, Art 54(3)(g).

[75] See Global Harmonization, above n 52, at 197–8 (discussing development of EU company law).

[76] ibid.

Companies are organizations which are created and administered according to legal requirements, and involve different categories of persons —shareholders, employees, creditors, and third parties—who are all concerned in some way with the activity of the undertaking.[77] The first objective of the approximation or harmonization of company law at the Community level is to ensure an equivalent degree of protection for the interests of these various constituencies.[78]

Most significant are the First Company Law Directive,[79] and the Second Company Law Directive.[80] For present purposes, the First Directive is important because it defines a system of public disclosure applicable to all companies—an area covered more by the securities laws in the US. The Second Directive deals with the raising, maintenance, and alteration of the capital of public limited companies (PLCs)—once again, essential for the present discussion.[81]

Other significant company law Directives include: the Third Company Law Directive,[82] introducing a common procedure for mergers; the Eleventh Company Law Directive,[83] providing for consolidated reporting; the Twelfth Company Law Directive,[84] dealing with single-member limited liability companies; and the Regulation on the European Economic Interest

[77] European Commission, *White Paper on the Preparation of the Associated Countries of Central and Eastern Europe for Integration into the Internal Market of the Union*, COM(95) 163 final 2, Annex, at 308.

[78] ibid. The basic legal approach to harmonization of company law has a twofold aim: (i) to remove obstacles to companies' freedom of establishment in order to expand and improve market competitivity; and (ii) to establish an equivalent degree of protection throughout the Community for the various constituencies. ibid at 309. See Treaty, Art 54, s 3g. The second approach is to allow enterprises to create new or combine existing cross-border operations on the basis of EU rather than national laws. Annex, above n 77, at 309. See Treaty, Arts 235, 100A

[79] First Council directive 68/151/EEC of 9 Mar 1968 on coordination of safeguards which, for the protection of the interests of members and others, are required by Member States companies within the meaning of the second paragraph of Art 58 of the Treaty, with a view to making such safeguards equivalent throughout the Community, OJ L 65 (1968).

[80] Second Council Directive 77/91/EEC of 13 Dec 1976 on coordination of safeguards which, for the protection of the interests of members and others, are required by Member States of companies within the meaning of the second paragraph of Art 58 of the Treaty, in respect of the formation of public limited liability companies and the maintenance and alteration of their capital, with a view to making such safeguards equivalent, OJ L 26 (1977), as amended by Council Directive 92/101/EEC, OJ L 347 (1992).

[81] Most specifically, the minimum subscribed capital of a PLC must be at least ECU 25,000. This is decidedly different from US law, under which no minimum capital is generally prescribed.

[82] Third Council Directive 78/885/EEC of 9 Oct 1978 based on Art 54(3)(g) of the Treaty concerning mergers of public limited liability companies, OJ L 295 (1978).

[83] Eleventh Council Directive 89/666/EEC of 21 Dec 1989 concerning disclosure requirements in respect of branches opened in a Member State by certain types of companies governed by the law of another Member State, OJ L 395 (1989).

[84] Twelfth Council Directive 89/667/EEC of 21 Dec 1989 concerning single member private limited companies, OJ L 395 (1989).

Grouping (EEIG),[85] creating a Community level instrument permitting cooperation of undertakings from different Member State jurisdictions.

3. *The Stock Exchange Directives*

The overall objective of these Directives is to provide a set of minimum standards capable of operating on a uniform basis throughout the EU and in a way which removes some of the barriers which would otherwise result from the existence of conflicting requirements in a number of different markets, so as to permit greater flexibility of access to the EU capital markets than might otherwise have been the case.

In July 2000, the European Commission proposed a simplification of the legislative framework governing stock exchange listings into a single directive.[86] The four major Directives covered are:

- The Directive on the conditions for the admission of securities to official stock exchange listing (79/279) (Admission Directive);[87]
- The Directive on the listing particulars to be published for the admission of securities to official stock exchange listing (80/390) (Listing Particulars Directive);[88]
- The Directive on information to be published on a regular basis by companies, the shares of which have been admitted to official stock-exchange listing (82/121) (Interim Reports Directive);[89] and
- The Directive on the information to be published when a major holding in a listed company is acquired or disposed of (88/627) (Major Holdings Directive).[90]

Directives not included are those not directly linked to the listing of or limited to listed securities, namely:

[85] Council Regulation 2137/85/EEC on the European Economic Interest Grouping (EEIG), OJ L 199 (1985).

[86] European Commission 'Securities: Commission proposes simplification of legislative framework', 24 July 2000; idem., Proposal for a Directive of the European Parliament and of the Council on the admission of securities to official stock exchange listing and on information to be published on those securities (codified version), 2000/0174 (COD), COM(2000) 126 final (2000).

[87] Council Directive 79/279/EEC of 5 Mar 1979, coordinating the conditions for the admission of securities to official stock exchange listing, OJ L 66 (1979)

[88] Council Directive 80/390/EEC of 17 Mar 1980 coordinating the requirements for the drawing up, scrutiny and distribution of the listing particulars to be published for the admission of securities to official stock exchange listing, OJ L (1980).

[89] Council Directive 82/121/EEC of 15 Feb 1982 on information to be published on a regular basis by companies the shares of which have been admitted to official stock exchange listing, OJ L (1982).

[90] Council Directive 88/627/EEC of 12 Dec 1988 on the information to be published when a major holding in a listed company is acquired or disposed of, OJ L (1988).

- The Directive on undertakings for collective investment in transferable securities (85/611/EEC) (the UCITS Directive);[91]
- The Investment Services Directive (93/22/EEC) (the ISD);[92]
- The Directive on investor-compensation schemes (97/9/EC) (Investor Compensation Schemes Directive);
- The Directive on prospectuses in the case of a public offer (89/298/EEC) (Public Offer Prospectus Directive);[93] and
- The Directive on insider dealing (89/592/EEC) (Insider Dealing Directive).[94]

The finalized consolidated listing Directive was adopted on 28 May 2001, in a substantially identical format to the initial proposal and repealing the underlying Directives.[95]

Specifically, the consolidated listing Directive details requirements respecting five major areas respecting listed securities, namely: official listing of securities[96] and information to be included;[97] conditions relating to official listing of securities;[98] ongoing obligations relating to securities admitted to official listing;[99] publication and communication of information;[100] and competent authorities and cooperation between Member

[91] UCITS, above n 66.

[92] Council Directive 93/22/EEC of 10 May 1993 on investment services in the securities field, OJ L 141 (1993).

[93] Council Directive 89/298/EEC of 17 Apr 1989 coordinating the requirements for the drawing-up, scrutiny and distribution of the prospectus to be published when transferable securities are offered to the public, OJ L 124 (1989).

[94] Council Directive 89/592/EEC of 13 Nov 1989 coordinating regulations on insider dealing, OJ L 334 (1989).

[95] Consolidated Stock Exchange Directive, above n 65.

[96] Title II. Issues addressed include: general conditions for admission (chs I and II, Arts 5–8); derogations (Ch III, Arts 9–10); and powers of national competent authorities (Ch IV), including decision of admission (s 1, Arts 11–15), information requested by authorities (s 2, Art 16), actions against issuers failing to comply with obligations (s 3, Art 17), suspension and discontinuance (s 4, Art 18) and judicial review (s 5, Art 19).

[97] Annex I.

[98] Title III. Issues addressed include: publication of listing particulars (ch. I), including exemptions (s 2, Art 23) and permitted omissions (s 3, Art 24), contents (s 4, Arts 25–34), control and circulation (s 5, Arts 35–6), mutual recognition and negotiations with non-Member States (ss 7–8, Arts 37–41); conditions for admission (ch II), including those relating to the company (s 1, Arts 42–4) and to the shares (s 2, Arts 45–51); conditions relating to debt securities (ch III, ss 1–3, Arts 52–59); and government debt securities (ch IV, Arts 60–3).

[99] Title IV. Issues addressed include: general obligations (ch II), including newly issued shares of the same class (s 1, Art 64), treatment of shareholders (s 2, Art 65), amendment of corporate documents (s 3, Art 66), annual accounts and annual report (s 4, Art 67), periodical information (s 7, Arts 70–1), semi-annual reporting requirements (s 8, Arts 72–7); obligations relating to debt securities and their issuers (ch. II, ss 1–2, Arts 78–84); and obligations related to major holdings (ch III), including disclosure requirements (s 2, Arts 89–91), voting rights (s 3, Art 92), exemptions (s 4, Arts 93–5), role of competent authorities (s 5, Art 96) and sanctions (s 6, Art 97).

[100] Title V. Issues addressed include: publication and communication of listing particulars (ch I), including procedures (s 1, Arts 98–100) and prior communication to competent authorities

States.[101] Information specified in Schedule A to Annex I to be included in listing particulars for equity securities includes: information on those responsible for the listing particulars and for auditing of accounts;[102] information concerning the listing and shares;[103] general information about the issuer and its capital;[104] information concerning the issuer's activities;[105] information about the issuer's assets, liabilities, financial position, profits and losses;[106] information concerning administration, management and supervision;[107] and information concerning recent developments and prospects.[108]

4. *Public Offer Prospectus Directive*

The Public Offer Prospectus Directive,[109] adopted in 1989 after 10 years of controversial negotiations,[110] sought to harmonize the disclosure standards of the Member States for public offerings of securities regardless of their listed or unlisted status. Like the consolidated listing Directive, its underlying policy is to protect investors by providing information necessary to assess the risks of investment in securities; to reinforce confidence in securities markets; to contribute to the correct functioning and development of securities markets; and to establish an equivalent level of securities disclosure among the Member States.[111] The Directive however has largely been ineffective and not used in practice.[112]

5. *The Investment Services Directive*

The most relevant of the passport directives (for present purposes) is the Investment Services Directive ('ISD'),[113] adopted in 1993. The ISD is intended to provide a 'single passport' for EU securities firms to conduct cross-border operations anywhere in the EU based on a licence issued by

(s 2, Art 101); publication and communication of information after listing (ch II, Art 102); and languages (ch III, Arts 103–4).

101 Title VI, Arts 105–7.

102 Annex 1, sch A, ch 1.

103 ibid, ch 2.

104 ibid, ch 3.

105 ibid, ch 4.

106 ibid, ch 5.

107 ibid, ch 6.

108 ibid, ch 7.

109 Council Directive 89/298/EEC of 17 Apr 1989 Coordinating the Requirements for the Drawing-up, Scrutiny and Distribution of the Prospectus to be Published When Transferable Securities are Offered to the Public, OJ L 124 (1989). See M Warren III *Regulatory Harmony in the European Communities: The Common Market Prospectus*, 16 Brooklyn J Int'l L (1990).

110 Global Harmonization, above n 52, at 215.

111 Public Offer Prospectus Directive, above n 67, at 8.

112 See Jackson and Pan, above n 27, at 680–3.

113 Council Directive 93/22/EEC on investment services in the securities field, OJ L 141 (1993).

their respective home States.[114] As originally proposed, the ISD was designed to achieve the goal of breaking down the various EU Member States' protectionist, non-tariff barriers to domestic market entry.

As adopted, the major provisions of the ISD are intended to provide: (i) common minimum authorization or licensing requirements among the EU Member States;[115] (ii) mutual recognition of the licence granted in the home State by all other Member States or 'host States';[116] (iii) prudential rules establishing common minimum financial soundness standards among the Member States;[117] (iv) certain guiding principles for adoption of conduct-of-business rules by the host States;[118] (v) direct access to each Member State's domestic stock exchange for both outside investment firms and banks;[119] (vi) requirements for concentration of securities trading in regulated markets which preserve investor choice to trade in less regulated markets;[120] (vii) minimum transparency rules for regulated markets;[121] and (viii) reciprocity.[122] for non-EU firms to participate in the newly integrated marketplace.

Although the ISD frees authorized investment firms from having to obtain host State authorization, it does impose certain regulatory conditions on those firms in connection with securing membership in or access to the host States' regulated markets, including rules concerning transactions in the host State market, professional standards, and rules and procedures for clearing and settlement of securities trades.[123]

6. *EMU and the Creation of a Single European Capital Market*

On 1 January, 1999, the individual currencies of the eleven EU Member States meeting the relevant criteria in the Maastricht Treaty and agreeing to do so, ceased to exist and were permanently fixed in exchange relationship, thereby creating a single European currency, the 'euro', and European Economic and Monetary Union ('EMU'). While to date significant differences still exist in European capital markets, with the introduction of the euro, financial Statements and offering documents have begun to become comparable. This shift is beginning to produce, when combined with the

[114] Manning Gilbert Warren III *The European Union's Investment Services Directive*, 15 U PA J INT'L BUS L 181 (1994). The ISD is intended to establish a level playing field amongst banks and securities firms in the EU, and especially to prevent banks from having a comparative advantage over securities firms as a result of the single passport of the 2BCD. See EU single market in financial services, above n 70, at 95.

[115] Investment Services Directive, Art 3.

[116] ibid, Art 14(1), (2).

[117] ibid, Art 10.

[118] ibid, Art 11.

[119] ibid, Art 15.

[120] ibid, Art 14(3), (4).

[121] ibid, Art

[122] ibid, Art 7.

[123] ibid, Art 15(2) ('Access to a regulated market, admission to membership thereof and continued access or membership shall be subject to compliance with . . . the professional standards imposed on staff and in conjunction with the market.')

painfully developed securities regulatory framework discussed in the previous sections, the development of a unified European capital market for the first time.

Prior to the signing of the Maastricht Treaty in 1992, there existed little impetus for Member States to actively implement the securities and company law directives. However, with the coming into force of the Treaty in 1994 and its requirements for adoption and implementation of the framework supporting freedom of capital movements necessary to underpin EMU, Continental Member States have adopted and implemented legislation quite foreign to the securities markets of their domestic systems. The result has been an increasing awareness of the use of capital markets and the realization that the legislative changes, when combined with the advent of the single currency, will change the nature of finance throughout the EU, but most especially in the Euro-11 (soon to be Euro-12, with the addition of Greece) members.

While the ultimate result is yet to be seen, significant movements have already taken place with the significant and continuing development of domestic capital markets in the EU. Further, new initiatives are coming rapidly seeking to take advantage of new opportunities and to place competitors at an advantage in the European markets that are in all likelihood to arrive in short order. Although numerous impediments to such developments remain (most notably in the area of taxation), activity is set to continue increasing at a rapid pace, putting pressure on the barriers that remain. One example of the recognition of continuing impediments and the pressure to remove them is the establishment of a triumverate of 'wise men' to review the EU capital markets and to develop proposals to remove remaining barriers to the creation of a single European capital market.

It is this 'real world' experience of the countries of the EU and their moves to the attainment of regional capital markets with an agreed and mutually acceptable issuing and trading framework that indicates the real advantages the path that might lie ahead in the globalization of capital markets. The development of European capital markets and other countries' nervousness respecting the same have provided the impetus to international organizations such as the International Organization of Securities Commissions (IOSCO) and the International Accounting Standards Committee and their previously recalcitrant members, such as the US, to consider the development of an internationally acceptable offering document.

IV. INTERNATIONAL DISCLOSURE STANDARDS FOR SECURITIES OFFERING AND LISTINGS

Originally formed in 1973 as an initiative of the US SEC to facilitate cooperation among securities regulators of the Americas, the International Organization of Securities Commissions (IOSCO) encompasses over 100 members representing securities regulatory authorities from developed and developing countries around the world, as well as over 50 affiliate members representing self-regulatory organizations (SROs) and stock and futures exchanges.[124] Today, IOSCO is the leading international financial organization coordinating cooperation, standardisation and establishment of minimum internationally agreed standards in the area of securities regulation.

In terms of functions, its members have agreed, through its permanent structures:[125] (i) to cooperate together to promote high standards of regulation in order to maintain just, efficient and sound markets; (ii) to exchange information on their respective experiences in order to promote the development of domestic markets; (iii) to unite their efforts to establish standards and an effective surveillance of international securities transactions; and (iv) to provide mutual assistance to promote the integrity of the markets by a rigorous application of the standards and by effective enforcement against offences.

Following the meetings of its Executive and Technical Committees in Paris in May 1998, IOSCO announced the release of four documents of significance to securities regulators and market participants:[126] (i) Objectives and Principles of Securities Regulation;[127] (ii) International Disclosure Standards for Cross–Border Offerings and Initial Listings by Foreign Issuers;[128] (iii) Risk Management and Control Guidance for Securities Firms and their Supervisors;[129] and (iv) Methodologies for Determining Minimum Capital Standards for Internationally Active Securities Firms.[130]

With the release of these four documents, IOSCO has sought to produce a largely complete and comprehensive body of internationally agreed principles and standards for securities regulation. Of most interest for present purposes are the *Objectives and Principles* and the *International Disclosure*

[124] See IOSCO, 1999 Annual Report (2000).

[125] IOSCO, General Information on IOSCO <http://www.iosco.org/index2.html>.

[126] IOSCO, Press Communique (27 May 1998) <http://www.iosco.org/press/presscomm980529.html>.

[127] IOSCO, Consultation Draft: Objectives and Principles of Securities Regulation (May 1998) <http://www.iosco.org> (hereinafter, 'IOSCO Principles').

[128] IOSCO, Report of the Technical Committee, International Disclosure Standards for Cross–Border Offerings and Initial Listings by Foreign Issuers (May 1998) <http://www.iosco.org>.

[129] IOSCO, Report of the Technical Committee, Risk Management and Control Guidance for Securities Firms and their Supervisors (May 1998) <http://www.iosco.org>.

[130] IOSCO, Report of the Technical Committee, Methodologies for Determining Minimum Capital Standards for Internationally Active Securities Firms (May 1998) <http://www.iosco.org>.

Standards. These two documents, taken together, establish the underlying standards for securities regulation and the form and content of an internationally acceptable offering document. The combination, accepted at IOSCO's Annual Meeting in September 1998 in Nairobi, Kenya, is in turn to be implemented by the membership through domestic legislation and regulation, with the intention to create a truly global set of standards for issuing and trading securities. According to IOSCO, in releasing the *International Disclosure Standards*, 'the Technical Committee has developed and released for public comment a set of international standards for non–financial Statement disclosure, which will greatly simplify cross–border offerings and initial listings on international markets.'[131]

A. *Objectives and Principles of Securities Regulation*

Following an initiative of the Group of Seven (G-7) at their Lyon Summit in 1995, the Group of Ten and representatives of 16 emerging market economies published a framework for promoting financial stability in domestic economies around the world.[132] As part of this initiative, international financial organizations such as IOSCO were instructed to develop internationally acceptable principles and standards for their respective disciplines. IOSCO's *Objectives and Principles* are the key standard in the area of securities regulation and reflect its membership's agreement that there are certain principles that form the basis for an effective system of regulation of securities and derivatives markets.

The document represents the joint efforts of IOSCO's Executive, Technical and Emerging Markets Committees and is intended to be a reference point for those who work in the financial markets, providing guidance for securities regulators, and a yardstick against which progress towards effective regulation can be measured. The document sets out the three objectives of securities regulation, and presents 30 principles for the practical implementation of these objectives. The IOSCO principles of securities regulation were formally adopted during its annual conference in September 1998.[133]

The IOSCO *Objectives and Principles of Securities Regulation* sets out three main objectives of securities regulation:[134] (i) the protection of investors; (ii) ensuring that markets are fair, efficient and transparent; and (iii) the reduction of systemic risk. To achieve these objectives, IOSCO has

[131] IOSCO Communique, above n 126.

[132] Group of Ten (G-10, A Strategy for the Formulation, Adoption and Implementation of Sound Principles and Practices to Strengthen Financial Systems, Report of the G-10 Working Party on Financial Stability in Emerging Markets (Apr 1997).

[133] IOSCO Principles, above n 127.

[134] ibid, at 6–8.

developed principles to be implemented as part of a legal framework for securities and capital markets.[135] Most significantly for present purposes, in order to provide adequate market information, issuers of securities must meet requirements for full, timely and accurate disclosure of financial results and other information material to investor decisions.[136] Legal safeguards should exist to ensure that holders of securities in a company are treated in a fair and equitable manner.[137] In addition, accounting and auditing standards need to be of a high and internationally acceptable quality.[138]

B. *International Disclosure Standards for Cross-border Offerings and Initial Listings by Foreign Issuers*

In order to build upon the general principles respecting offering and listings standards, IOSCO has developed a framework for minimum content of public offer prospectuses. This latter document is intended to set a basic framework for international offering documents acceptable to regulators and stock exchanges around the world. Such a framework could serve as an internationally acceptable basis for the further development of stock exchange listing requirements and prospectus regulations throughout the world.

Specifically:

> The International Organization of Securities Commissions (IOSCO) believes it is important for securities regulators to facilitate cross border offerings and listings by multinational issuers by enhancing comparability of information, while ensuring a high level of investor protection. An important factor in achieving these goals is the development of a generally accepted body of non-financial Statement disclosure standards that could be addressed in a single disclosure document to be used by foreign issuers in cross-border offerings and initial listings, subject to the host country review or approval processes.[139]

According to IOSCO, this report presents a set of non–financial Statement disclosure standards (financial Statements standards are the subject of another project) that will apply to foreign companies seeking to enter a host–country market, facilitating cross-border offerings and initial listings.[140] The intention is that the adoption of these standards will allow issuers to prepare a single disclosure document that will serve as an 'international passport' to capital raising and listing in more than one jurisdiction at a time. If successful, the implementation of these standards will represent

[135] ibid at 9 and Annexure 3 (listing areas of implementation necessary as a precondition).

[136] IOSCO Principles, above n 127, Principle 14.

[137] ibid, Principle 15.

[138] ibid, Principle 16.

[139] IOSCO, International Disclosure for Cross-border Offerings and Initial Listings by Foreign Issuers (May 1998) (hereinafter 'IDS'), at 3.

[140] IOSCO Communique, above n 126.

an important step forward in reducing the costs of capital raising for companies, enabling them to issue or list shares in multiple jurisdictions without concern for the burdens of complying with a multiplicity of non-financial Statement disclosure requirements.

Following the receipt of comments from the IOSCO Emerging Markets Committee and from the international financial community, the standards were approved by the membership of the entire organization, including the US SEC.[141]

1. *Scope of the Standards*

Part I sets out *International Disclosure Standards (IDS)* for use by companies in connection with cross-border public offerings and listings of equity securities. The Standards are to apply to listings and public offers and sales of equity securities for cash; and unless otherwise indicated, the Standards are intended to be used for prospectuses, offering and initial listing documents and registration Statements.[142] The Standards relate to non-financial Statement disclosure requirements and do not address a number of issues, including:[143] (i) which bodies of accounting or auditing principles may be followed by the issuer in preparation of its financial Statements; (ii) disclosure requirements that may apply in some countries in connection with other types of transactions, such as business combinations, tender offers, exchange offers, 'going private' transactions or interested party transactions; (iii) collective investment schemes or 'start-up' companies with no history of operations; (iv) continuous reporting disclosure mandates which may arise, for example, out of insider trading laws, requirements to disclose material developments or antifraud prohibitions; and (v) suitability criteria that may be imposed by stock exchanges in connection with listings of equity securities, such as the company's operating history, asset size, profitability, market float, share price, etc.

Companies engaged in specialized industries (ie banking, insurance, mining and oil and gas companies) may be required to provide additional information in certain countries, and the sources of these requirements are set forth in Part II, which addresses disclosure issues outside of the Standards and includes information of a general nature and other disclosure requirements that may apply in certain countries. The disclosure requirements for certificates representing shares, such as depository receipts, voting trust certificates or similar forms of ownership representation, are also referenced in Part II.

[141] Securities Exchange Act, Release No 34-41936 (2000).
[142] IDS, above n 139, at 3.
[143] ibid at 3–4.

The Standards are intended to apply to cross-border offering and listings. Under the IDS, an offering or listing of securities is considered to be 'cross-border' 'when it is directed to one or more countries other than the company's home country (whether or not the offering or listing also is being made concurrently in the company's home country).'[144] As a general matter, according to IOSCO, the IDS can be applied in a particular host country to offerings or listings by all foreign companies, subject to certain exceptions.[145]

2. *Additional Requirements*

The IDS were issued with a recommendation that IOSCO members accept in their respective home jurisdictions a disclosure document containing the information set forth in the Standards.[146] According to IOSCO, additional actions, however, may be needed in some jurisdictions to implement the Standards, and issuers are encouraged to verify that the Standards are in effect in the host country jurisdiction prior to their use.[147] While the IDS are not necessarily intended to substitute for or to replace disclosure requirements applicable to any jurisdiction's domestic issuers, they are intended to provide alternative standards for the preparation of a single disclosure document by foreign issuers.[148]

In addition to the specific disclosures required in the Standards, according to IOSCO, most countries rely on an overriding principle that 'in connection with a registration or listing of securities or a public offering of

[144] ibid at 4.

[145] ibid at 4. In the document, IOSCO notes the following exceptions:
(i) Australia: the Standards will not apply to companies incorporated in New Zealand that are listed or See king to be listed on an Australian Securities Exchange.
(ii) Canada: the Standards will not apply to companies organized in the United States that use the Canadian Multijurisdictional Disclosure System with the United States, described in National Policy No. 45. The Standards will not apply to a company legally organized, incorporated or established in Canada for offerings within Canada.
(iii) European Union: offerings or listings by a company registered in an EU member State that only take place within EU member States will not be considered to be cross-border (but See also Item XX, Mutual recognition in the European Union in Part II).
(iv) Hong Kong, the Standards will only apply to companies whose primary listing is on a stock exchange approved under the Stock Exchange of Hong Kong's Listing Rule 19.30 as being an exchange that is a 'regulated, regularly operating, open stock market recognized for this purpose by the Exchange' and the issuer 'conducts its business and makes disclosure according to the accepted standards in Hong Kong.'
(v) United States, the Standards will not apply to (1) companies that are organized in a foreign country but do not meet the Securities and Exchange Commission's definition of a 'foreign private issuer' as set forth in Rule 405 under the Securities Act of 1933, as amended, or in Rule 3b-4 under the Securities Exchange Act of 1934, as amended; or (2) companies organized in Canada that register under the US federal securities laws using the rules and forms provided for in the US Multijurisdictional Disclosure System with Canada.

[146] ibid at 3. [147] ibid. [148] See ibid at 3.

securities, a company should disclose all information that would be material to an investor's investment decision and that is necessary for full and fair disclosure.'[149] Accordingly, information called for by specific requirements contained in the Standards may need to be expanded under this general principle of disclosure of material information, where supplemental information is deemed to be material to investors and necessary to keep the mandated disclosure provided pursuant to specific requirements from being misleading.[150]

The Standards also address omission of information and supplementary information.[151] If a disclosure requirement is inapplicable to an issuer's sphere of activity or legal form, no information need be provided in response to that requirement, although equivalent information should be given, if possible. Any significant change or any inaccuracy in the contents of the document which may materially affect the company or its securities, that occurs between the date of publication of the document and the date of sale or listing also must be adequately disclosed and made public.

3. The Standards

Following an introduction (summarized in the previous section) and a glossary of terms,[152] the Standards, in Part I, outline the contents of an acceptable document.[153] Part II provides country specific information on areas not covered within the standards, necessary to validate the document in a given jurisdiction, which should be incorporated as a 'wrapper' to the IDS prospectus. In outline form, the cross-border prospectus is to comprise the following ten information categories: (i) identity of directors, senior management and advisers; (ii) offer statistics and expected timetable; (iii)

[149] ibid at 4–5. [150] ibid at 5. [151] ibid at 5.

[152] The following terms are defined for consistency throughout the Standards: affiliate; beneficial owner; company; directors and senior management; document; equity securities; group; home country; host country; and pre-emptive issue. ibid at 6–7. Of most interest for present purposes are 'equity securities', and 'home' and 'host' country. The term 'equity securities' includes common or ordinary shares, preferred or preference shares, options or warrants to subscribe for equity securities, and any securities, other than debt securities, which are convertible into or exercisable or redeemable for equity securities of the same company or another company. If the equity securities available upon conversion, exercise or redemption are those of another company, the disclosure standards also apply to the other company. The standards do not apply to debt securities or debt which is convertible into or exercisable or redeemable for equity or debt securities. ibid at 6. 'Home country' refers to the jurisdiction in which the company is legally organized, incorporated or established and, if different, the jurisdiction where it has its principal listing. 'Host country' refers to jurisdictions, other than the home country, in which the company is See king to offer, register or list its securities. ibid at 7.

[153] Although IOSCO States that the information headings and order of presentation are not mandatory, it recommends that the format of the Standards be followed to enhance comparability, assuming that all information contained in a given document is provided in a language acceptable to the host country. ibid at 5.

key information; (iv) information on the company; (v) operating and financial review and prospects; (vi) directors and employees; (vii) major shareholders and related party transactions; (viii) financial information; (ix) the offer and listing; and (x) additional information.

The purpose of section I, the standard addressing identity of directors, senior management and advisers, is to identify the company representatives and other individuals involved in the company's listing or registration.[154] The standard requires identification of directors and senior management, advisers (principal bankers and legal advisers), and auditors.

Section II, offer statistics and expected timetable, is intended to provide key information regarding the conduct of any offering and the identification of important dates relating to that offering.[155] The standard requires description of offer statistics, and the method and expected timetable of the offer.

Section III, key information, summarises key information about the company's financial condition, capitalisation and risk factors, and must be restated if the financial Statements are restated to reflect materials changes in the company's group structure or accounting policies.[156] Compliance with the standard requires provision of selected financial data for the five most recent years in the same currency as the financial statements,[157] a statement of capitalization and indebtedness, the estimated net amount of the proceeds broken down into each principal intended use thereof, prominently disclose risk factors that are specific to the company or its industry and make an offering speculative or one of high risk, in a section headed 'Risk Factors,' intended to be a summary of more detailed discussion contained elsewhere in the document.[158]

Section IV provides information on the company. The purpose of this standard is to provide information about the company's business operations, the products it makes or the services it provides, and the factors which affect the business. It also is intended to provide information regarding the adequacy and suitability of the company's properties, plants and equipment, as well as its plans for future increases or decreases in such capacity.[159] Information must be provided on the history and development of the company, an overview of the company's business, the company's organizational structure and details on group affiliation (if any), and infor-

154 ibid at 8. 155 ibid at 8. 156 ibid at 9

157 Information is to include, at a minimum: net sales or operating revenues; income (loss) from operations; income (loss) from continuing operations; net income (loss); net income (loss) from operations per share; income (loss) from continuing operations per share; total assets; net assets; capital stock (excluding long term debt and redeemable preferred stock); number of shares as adjusted to reflect changes in capital; dividends declared per share in both the currency of the financial Statements and the host country currency, including the formula used for any adjustments to dividends declared; and diluted net income per share. ibid at 9–10.

158 ibid at 10–11. 159 ibid at 11.

mation regarding any material tangible fixed assets, including leased properties, and any major encumbrances thereon, as well as any environmental issues that may affect the company's utilization of its assets.[160]

Section V, operating and financial review and prospects, provides management's explanation of factors that have affected the company's financial condition and results of operations for the historical periods covered by the financial Statements, and management's assessment of factors and trends which are anticipated to have a material effect on the company's financial condition and results of operations in future periods.[161] Information should discuss the company's financial condition, changes in financial condition and results of operations for each year and interim period for which financial Statements are required, including the causes of material changes from year to year in financial Statement line items, to the extent necessary for an understanding of the company's business as a whole. Information must be provided on operating results, liquidity and capital resources, research and development policies, and significant recent trends in its financial and operating environment, as well as such other information that is necessary for an investor's understanding of the company's financial condition, changes in financial condition and results of operation.[162]

Section VI, directors and employees, provides information concerning the company's directors and managers that will allow investors to assess such individuals' experience, qualifications and levels of compensation, as well as their relationship with the company.[163] Information concerning the company's employees is also required.

Section VII, major shareholders and related party transactions, provides information regarding the major shareholders and others that control or may control the company, as well as information regarding transactions the company has entered into with persons affiliated with the company and whether the terms of such transactions are fair to the company.[164]

Section VIII, financial information, specifies which financial statements must be included in the document, as well as the periods to be covered, the age of the financial statements and other information of a financial nature. The comprehensive bodies of accounting and auditing principles that will be accepted for use in preparation and audit of the financial statements will be determined by the host country. Financial information must include consolidated statements, audited by an independent auditor and accompanied by an audit report, and include comparative financial statements that cover the latest three financial years, audited in accordance with a comprehensive body of auditing standards, as well disclosure of any significant

[160] ibid at 11–13.
[161] ibid at 13.
[162] ibid at 13–15.
[163] ibid at 15. See ibid at 15–17.
[164] ibid at 17. See ibid at 17–19.

changes since the date of the annual financial Statements, and/or since the date of the most recent interim financial Statements, if any, included in the document.[165]

Section IX, the offer and listing, provides information regarding the offer or listing of securities, the plan for distribution of the securities and related matters.[166] Extensive information must be presented regarding the offer and listing details, plan of distribution, all stock exchanges and other regulated markets on which the securities to be offered or listed are traded, selling shareholders, dilution, and expenses of the issue.[167]

Finally, section X, additional information, provides information, mostly of a statutory nature, that is not covered elsewhere in the document.[168] The standard requires detailed information on share capital; memorandum and articles of association; material contracts; relevant exchange controls; taxes (including withholding provisions) to which shareholders in the host country may be subject and whether the company assumes responsibility for the withholding of tax at the source and regarding applicable provisions of any reciprocal tax treaties between the home and host countries, or a statement, if applicable, that there are no such treaties; and any dividend restrictions, the date on which the entitlement to dividends arises, if known, and any procedures for non-resident holders to claim dividends, including paying agents of the company.[169] Statements of experts must be attributed and the experts identified, and the company must provide an indication of where the documents concerning the company which are referred to in the document may be inspected, translated into or summarised in the language of the host country.[170]

Overall, while significant, the non-financial standards provided by the IDS will fail to serve as the basis for an 'international passport prospectus' unless common financial standards are also used.

C. *International Harmonization of Accounting Standards*

Accounting standards provide the essential means of communication essential for valuation of companies regarded as necessary to any sort of investor choice regarding investment in equities and therefore necessarily underlie any efforts to harmonize and/or standard international offering requirements. At present, accounting standards are nationally determined, so in effect, preparers and users of financial Statements from different countries essentially speak different languages.[171] Major initiatives however are

165 See ibid at 19–21.
166 ibid at 21.
167 See ibid at 21–5.
168 ibid at 25.
169 See ibid at 25–8.
170 See ibid at 28.
171 See Cheney *Western Accounting Arrives in Eastern Europe*, J ACCT (Sept 1990) (describing accounting at the 'language of production and transaction' and discussing difficulties in integrating Eastern Europe and Western countries due to differences in accounting).

underway to establish internationally agreed accounting standards, with the most significant achievements to date involving, respectively, the EU and IOSCO and the International Accounting Standards Committee (IASC).

The Office of the Chief Accountant of the US SEC surveyed international accounting and auditing standards in 1987 and found significant disparities in a number of respects.[172] In general terms, systems of accounting rules in different countries at the time could be grouped into two categories:[173] (i) countries where business finance is provided more by loans than by equity capital, where accounting rules are dominated by taxation considerations and where legal systems customarily incorporate codes with detailed rules for matters such as accounting;[174] and (ii) countries in which equity sources of finance are more important, accounting measurements are not dominated by taxation considerations because tax breaks can enjoyed independently of the mechanism of reporting, and common law traditions prevail.[175] Overall, however, at the time of the SEC's study, no one system seemed to have such clear merits as to deserve adoption by the entire world.

The task of harmonization is especially important in the area of securities regulation because of the critical link between information and stability in the world's securities markets.[176] The disharmony in accounting standards that exists today creates difficulties for both users and preparers of financial Statements,[177] and presents obstacles to the process of international capital formation.[178] Overall, the usefulness of financial Statements prepared on the basis of varying accounting standards is limited because it

[172] SEC, Internationalization of the Securities Markets (1987), ch 4. At least as a partial result of this study, the SEC insists, in connection with financial Statements used by foreign issuers, that assurances be provided that the auditing standards followed are the equivalent to US generally accepted accounting standards (GAAS). ibid at IV-34. See generally Gonzalez and Olive, above n 28.

[173] Brian Carlsberg, *Harmonising Accounts Worldwide* FINANCIAL TIMES, 12 Jan 1996, at XII.

[174] Reporting under these systems often leads to a lack of full transparency for investors due to their basis on the tax systems. Major countries in this category include France, Germany, and Japan. ibid.

[175] These countries generally have private sector mechanisms for setting accounting standards, usually within an overall statutory framework, and capital market pressures lead to the increased availability of information to investors. Major countries in this category include the US, the UK, Australia, and the Netherlands. ibid.

[176] UN Centre on Transnational Corporations, International Accounting and Reporting Issues: 1989 Review iii (1990). See also Thomas, International Accounting and Reporting—Developments Leading to the Harmonization of Standards, 15 NYU INT'L L & POL. (Spring 1983).

[177] T Evans, M Taylor, and O Holzmann, International Accounting and Reporting 85–6 (1985).

[178] See SEC, Internationalization, above n 172, at IV-8. A study of international accounting problems has confirmed that the lack of international accounting standards greatly diminishes the utility of financial Statements in world markets. See Scott and Torberg Eighty-eight International Accounting Problems in Rank Order of Importance—a DELPHI Evaluation (1980).

is difficult to know what the information means and time consuming to determine what it does mean.[179] Further, from the standpoint of preparers of financial Statements and the companies involved, disharmony of accounting standards is an impediment to both international securities offerings and cross-border mergers and acquisitions.[180]

Globalization of the stock and other trading markets is driving the movement toward the international harmonization of accounting standards. Further, businesses and capital markets desire both uniformity and higher quality, thereby stemming fears of regulatory arbitrage and a race for the 'lowest common denominator'.[181]

1. *Harmonization of Accounting Standards in the EU*

The EU has undertaken a number of initiatives to improve financial reporting among its Member States from both a qualitative and a quantitative standpoint. Accounting harmonization is part of the company law harmonization program aimed at furthering freedom of establishment, and as such, is aimed not only toward the equivalent protection of all investors, but of all third parties dealing with Member States' companies.[182]

EU legislative harmonization in the accounting field presupposes the existence of a national accounting system.[183] EU accounting directives include the First Company Law Directive, discussed above; the Fourth Company Law Directive;[184] the Eighth Company Law Directive;[185] the Insurance Accounting Directive;[186] the Seventh Company Law

[179] The case of Daimler-Benz is illustrative in this context: in 1994, its reported profit under German accounting rules was DM 895 million, whereas its profit under US accounting rules was DM 1,052 million In 1983, however, accounting under German rules showed a profit of DM 615 million, but US rules led to a loss of DM 1,839 million. Carlsberg, above n 173, at XII. See generally Gonzales and Olive, above n 28.

[180] A survey of multinational corporations indicated that the greatest potential benefit of harmonization would be the acceptance by stock exchanges around the world of 'one set of accounts' complying with international accounting standards, instead of requiring different financial information prepared in accordance with local accounting standards. Support for International Standards, J ACCT (Apr 1990).

[181] International Accounting Standards, at 540 (quoting Dennis Beresford, chairman of the UK Financial Accounting Standards Board (FASB)).

[182] Annex, at 315.

[183] ibid. These include: a register for undertakings and the scope of undertakings concerned, and rules of accounting, auditing, and publication.

[184] Fourth Council Directive 78/660/EEC of 25 July 1978 based on Art 54(3)(g) of the Treaty on the annual accounts of certain types of companies, OJ L 222 (1978), as amended by Directive 84/569/EEC, OJ L 314 (1984), Directive 90/604/EEC, OJ L 317 (1990), Directive 90/605/EEC, OJ L 317 (1990), and Directive 94/8/EU, OJ L 82 (1994).

[185] Eighth Council Directive 84/253/EEC of 10 Apr 1984 based on Art 54(3)(g) of the Treaty on the approval of persons responsible for carrying out the statutory audits of accounting documents, OJ L 126 (1984).

[186] Council Directive 91/674/EEC of 19 Dec 1991 on the annual accounts and consolidated

Directive;[187] and the Bank Accounting Directive.[188] As insurance and banking matters are beyond the scope of the present discussion, the two directives dealing with specific accounting procedures in these areas will not be discussed.

For present purposes, in addition to the financial Statements required in connection with listing applications, the Fourth Company Law Directive,[189] adopted in August 1978, requires limited liability companies to publish or otherwise make available to the public at no cost both their annual accounts and an annual report.[190] The annual accounts must comprise a balance sheet, profit and loss account (both presented on a comparative basis with the preceding year) and notes, including specified disclosures relating to, inter alia, the company's principal accounting policies,[191] and must give 'a true and fair view of the company's . . . financial position and profit or loss'.[192] The annual report must include a fair review of the development of the company's business and position; describe the important events since the end of the financial year, and set forth information relating to future developments as well as activities in the field of research and development.[193] The annual accounts must be audited by a person or persons authorized by national law to audit accounts.[194] The layout of the balance sheet,[195] and of the profit and loss statement,[196] and the general content of the notes[197] are specified. A number of accounting principles, including those relating to valuation,[198] research and development,[199] inventory,[200] and depreciation,[201] are prescribed.

The Eighth Company Law Directive[202] requires auditors to meet specified standards of professional education and experience as well as requires, in most instances, that they take and pass a comprehensive examination. The preamble to the Directive, however, candidly admits that while in some members 'statutory audits of the accounts of companies is entrusted to highly qualified persons, this is not the rule in all Community countries'.[203]

The Seventh Company Law Directive,[204] adopted in 1983, requires companies with subsidiaries to present their financial Statements on a consolidated basis. The proposed Fifth Company Law Directive also

accounts of insurance undertakings, OJ L 374 (1991). Insurance matters are beyond the scope of the present discussion of financial services.

[187] Seventh Council Directive 83/349/EEC of 13 June 1983 based on Art 54(3)(g) of the Treaty on consolidated accounts, OJ L 193 (1993).

[188] Council Directive 86/635/EEC of 8 Dec 1986 on the annual accounts and consolidated accounts of banks and other financial institutions, OJ L 372 (1986).

[189] Council Directive 78/660 of 25 July 1978, OJ L (1978).

[190] ibid Art 47.

[191] ibid Art 2, ss 4(4), 43.

[192] ibid Art 2, para 3.

[193] ibid at Art 46.

[194] ibid at Art 51.

[195] ibid at Arts 9–10.

[196] ibid Arts 23–4.

[197] ibid Art 43.

[198] ibid s 7.

[199] ibid Art 43.

[200] ibid Art 40.

[201] ibid Art 35(b).

[202] 27 OJ L 126 (1984).

[203] ibid.

[204] 26 OJ L 126 (1984).

contains provisions which would require auditors undertaking annual reports to be independent; however, due to the controversial nature of the employee participation provisions contained in the Directive, it is unlikely to be adopted.

In 1995, the Commission presented the outline for a 'new accounting strategy',[205] which was subsequently endorsed by the Council of Ministers in June 1996. Key objectives of the strategy are 'easier access for European companies to international capital markets and improved comparability of consolidated accounts prepared by those companies which are important players in the Single Market'.[206] Under this 'new strategy', the Commission has determined to associate its work with that of the IASC and IOSCO (described below) in pursuit of international accounting standards, rather than establishing a European Accounting Standards Board or a new layer of EU accounting standards. In addition, the Commission's work in the area of accounting standards has been significantly spurred by the needs of EMU, which formally began on 1 January 1999.

According to Commissioner Mario Monti:

> The accountancy sector has a fundamental role to play in an efficient Single Market. The preparation, publication and widespread circulation of financial information relating to companies allows economic actors to make appropriate choices and constitutes the necessary basis for management to take the right decisions.[207]

As part of its 'new accounting strategy', the Commission adopted an Interpretative Communication[208] in January 1998[209] covering three main issues: consolidated accounts, the relationship between the Accounting Directives and IAS, and environmental issues in financial reporting. The Communication conclusions regarding compatibility with IAS are based on the comparison undertaken between the E.U. Accounting Directives and IAS by a special Task Force of the Contact Committee on the Accounting Directives.[210] In addition, the Commission's work in the area of accounting standards has been significantly spurred by the needs of EMU. In this regard, the Commission has produced two sets of guidelines to assist

[205] European Commission, Accounting Harmonization: A New Strategy vis-à-vis International Harmonization, Communication from the Commission, COM 95 (508), Nov 1995. See European Commission, 'Commission Proposes a New Strategy for the Improvement of the Financial Reporting Framework for Companies in Europe', Press Rel IP/95/1234 (14 Nov 1995).

[206] ibid.

[207] 'Speech by Commissioner Mario Monti at the Conference on the Role, the Position and the Liability of the Statutory Auditor in the EU,' Brussels, 6 Dec 1996, EC, Speech/96/322, Rapid (6 Dec 1996).

[208] European Commission, Interpretative Communication Concerning Certain Articles of the Fourth and Seventh Council Directives on Accounting, XV/7009/97.

[209] European Commission, 'Accounting: Interpretative Communication Concerning Directives on Annual and Consolidated Accounts', Press Rel IP: 98/75, RAPID (22 Jan 1998).

[210] European Commission, An Examination of the Conformity Between the International Accounting Standards and the European Accounting Directives (1996).

companies in dealing with the practical financial implications of the advent of the euro.[211]

Overall, despite significant general progress in establishing minimum accounting standards, the EU system has not reached the level of a coherent and comprehensive system and recognition of this fact has led to the decision to adopt IAS.

2. *International Accounting Standards Committee (IASC)*

Formed initially in 1973 by agreement among the accounting bodies of ten industrialized countries,[212] by 1989, the IASC had grown to include approximately 100 accountancy bodies from 80 countries.[213] The IASC is engaged in an effort to harmonize and improve accounting principles 'for the benefit of the public.'[214] This task is especially difficult for two reasons: first, the IASC seeks harmonization on a worldwide basis,[215] and second, since the IASC has no official status, its standards are essentially recommendations.[216] Further, the IASC standards are generally broad and allow alternative practices; hence, they achieve no real uniformity.[217]

The IASC's overall objectives are to formulate and publish accounting standards to be observed in the presentation of financial Statements and to promote their world-wide acceptance, and to work generally for the improvement and harmonization of regulations, accounting standards, and procedures relating to the presentation of financial Statements.[218] By agreement, members of IASC are bound to persuade governments and other standard setting bodies that financial Statements should comply with the international accounting standards (IAS) promulgated by the IASC.[219] These standards are not binding on nations or the IASC members themselves, and the IASC has no enforcement authority.[220]

[211] See European Commission, Directorate General XV, Accounting for the Introduction of the Euro (1997) and Preparing Financial Information Systems for the Euro, XV/7038/97 (15 Dec 1997).

[212] The founding members were Australia, Canada, France, Germany, Japan, Mexico, The Netherlands, the UK, Ireland, and the US Objectives and Procedures, s 9000.24.

[213] Collins *The Move to Globalization*, J ACCT 83 (Mar 1989). Note that the membership of the IASC consists of accountancy bodies rather than nations. T Evans, above n 177, at 89.

[214] Int'l Acctg. Stans Comm., 'Objectives and Procedures', s 9000.33 (Jan 1983).

[215] See IASC, *Moves to United Worldwide Standards*, 165 J ACCT 22, 26 (June 1988).

[216] See Herbert Developments in the Harmonization of Accounting Standards, ALI-ABA Conference on the Internationalization of Capital Markets, 102 (1981).

[217] Note, however, that the IASC in recent years has been making efforts to eliminate alternatives, thereby increasing the possibility of real harmonization. See Carlsberg, above n 127, at XII.

[218] IASC Constitution No 2, in Objectives and Procedures, Appendix 2, s 9000.58.

[219] Preface to Statements of International Accounting Standards No 4, in Objectives and Procedures, s 9000.60.

[220] Preface to Statements of International Accounting Standards No 19, in Objectives and Procedures, s 9000.60, Appendix 4.

The reaction of nations to the IASs of the IASC has been divided into three categories: (i) for some countries that do not have a developed national system of accounting, the IASs have been given essentially the same status given domestic standards;[221] (ii) a number of countries have accounting systems that are for the most part compatible with IASs;[222] and (iii) some countries have well-developed accounting standards that in large part are incompatible with IASs.[223] Given the general reception and the overall necessity of harmonization, increasing use of IASs appears likely.[224]

3. *International Federation of Accountants (IFAC)*

The IFAC, organized in 1977, includes the International Auditing Practices Committee (IAPC), which is charged with the responsibility of developing and issuing guidelines on generally accepted auditing practices and the content of audit reports.[225] Overall, the problems facing the IAPC are quite similar to those facing IASC; however, the focus of the IAPC is on auditing rather than on accounting standards.

4. *Cooperation Between IOSCO and IASC*

In the area of international accounting standards for financial reporting connected with stock exchange listings, the barriers created by the lack of a single financial language are especially significant to the process of international capital formation. IOSCO, however, had always withheld any endorsement of the various IASs, feeling that a core set of standards that dealt comprehensively with all the main financial reporting issues should be completed first.[226] In 1993, IOSCO agreed on 'the necessary components of a reasonably complete set of accounting standards (core standards) that would comprise a comprehensive body of principles for enterprises undertaking cross-border offerings and listings'.[227] IOSCO's list identified 40 core standards.

The IASC, however, was unwilling to undertake such a process, until July 1995, at which time the IASC and IOSCO published a joint agreement agreeing to complete a comprehensive set of core standards agreed between

[221] T Evans, above n 177, at 94. Cf Cheney, Western Accounting Arrives in Eastern Europe.
[222] T Evans, above n 177, at 95 (eg US, Canada, and the UK).
[223] ibid (eg Japan, although this may be changing somewhat).
[224] Note that the London Stock Exchange began accepting IASs soon after the foundation of IASC. See Carlsberg, above n 127, at XII. The US, Canada, and Japan, however, still refuse to permit the use of IASs for stock exchange purposes. ibid.
[225] See Preface to International Auditing Guidelines of the International Federation of Accountants, AICPA Professional Standards, s 8000.01-02 (1 July 1979).
[226] Carlsberg, above n 127, at XII.
[227] IASC.

the two organizations by 1999.[228] In July 1995, the IASC's 16-member board and IOSCO's technical committee agreed that there is 'a compelling need' for high-quality, comprehensive international accounting standards.[229] In July 1995, IOSCO announced publicly:

> The [IASC] Board has developed a work plan that the Technical Committee agrees will result, upon successful completion, in IAS comprising a comprehensive core set of standards. Completion of comprehensive core standards that are acceptable to the [IOSCO] Technical Committee will allow the Technical Committee to recommend endorsement of IAS for cross border capital raising and listing purposes in all global markets. IOSCO has already endorsed IAS 7, Cash Flow Statements, and has indicated to the IASC that 14 of the existing International Accounting Standards do not require additional improvement, providing that the other core standards are successfully completed.

Under the agreement, IASC and IOSCO agreed to collaborate to produce a comprehensive set of core standards for the global listing of securities, which then would be submitted to IOSCO for endorsement by its membership.[230] Overall, the two groups' goal is the development of financial Statements, prepared in accordance with such international rules, that can be read world-wide in cross-border securities listings as an alternative to the use of national accounting standards, thereby resulting in an increase in market efficiencies.[231]

In July 1995, the completion of the core standards work programme was scheduled for June 1999.[232] The participants in the core standards development process thereafter urged IASC to accelerate the timetable, and in March 1996 the IASC announced that its Board agreed to set a new date of March 1998.[233] This date however was subsequently delayed again to 1999.

As of October 1998, the IASC and its membership had formally

[228] IASC concluded that completion of this core set was a desirable objective for IASC in any event, and acceptance of this goal made an agreement possible under which both IOSCO and IASC would cooperate in order to fulfil an objective that was in the best interest of both organisations. ibid. The completion date for this agreement has now been advanced to March 1998. See Steve Burkholder *International Accounting Standards Panel Accelerates Release of Rules*, 28 SEC REG & L REP 540 (19 Apr 1996).

[229] ibid at 540.

[230] International Accounting Standards Panel, at 540. Highlights of the IASC work plan include: (i) issuance of a final Statement on international accounting standards on income taxes in June 1996; (ii) revised standards on intangible assets, research and development, and goodwill, also in June 1996; (iii) international accounting standards on earnings per share in January 1997, following issuance of a disclosure document in September 1996; (iv) final standards on business segment reporting in March 1997; and (v) final rules on financial instruments and investments, interim reporting, discontinued operations, and provisioning and contingencies, all in Mar 1998. ibid.

[231] International Accounting Standards Panel, at 540 (citing joint IOSCO/IASC Statement of July 1995)

[232] ibid.

[233] ibid at 12.

approved 36 of 40 proposed core standards. Of the four outstanding standards, that applicable to business combinations (including goodwill)[234] was finalized in July 1998, and approved by the membership of IASC. The core standards relating to the Financial Instruments Project, with respect to standards dealing with hedging,[235] investments,[236] and financial instruments/off-balance sheet items[237] were all eventually finalized and accepted during 1998 and 1999, in order to meet the revised March 1999 completion deadline.

The Core Standards as set forth in IOSCO's 1993 list are grouped into five major categories: general; income Statement; balance sheet; cash flow Statement; and other.

General standards deal with the following areas: (i) disclosure of accounting policies;[238] (ii) changes in accounting policies;[239] and (iii) information disclosed in financial Statements.[240]

Core standards related to the income Statement are addressed to: (i) revenue recognition;[241] (ii) construction contracts;[242] (iii) production and purchase costs;[243] (iv) depreciation;[244] (v) impairment;[245] (vi) taxes;[246] (vii) extraordinary items;[247] (viii) government grants;[248] (viii) retirement benefits;[249] (ix) other employee benefits;[250] (x) research and development;[251] (xi) interest;[252] and (xii) hedging.[253]

234 IAS 22, Business Combinations (1.1.85) (revised July 1998).

235 IAS 39, Financial Instruments: Recognition and Measurement (1998).

236 ibid.

237 IAS 32, Financial Instruments: Disclosures and Presentation (1.1.96) (revised 1998).

238 IAS 1, Presentation of Financial Statements (1.7.98) (revised 1997) (replaced IAS 1, Disclosure of Accounting Policies, which remained in effect until 1.7.98).

239 IAS 8, Profit or Loss for the Period, Fundamental Errors and Changes in Accounting Policies (1.1.79).

240 IAS 1, above n 238.

241 IAS 18, Revenue (1.1.84).

242 IAS 11, Construction Contracts (1.1.80).

243 IAS 2, Inventories (1.1.76) (revised 1993).

244 IAS 4, Depreciation (1.1.77) (revised 1974) and IAS 16, Property, Plant and Equipment (1.1.83) (revised 1993) (currently being revised).

245 IAS 36, Impairment of Assets (1.7.99) (issued June 1998. Effective for financial reporting periods beginning 1 July 1999).

246 IAS 12, Income Taxes (1.1.98) (this replaced IAS 12, Accounting for Taxes on Income, which remained in effect until 1.1.98) (revised 1996 and effective for financial reporting periods beginning on or after 1 Jan 1998).

247 IAS 8, Profit or Loss for the Period, Fundamental Errors and Changes in Accounting Policies (1.1.79) (revised 1993).

248 IAS 20, Accounting for Government Grants and Disclosure of Government Assistance (1.1.84) (revised 1983).

249 IAS 19, Employee Benefits (1.1.85) (revised Jan 1998 and effective for Reporting Periods beginning 1 Jan 1999).

250 IAS 19, ibid.

251 LAS 38, Intangible Assets (1.7.99) (issued Sept 1998 and effective for annual financial Statements covering periods beginning on or after 1 July 1999).

252 IAS 23, Borrowing Costs (1.1.86) (revised 1993).

253 E62, Financial Instruments: Recognition and Measurement (Exposure Draft June 1998); IAS 39, Financial Instruments: Recognition and Measurement (1998).

Standards governing the balance sheet address: (i) property, plant and equipment;[254] (ii) leases;[255] (iii) inventories;[256] (iv) deferred taxes;[257] (iv) foreign currency;[258] (v) investments;[259] (vi) financial instruments/off balance sheet items;[260] (vii) joint ventures;[261] (viii) contingencies;[262] (viii) events occurring after the balance sheet date;[263] (ix) current assets and current liabilities;[264] (x) business combinations (including goodwill);[265] and (xi) intangibles other than R&D and goodwill.[266]

A single standard details cash flow statement contents.[267]

Other relevant core standards cover: (i) consolidated financial Statements;[268] (ii) subsidiaries in hyperinflationary economies;[269] (iii) associates and equity accounting;[270] (iv) segment reporting;[271] (v) interim reporting;[272] (vi) earnings per share;[273] (vii) related party disclosures;[274] (viii) discontinuing operations;[275] (ix) fundamental errors;[276] and (x) changes in estimates.[277]

[254] IAS 16, Property, Plant and Equipment (1.1.83) (revised 1998).

[255] IAS 17, Accounting for Leases (1.1.84) (to be superseded by IAS 17 [revised 1997], Leases, effective 1.1.99).

[256] IAS 2, above n 243.

[257] IAS 12, above n 246.

[258] IAS 21, The Effects of Changes in Foreign Exchange Rates (1.1.85) (revised 1993).

[259] IAS 39, above n 235.

[260] IAS 39, above n 236. See discussion of E62 below.

[261] IAS 31, Financial Reporting of Interests In Joint Ventures (1.1.92) (revised 1990).

[262] IAS 37, Provisions, Contingent Liabilities and Contingent Assets (1.7.99) (issued September 1998 and effective for annual financial Statements covering periods beginning on or after 1 July 1999).

[263] IAS 10, Contingencies and Events Occurring after the Balance Sheet Date (1.1.80) (revised 1974). The portion of IAS 10 dealing with contingencies is being revised in the current IASC project on Provisions, Contingent Liabilities and Contingent Assets. The portion on subsequent events is being revised in a separate IASC project on that subject.

[264] IAS 1, above n 238.

[265] IAS 22, above n 235. Revision to IAS 22 was approved in principle by the Board in July 1998, subject to mail ballot on a final draft.

[266] IAS 38, above n 252.

[267] IAS 7, Cash Flow Statements (1.1.79) (revised 1992).

[268] IAS 27, Consolidated Financial Statements and Accounting for Investments in Subsidiaries (1.1.90) (revised 1988).

[269] IAS 21, above n 258, and IAS 29, Financial Reporting in Hyperinflationary Economies (1.1.90) (revised 1989).

[270] IAS 28, Accounting for Investments in Associates (1.1.90) (revised 1988).

[271] IAS 14, Segment Reporting (1.7.98) (revised in 1997 and effective for financial reporting periods beginning on or after 1 July 1998) (this replaced IAS 14, Reporting Financial Information by Segment, which remained effective until 1 July 1998).

[272] IAS 34, Interim Financial Reporting (1.1.99) (issued Feb 1998 and effective for financial reporting periods beginning 1 Jan 1999).

[273] IAS 33, Earnings Per Share (1.1.98) (issued Feb 1997 and effective for financial reporting periods beginning 1 Jan 1998).

[274] IAS 24, Related Party Disclosures (1.1.86) (revised 1984).

[275] IAS 35, Discontinuing Operations (1.1.99) (issued June 1998 and effective for financial reporting periods beginning 1 Jan 1999).

[276] IAS 8, above n 247.

[277] IAS 8, ibid.

The IASC proposal has been submitted and approved by the membership of IOSCO[278] and has also been reviewed both by domestic authorities and other international institutions and organizations, such as the the Basel Committee on Banking Supervision.[279] Although IOSCO endorsement of comprehensive IAS was not guaranteed, IOSCO did commit to undertake a review of the completed project, and upon completion of the IASC core standards working programme, IOSCO evaluated the resulting standards.[280] The IOSCO evaluation commenced after the final draft standards was completed and resulted in substantial approval. The standards were subsequently approved by the full membership of IOSCO (including the US SEC), with a recommendation for implementation in member jurisdictions.[281] As a result, there exists the clear possibility for the eventual employment of core standards developed by IASC and approved by IOSCO being thereafter acceptable by the SEC for acceptance in the US capital markets.

V. IMPLEMENTATION OF INTERNATIONAL STANDARDS FOR OFFERINGS AND LISTINGS OF SECURITIES

International standards may be interesting from an academic standpoint, but real impact on financial markets only come with domestic implementation in the world's most significant capital markets, namely the US and the EU.

Recognizing the importance of implementation, in May 2000, IOSCO produced a *Report on Implementation of IDS*.[282] The Report surveyed the progress of implementation of IDS among the 17 members of the Working Party.[283] Sixteen indicated either that they: (1) currently accept documents prepared in accordance with the IDSs from foreign companies, or (2) have taken steps to be in a position to do so at some point in 2000.

According to information supplied by those surveyed, progress in implementation fell into five categories: (1) those that had implemented IDS through changes in law or rules by May 2000 (four jurisdictions: Spain, the

278 IOSCO Technical Committee, IASC Standards—Assessment Report (May 20000; See IOSCO, Final Communique of the 25th Annual Conference of the International Organization of Securities Commissions (IOSCO) (May 2000).

279 Basel Committee on Banking Supervision, Report to G7 Finance Ministers and Central Bank Governors on International Accounting Standards (Apr 2000).

280 IOSCO Technical Committee, IASC Standards—Assessment Report (May 2000)

281 IOSCO, Resolution Concerning the Use of IASC Standards for the Purpose of Multinational Securities Offerings and Cross-border Listings (May 2000).

282 IOSCO, Report on Implementation of IDS (May 2000).

283 The 17 Working Party members surveyed were: Australia, Belgium, France, Germany, Hong Kong, Italy, Japan, Luxembourg, Mexico, the Netherlands, Ontario, Quebec, Spain, Sweden, Switzerland, the United Kingdom, and the United States.

U.K., Mexico, and Italy); (2) those that were in the process of implementing IDS through changes in law or rules by the end of 2000 (two jurisdictions: France and the US); (3) those that permitted use of IDS without any need for rule changes, through discretionary authority or other means (eight jurisdictions: Australia, Belgium, Germany, Hong Kong, Japan, Luxembourg, the Netherlands, and Switzerland); (4) those that planned to undertake rule changes to implement IDS but in the interim would permit use through discretionary authority (two jurisdictions: Ontario and Quebec); and (5) those that would not allow use of IDS (one jurisdiction: Sweden).

According to the survey participants, of the four jurisdictions which had made changes to laws and/or rules: two (Spain, UK) permit optional use of the IDSs by foreign companies; one (Mexico) requires use of IDS by both foreign and domestic companies; and one (Italy) revised its listing rules in a manner that conforms to the IDS requirements (although without specific reference to the IDSs) and those listing rules apply to both foreign and domestic companies. As of May 2000, France and the US were in the process of changing laws and/or rules to permit use of the IDS, with the changes effective sometime in 2000.

According to the respondents, Australia, Belgium, Germany, Hong Kong, Japan, Luxembourg, the Netherlands, and Switzerland currently permit (either through discretionary authority or other means) foreign companies to use the IDS without the necessity of changing their laws or rules. Japanese officials Stated that its foreign company disclosure forms had been amended to be more comparable to the IDS and disclosure that complies fully with the IDS would be accepted under discretionary authority. Switzerland noted plans to make follow-up changes to its laws or rules.

Two Canadian provinces, Ontario and Quebec, Stated that rulemaking activities were planned in cooperation with other provincial securities regulators to permit use of the IDS by foreign companies. In the interim period, both would consider exercising their discretionary authority to permit a foreign company to use the IDS to access their markets.

Sweden noted that the content of the IDS would satisfy most, but not all, of its requirements for an offering, but that companies would have to provide additional information on the topics covered by the IDS before documents based on those standards would be accepted.

In relation to domestic companies, according to the IOSCO survey, two (Italy and Mexico) require disclosure that conforms with the IDS requirements. Eight (Australia, Belgium, Germany, Luxembourg, the Netherlands, Spain, Switzerland, and the UK would permit domestic companies to use the IDSs, although with conditions in some cases.

An informal survey of implementation of IDS conducted by Samuel

Wolff of Akin, Gump, Strauss, Hauer & Feld was published in February 2001.[284]

Of the respondents to the informal survey, Wolff found four in which IDS had been implemented through rule and/or legislative changes applicable to foreign and domestic issuers:[285] two (Italy and Mexico) required use of IDS for both foreign and domestic issuers; one (Argentina) required IDS for foreign issuers and intended to apply the same requirements to domestic issuers by sometime in 2002; and one (Singapore) required IDS with modifications for both foreign and domestic issuers.

Of the respondents, Wolf found five jurisdictions which had implemented IDS for foreign issuers only by rule and/or legislative change:[286] in two (the US and Switzerland), IDS were optional for foreign issuers, but different standards applied to domestic issuers, though foreign issuers could also comply with the domestic requirements; in one (France), changes were in progress during 2001 to allow use of IDS by foreign issuers; one (Spain) required use of IDS for foreign issuers; and one (the U.K.) listing rules exempt foreign issuers complying with IDS from certain provisions, but would nonetheless be required to furnish listing particulars in accordance with the remaining provisions of the listing rules.[287]

Of the respondents, Wolf found seven in which no legislative and/or rules changes were anticipated, but IDS were acceptable for issuers: in four (Luxembourg, Hong Kong, the Netherlands and Belgium), IDS would be accepted under discretionary authority; in one (Germany), IDS were deemed to meet listing requirements; in one (Japan), IDS would be accepted on a discretionary basis, but only if in Japanese in proper format; and in one (Australia), Wolf was not able to confirm the response to the IOSCO survey indicating that IDS would be accepted under discretionary authority.

In one jurisdiction (South Africa), it was unclear whether IDS would be accepted, and IDS were not acceptable in four jurisdictions (Israel, Canada, India, and Taiwan).

From these surveys, use of IDS by different jurisdictions appears to be falling into four categories: (1) required for all companies, foreign and domestic; (2) optional for all companies, foreign and domestic; (3) inapplicable to domestic companies, but required for foreign companies; and (4) inapplicable to domestic companies and optional for foreign companies.

Wolff concludes:

[284] S Wolff *Implementation of International Disclosure Standards*, 22 U Pa J Int'l Econ L 91 (2001). Wolff surveyed 20 IOSCO member organizations ibid at 94.

[285] See ibid at 95–104.

[286] ibid.

[287] Public offerings without listing are governed by POS Regulations (based on EU POP Directive), to which no change had been made in respect to IDS.

the record so far, two and one-half years after promulgation of the IOSCO Standards, is mixed at best . . .While some progress has been made toward the implementation of International Disclosure Standards, the more toward implementation has probably been slower than IOSCO contemplated. There is still a hodgepodge of prospectus and listing rules which foreign issuers have to sort through as before on a country-by-country basis to determine applicable disclosure standards. More often than not, there is no reference at all to the IOSCO Standards.[288]

While Wolf's conclusion does not appear optimistic, closer analysis of implementation of IDS and IAS in the two most significant capital markets (the US and the E.U.) actually suggests that significant progress is in fact being made.

A. *International Disclosure Standards*

1. *US*

The principal securities legislation in the US remains the Securities Act of 1933 (the '1933 Act') and the Securities Exchange Act of 1934 (the '1934 Act'), the former regulating the initial public offering of securities and the latter secondary dealings in them. Although much amended by subsequent Congresses and added to by rules and regulations of the Securities and Exchange Commission (SEC), the original purpose of the legislation remains unchanged, namely to protect investors by requiring the provision of accurate and timely information.[289] Specifically in relation disclosure in securities offerings, providing shareholders with better tools with which to scrutinize companies issuing securities (especially public/listed corporations) was one of the US Congress's central purposes in adopting the 1933 and 1934 Acts.[290] The key obligation imposed by the 1933 Act is the requirement for registration of any offering of securities, absent a specific exemption.[291] Initial disclosure obligations are supported by a liability framework, including both criminal and civil (private and administrative) actions, as well as requirements for on-going disclosure of public companies under the 1934 Act. General disclosure requirements are contained in Regulation S-K. In order to increase the attractiveness of US capital markets for non-US issuers, the SEC has made a number of accommodations over the years, including respecting disclosure standards.[292]

[288] Wolff, above n 284, at 105.
[289] A Alcock *Rise and Fall of Private Actions under Rule* 10b-5, JBL 1998, May, 230–49, 230.
[290] HR Rep No 85, 73rd Congress, 1st sess, 1933.
[291] 1933 Act, above n 191, s 5.
[292] Accommodations include:

- Interim reporting on the basis of home country and stock exchange practice rather than quarterly;

On 28 September 1999, the US SEC adopted a complete revision of Form F-20,[293] which contains the basic disclosure requirements applicable to foreign private issuers under the US Securities Acts, largely along the lines proposed previously in February 1999.[294] Under the SEC Final Rule and Form F-20 thereunder, the IOSCO IDS are substantially implemented into US securities regulation, although the F-20 requirements remain more detailed and stringent than those of IDS. According to Allan Beller of Cleary, Gottlieb, Steen & Hamilton:

> foreign issuers that register with the Commission for the first time will not find the new disclosure regime any more hospitable than the old . . . Unless the IOSCO Standards are adopted for home-country disclosure, most issuers will probably continue to prepare substantially different offering documents and annual reports to satisfy home-country requirements and to satisfy US requirements.[295]

Most significantly, the F-20 revision does not address issues respecting financial information, with reconciliation to US GAAP continuing to be required. Nonetheless, IDS have been implemented in the US.

2. *Europe*

As a result of EMU, EU Member States and the European Commission have re-examined the Single Market project and sought to take steps to remedy structural problems not addressed in the earlier SEA and Maastricht processes.

The European Council endorsed the European Commission's Single Market Action Plan on 16–17 June 1997 in Amsterdam. The Action Plan establishes four 'Strategic Targets' for implementation under a three-phase timetable: making rules more effective, addressing key market distortions, removing obstacles to integration, and delivering a 'Single Market' for the

- Exemption from proxy rules and the insider reporting and short swing profit recovery provision;
- Aggregate executive compensation disclosure rather than individual disclosure, if permitted in issuer's home country;
- Acceptance of 3 IAS: cash flow Statements (7), business combinations (22) and operations in hyperinflationary economies (21);
- Offering document financial Statements updated principally on a semi-annual rather than a quarterly basis; and
- Exemption from 34 Act registration under Section 12(g) for foreign private issuers that have not engaged in a US public offering or whose securities are not traded on a national exchange or NASDAQ.

[293] Securities Act of 1933, Release No. 33-7745 (28 Sept 1999).

[294] Securities Act of 1933, Release No. 33-7637 (2 Feb 1999).

[295] A Beller 'SEC Adopts New Disclosure Requirements for Non-US Issuers,' 32nd Annual Institute on Securities Regulation, Practising Law Institute, Corp L & Prac Course Handbook Series, 1213 PLI/Corp 183, 186 (Nov 2000).

benefit of all citizens of EU Member States.[296] As one aspect of the Single Market Action Plan, the Commission developed a Framework for Action for creating a single market in financial services in 1998.[297] A Financial Services Policy Group (FSPG) was established in January 1999 to develop specific recommendations. Following meetings of the FSPG, the Commission produced its Financial Services Action Plan for the establishment of a single market in financial services by 2005.[298] Included within the FSAP were decisions to focus on, inter alia, developing a single prospectus for securities offerings and a single set of financial statements for listed companies. The Commission, the FSPG and a variety of specially created groups of market experts have since moved forward with proposals in a wide variety of areas, including the development of a single prospectus and single set of financial statements.[299] Most significantly, the Commission established a so-called 'Committee of Wise Men' or the Lamfalussy Committee, chaired by Baron Alexandre Lamfalussy.[300] The recommendations (including for a controversial new legislative process for EU securities legislation) of the Lamfalussy Committee were endorsed by the European Council in Stockholm in March 2001.[301] Key recommendations of the Lamfalussy Committee include adoption by end 2003 of a single prospectus for issuers and modernization of admission to listing. Other key recommendations include Home country control for all wholesale members and definition of professional investor, modernization of investment rules for UCITS, adoption of IAS, and the creation of a single passport for recognized stock markets. Recommendations so far have resulted in the creation of a Committee of European Securities Regulators[302] and a European Securities Committee.[303]

296 See Single Market Action Plan <http://europa.eu.int/comm/internal_market/en/update/strategy/action/plan.htm>.

297 Communication of the European Commission, 'Financial Services: Building a Framework for Action', COM(1998)625 (Oct 1998)

298 Communication of the European Commission, 'Financial Services: Implementing the Framework for Financial Markets: Action Plan', COM(1999) 232 (May 1999).

299 See European Commission, 'Financial Services Priorities and Progress: Third Report', COM(2000) 692/2 final (Nov. 2000); idem, 'Progress on Financial Services: Second Report', COM(2000) 336 (May 2000); idem, 'Financial Services Action Plan: Progress Report' (Nov 1999).

300 Committee of Wise Men, 'Final Report of the Committee of Wise Men on the Regulation of European Securities Markets' (Feb 2001); idem, 'Initial Report of the Committee of Wise Men on the Regulation of European Securities Markets' (Nov 2000).

301 European Commission, 'Results of the Council of Economics and Finance Ministers, 22 March 2001, Stockholm—Securities legislation' (23 Mar 2001).

302 Commission Decision 2001/527/EC of 6 June 2001 establishing the Committee of European Securities Regulators, OJ L 191 (2001).

303 Commission Decision 2001/528/EC of 6 June 2001 establishing the European Securities Committee, OJ L 191 (2001).

As noted above, as one aspect of the creation of a single prospectus, the Commission has codified the four basic listing Directives.[304] As a very significant follow-on development, the Commission, following the Lamfalussy recommendations, proposed a single prospectus valid EU-wide, covering all listing and public offers of securities. According to the Commission, the key features are:[305]

(1) Definition of clear conditions for offering securities to the public and for admission to trading;
(2) Harmonization of the essential definitions in order to avoid loopholes and different approaches, thus ensuring a level playing field throughout the EU;
(3) Introduction of enhanced disclosure standards in line with international standards (IOSCO) for public offer of securities and admission to trading;
(4) Introduction of the registration document system for issuers whose securities are admitted to trading on regulated markets in order to ensure a yearly update of the key information concerning the issuer;
(5) Concentration of the responsibilities in the Home State's administrative competent authority; and
(6) The 'single passport' enabling the possibility to offer or admit securities to trading on the basis of a simple notification of the prospectus approved by the home competent authority.

Significantly, the requirements for information included in the prospectus are identical to those of the IOSCO IDS, albeit with much less detail present in the Commission proposal.[306] At present, the ideas included within the proposed prospectus Directive, while enjoying general support, are generating conflict amongst market practitioners, especially in respect to the lack of detail included in the initial proposal and in respect to potential liability for issuers using such a mechanism and the related lack of clarity in respect to general issues of enforcement outside of initial approval.[307]

In addition to proposals on accounting standards and prospectuses, the

[304] Directive 2001/34/EC of the European Parliament and of the Council of 28 May 2001 on the admission of securities to official stock exchange listing and on information to be published on those securities, OJ L 184 (2001).

[305] European Commission, 'Financial services: Commission proposes single prospectus valid EU-wide', 30 May 2001; idem, Proposal for a Directive of the European Parliament and of the Council on the prospectus to be published when securities are offered to the public or admitted to trading, COM (2001) 280 final (COD) (May 2001).

[306] Annex I (prospectus), Annex II (registration document) & Annex III (securities note).

[307] As one simple example, the proposal refers intends to amend significantly both Directive 80/390/EEC on listing particulars and Directive 89/298/EEC on public offers of securities. As noted, the listing particulars Directive has been consolidated and repealed. Interestingly, no mention is made of the consolidated Directive.

Commission has also initiated consultation on on-going disclosure obligations of listed companies.[308]

B. Accounting and Auditing Standards

As noted, the IAS core programme has been approved by IOSCO, reviewed and largely recommended by the Basel Committee, and included as one of the key standards for sound financial systems by the Financial Stability Forum.[309] In addition, they have been accepted for international offerings and listings by a wide range of stock exchanges around the world.[310] Among the largest capital markets in the world, the EU has determined to use IAS as the basis for reporting by all EU-listed companies by 2005, while the US is currently discussing future usage of IAS in its markets.

1. Europe

In the EU, the Accounting Directives have provided a base level of minimum standards for accounting; however, as noted above, they never reached the level of a complete, coherent, integrated system of accounting, with the result being that the accounting standards and practices varied significantly across Member States.

As a result of this realization and of the increasing emphasis on the importance of developing a single capital market in the Euro Area and the EU as a whole, the Commission investigated whether to develop a complete system of European accounting standards—an European GAAP, perhaps through an European Accounting Standards Board or similar organization—or whether to instead rely on the work of the IASC. In the event, the decision taken was to work with the IASC process and IAS. As the most concrete step to date, the Commission determined in 2001 to adopt the use of IAS as a requirement applying to all companies listed on any securities exchange within the EU by the end of 2005[311]—a requirement that will

[308] European Commission, Internal Market Directorate General *Towards an EU Regime on Transparency Obligations of Issuers whose Securities are Admitted to Trading on a Regulated Market*, MARKT/11.07.2001 (July 2001).

[309] Financial Stability Forum, International Standards and Codes to Strengthen Financial Systems (June 2001). See also the FSF Compendium of Standards, available at <www.fsforum.org>. The FSF is the key coordinating organisation for international financial standards, now a key aspect of the so-called 'new international financial architecture (NIFA)'. See *eg*, M Giovanoli 'A New Architecture for the Global Financial Market: Legal Aspects of International Financial Standard Setting' in M Giovanoli (ed) *International Monetary Law: Issues for the New Millennium* (Oxford: OUP 2000) ch 1.

[310] For a current summary, see the IASC website at <www.iasc.org.hk>.

[311] European Commission, Proposal for a Regulation of the European Parliament and of the Council on the application of international accounting standards, COM(2001) 80 final, 2001/0044 (COD) (13 Feb 2001).

fundamentally effect the financial reporting of approximately 7,000 EU-listed companies.

As a result of the Commission's determination to work directly with the international standards-setting process and to require all EU-listed companies to report according to IAS by 2005, recent and developing international efforts in this area are of considerable interest and importance.

2. *US*

In the US, the SEC has responsibility for setting accounting standards for securities issuers, which it in turn delegates to the Financial Accounting Standards Board (FASB). The FASB in turn establishes US GAAP, which govern accounting practices in the US.

Historically, by far the greatest barrier to foreign issuer access to the US capital markets has been the requirement for use of US GAAP for required financial information and reporting.[312] In order to partially address these concerns, the SEC has allowed foreign issuers to use either GAAP or home country (or IAS) reconciled to GAAP. Reconciliation, however, is an expensive and time-consuming process and can still be regarded as the major barrier to foreign issuer access to US markets.

Notwithstanding IOSCO endorsement of IAS (and participation of the US SEC in that process), the US SEC is considering the IAS package independently with no underlying legal obligation to follow IOSCO endorsement. Congressional testimony of SEC officials indicates that in order for IAS to be adopted, the standards must (1) constitute a comprehensive basis of accounting; (2) be of high quality and result in comparability and transparency and provide for full disclosure; and (3) be rigorously interpreted and applied.[313] The SEC has repeatedly stated that its decision to adopt IAS would be premised upon an evaluation of the impact of IAS upon capital formation, cost of capital for domestic registrants, and investor protection.[314] The SEC concluded that:

[312] See Gonzales and Olive, above n 28.

[313] See, eg, Remarks by Jane B Adams, Deputy Chief Accountant, Office of the Chief Accountant, US Securities and Exchange Commission, at the 17th Annual SEC and Financial Reporting Institute Conference, Leventhal School of Accounting, University of Southern California, Los Angeles (14 May 1998). These factors have been repeated on numerous occasions in SEC testimony and speeches since April 1996, when the SEC released a Statement in support of the efforts of IOSCO and the IASC. See SEC News Digest, SEC Statement Regarding International Accounting Standards, Issue 96–67, reprinted in 1996 SEC LEXIS 873 (11 Apr 1996).

[314] See, eg, Remarks by Mary B Tokar, Senior Associate Chief Accountant, Office of the Chief Accountant, US Securities and Exchange Commission, at the 2nd Annual International Accounting Standards Conference, Belgium (10 Mar 1998).

The IASC's efforts have already contributed greatly to raising the level of accounting standards worldwide and reducing the number of differences between international standards and accounting principles used in the United States. These and other efforts at the international level are encouraging development of accounting principles that have the needs of investors and capital markets as their primary focus.[315]

The SEC at present has a request for public comment respecting adoption of IAS pending.[316] In respect to the IAS proposal, the US is looking at four options:

(1) retain the current reconciliation system;
(2) remove some reconciliation requirements for selected IAS;
(3) allow IAS for recognition and measurement, with GAAP and SEC supplemental footnote disclosure; or
(4) allow IAS without reconciliation.

The first (no change) and last (adopt IAS for foreign issuers) are both unlikely. In respect to the first, the SEC (through IOSCO) has endorsed the use of IAS for foreign issuers. As a result of this, combined with congressional pressure, it would seem as if the SEC will have to make some allowances in respect to IAS. In respect to the last, given the comments of both the SEC and domestic constituents, it appears unlikely that IAS will be adopted wholesale, at least at this point in time.

It therefore seems probable that the SEC will allow use of IAS to some extent by foreign issuers. The SEC may decide to endorse certain IASC core standards but not endorse other standards. Notably, the SEC has previously endorsed three IASC standards for partial use by foreign issuers without requiring reconciliation to US GAAP.[317] The SEC could decide to endorse IAS for use by foreign issuers coupled with a requirement that issuers explore US GAAP on particular issues not addressed or inadequately addressed in the opinion of the SEC. The SEC could also exclude one or more of the core standards adopted by IOSCO from domestic endorsement.

VI. CONCLUSION: GLOBALIZATION OF SECURITIES OFFERINGS?

As noted at the outset, the key issue is globalization of financial markets, specifically the market for securities offerings and listings, at present largely impossible due to disparities between domestic legal and regulatory standards. Essential to true 'globalization' of securities offerings and listings is

[315] See SEC International Accounting Report, above n 172, at 23.
[316] See Tokar, above n 314, at 5.
[317] See *A Window of Opportunity*, CORP ACCOUNTING INT'L 10 (Apr 1996).

the issue of whether, for the first time, international efforts may lead to the development of an agreed format for the content of an international offering/listing document acceptable in jurisdictions around the world, ie a 'global prospectus' or 'international passport prospectus'. Three trends underscore the forces supporting the growing pressure for such a mechanism: cross-border mergers and acquisitions, mergers and alliances between stock exchanges around the world, and the development of 'global shares', traded on multiple markets. As a preliminary matter, however, it is necessary to look at the current status of international securities offerings in order to determine whether, despite current disparities, truly global offerings do in fact exist.

A. *'Global Offerings' in Practice*

In February 2001, Howell Jackson of Harvard University and Eric Pan of Covington & Burling published the results of an investigation into how European corporate issuers are currently (as of 1999) raising capital in European transactions.[318] Jackson and Pan conclude: 'the most notable feature of capital-raising practices in Europe in 1999 is the fact that market forces, and not formal legal requirements, appear to be the most important determinant of the manner in which European issuers raise capital in pan-European offerings.'[319] They conclude that the practices in Europe have two significant implications for the debate over regulatory competition:[320] first, competition seems to be following a pattern of higher standards, rather than a feared 'race to the bottom'; and second, market practices are moving towards a level and system of disclosure similar to that found in US private placements, supported by effective linkages between national markets through secondary market access.

Overall, Jackson and Pan's research suggests that

> the overwhelming number of European equity offerings consist of a distribution to local investors (including retail investors) plus a pan-European offering limited to institutional investors across Europe (and elsewhere in the world, often including US institutional investors under Rule 144A),

termed an 'International-style Offering'.[321] Essentially, the mutual recognition provisions of the European prospectus and stock exchange directives are not useful in practice due to State barriers and technical issues; instead, it is simpler and more effective to rely on the Euromarkets and exemptions for professional investors required under the Public Offer Prospectus

[318] H Jackson and E Pan, above n 27. This is the first part of a two part study, investigating European corporate capital raising in Europe (the subject of Part I) and in the US (the subject of Part II—yet to be published).

[319] ibid at 654.

[320] ibid at 655–56.

[321] ibid at 681.

Directive.[322] Further, market practice allows transfers from professional purchasers to domestic retail purchasers, through loose resale restrictions (termed by the authors, 'resale leakage') and also through European stock exchange access provisions of the ISD (termed by the authors 'secondary market linkages').[323]

While Jackson and Pan's subsequent study has not yet been published, a review of market practices suggests that at present securities offerings take six primary forms: (1) domestic offerings by domestic companies to domestic investors, subject to domestic regulatory standards; (2) foreign offerings by foreign companies to investors in another jurisdiction, subject to domestic standards which have in some cases been relaxed to encourage such activities (eg Regulation S/Rule 144A in the US); (3) international or Euromarkets offerings by companies of any jurisdiction to international institutional investors, structured to avoid domestic regulatory standards through exemptions for certain transactions and investors and typically following US private placement standards (as noted by Jackson and Pan); (4) international-style offerings (as described by Jackson and Pan) by companies of any jurisdiction, to domestic (including retail) investors in the company's home jurisdiction, plus institutional investors across the EU through the Euromarkets, and often to US institutional investors through the Regulation S/Rule 144A mechanism; (5) so-called 'global offerings', in reality a series of domestic offerings to domestic investors in various jurisdictions subject to domestic regulatory requirements, often combined with an international or international-style offering, and sometimes structured around a 'global share' tradable across various domestic exchanges; and (6) internet offerings, which typically reflect domestic or international-style structures.

By contrast, a true global offering would involve a single coordinated offering to investors around the world based upon identical standards respecting not only offering/listing but also marketing requirements and based upon a freely tradable global share structure. At present, due to conflicting domestic requirements, such an offering is not possible, even absent considerations of subsequent on-going reporting or liability concerns.

B. Stock Exchange Consolidation

In the past several years, in addition to growing numbers of international and multi-jurisdictional offerings of securities and drives towards truly 'global' offerings, securities exchanges around the world have been moving to encourage listings by foreign companies and to expand operations internationally, through organic growth, mergers and alliances.

[322] ibid at 680–3. [323] ibid at 687–90

The first method, attracting foreign listings, has been favoured by the New York Stock Exchange (NYSE) NYSE and the London Stock Exchange (LSE). The difficulty here, namely for the NYSE, has been US inflexibility in respect to requirements for listing and accounting standards—exactly the issues addressed above.

The second method, international expansion, is illustrated by NASDAQ's drive to organically establish linked exchanges in the major securities markets around the world. Because of varying legal requirements in the major financial jurisdictions (ie the US, the EU and Japan), this has not been overly successful—once again, exactly the issues discussed above.

The third key method is the recent spate of mergers and alliances between exchanges around the world. In respect to consolidation of exchanges, this trend began with NASDAQ's drive to establish linked exchanges in the major securities markets around the world in order to avoid certain of the difficulties associated with organic expansion. Other key examples are the merger of the Paris, Amsterdam and Brussels bourses to form 'Euronext' and the ongoing efforts on the parts of the Frankfurt and London exchanges to expand their respective international reaches. While these latter moves are being driven by changes in the EU (especially EMU), the trend has now spread internationally, with the mooted creation of GEM (Global Equity Market), combining, inter alia, the New York Stock Exchange and EuroNext.

As with the move towards fully global offerings of securities, international expansion by historically domestic stock exchanges has been driven by investors (especially institutions) and companies seeking to diversify risk and maximise opportunities for capital raising and generation of returns. Put simply, the overall goal is 'a single 24-hour market in which the shares of the world's biggest blue-chip firms can be traded cheaply and efficiently'.[324]

A number of key impediments exist however, of which differing regulatory and financial standards are the most significant. In addition, other significant impediments include settlement and custody and nationalistic protectionism and pride. Interestingly, however, in terms of regulation, what does not seem to be happening is the classic fear of a 'race to the bottom' (as was seen historically in US corporate law). Rather, there seems to be a move towards higher standards, rather than lower, with two major systems appearing most competitive: that of the US and that of the UK—the two systems with historically the highest standards of securities regulation and also the two predominant financial centres of their respective continents.

[324] *Stock Exchanges: The Battle for Efficient Markets*, THE ECONOMIST, 17 June 2000, 86.

C. *Cross-border Mergers and Acquisitions*

In respect to cross-border M&A, the growing importance and usefulness of such a mechanism is underscored by recent cross-border merger activities, of which the Daimler Benz-Chrysler and British Petroleum-Amoco mergers are the most high profile instances.[325] While in the area of international bonds, a de facto global prospectus has been in existence for some time (through the mechanisms of the Eurobond markets), this article argues that the development of a global prospectus for international equity offerings may soon be a reality. In fact, in some ways as discussed below, it already has and is set to continue, essentially because of support from the various concerned constituencies in major markets around the world.

D. *Proposals to Support the Development of Global Offerings*

According to Hal Scott of Harvard University,

> [i]n fully internationalized securities markets, issuers in public primary markets should be able to issue securities to investors worldwide using one set of optimal distribution procedures and disclosure documents, and subject to one set of liability standards and enforcement remedies.[326]

Scott argues that 'the imposition of US rules for disclosure, distribution, and enforcement, within and to some extent outside the United States, impedes the achievement of [this goal]'—and in fact at present makes achievement of the goal impossible.[327] According to Scott, an issuer can at present deal with diverse national distribution requirements in three ways, none of which are entirely satisfactory:[328] (1) abstain entirely from issuing in the US market; (2) distribute in foreign markets under foreign rules and in the US market under US marketing standards, which may result in the US distribution occurring later in the US than elsewhere; or (3) refrain from issuing marketing materials, other than a US-compliant prospectus, in any market until the registration Statement is effective in the US As a result of the current impasse, Scott analyses three possible alternatives:[329] (1) harmonization to an agreed common set of rules; (2) mutual recognition of domestic rules; and (3) off-shore free zones in which issuers issue securities to investors from any country under a single set of market-determined rules. In respect to harmonization, Scott is dismissive of the likely success of IDS.[330] While this can be disputed, he also suggests that more significant

325 For discussion and analysis, see B Black *The First International Merger Wave (and the Fifth and Last US Wave)*, 54 U MIAMI L REV 799 (2000).

326 H Scott *Internationalisation of Primary Public Securities Markets* 63-SUM LAW & CONTEMP PROBS 71 (2000).

327 ibid at 72–3.

328 ibid at 74–5.

329 ibid at 78–103.

330 See ibid at 78–9.

impediments remain in respect to, first, standardization of distribution procedures, second, standardization of enforcement, and third, interpretation, updating and potential to stifle competition.[331]

In respect to mutual recognition, Scott concludes (along with most others) that the neither the MJDS nor the EU passport system have not been satisfactory in practice.[332] In relation to the possible extension of mutual recognition beyond the MJDS or the EU, Scott concludes that the US is unlikely to converge its standards with those of others, that any mutual recognition must be limited to true home country companies, and non-standardized distribution and enforcement rules would remain.[333]

Scott's preferred alternative is the creation of an off-shore free-zone, in which countries would permit issuers to offer securities to the public (including residents of their own countries) offshore, subject only to minimum disclosure standards, which would require substantial changes in current US rules embodied principally in Regulation S.[334]

John Coffee, Jr of Columbia University has argued that global convergence of shareholder protection norms is more likely to come from stock exchange regulation than corporate law.[335]

Marc Steinberg of Southern Methodist University and Lee Michaels develop a proposal combining elements of mutual recognition and harmonization.[336] First, IOSCO should develop a common prospectus or offering document, with different standards for companies from developed, semi-developed and emerging markets.[337] Second, '[e]ach nation's antifraud provisions would apply to enable regulators (and where authorized, investors) to pursue relief for disclosure deficiencies or other wrongs.'[338]

While all of these are potentially valid suggests, the recent use of 'global shares' may indicate a different path forward.

E. Global Shares

Global shares are used by a number of companies, including DaimlerChrysler and most recently Deutsche Bank. Under the global share structure, companies issue a single, interchangeable and freely tradable class of shares, which are in turn listed on multiple exchanges pursuant to the individual requirements of the individual exchanges (eg the NYSE, the LSE and Deutsche Bourse). Shares are created pursuant to the law of the jurisdiction of incorporation, which governs internal matters, and listed pursuant to the

[331] ibid at 79-81.
[332] See ibid at 80–4.
[333] See ibid at 85–92.
[334] ibid at 92.
[335] J Coffee, Jr above n 9, 704.
[336] M Steinberg and L Michaels *Disclosure in Global Securities Offerings: An Analysis of Jurisdictional Approaches, Commonality and Reciprocity*, 20 MICH J INT'L L 207 (1999).
[337] See ibid at 262–4.
[338] ibid at 262.

requirements of the securities regulatory systems in the jurisdictions of the respective stock exchanges, which also typically requires certain standards of corporate governance and ongoing disclosure. Enforcement of securities violations is pursuant to the rules and structures of the jurisdictions in which the listings take place, although the jurisdiction of incorporation governs in certain circumstances. Shares are then traded through linkages between the clearing and settlement structures associated with each listing exchange, with a register maintained under the rules of the jurisdiction of incorporation.

This sort of structure, while complex, is quite appealing, in that it also companies to access investors in a variety of markets, while at the same time encouraging liquidity through identity of shares traded on all listing markets. Standards of corporate governance in turn are maintained by both the rules of the listing jurisdiction (in order to ensure adequate disclosure and appropriate investor protection) and the law of the jurisdiction of incorporation.

At this point in time, the major impediment to the further development of this sort of structure lies in the disparity of offering/listing rules (making a simultaneous global offering/listing still impossible), in the lack of international linkages between securities clearing and settlement systems (making inter-exchange trading impossible in some cases), and in disparity between accounting systems across various jurisdictions (making it necessary, in some cases, to produce multiple sets of accounts). Nonetheless, it is this sort of model that most exchanges likely will move towards as consolidation and expansion continue.

F. A Modest Proposal based upon Pragmatism and Public Policy

Based upon the analysis above, this author suggests the following as a possible pragmatic approach to the development of mechanisms to support true global offerings, while at the same time maintaining high standards of disclosure and adequate investor protection across jurisdictions.

Countries should continue to implement the IOSCO IDS, along with improving IAS to an acceptable level within a short period. Companies (whether domestic or foreign) seeking to sell securities to the public (either through a stock exchange listing or through a public offering) should be required to use IDS in conjunction with IAS or have the option to use domestic standards (if such exist). Companies would have to comply with the distribution rules of each jurisdiction in which it is desired to list or make an offering to the public (as is presently the case). IOSCO (and where relevant, regional organizations such as the EU) would seek to develop harmonized distribution standards, a process that in all likelihood will be facilitated and encouraged by consolidation and international expansion on the part of securities exchanges. In the interim, companies and their legal advisors are well-equipped to deal with divergent systems. By accessing the public markets of a given jurisdiction, companies would become subject to the domestic enforcement standards applicable. The risks would be limited by registration requirements of exchanges and securities regulators. For institutional investors (the major constituency of the Euromarkets), exemptions/relaxations should be in place to reduce the more stringent disclosure requirements appropriate for the public (and used in all listings). This however will necessitate convergence in respect to definitions of public offers.

Clearly, companies are better placed than individual investors to monitor their potential legal and regulatory risks. Companies would also be subject to the legal regime of their jurisdiction of incorporation and/or domicile. As stock exchange linkages develop, standards of enforcement will move upwards, as individual exchanges seek partners with exchanges from countries with higher regulatory standards or choose such standards for market reasons. Institutional investors pursuant to exemptions from the stringent requirements of public offerings in turn would rely on the standards of the home jurisdiction, as well as listing jurisdictions, as appropriate in the given case. The end result is a placing of the burden on companies in the context of listings and public offerings and allowing the public in a given jurisdiction to use the rules available in their own jurisdiction for enforcement. Institutional investors operating outside of the standards appropriate for the investing public should be able to enforce on the basis of the home jurisdiction of the issuer, as well as on the basis of the rules of any jurisdiction on which the issuer is listed.

The US should continue to emphasize high minimum standards for disclosure and enforcement, but should be flexible in their actual form and work through IOSCO to achieve harmonization of standards. Mutual recognition will in all likelihood increase as minimum international standards are established, implemented and enforced, reflecting the experiences of the EU in its on-going project to create a single European capital market.

THE FIGHT AGAINST THE FINANCING OF TERRORISM BETWEEN JUDICIAL AND REGULATORY COOPERATION

ANNA GARDELLA*

CHAPTER OUTLINE

* Research Fellow in International Law, School of Law, Università Cattolica di Milano; PhD International Law, Università Statale di Milano; LLM, Harvard Law School; D.E.Sup., Droit et économie des Communautés europééennes, Université de Paris I, Panthéon-Sorbonne; J.D., Università di Genova.

This is a revised version of the paper presented at the Symposium *Enforcing international law norms against terrorism*, held in Milan at the Università Cattolica on 10 and 11 May, 2002.

The author would like to thank Andrea Bianchi, Francesco Bestagno, Luca G. Radicati di Brozolo, Fabio Recine, and Antonio Sáinz de Vicuña for their comments on an earlier draft. Errors and omissions are, however, exclusively the author's responsibility.

I. INTRODUCTION

The financing of terrorist groups has recently attracted the attention of the international legal community, as one aspect of the multifaceted fight against international terrorism. The increased focus on the prevention, in addition to the repression, of terrorist acts, has necessarily involved the conclusion of legal instruments aimed at the suppression of the financing of terrorism, given its strategic role in depriving terrorist organizations of the necessary funds to carry out their activities.

Combating the financing of terrorism, however, is not an easy task. The different patterns of funding put in place by terrorist groups, principally characterized by the cross-border abuse of the financial system, require a multi-disciplinary approach concentrated on criminal and financial law and regulation, as well as coordinated multi-jurisdictional efforts. Whereas international cooperation plays a fundamental role in identifying criminal conduct and in ensuring that the offenders are brought to justice, effective and reciprocal financial regulation is essential to prevent abuses of the financial system for illicit purposes. These latter features are not distinctive traits of the struggle against the financing of terrorism, since they are common to ordinary financial crimes and to money laundering in particular. For this reason, the fight against the funding of terrorism is largely inspired by, and is currently conducted within the legal framework against money laundering, as will be illustrated in the following paragraphs.

The lack of regulation of the financial system, or its unsatisfactory implementation, offer attractive opportunities to terrorists to achieve their criminal goals, enabling a profitable management of financial resources as well as their transfer through banking channels (without material shipment) to the jurisdiction where the preparation of terrorist activities is to take place. All of this occurs without leaving a trace of the criminals' identity, or of the origin and destination of the money. Regardless of the stringent rules in force in the most advanced financial centres, the financing of terrorism takes advantage of the arbitrage opportunities offered by unregulated or insufficiently regulated jurisdictions. For this reason, a multi-jurisdictional approach, characterized by reciprocity and a high degree of international cooperation, is critical to the struggle against financial crime in general.

International fora are therefore the most appropriate places to develop a comprehensive legal framework which duly takes into account both the inter-disciplinary and cross-border elements of the puzzle. In addition to the existing legal machinery to fight money laundering, mandatory provisions in UN Security Council Resolutions, as implemented by regional organizations (such as the European Union), together with international conventions and ad hoc recommendations adopted by specialized international bodies (such as the Financial Action Task Force), are the most relevant instruments available to national authorities in fighting against the financing of terrorism.[1]

Combating the financing of terrorism may turn out to be more troublesome than ordinary financial crime. Additional hurdles which challenge the current legal framework set up against financial criminality, are represented by the involvement, in the financing of terrorism, of legitimate entities and legitimate financial resources; by the use of small amounts of money, below the existing alert thresholds, which can be easily concealed; and by resort to underground banking networks which escape the existing monitoring and controlling schemes. In this context, the countering of terrorism financing is made more complex by the need to balance the public interest to defeat terrorism against the conflicting, but equally important societal needs, of preserving individual civil liberties and privacy.

In the light of the above considerations, the goal of the present paper is to provide an overview of the many issues involved in the fight against the financing of terrorism as well as to envisage effective remedies. Part I describes the financial resources which fuel terrorist groups, in particular the coexistence of illegitimate and legitimate sources of income and the fund-raising role played by charities and legitimate business. To combat these forms of assistance, the need to make the financing of terrorist groups a criminal offence in domestic legislation will be underlined. Part II starts with a survey of the legal instruments already available in criminal law within the existing anti-money laundering schemes, and then focuses on actions taken internationally in the aftermath of the September 11th attacks to adapt the existing legal tools to the fight against international terrorism. For this purpose, particular emphasis will be placed on the UN Security Council's Resolution 1373 and on the 1999 UN Convention on the suppression of the financing of terrorism. Part III analyses the financing of terrorism from the perspective of regulation. In doing so, attention will primarily be directed at the legislative shortcomings vis-à-vis the peculiarities of terrorist

[1] For an overview of the several international institutions actively involved in the fight against the financing of terrorism, see J Fisher *Recent International Developments in the Fight Against Money Laundering*, 17 JOURN INT'L BANKING LAW 67 (2002); see also the Special Issue entirely dedicated to *The Funding of Terror: The Legal Implications of the Financial War on Terror* 6 JOURNAL OF MONEY LAUNDERING CONTROL (2003).

funding, which have called into question the adequacy of the current regulation of the financial system and have drawn global attention to the need to enact harmonized regulatory and supervisory standards and to enhance international cooperation also in the form of information-sharing. In the concluding remarks (Part IV), it will be emphasised that effective enforcement and implementation at the national level of the international legal norms adopted is necessary, rather than further legislative initiatives.

II. THE FINANCIAL RESOURCES OF TERRORIST GROUPS

A. The Financial Resources of Terrorist Groups

An extensive analysis of the funding methods of terrorist groups and of the financial resources supporting terrorist activities has been carried out by the Financial Action Task Force (FATF). Therefore, the following illustration to a large extent relies on the outcomes of its survey. The FAFT is an intergovernmental organization established in 1989 by the G-7 States, working as a policy-making group entrusted with the task of suggesting legislative and regulatory action to counter money laundering.[2] The FATF is internationally recognized as the leading institution in the combat of money laundering. The '*summa*' of its work is represented by the 'Forty Recommendations',[3] originally issued in 1990, and subsequently subject to a review process in 1996 in order to update their content consistent with evolving patterns of money laundering. A further round of consultation for review of the Forty Recommendations was launched in 2002, and the current version was approved in June 2003.[4] The Forty Recommendations are a body of international standards which, despite not being formally binding on the member States of the FATF, hold great authority and are highly considered by national legislators.[5] Indeed, their nature as 'soft law'

[2] At the time of writing, the FAFT's membership consists of 31 countries and two regional organisations (EC and Gulf Cooperation Council).

[3] The Forty Recommendations are a comprehensive legal framework designed to be of universal application, encompassing measures concerning the criminal justice system and law enforcement, the financial system and its regulation, and international regulation. The text of the Forty Recommendations is *available at* <www.fatf-gafi.org>.

[4] See respectively, Review of the FATF Forty Recommendations, Consultation Paper, of 30 May 2002; and The Forty Recommendations of 20 June 2003, both available at <www.fatf-gafi.org>.

[5] Suffice it here to recall that the Forty Recommendations have so far been endorsed by 130 States, and that references to the activity of FATF is contained in above national and national legislation; for instance see recital 14 of Directive 2001/97/EC of 14 Dec 2001 amending Directive 91/308, on prevention of the use of the financial system for the purpose of money laundering in OJ Eur Comm L 344 of 28 Dec 2001 at 76; see also Italian law decree n 369, of 12 Oct 2001, introducing urgent measures to counter the financing of terrorism, converted into law by Law n 431 of 14 Dec 2001, in OJ n 290 of 14 Dec 2001. The decree specifies that special attention in updating national law will be paid to the outcomes of the FATF work.

does not prevent them from being recognized as the international anti-money laundering framework. 'Soft law' is usually defined as consisting of international standards, declarations of principles, and statements generally adopted by international organizations in matters related to the protection of human rights, economic relations and the environment, which embody a common core of principles, approaches or concerns of the international community. Although it might be considered as 'second best' in respect of formal and binding international treaties,[6] it is not tantamount to 'weak law'; on the contrary, 'soft law' responds to the logic that sometimes 'less is more'. In matters where the views of States may not yet be sufficiently mature to form the basis of formal agreements, soft law lays down informal commitments with which States can spontaneously comply, or which may be a starting point towards further international efforts to be later translated into 'hard law' such as a treaty.[7] The FATF Recommendations fit this scheme and go even further, constituting the general and primary reference for international and domestic legislation. For this reason the efforts undertaken by the FAFT are a chief reference also in the present paper.

Starting from its *Report on Money Laundering Typologies 1999–2000*,[8] analysis by the FATF has included issues concerned with the financing of terrorism, due to the connections with money laundering typologies. After the September 11th attacks, at an extraordinary session held on 29–30 October 2001 in Washington DC, in light of its expertise in the field of money laundering control and prevention, the FATF undertook to extend its mandate to the financing of terrorism, and immediately issued the 'Eight Special Recommendations' which specifically address terrorist financing.[9] This has been the first specific contribution of the FATF to the fight against the financing of terrorism, to which it is still actively committed. In order to ensure the swift and effective implementation of the Eight Special Recommendations, the FATF has adopted a Plan of Action providing for, inter alia, a self-assessment exercise addressed both to Member and non-

[6] The debate on whether 'soft law' is a good or a bad thing has been extensively developed; against the resort to 'soft law', perceived as a threat to the prescriptive nature of international law, see P Weil *Towards Relative Normativity in International Law?* (1983) 77 AM JOURN INT'L LAW 413.

[7] See, G Abi-Saab 'Éloge du "droit assourdi". Quelques réflexions sur le rôle de la *soft law* en droit international contemporain', in *Nouveaux itinéraires en droit. Hommage à François Rigaux* (Bruxelles: Bruylant, 1993) 59; RJ Dupuy 'Droit déclaratoire et droit programmatoire: de la coutume sauvage à la soft law' in Dupuy *Dialectique du droit international* (Paris: Pedone, 1999) 107; A Cassese *International Law* (OUP Oxford 2002) 160; A Bianchi 'Globalization of Human Rights: the Role of Non-State Actors' in G Teubner (ed) *Global Law without a State* (Dartmouth Aldershot 1997) 405.

[8] See FATF-XI, *Report on Money Laundering Typologies 1999–2000*, 3 Feb 2000, available at <www.fatf-gafi.org>.

[9] Available at <www.fatf-gafi.org>.

Member States directed at evaluating the degree of compliance with the Special Recommendations.[10]

According to the *Reports on Money Laundering Typologies* adopted by the FATF for the years 2001–2 and 2002–3,[11] terrorist organizations rely both on illegal and legal sources of income. With respect to illegal sources of income, the reports point out the link with trans-national criminality, since they derive from criminal 'revenue-generating' activities, such as narcotics trafficking,[12] large-scale smuggling, various frauds (such as credit card duplication), kidnapping, extortions and so on. The 2001–2 Report underlines that there is little difference between terrorists and other criminals in the use of the proceeds of crime, since both aim to launder the dirty money, generated by such offences, in order to either make profits or to invest such money in other criminal plans. According to the FATF findings, laundering typologies used by terrorists do not differ from those followed by ordinary criminals. Therefore, to the extent that terrorists are funded by criminal 'revenue-generating' activities, the fight against the financing of terrorism can be conducted within the existing framework against money laundering.

Terrorist funding, however, also largely relies on legal financial resources, solicited and collected by associations having a charitable or non-profit status. These funds, which derive from membership subscriptions, donations, sales of publications, cultural and social events and appeals to wealthy members of the community, are then diverted to the terrorist cause by the charitable or non-profit association. Therefore, fundraising campaigns promoted for charitable purposes often become willingly or unwittingly a privileged vehicle to collect and transfer money to terrorists, and the lawful origin of the funds makes it difficult to detect the sums destined for terrorist organizations. Besides charities, front-stores

[10] The other steps envisaged by the Action Plan agreed upon at the Washington meeting include (i) the development of additional guidance for financial institutions to detect the mechanisms used in the financing of terrorism; (ii) the identification of jurisdictions that lack appropriate measures to combat terrorist financing and discussion of the available remedies to impose compliance; (iii) regular publication by the member States of the amount of suspected terrorist assets frozen; (iv) the provision by FATF members of technical assistance to non-members, as necessary to assist them in complying with the Eight Recommendations. For a review of the FATF's counter-terrorism activity, see FATF Annual Report 2001–2 of 21 June 2002, and FATF Annual Report 2002–3 of 20 June 2003, both *available at* <www.fatf-gafi.or>.

[11] Respectively FATF-XIII, *Report on Money Laundering Typologies, 2001–2002* of 1 Feb 2002, and FATF-XIII, *Report on Money Laundering Typologies, 2002–2003* of 14 Feb 2003, both available at <www.fatf-gafi.org>.

[12] Explicit mention to this modality of self-financing is made in UN Security Resolution 1333 of 19 Dec 2000, where it is acknowledged that 'the Taliban benefits directly from the cultivation of illicit opium by imposing a tax on its production and indirectly benefits from the processing and trafficking of such opium and [. . .] that these substantial resources strengthen the Taliban's capacity to harbour terrorists'.

exercising cross-border business are employed by terrorists as a conduit for the funding of terrorism through legitimate resources; the under-invoicing and over-invoicing of the traded goods allow the allocation of hidden balances to terrorist groups through underground banking channels.[13]

Paradoxically, the legal origin of these economic resources hinders the detection, and prevention of such funds from reaching terrorist organizations, since anti-money laundering control and reporting schemes are not triggered without any criminal activity being at their source. Before the legal money reaches terrorist groups, and even at that time, no crime has yet been committed, and this prevents financial institutions from identifying suspicious transactions in accordance with money laundering provisions.[14] Such an undisturbed freedom to move sums of money within the financial system has undoubtedly increased the funding of terrorist groups through legal channels, making financing through 'clean' resources a convenient tool for supporting terrorism. The lack of provisions proscribing terrorism financing has also had the adverse effect of formally allowing terrorist groups to carry on 'safe and sound' fundraising campaigns in the territory of the State against which the terror plans were eventually directed, exposing governments to adverse political criticism. As will be further illustrated,[15] to redress such an intolerable situation the envisaged remedy has been to make the financing of terrorism an independent crime, a solution which builds on the existing legal framework against money laundering by introducing the specific crime of terrorist financing within its predicate offences.[16]

B. Specific Problems Raised by Charitable Associations in the Enforcement of Measures Against the Financing of Terrorism

The misuse of non-profit and charitable associations is the most distinctive feature of the financing of terrorism and undisputedly the aspect which creates the most serious challenges from a law enforcement and crime prevention perspective. Notwithstanding the normative progress made by the criminalization of the financing of terrorism, which is primarily targeted

[13] For a description of these techniques see J Trehan *Terrorism and the Funding of Terrorism in Kashmir* 5 JOURN OF MONEY LAUNDERING CONTROL 201 (2002); K Alexander *United States Financial Sanctions and International Terrorism, Part 2*, 17 BUTTERWORTHS JOURN INT'L BANKING FIN LAW 213 (2002), as well as FATF—XIII *Report on Money Laundering Typologies, 2001–2002* cit and FATF—XIV *Report on Money Laundering Typologies, 2002–2003* cit.

[14] See also J Jackson *11th Sept. 2001: Will it Make a Difference to the Global Anti-Money Laundering Movement?*, 5 JOURN OF MONEY LAUNDERING CONTROL 9, at 11 (2002).

[15] See below, para 5, 6.

[16] On the need to include terrorist financing as a predicate offence of money laundering, see FATF—*XIII, Report on Money Laundering Typologies, 2001–2002* cit, at 6; as well as S/RES/ 1373.

at stopping the funding of terrorist organizations through legitimate resources, the reality of enforcement does not correspond to the written law. The ideological and religious elements supporting terrorist acts make these private entities, willingly or unwittingly, a crucial link between civil society and terrorist organizations. Under the cover of the legitimate goal of their front activities, non-profit and religious entities may act freely and above suspicion to support terrorist groups. The protections granted by the constitutional and internationally recognized rights of freedom of association and of freedom of religion normally shield these entities from administrative control of their activities. These circumstances easily expose charities and non-profit organizations to misuse by terrorist financiers, thus representing a crucial weak point in the struggle against the funding of terrorist groups.

That non-profit associations are particularly vulnerable to misuse for purposes of the financing of terrorism is commonly acknowledged and is reflected in the recitals of the UN Convention on the Suppression of the Financing of Terrorism, signed in New York on 9 December 1999 (the 'New York Convention')[17] as well as in FATF Special Recommendation VIII, whereby countries are urged to review the adequacy of their laws and regulations governing such entities.[18] With a view to helping Member and non-Member States to comply and to ensure its swift implementation, the FATF issued an 'International Best Practices' guideline, in October 2002.[19] Consistent with domestic constitutional constraints, the FATF urges the establishment of measures setting up transparency and accountability mechanisms for oversight of the activities carried out by such entities. These measures should enable authorities to verify the actual use of the funds collected by or donated to non-profit associations and specifically verify that they are actually employed in the accomplishment of the promoted charitable programmes and are not diverted to support terrorist acts. In this respect, special efforts are required to monitor those non-profit associations

[17] See recital n 6, recalling that financing of terrorism may be direct or 'indirect through organizations which also have or claim to have charitable, social or cultural goals or which are also engaged in unlawful activities [. . .]'

[18] See Special Recommendation VIII which reads 'Countries should review the adequacy of laws and regulations that relate to entities that be abused for the financing of terrorism. Non-profit organisations are particularly vulnerable, and countries should ensure that they cannot be misused: (i) by terrorist organisations posing as legitimate entities; (ii) to exploit legitimate entities as conduits for terrorist financing, including for the purpose of escaping asset freezing measures; and (iii) to conceal or obscure the clandestine diversion of funds intended for legitimate purposes to terrorist organisations.'

[19] See FATF *Combating the abuse of non-profit organisations. International Best Practices*, of 11 Oct 2002, available at <www.fatf-gafi.org>. Responses submitted by FATF members States to the self-assessment exercise evidenced difficulties encountered by domestic legal systems in implementing Special Recommendation VIII specifically focused on the misuse of non-profit organisations; see FATF *Annual Report, 2001–2002*, at 5.

directing their activities to beneficiaries established in foreign countries to who the funds are transferred. In this regard, the FATF recommends that international cooperation be reinforced, especially in the form of information sharing between the administrative agencies of different jurisdictions.

Despite the valuable efforts undertaken by the FATF in the identification of remedies to the major shortcomings of the current legislation which expose non-profit associations to misuse by terrorist financers, the envisaged monitoring task may turn out to be ineffective, either because of constitutional constraints—ie prohibition of interference on the free exercise of civil liberties—or because of the practical hurdles of identifying and overseeing such entities. Notwithstanding the normative solution to the prevention of terrorist financing, the trade-off between the expenses jurisdictions would incur in pursuing this goal and the ascertained number of cases of actual misuse of non-profit associations may call into question the proportionate character of the envisaged remedies also in the light of their intrusive nature on the activities of legitimate associations.

III. THE CRIMINAL LAW APPROACH TO COUNTER THE FINANCING OF TERRORISM

A. *The Existing Anti-Money Laundering Regime and the Limits of its Application Against the Financing of Terrorism*

To the extent that terrorist organizations do rely on illegal sources of income, the similarities with the operating and financing modalities of international criminality[20] have made resort to the existing legal framework against money laundering a natural remedy to counter the funding of terrorism. Although experts have rightly questioned its adequacy to combat all forms of terrorism financing, notably those depending on resources of legitimate origin,[21] it has the unquestionable merit of being a valuable and

[20] The connection between international terrorism and transnational organized crime has been stressed in several UN declarations, see A/RES/46/51, 9 Dec 1991 (UN Doc A/46/654); A/RES/49/60, 9 Dec 1994, *Measures to eliminate international terrorism*; A/RES/55/25 of 8 Jan 2001, adopting the UN Convention against Transnational Organized Crime of 15 Nov 2000, whose ratification is urged by FATF Recommendation n 35; A/RES/55/59 of 17 Jan 2001, *Vienna Declaration on Crime Prevention and Justice: Meeting the Challenges of the Twenty-first Century*; see also A/RES/45/117 adopting the model treaty on Mutual Assistance in Criminal Matters, recalling the need to strengthen cooperation in mutual legal assistance against criminal acts of terrorist character. At the domestic level—with specific reference to US law—similarities between international terrorism and transnational organised crime had suggested the application of the Racketeer Influenced and Corrupt Organization Act ('RICO'), see Z Joseph 'The Application of RICO to International Terrorism' 58 Fordham L Rev 1071 (1990); SC Warneck 'A Preemptive Strike: Using RICO and the AEDPA to Attack the Financial Strength of International Terrorist Organizations', 78 BUL Rev 177 (1998).

[21] See FATF-XII, *Report on Money Laundering Typologies, 2000-2001* of 1 Feb 2001, at 19 and 20.

already available international legal framework, encompassing both the criminal and financial aspect of this complex offence.[22]

Money laundering may be defined as a process aiming at concealing the existence, illegal sources or illegal application of income, in order to disguise that income, make it appear legitimate and inject it into the legal economy. The first international instrument to proscribe money laundering was the UN Convention against illicit traffic in narcotic drugs and psychotropic substances signed in Vienna on 19 December 1988 (hereinafter the 'Vienna Convention'), which in addition to the prohibition of cultivation and export of psychotropic substances, had the merit, having regard to the amounts of money generated by such commerce, of specifically addressing the economic aspects of drug trafficking. In order to prevent the legitimate use of the proceeds of crime, the Vienna Convention adopted a scheme essentially based on three main concepts, notably (i) the obligation to establish money laundering as a separate crime by the national legal systems; (ii) the freezing and seizing of the assets deriving from or constituting the proceeds of crime; and (iii) the enhancement of inter-State cooperation and mutual legal assistance in penal matters.

This basic scheme has been adopted by subsequent international instruments combating money laundering and in particular by the Council of Europe Convention on Laundering, Search, Seizure and Confiscation of the Proceeds of Crime of 8 November 1990 (hereinafter the 'Strasbourg Convention').[23] This Convention is of paramount importance in that it intends to be a broad and general instrument to prevent the use of proceeds of crime beyond the specific focus on drug-related crimes. To this end, the Strasbourg Convention expands the scope of application of the Vienna Convention, subjecting to the money laundering regime additional predicate offences which are not associated with narcotic trafficking, but which are also capable of generating large profits. This step was taken in the belief that the fight against serious crime has become an increasingly international problem, which calls for the use of modern and effective methods on an international scale, and in particular of the deprivation of criminals of the proceeds of crime.[24]

[22] On the national and international aspects of anti-money laundering regimes see the extensive and in-depth study of G Stessens *Money Laundering. A New International Law Enforcement Model* (CUP Cambridge 1999); K Hinterseer *Criminal Finance. The Political Economy of Money Laundering in a Comparative Legal Context* (Kluwer Law International The Hague, London, New York, 2002).

[23] ETS, n 141; for commentary see V Delicato 'Reato di Riciclaggio e Cooperazione Internazionale: l'Applicazione in Italia della Convenzione del Consiglio d'Europa del 1990' (1995) 31 Riv dir int priv proc 341; E Müller-Rappard 'Inter-State Cooperation in Penal Matters Within the Council of Europe Framework' in M Cherif Bassiouni (ed) *International Criminal Law*, 2nd edn, vol II, *Procedural and Enforcement Mechanisms* (Transnational Publishers, Ardsley, New York, 1999) 331, spec at 349 et seq.

[24] See preamble of the Strasbourg Convention.

The treaty framework is completed by a set of rules on international cooperation covering all procedural stages including investigative assistance as well as the search, seizure and confiscation of the proceeds of crime, accompanied by provisions governing extradition, assistance in evidence gathering and execution of penal sanctions. It is worth noting that the picture of international cooperation in criminal matters is completed by provisions encouraging contracting States to enter Mutual Legal Assistance Treaties (MLATs), establishing more detailed provisions to be of aid to law enforcement authorities.[25]

Indisputably, effective inter-State cooperation is necessary to track money and other assets originating from crimes in order to enable their seizure and confiscation as envisaged by the Conventions. In this regard, one of the most powerful provisions contained in both Conventions is the express waiver of banking secrecy, which removes one of the major obstacles to tracing the proceeds of crime, thus preventing a State Party from declining assistance on this basis.[26] This is a remarkable step in the struggle against criminality and a demonstration that the international community is increasingly aware of the seriousness of the phenomenon of money laundering, which compels the adoption of extraordinary measures. Unilateral efforts to pierce banking secrecy, through extraterritorial discovery orders adopted by various jurisdictions, and in particular by US authorities, have raised issues of compatibility with international law as well as causing diplomatic tension with jurisdictions providing banking secrecy as a means of protecting financial privacy and fostering economic policy.[27]

[25] For a review of the principal forms of cooperation contemplated in both the Vienna and Strasbourg Conventions and in bilateral Mutual Legal Assistance Treaties (MLATs), see M Cherif Bassiouni and DS Gualtieri 'International and National Responses to the Globalization of Money Laundering' in M Cherif Bassiouni (ed), *International Criminal Law*, 2nd edn, vol II, *Procedural and Enforcement Mechanisms* (Transnational Publishers Ardsley 1999) 675.

[26] See Art 7, para 5 of the Vienna Convention stating that 'A Party shall not decline to act under the provision of this paragraph on the ground of bank secrecy'; see also Art 5, para 3 compelling States Parties to the Convention to empower courts or other competent authorities 'to order that bank, financial institution or commercial records be made available or be seized'. See also Art 18, para 7 of the Council of Europe Convention excluding banking secrecy as a legitimate ground for refusal of inter-State cooperation; the provision reads 'A Party shall not invoke bank secrecy as a ground to refuse any cooperation under this chapter. Where its domestic law so requires, a Party may require that a request for cooperation which would involve the lifting of bank secrecy be authorised by either a judge or another judicial authority, including public prosecutors, any of these authorities acting in relation to criminal offences.' For a review of the issues connected to bank secrecy in the context of the fight against money laundering see G Stessens *Money Laundering. A New International Law Enforcement Model* (CUP Cambridge 1999) 311.

[27] For a review of the relevant US case-law and for a comment of the underlining issues, see CT Jones, 'Compulsion over Comity: The United States' Assault on Foreign Bank Secrecy' (1992) 12 J Int'l L Bus 454; C McLachlan 'The Jurisdictional Limits of Disclosure Orders in Transnational Fraud Litigation' (1998) 47 Int'l & Comp LQ 3.

Therefore, international cooperation has been the only available solution to accommodate these conflicting interests. Various jurisdictions which protect banking secrecy, in particular Switzerland, have ratified the Vienna Convention, the Strasbourg Convention and have concluded bilateral MLATs explicitly providing for the lifting of banking secrecy in relation to such criminal matters, due to concern at the seriousness of the threats posed by transnational criminality to the soundness and reputation of the financial system, particularly when financial institutions are used for sheltering illegally-derived proceeds.[28] Piercing of banking secrecy is provided also by the 1990 UN Model Treaty on Mutual Assistance in Criminal Matters.[29] It is worth noting that such international law-making processes have also resulted in amendments to domestic laws on banking secrecy in order to comply with the normative contents of these international instruments.[30]

However valuable the regime provided by the Vienna and Strasbourg Conventions, it can only be of partial aid in the struggle against the funding of terrorism, given that it does not cover the financing of terrorism through legitimate resources absent the establishment of a specific crime of terrorist financing.

Adoption of specific measures at the international level to combat the financing of terrorism is therefore a necessary step to complete and to adjust the anti-money laundering regime to the peculiarities of the funding of terrorism.[31] UN Security Council Resolution 1373 and the FATF have envisaged the criminalization of terrorism financing as the first step to be taken to fight the financing of terrorism, given that it would enable domestic jurisdictions to apply the mechanisms provided by the anti-money laundering regimes which cannot otherwise be applied without the specific proscription of such an offence.

From a criminal law standpoint, contrary to the classic money laundering scenario where the laundering process is undertaken *after*, and as a consequence of, economic crimes which have been already committed, in

[28] The bilateral MLAT between US and Switzerland has proved to be particularly effective, see KM Singh, 'Nowhere to Hide: Judicial Assistance in Piercing the Veil of Swiss Banking Secrecy' (1991) 71 BUL Rev 847.

[29] See A/RES/45/117 of 14 Dec 1990. Art 4(f) expressly excludes that assistance be refused 'solely on the ground of secrecy of banks and similar financial institutions'.

[30] For an overview of the content and of the amendments to the Swiss Criminal Code with regard to banking secrecy, see F Beck and M Jagmetti 'Il segreto bancario in Svizzera' (1993) 7 Diritto del Commercio Internazionale 279; P Bernasconi 'Il Segreto Bancario Svizzero nella Collaborazione Giudiziaria Internazinale in Materia Penale e Fiscale' (1995) 66 Diritto e Pratica Tributaria, I, 1934; D Poncet and C Lombardini 'Segreto bancario e modifiche recenti nel diritto di cooperazione penale nella Confederazione elvetica (1998) 51 Banca Borsa e titoli di credito, I, 488.

[31] The need of specific measures to complement anti-money laundering scheme had been raised by FATF experts who consider the financing of terrorism as a of money laundering, as such requiring ad hoc measures; see FATF-XII, *Report on Money Laundering Typologies, 2000–2001*, at 20.

the case of terrorist financing, the acts of financial assistance—where the laundering activity may take place—occur *before* an act of terrorism (if any) is actually committed. Therefore, the argument has been made that the crime of financial assistance to terrorists does not fall, strictly speaking, into the category of predicate offences,[32] it being quite obvious that the crime of financing of terrorism has to do with disguising the *destination* of the funds rather than their illicit *origin*. Hence, the criminalization of terrorist financing has arguably the effect of ultimately expanding the scope of application of the anti-money laundering regime, in order to apply the existing monitoring and law enforcement schemes to a new criminal hypothesis.[33]

From another perspective, it should be stressed that in order to be effective, the criminalization of the financing of terrorism must be established at the international level, since sporadic prohibitions of financing of terrorism by single jurisdictions risk being inadequate vis-à-vis the global ramifications of terrorism and the dual criminality requirement for the exercise of jurisdiction in criminal matters.[34] Therefore, a multilateral approach, requiring a high degree of consensus on the introduction of this crime is crucial to effective enforcement of the measures enacted against the financing of terrorism, and against terrorism more generally.[35]

B. *The Criminalization of the Financing of Terrorism Under US Law and the Limits of Unilateral Action*

Even before the law-making developments following the events of 11 September, steps against the funding of terrorist groups had been taken at the domestic level in the context of the struggle against international terrorism. Special rules proscribing support to terrorists under any form, as well as transactions with such organizations or State sponsors of terrorism had been enacted in US law. Federal law had criminalized financial assistance to terrorism since 1994 in 18 USC 2339A, subsequently amended by the comprehensive Anti-terrorism and Effective Death Penalty Act of 1996 ('AEDPA'),[36] which was passed one year after the bombing of the federal

[32] JJ Norton and H Shams *Money Laundering Law and Terrorist Financing: Post-Sept. 11 Responses—Let Us Step Back and Take a Deep Breath?* 36 INT'L LAWYER 103 (2002).

[33] See also, J Jackson, *11th Sept. 2001: Will it Make a Difference to the Global Anti-Money Laundering Movement?* (2002) 5 JOURN OF MONEY LAUNDERING CONTROL 10.

[34] On dual criminality see C van den Wyngaert, 'Double Criminality as a Requirement to Jurisdiction', in N Jareborg (ed), *Double Criminality. Studies in International Criminal Law* (Iustus Forlag Uppsala 1989) 43; reprinted in J Dugard and C van den Wyngaert (eds) *International Criminal Law and Procedure* (Brookfield Aldershot 1996) 131.

[35] See JA Carberry *Terrorism: A Global Phenomenon Mandating a Unified International Response*, 6 IND J GLOBAL LEG STUD 685 (1999) (arguing in favour of a unified and integrated response to terrorism, demanding a high degree of cooperation).

[36] Public Law n 104–32 [S.735], of 24 Apr 1996.

building in Oklahoma City. This statute, targeting foreign terrorist organizations on the assumption that these groups 'raise significant funds within the United States, or use the United States as a conduit for the receipt of funds raised in other nations' and 'are so tainted by their criminal conduct that any contribution to such an organization facilitates that conduct', sets forth rules aiming at preventing such material support. Thus, proscribed conduct includes the supply of material support or resources to terrorists (18 USC 2339A); the provision of material support or resources to designated terrorist organizations (18 USC 2339B); the provision or collection of funds (18 USC 2339C); and the engagement in financial transactions with terrorists (18 USC 2332d).[37] Whereas § 2339A, as amended by the USA Patriot Act of 2001,[38] sanctions by up to 15 years' imprisonment for whoever provides material support or resources or conceals or disguises the nature, location, source or ownership of material support or resources, knowing or intending that they are to be used in preparation for, or in carrying out, specific mentioned crimes related to terrorism, § 2339B is directed against whoever in the United States or subject to its jurisdiction provides material support or resources to a *foreign* terrorist organization, or attempts or conspires to do so. With respect to the financial aspects of both offences, 'material support or resources' means 'currency or monetary instruments or financial securities, financial services [. . .]'.[39] The offence codified by § 2339A appears broad and generic, whereas the offence proscribed by § 2339B expressly targets foreign terrorist organizations.[40] These are specifically designated by the Secretary of State in accordance with the administrative procedure laid down in the AEDPA, in the light of the threat posed by such organizations to the security of United States nationals and the national security of the United States. Despite the delicate issues that such a designation process is likely to raise in terms of respect

[37] Similar provisions were already proscribed by the Prevention of Terrorism Act 1989 adopted by the United Kingdom; for a review, see D Schiff *Managing Terrorism the British Way*, in R Higgins and M Flory *Terrorism and International Law* (Routledge London/New York 1997) 129.

[38] Uniting and Strengthening America by Providing Appropriate Tools Required to Intercept and Obstruct Terrorism (USA PATRIOT ACT) Act of 2001, Public Law 107–56 26 Oct 2001, see below para 9.1.

[39] See 18 USC. 2339A, letter (b), the list also includes 'lodging, training, expert advice or assistance, safehouse, false documentation or identification, communications equipment, facilities, weapons, lethal substances, explosives, personnel, transportation and other physical assets, except medicine or religious materials.'

[40] For a commentary see J Benson *Send Me Money: Controlling International Terrorism by Restricting Fundraising in the United States* 21 Hous J Int'l L 321, at 327 (1999). The author illustrates also that in the wake of the federal legislation single States, such as Illinois, Maryland, Wisconsin enacted anti-terrorism statutes proscribing terrorist fundraising; W Patton *Preventing Terrorist Fundraising in the United States* 30 GW J Int'l L & Econ 127 (1996) (with references also to the British legislation).

for civil liberties and due process,[41] the designation of an entity as a foreign terrorist organization may be immediately sanctioned and financial institutions may be ordered to freeze assets which are connected to such criminal entities.[42] The conduct proscribed by § 2339C is even broader and is closer to the notion of terrorism financing set forth by the New York Convention. It targets 'whoever . . . by any means, directly or indirectly, unlawfully and wilfully provides or collects funds with the intention that such funds be used, or with the knowledge that such funds are to be used, in full or in part, in order to carry out' terrorist acts, regardless of the circumstance that the funds are actually used to carry out a predicate act.

The offence provided at 18 USC. § 2332d operates at a different level in that it prevents any United States person from engaging in financial transactions with the governments of those countries designated by the competent US agencies as a State sponsor of international terrorism. The same effort of isolating State sponsors of terrorism is pursued by the obligation imposed on United States representatives within international financial institutions, such as the IMF and the World Bank, to oppose any loan or other use of the funds of the respective institution to or for a country which has been designated as sponsor of terrorism.[43]

A third provision relates to the issue of State-sponsored financing of terrorism from a reparatory standpoint, by allowing the lifting of sovereign immunity of those States supporting terrorist activities.[44] Although this provision is significant from the standpoint of general international law, its

[41] See 8 USC 1189. The analysis of the relationship of the AEDPA procedure with human rights standards, however exceeds the scope of the present paper. Lack of review procedures and absence of a common set of rules in accordance to which individuals and groups are designated to be terrorists, have raised criticism also outside the US, in Sweden and France and created diplomatic tension. These countries have challenged the accuracy of the modalities of designation and claimed the disregard of human rights in such a process, see K Alexander *United States Financial Sanctions and International Terrorism, Part* 2, 17 BUTTERWORTHS JOURN INT'L BANKING FIN LAW 219 (2002).

[42] See 8 USC 1189, which, in respect of the freezing of assets reads 'Upon notification . . . the Secretary of the Treasury may require United States financial institutions possessing or controlling any assets of any foreign organization included in the notification to block all financial transaction involving those assets until further directive from either the Secretary of the Treasury, Act of Congress, or order of the Court.'

[43] See 22 USC 262p-4q.

[44] The AEDPA added s 1605(a)(7) to the Foreign Sovereign Immunities Act which States that the District Courts of the United States may exercise jurisdiction over all claims 'in which money damages are sought against a foreign State for personal injury or death that was caused by an act of torture, extrajudicial killing, aircraft sabotage, hostage taking, *or the provision of material support or resources* (as defined in s 2339A of title 18) for such an act if such act or provision of material support is engaged in by an official, employee, or agent of such foreign State while acting within the scope of his or her office, employment or agency, except that the court shall decline to hear a claim under this paragraph . . . (A) if the foreign State was not designated as a State sponsor of terrorism . . . at the time the act occurred, unless later designated as a result of such act . . .' (emphasis added).

effectiveness in the fight against international terrorism is disputable. Suffice it to note here the political nature of such a provision, intended to offer relief to the victims (US nationals) of terrorist acts, rather than actually combating State sponsorship of terrorism. In this regard it should be underlined that even the collection of damages by the victims of terrorism, contemplated by the provision, has long remained ineffective because of the disputes which have arisen within the US itself, in respect of the actual enforcement of the judgments awarding damages against foreign States.[45]

Normative endeavours to fight the financing of terrorist groups, therefore, rather than focusing on State sponsorship of terrorism, concentrate on the non-State actors and their financing patterns, by providing *ex ante* and more effective responses in the tools available within criminal law.[46] In this regard, although US domestic law has the merit of addressing terrorist financing as a separate and complementary issue in the fight against international terrorism, its unilateral approach may undermine its effectiveness. In the absence of reciprocal engagements and cooperation schemes with foreign States, the inherent territorial scope of criminal jurisdiction may impair the strength of such internal proscriptions. Even the extraterritorial reach attached to these provisions[47] may prove ineffective against the

[45] The major difficulties have come from the executive branch which on several occasions has opposed the actual collection of the large awards made by the judiciary as a result of suits filed by victims of terrorist attacks; see *Alejandre v Republic of Cuba*, 996 F Supp 1239 (S D Fla 1997); *Flatow v Islamic Republic of Iran*, 999 F Supp 1 (DDC 1998); *Cicippio v Islamic Republic of Iran*, 18 F Supp 2d 62 (DDC 1998). For further references see, *State Jurisdiction and Jurisdiction Immunities* (2000) 94 AM JOURN INT'L LAW 117; *Lawsuit by US Hostage Against Iran* (2002) 96 AM JOURN INT'L LAW 463, discussing *Roeder v Iran*, Complaint No 1:00CV03110 (EGS) (DDC 29 Dec 2000), and 'Terrorist-Exception Cases in 2002', ibid 964, on *Price v Socialist People's Lybian Arab Jamahiriya*, 110 F Supp 2d 10 (DDC 2000); *2002 Victims of Terrorism Law* (2003) 97 AM JOURN INT'L LAW 187, on *Hegna v Iran*, N 00-00716, slip op (DDC 22 Jan 2002); McKay *A New Take on Antiterrorism: Smith v Socialist People's Libyan Arab Jamahiriya* (1997) 13 AM U INT'L L REV 439; WP Hoye *Fighting Fire with . . . Mire? Civil Remedies and the New War on State-Sponsored Terrorism* 12 DUKE J COMP & INT'L L 105 (2002); SP Vitrano *Hell-Bent on Awarding Recovery to Terrorism Victims: the Evolution and Application of the Anti-terrorism Amendments to the Foreign Sovereign Immunity Act* 19 DICK J INT'L L 213 (2000), also for references to the relevant case-law; L Fisler Damrosch, *Sanctions Against Perpetrators of Terrorism* 22 HOUS J INT'L L 63 (1999) (for an examination of this provision from the perspective of the strengthening of economic pressure against State sponsors of terrorism); for a critique of this exception to sovereign immunity see, D Gartenstein-Ross *A Critique of the Terrorism Exception to the Foreign Sovereign Immunity Act*, 34 NYU J INT'L L & POL 887 (2002).

[46] See also A Einisman *Ineffectiveness at Its Best: Fighting Terrorism with Economic Sanctions* 9 MINN J GLOBAL TRADE 299 (2000) (arguing against the resort to economic sanctions in the fight of international terrorism, also in the light of the declining role of State-sponsored terrorism replaced by independent groups).

[47] See for instance Section 303(d) which establishes 'extraterritorial Federal jurisdiction over an offence under this section'. An extraterritorial character may also be attributed to the prohibition of financial transactions with terrorists, addressed to 'whoever, being a United States person', broadly defined as to include '(a) United States citizens or nationals; (b) permanent resident aliens; (c) juridical persons organized under the laws of the United States; or (d) any person in the United States' (AEDPA, Section 321).

financing of terrorism. Not surprisingly, considering the trans-national ramifications of terrorist groups, the need for inter-State cooperation for an effective response to terrorism financing is acknowledged by US law itself.[48]

The limits of unilateral action, regardless of the extraterritorial reach of the enacted provisions, are expressly admitted also by Presidential Executive Order 13224 of 24 September 2001, issued by President Bush in the immediate aftermath of the events of 11 September.[49] The Executive Order, adopted in accordance with the International Emergency Economic Power Act, promptly reacted to the attacks of 11 September, from the perspective of the financing of terrorists, by imposing the freezing of assets belonging to designated terrorists or terrorist organizations that 'are in the United States or that hereafter come within the United States, or that hereafter come within the possession or control of United States persons' and by prohibiting any transaction or dealing with the blocked assets.[50] Section 4 of the Executive Order prohibits donations to designated terrorist organizations, thus directly intervening in the misuse of charities for terrorist funding purposes. Lastly, it is worth mentioning section 6 of the Executive Order which calls for cooperation and coordination between the agencies involved as well as for a reinforced and flexible international cooperation focused on the sharing of information on the funding activities in support of terrorism.

C. *The International Criminalization of the Financing of Terrorism*

Terrorist financing is today proscribed as a separate and autonomous crime by most jurisdictions around the world, due to the joint pressure exercised by the United Nations, the FATF and regional organizations, such as the European Union, in the aftermath of the 11 September attacks.

The cornerstone of the recent normative developments is UN Security Council Resolution 1373 of 28 September 2001,[51] adopted a few days after the terrorist acts against the United States. The Security Council, acting on the basis of Chapter VII of the Charter, having acknowledged that acts 'of international terrorism constitute a threat to the international peace and security', addressed the issue of the financing of terrorist organizations, by

48 See AEDPA, Section 18 USC 2339B (a)(5) note.

49 Available at <www.whitehouse.gov>.

50 See Executive Order n 13224, s 1. The order as well as the freezing of funds and assets is extensively commented upon by LG Radicati di Brozolo and M Megliani, above, therefore it will not be dealt with in the present paper. On the US financial sanctions, see also K Alexander *United States Financial Sanctions and International Terrorism, Part 1* 17 BUTTERWORTHS JOURN INT'L BANKING AND FINANCIAL LAW 80, 81 (2002); JJ Savage *Executive Use of the International Emergency Economic Powers Act—Evolution through the Terrorist and Taliban Sanctions* 10 CURRENTS INT'L TRADE LJ 28, 36 (2001).

51 See S/RES/1373 of 28 Sept 2001; reaffirmed by S/RES/1390/2002 of 16 Jan 2002.

putting on an equal footing the funding and the planning of terrorist acts. This is explicitly stated in paragraph 5 of the Resolution where it is declared that 'acts, methods and practices of terrorism are contrary to the purposes and principles of the United Nations and that knowingly financing, planning and inciting terrorist acts are also contrary to the purposes and principles of the United Nations'.

Resolution 1373 envisages specific measures against the financing of terrorism to be adopted by *all* States. Such measures are directly targeted to prevent any kind of financial assets from reaching and fuelling terrorist organizations, resorting to substantive criminal and conservatory measures. The strategy envisioned by the Security Council, to be undertaken by all States, is basically threefold and consists of (a) the criminalisation of the wilful provision or collection, by any means, directly or indirectly, of funds by their nationals or in their territories with the intention that the funds should be used in order to carry out terrorist acts; (b) the freezing of funds and other financial assets or economic resources of persons who commit, or attempt to commit, terrorist acts,[52] and (c) the prohibition that their nationals and entities within their territories make any fund, financial assets or economic resources or financial or other services available, directly or indirectly, for the benefit of persons involved in the commission of terrorist acts. Ancillary to these provisions is the requirement that *all* States (i) deny safe haven to those who finance terrorist acts in addition to those who plan, support and commit such acts, and (ii) extend repressive judicial measures to those who finance the organizations, so that they are actually brought to justice and are subjected to a punishment adequate to the seriousness of the crime committed. In order to achieve these goals, the Resolution urges the ratification of the New York Convention on the suppression of the financing of terrorism, the principal obligations of which are duplicated by the Resolution.[53]

This approach has subsequently been implemented by regional international organizations. The European Union promptly reacted to the UN Security Council Resolution, by enacting specific measures; notably Common Position 2001/931/CFSP,[54] Regulation 2580/2001/EC on the freezing of assets belonging to terrorist entities and individuals,[55] and

[52] The freezing of terrorists' assets had already been ordered by the Security Council directly addressed to the Talibans (S/RES/1267 of 15 Oct 1999) and to 'Usama Bin Laden and individuals and entities associated with him . . . including those in the Al-Qaida organization' (S/RES/1333 of 19 Dec 2000).

[53] See below, para 8.

[54] Council Common Position on the application of specific measures to combat terrorism, in OJ Eur Comm L 344 of 27 Dec 2001, at 93.

[55] *Regulation of 27 Dec 2001*, in OJ EUR COMM L 344 of 28 Dec 2001 at 70, on which see the comments by LG Radicati di Brozolo and M Megliani, above.

Directive 2001/97/EC on money laundering.[56] A mechanism for evaluating the legal systems and their implementation at national level in the fight against terrorism has been recently adopted.[57]

The contribution of the FATF to counter the financing of terrorism is particularly valuable both from a policy-making perspective and from a compliance monitoring standpoint. The Special Recommendations include (a) the criminalization of the financing of terrorism and associated money laundering;[58] (b) the freezing of all funds belonging to terrorist organizations;[59] (c) the ratification of the New York Convention on the suppression of terrorism financing[60] and (d) the intensification of inter-State cooperation.[61]

In addition the FATF has launched a self-assessment questionnaire in order to verify the level of compliance with the Special Recommendations which reports positive results. Responses submitted by both FATF Member States and States who are members of FATF-like organizations show an encouraging level of implementation of the Special Recommendations in domestic legal systems.[62] Similarly encouraging responses come from the reports submitted by UN Member States to the ad hoc Counter-Terrorism

[56] On the initiatives undertaken at Community level, see the contribution by A Reinisch, above.

[57] Council Decision 2002/996/JHA of 28 Nov 2002 in OJ EUR COMM L 349 of 24 Dec 2002.

[58] Recommendation II reads: 'Each country should criminalise the financing of terrorism, terrorist acts and terrorist organisations. Countries should ensure that such offences are designated as money laundering predicate offences.'

[59] Recommendation III reads 'Each country should implement measures to freeze without delay funds or other money assets of terrorists who finance terrorism and terrorist organisations in accordance with the United Nations resolutions relating to the prevention and the suppression of the financing of terrorist acts. Each country should also adopt and implement measures, including legislative ones, which would enable the competent authorities to seize and confiscate property that is the proceeds of, or used in, or intended or allocated for use in, the financing of terrorism, terrorist acts or terrorist organisations.'

[60] Recommendation I reads: 'Each country should take immediate steps to ratify and implement fully the 1999 United Nations International Convention for the Suppression of the Financing of Terrorism. Countries should also immediately implement the United Nations resolutions relating to the prevention and suppression of the financing of terrorist acts, particularly United Nations Security Council Resolution 1373.'

[61] Recommendation V reads: 'Each country should afford another country, on the basis of a treaty, arrangements or mechanism for mutual legal assistance or information exchange, the greatest possible measure of assistance in connection with criminal, civil enforcement, and administrative investigations, inquiries and proceedings relating to the financing of terrorism, terrorist acts and terrorist organisations. Countries should also take all possible measures to ensure that they do not provide safe havens for individuals charged with the financing of terrorism, terrorist acts or terrorist organisations, and should have procedures in place to extradite, where possible, such individuals.'

[62] See FATF Annual Report 2001–2002 at 5. The highest levels of compliance has been achieved by FATF Recommendations concerning freezing of terrorist assets, followed by the recommendation regarding international cooperation and that urging the criminalization of the financing of terrorism.

Committee entrusted with the task of monitoring the implementation of UN Security Council Resolution 1373. Both sources show that many jurisdictions have established in their domestic law the financing of terrorism as an independent and autonomous crime[63] and have ratified the UN 1999 Convention (which was more or less ignored by the international community before the events of 11 September), thus speeding up its entry into force on 10 April 2002.[64]

These encouraging data, however, do not actually correspond to the reality of the situation. An accurate analysis shows that in many cases the domestic implementation of the UN Resolution No 1373 equates only to formal compliance and has not attained the intended degree of uniformity across jurisdictions. This is largely attributable to the different degrees of development of the domestic legal systems, resulting in disparities in technical and administrative skills and in belowstructural support. Such environmental hurdles may lead to trans-national divergence between implementing measures, which in light of the cross-border nature of the financing of terrorism and of the requirement of double criminality to promote international criminal proceedings, may impair the effectiveness of the international legal framework.[65]

Lack of consensus has been reported, for instance, on the definition of financing of terrorism, which many States assumed to be already covered by anti-money laundering or by other criminal provisions. Taking into

[63] For instance see Art 1 of Italian Law of 15 Dec 2001, n 438, which by introducing new Article 270-*bis* in the Criminal Code, proscribes the crime of international terrorism sanctioning whoever promotes, establishes, manages, directs or funds organisations pursuing international terrorism; see also § 2339C of 18 US Code. For a commentary on the new provisions introduced in Luxembourg see A Schmitt and F Sudret *Cutting the Financial Roots of Terrorism: Introduction of a New Bill in Luxembourg* 17 J INT'L BANKING LAW 382 (2002); for Canadian law see E Machado *A Note on the Terrorism Financing Offences in Bill C-36* 60 UNIV TORONTO FACULTY L REV 103 (2002); BP Bedard and AJ Kilgour *Tracking Funds: Canada's Recent Initiatives to Combat Money Laundering and the Financing of Terrorism* 17 J INT'L BANKING LAW 117 (2002); and on the recent initiatives in Switzerland refer to EHG. Hüpke *Keeping Dirty Money and Terrorist Funds Away: the Proposed Money Laundering Regulation of the Swiss Federal Banking Commission* 10 J FINANCIAL REGULATION AND COMPLIANCE 317 (2002).

[64] It is worth mentioning, however, that many States particularly exposed to terrorist financing activities, such as Switzerland, Saudi Arabia, Jordan, Bahamnas, China, Luxembourg, the Philippines, and Tunisia, as well as Belgium, Germany, and Greece, have not yet ratified the Convention, thus threatening its overall effectiveness. Fort further details see <http://untreaty.un.org/ENGLISH/Status/Chapter_xviii/treaty11.asp>.

[65] See W Gehr 'Recurrent Issues (Briefing for Member States) 4 Apr 2002', available at <www.un.org>. See also the realistic criticism expressed by K Alexander *United States Financial Sanctions and International Terrorism*, Part 2 17 BUTTERWORTHS J INT'L BANKING FIN LAW 218 (2002); M Kantor 'Effective Enforcement of International Obligations to Suppress the Financing of Terror—Prepared in conjunction with the ASIL Presidential Task Force on Terrorism—(2002)', available at <www.asil.org>, visited on 15 Oct 2002. Both authors warn against the risk that efforts undertaken internationally are confined solely to the law-making level without sufficient concern as to the implementation of those norms.

account the recommendation to ratify the New York Convention, a possible solution to enhance the uniform implementation of the Resolution might be to take the definition of the crime provided for in the New York Convention as guidance for national legislators.

Under Article 2 of the New York Convention, the crime of financing of terrorism is committed by any person who 'by any means, directly or indirectly, unlawfully and wilfully, provides or collects funds with the intention that they should be used or in the knowledge that they are to be used, in full or in part, in order to carry out' terrorist activities. It is worth noting that while the Convention requires the criminal intent in the supply of funds, it does not require their actual employment for terrorist acts.[66] Some national legislators, however, have adopted more stringent provisions. While the New York Convention prohibits the use of funds for 'terrorist activities', UK, Canadian and US laws have codified a broader notion of this crime, proscribing the financing of 'terrorist groups', besides that of 'terrorist activities'. The 'organizational approach' endorsed by the proscription of the financing of the group of terrorists in addition to the terrorist acts, may prove more efficient against terrorism since it does not require any particular link with subsequent terrorist activities.[67]

IV. THE ROLE OF FINANCIAL INSTITUTIONS IN FIGHTING THE FINANCING OF TERRORISM

A. The International Framework

The economic feature of the crime of money laundering, ultimately aimed at disguising the revenue's illicit origin with a view to injecting it into the legitimate economy, makes it a complex offence which calls for an interdisciplinary approach. The criminal law aspects examined so far cannot be successfully enforced unless they are complemented by efficient regulatory provisions tackling the abuse of financial institutions involved in the commission of these crimes. It is a common understanding that banks may be 'unwittingly used as intermediaries for the transfer of funds derived from criminal activity'[68] and that in order to preserve financial stability, soundness and the reputation of banks, supervisors have to take steps to avoid the abuse of the financial system for criminal purposes. The achievement of this goal necessarily relies on the cooperation of the private sector,

66 Art 2, para 3 of the New York Convention.

67 An analysis of Canadian, UK and US law, compared with the New York Convention, has been carried out by KE Davis *Legislating against the Financing of Terrorism: Pitfalls and Prospects* 10 Journ Fin Crime 269, at 271 (2003).

68 Bank of International Settlements, *Prevention of Criminal Use of the Banking System for the Purpose of Money-Laundering*, 12 Dec 1988, available at <www.bis.org>.

ie. on financial institutions themselves. In line with this, the comprehensive framework against money laundering, condensed in the FATF's Forty Recommendations,[69] is a prominent contribution to this interdisciplinary approach, since it takes into due account both the criminal and the financial profiles of the struggle to this crime. Section B of the FATF standards specifically addresses the role of the financial system in combating money laundering, by imposing on financial institutions reporting obligations in relation to suspicious transactions and the adoption of transparency requirements in the management of banking relationships.[70]

These deal in particular with the control of the client's identity, the so-called 'know-your-customer' principle (or 'KYC'), which, in the case of accounts opened on behalf of juridical persons, imposes the identification of the beneficial owner, as well as the actual existence of the legal entity. The implementation of the KYC principle has been conducive to the elimination of anonymous bank accounts and to the lifting of bank secrecy in investigations on money laundering offences,[71] thus removing traditional major obstacles to the tracking of funds and the reconstruction of suspicious transactions. In this context, financial institutions are also required to retain for at least five years the necessary transaction records, in order to be able to expeditiously comply with the authorities' requests. The risks of misuse of banking institutions for money laundering purposes have required further reporting duties to the competent authorities regarding all 'complex, unusual large transactions, and all unusual patterns of transactions, which have no apparent economic or visible lawful purposes'.[72] Lastly, due to their particular suitability for concealing tracks, the Forty Recommendations also draw attention to the misuse of corporate vehicles such as shell corporations and the use of bearer shares and other negotiable instruments.

These standards have had a critical impact at the domestic and regional level where they have received widespread implementation by legislators. Particularly telling is Directive 91/308/EEC on money laundering,[73]

[69] See above at para 2.

[70] On the role of financial institutions in the prevention of money laundering see extensively G Stessens *Money Laundering. A New International Law Enforcement Model* (CUP Cambridge 1999) 143 ff.

[71] The lifting of banking secrecy is provided for by both the Vienna and the Strasbourg Convention as well as by several MLATS specifically dealing with money laundering offence, see above para 4.

[72] See FATF Forty Recommendations, Recommendation n 14. For an in-depth analysis of the Italian framework of banking supervision with concern to money laundering, accounting for the different authorities involved and the tasks respectively entrusted to them see A Urbani 'Supervisione Bancaria e Lotta al Riciclaggio' (2002) 55 Banca, Borsa e Titoli di Credito, I, 480.

[73] Council Directive 91/308/CEE of 10 June 1991 on prevention of the use of the financial system for purpose of money laundering, in OJ Eur Comm L 166 of 28 June 1991, 77, as recently amended by Directive 2001/97/EC, in OJEC L 344 of 28 Dec 2001, 76.

adopted in light of the Community liberalization of financial services and of the ensuing increased circulation of capital. To prevent criminal activities benefiting from such cross-border liberalization, the Directive provides for transparency requirements, due diligence provisions and reporting duties inspired by the FATF Forty Recommendations, to be complied with by the financial institutions admitted to operate on the common market.

To complete the picture of the initiatives to protect the financial system from abuses, special consideration must be given to the activity of the FATF in controlling the actual implementation of the Forty Recommendations, in order to assess effective progress in the fight against money laundering. Even though, as observed before,[74] the standards laid down by this intergovernmental body are 'soft law' and are not legally binding, they nonetheless hold special authority with national legislators and enjoy a general international consensus. As a result of the country by country review, FATF singles out a list of 'non-cooperative countries', which are encouraged to comply with the recommendations. It is hardly questionable that those jurisdictions which disregard internationally agreed standards on financial supervision, transparency requirements and suspicious transactions reporting duties largely impair the effectiveness of the abovenational framework to combat money laundering, thus allowing criminals to structure their transactions in such a way as to take advantage of the loopholes in the global financial system.[75] Coordinated international pressure to isolate these countries is therefore a powerful tool to obtain their cooperation.

B. The 1999 UN Convention on the Suppression of the Financing of Terrorism

The legislative enactments against money laundering and the funding of terrorism, accounted for in the previous paragraphs, were important terms of reference in the drafting of the UN Convention on the Suppression of the Financing of Terrorism. This international treaty is the last part of the normative piecemeal approach to international terrorism consisting in several 'sectoral' conventions, each of which deals with specific aspects of terrorist acts.

The New York Convention specifically addresses the issue of terrorist financing, thus filling an important gap of the international legal framework against international terrorism. It is a comprehensive and valuable tool for combating terrorist financing since it concentrates in one legal instrument the criminal approach endorsed by the anti-money laundering

[74] See above at para 2.

[75] See FATF, Report on Non-Cooperative Countries and Territories, 14 Feb 2000, available at <www.fatf-gafi.org>.

conventions and the obligations imposed on financial institutions to prevent the sheltering of the proceeds of crime.

With regard to the first aspect, besides the cornerstone provision of Article 2, which establishes terrorism financing as an autonomous offence,[76] the New York Convention contains a definition of terrorism which delimits the substantive scope of application of the treaty. 'Terrorism' is defined as 'any act intended to cause death or serious bodily injury to a civilian, or to any other person not taking an active part in the hostilities in a situation of armed conflict, when the purpose of such act, by its nature or context, is to intimidate a population, or to compel a government or an international organization to do or to abstain from doing any act'.[77] Although the effort to set out a definition must be praised as an attempt to reduce the ambiguities which characterise the notion of terrorism and to clarify when the treaty applies, the notion of terrorism is still inevitably loose and prone to divergences of interpretation.

Having defined its ambit of application, the Convention sets provisions reinforcing inter-State cooperation in the tracing, freezing and confiscation of assets and funds of terrorist groups. In addition, States Parties to the Conventions are required to afford one another the greatest measure of assistance in connection with investigations or criminal or extradition proceedings, including assistance in obtaining evidence. In this respect, it is worth mentioning that like anti-money laundering conventions, the New York Convention explicitly provides for the waiver of banking secrecy.[78] Consistently with existing international legal instruments against terrorism—but unlike ordinary treaties on criminal matters—the New York Convention prohibits the refusal of extradition or other forms of mutual legal assistance on the ground of the political offence exception.[79]

[76] See above at para 6.

[77] Art 2(b) of the New York Convention; the Convention also makes reference to the offences contained in international treaties against terrorism listed in the Annex to the Convention. It should be noted, however, that many States made reservations on the application of the Convention in relation to some of the international treaties listed in the Annex.

[78] See Art 12(2) which reads 'States may not refuse a request of mutual legal assistance on the ground of bank secrecy.'

[79] This is explicitly provided at Art 14 of the New York Convention which reads that '[n]one of the offences set forth in article 2 shall be regarded for the purposes of extradition or mutual legal assistance as a political offence inspired by political motives. Accordingly, a request for extradition or for mutual legal assistance based on such an offence may not be refused on the sole ground that it concerns a political offence or an offence connected with a political offence or an offence inspired by political motives.' On the political offence exception in relation to acts of terrorism see C van den Wyngaert, 'The Political Offences Exception to Extradition: How to Plug the "Terrorist's Loophole" Without Departing from Fundamental Human Rights' (1989) 19 Israel Yearbook on Human Rights 297 , reprinted in J Dougard and C van den Wygaert (eds) International Criminal Law and Procedure (Dartmouth Aldershot 1996) 191; and F Mosconi 'La Convenzione europea per la repressione del terrorismo' (1979) 62 Riv dir int 303.

Coming to the financial aspects of the offence of the funding of terrorism, the New York Convention reflects the previously examined endeavours undertaken at the international level by specialized institutions such as the FATF's Forty Recommendations, the Basel Committee's Principles against money laundering, the European Community Directive and national legislation. In this respect, the innovative feature of the New York Convention is to reproduce such international standards in a legally binding treaty.

Accordingly, Article 18 of the Convention singles out a minimum core of principles and practices to combat the financing of terrorism, consisting of requirements of transparency and due diligence in respect of the identity of customers, as well as obligations to detect and report suspicious transactions. For these purposes, the New York Convention provides that States Parties 'shall consider' adopting regulations to prevent the opening of anonymous bank accounts and to ensure the full implementation of the KYC principle with regard to individuals and legal entities. The enactment of regulations imposing 'on financial institutions the obligation to report promptly to the competent authorities all complex, unusual, large transactions and unusual patterns of transactions' and to 'maintain, for at least five years, all necessary records on transactions' (Article 18.1(b)(iii) and (iv)) is also envisaged. An enhanced supervision of financial institutions and the licensing of all money transmission agencies should also be 'considered' by the States Parties (Article 18.2(a)).

Despite the merit of codifying a minimum core of regulatory anti-money laundering measures in a formal treaty, the New York Convention does not go beyond that. Both the style of wording and the content of the envisioned measures are closer to soft law standards than to formal obligations. Formulations such as 'States Parties shall consider . . . adopting', or 'utilize the most efficient measures *available*' (Art 18.1 (b)) call into question the prescriptive nature of the provisions. Also their content appears vague and ambiguous, thus leaving the States Parties a significant discretion in their implementation. The need for the FATF guidance is therefore inevitable, to ensure uniformity of national laws. Far from replacing the FATF regulatory standards by an autonomous body of rules, the New York Convention is still dependent on the work of this specialized institution in order to adapt the domestic legal systems of the States Parties to the minimum core of practices mentioned in the treaty. The reliance of the Convention on the work of FATF should not necessarily be seen as a weakness of the treaty; rather it could be argued that in an evolving and technical field such as criminal finance, rigid (non-amendable) rules are ill-suited to efficiently fight the phenomenon, and that an adjustable set of standards is more desirable. Put differently, it is legitimate to maintain that in this branch of the law, a strict observance of the hierarchy of the sources of international law is incompatible with the pragmatic goal that is pursued. The New York

Convention is not a self-sufficient instrument to combat the financing of terrorism. It needs to be complemented by the work of specialized institutions such as the FATF, with regard to normative developments and the continuous monitoring of the law's actual enforcement. This continuous reliance upon external assistance is compelled by the evolutionary patterns of criminal finance requiring an ongoing normative update. Suffice it here to remark that the provisions of the New York Convention are to some extent already unsatisfactory confronted with the last version of the FATF Forty Recommendations adopted in June 2003. Should the New York Convention be considered an autonomous and self-contained body of rules, the leeway left to the States Parties in its implementation and the degree of obsolescence of its provisions would inevitably lead to divergences of domestic laws, of which terrorist financiers would certainly take advantage.

C. The Need for an Ongoing Update of the Regulation to Track Transfer of Funds: Alternative Remittance, Underground Banking Systems, Wire Transfers

In the light of the above considerations, the entry into force of the New York Convention is not sufficient alone to combat the financing of terrorism, since it needs a constant and coordinated updating of due diligence requirements, reporting duties and regulation of the financial system to be implemented by the contracting States. For this purpose, the standards issued by specialized bodies such as the FATF are an essential guidance to the States engaged in the war on the financing of terrorism.

It is acknowledged that anti-money laundering schemes have been successful and effective in reducing the criminal patterns covered by the enacted provisions, but this has shifted criminal transactions to unregulated financial channels which are particularly suitable for money laundering purposes.

To stop this migration, the solution consists in bringing unregulated activities within the scope of the existing legislation, by widening the range of subjects affected by anti-money laundering control obligations. Alternative remittance services have therefore become the principal target of regulatory endeavours with a view to ensuring that they be licensed, registered and subject to anti-money laundering obligations.[80] This is the

[80] See FATF Special Recommendation VI which reads '[e]ach country should take measures to ensure that persons or legal entities, including agents, that provide a service for the transmission of money or value, including transmission through an informal money or value transfer system or network, should be licensed or registered and subject to all the FATF Recommendations that apply to banks and non-bank financial institutions. Each country should ensure that persons or legal entities that carry out this service illegally are subject to administrative, civil or criminal sanctions.'

object of FATF Special Recommendation VI, aimed at 'persons and legal entities . . . that provide a service for the transmission of money for value', which recommends that they should be subject to 'all FATF Recommendations that apply to banks and non-bank financial institutions'. At the EU level this has required amendments to Directive 91/308/EEC on money laundering so as to update the notion of credit institution in accordance with the definition contained in Article 1 of Directive 2000/12/EC[81] and to expand the notion of 'financial institution', which now covers currency exchange offices and money transmittance/remittance offices.[82]

Underground or parallel banking systems, employed by terrorists, financiers and other criminals for cross-border money transfers, have also been affected by the post 11 September normative endeavours. In consideration of the poor legal and economic environment in which they operate, however, one can legitimately manifest some scepticism as to the actual implementation and enforcement of the envisioned measures, admittedly a very difficult task.

The underground banking system, known as hawala, hindu, chop shop and chitti banking, is common in some Asian and South Asian countries such as India, Pakistan, Hong Kong and China. Here it has socio-cultural roots which rely on trust and on strong family ties. While it may pursue legitimate business aims, providing good service (it is for instance commonly used by overseas workers for remittances to their families), especially in those jurisdictions where the regulated financial sector is insufficient, costly or not present in the whole territory, its informal nature and its international structure make it a suitable channel for money laundering purposes. Expedited (often 'real time') cross-border transfer of funds and complete anonymity are attractive features to terrorist financiers, who are thus enabled to move money across jurisdictions without any paper trail.[83] Underground bankers are established in many different countries and are linked with each other; they debit and credit funds on their accounts for

[81] Directive 2000/12/EC of the Council of 20 Mar 2000 on the taking up and pursuit of the business of credit institutions, in OJ EUR COMM L 125 of 26 May 2000 at 1.

[82] For a general overview of the new EU instruments to combat money laundering, see S Mohamed *Legal Instruments to Combat Money Laundering in the EU Financial Market* 10 JOURN MONEY LAUNDERING CONTROL 66 (2002); J Fisher *Recent International Developments in the Fight Against Money Laundering* 17 JOURN INT'L BANKING LAW 67 (2002).

[83] For an overview of the functioning mechanisms of underground banking systems, see J Trehan *Underground and Parallel Banking System* 10 JOURN MONEY LAUNDERING CONTROL 76 (2002); FATFT, Report on Money Laundering Typologies 1999–2000, 3 Feb 2001, at 4–8, available at <www.fatf-gafi.org>; K Alexander *United States Financial Sanctions and International Terrorism, Part 2* 17 BUTTERWORTHS JOURN INT'L BANKING FIN LAW 215 (2002); F El Sheikh *The Underground Banking Systems and their Impact on Control of Money Laundering: With Special Reference to Islamic Banking* 5 JOURN MONEY LAUNDERING CONTROL 42 (2002).

movements of money in connection with their legitimate trade or illicit trafficking. Communication of the accomplishment of the transfer of money is given by secret codes.

So far, to counter resort to these underground networks, attempts have been made in developing countries to strengthen exchange control regulations and to make formal banking channels more attractive. In some countries they have also been outlawed. In developed countries, the freezing and confiscation of assets in pursuance of anti-money laundering statutes are considered viable remedies.[84]

The war on terrorism has brought about new efforts aimed at the uncovering and regulation of underground banking networks. To begin with, it is worth noting that as clarified by the Interpretative Note to Special Recommendation VI,[85] the definition of 'alternative remittance', by referring to 'informal money or value transfer system or network', intends to include also underground or parallel banking systems. To this end, the International Best Practices released by the FATF in June 2003, to combat the abuse of alternative remittance systems, is largely dedicated to the ways of dealing with these informal networks. When the informal systems operate openly, registration with the competent authority is the recommended minimum requirement. In addition, on the assumption that rigid and disproportionate regulatory obligations push money transfer mechanisms underground, flexible oversight and avoidance of excessively burdensome compliance are envisaged remedies. With regard to banking networks operating underground, the task is more difficult, the first issue being their identification. For this purpose, critical is the sharing of information between the investigative units and the regulatory agencies involved. Regulatory efforts, if any, will come later, once the network has been tracked by the competent authorities.

A further measure envisioned by the FATF to avoid terrorist financiers taking advantage of the loopholes in the system to freely transfer funds across frontiers, is enhanced scrutiny of wire transfers. In the effort to track the complex cross-border movements of funds, credit institutions, including money remitters, are urged to acquire accurate information on the originator and on the transaction and to include them on fund transfers and related messages that are sent through the whole payment chain. The

[84] For further references, see J Trehan *Underground and Parallel Banking System* 10 JOURN MONEY LAUNDERING CONTROL 81, 82 (2002). See also K Alexander, United States Financial Sanctions and International Terrorism, Part 2, at 215 warning that the war on financing of terrorism could be lost absent international coordinated efforts tackling informal money networks.

[85] Interpretative Note to FATF Special Recommendation VI: Alternative Remittance, available at <www.fatf-gafi.org>.

Interpretative Note to Special Recommendation VII has provided practical guidance to its effective implementation.[86]

The need to keep pace with evolving money laundering patterns has directed attention not just to financial entities but also to professionals, such as lawyers, accountants, tax advisors and public notaries, who are particularly vulnerable to being involved in money laundering transactions in connection with their services. The solution adopted has been to expand the anti-money laundering regime to these professionals.[87]

D. Measures Adopted by States to Promote Compliance with International Legal Standards

The lack or paucity of financial regulation is a major threat to the fight against the financing of terrorism. In the previous paragraph, measures to be taken at the domestic level in order to bring unregulated financial services within the control of regulators have been discussed. This level of action, however, is unlikely to be sufficient in respect of off-shore centres and of poorly regulated jurisdictions, which offer a set of 'legal facilities'—such as bank secrecy, shell corporations, absence of customer due diligence—which attract terrorist financiers, attempting to hide wealth and to eliminate traces of fund movements.[88] Isolation of such centres, in the form of prevention of their financial institutions from accessing regulated financial systems, is therefore envisaged as an efficient disincentive to non-compliance with internationally agreed standards.[89] This is the approach endorsed by the USA Patriot Act, a comprehensive anti-terrorism act which

[86] Interpretative Note to FATF Special Recommendation VII: wire transfers; available at <www.fatf-gafi.org>.

[87] See Art 2a of Directive 91/308/EC introduced by Directive 2001/97/EC. It is worth noting, however, that notaries and other independent legal professionals are subject to anti-money laundering obligations in as much as they participate 'in financial or corporate transactions, including providing tax advice, where there is the greatest risk of the services of those legal professional being misused for the purpose of laundering the proceeds of criminal activity', see recital 16 and Art 2 *(a)5*, although such duties do not apply to lawyers 'ascertaining the legal position of a client or representing a client in legal proceedings', unless legal advice is provided for money laundering purposes (see preamble 17).

[88] See E Ceriana 'Profili Internazionali del Segreto Bancario nell'Ottica della Lotta all'Evasione e al Riciclaggio del Denaro di Provenienza Illecita' (1994) 65 Diritto e Pratica Tributaria, II, at 82(on banking secrecy in off-shore centres and its interplay with tax evasion and money laundering; recently on the interaction of off-shore centres and terrorist financing), see also J Johnson, *11th Sept. and Revelations from the Enron Collapse Add to the Mounting Pressure on the Offshore Financial Centres* 10 JOURN FIN REGULATION AND COMPLIANCE 341 (2002).

[89] *Contra* see JJ Norton, H Shams *Money Laundering Law and Terrorist Financing: Post-Sept. 11 Responses—Let Us Step Back and Take a Deep Breath?* 36 INT'L LAWYER 103 (2002) (arguing that this approach runs counter to the policy of liberalisation pursued since the end of the Second World War, originating in the consideration that the post-First World War isolation of Germany had been one of the causes leading to the Second World War).

also strengthens the countering of international money laundering,[90] by far-reaching provisions which subject to in-depth scrutiny banks established in off-shore and non-cooperative countries attempting to open correspondent or payable through accounts with US financial institutions.

A correspondent account enables a correspondent bank to provide banking services—receipt of deposits, payments and other transactions—on behalf of a respondent bank established abroad; a payable through account opened at a depository institution by a foreign financial institution, enables customers of the latter to engage directly or through sub-accounts in banking activities, usually in connection with business activities carried on in the foreign country. Although these inter-bank accounts are generally set up for legitimate business purposes, they may turn into money laundering gateways.[91] To avoid this risk of abuse, the USA Patriot Act imposes on domestic financial institutions acting as correspondent banks of foreign financial institutions based in targeted jurisdictions (off-shore non-cooperative countries), enhanced due diligence policies, procedures and controls. In particular US credit institutions should take reasonable steps to ascertain the identity of each of the owners of the foreign bank, exercise enhanced scrutiny of such accounts to guard against money laundering and to make sure that the foreign bank does not provide correspondent accounts to other foreign banks and, if so, to identify those foreign banks. With respect to the establishment of a payable-through account relationship, US banks are required to ascertain the ultimate identity of the customer, the source of the funds deposited in the account by their customers, and to exercise reinforced anti-money laundering scrutiny.[92] Additional provisions of the USA Patriot Act are concerned with foreign shell banks —banks without a physical presence in any country—and prohibit them from holding accounts with US financial institutions; subject to the same prohibition are also foreign banks servicing shell banks.[93]

[90] For comments on the anti-money laundering provisions see K Alexander, *United States Financial Sanctions and International Terrorism, Part 1* 17 BUTTERWORTHS JOURN INT'L BANKING AND FINANCIAL LAW 83 et seq (2002).; A Rueda, *International Money Laundering Law Enforcement & the USA PATRIOT Act of 2001* (2001) 10 MSU-DCL INT'L L 141; FN Baldwin, Jr, *Money Laundering Countermeasures with Primary Focus upon Terrorism and the USA Patriot Act 2001*, 6 JOURN MONEY LAUNDERING CONTROL 105 (2002).

[91] See FATF—XIII Report on Money Laundering Typologies 2001–2, at 8; on correspondent accounts and their misuse for terrorist purposes, see R Cranston *Principles of Banking Law* (2nd edn, Clarendon Press Oxford 2002) 44.

[92] See USA PATRIOT Act, s 312. For an in-depth analysis of the anti-money laundering measures provided by the USA PATRIOT Act, see K Alexander 'United States Financial Sanctions and International Terrorism, Part 1', at 83 et seq; A Rueda 'International Money Laundering Law Enforcement & the USA PATRIOT Act of 2001' 10 *MSU-DCL Int'l L* 141 (2001); see also J Jackson *In Pursuit of Dirty Money: Identifying Weaknesses in the Global Financial System*, 4 JOURN MONEY LAUNDERING CONTROL 122, spec 124 (2001), J Abrahamson *Capitol Outlook* 17 BUTTERWORTHS JOURN INT'L BANKING FIN LAW 102 (2002).

[93] See USA PATRIOT Act, s 313.

Under Section 317 of the USA PATRIOT Act, these regulatory obligations are assisted by an aggressive extra-territorial approach enabling the exercise of jurisdiction over matters presenting only tenuous links with the US, which might consist of the simple existence of a bank account in the US.[94]

The ultimate goal pursued by the outlined measures of the USA PATRIOT Act is indirectly to impose compliance with international agreed standards on foreign banks based in non-cooperative jurisdictions, perceived as the only protection against transnational abuse of the financial system. Besides the long-arm provisions set forth in the Statute, the enforcement of the American legal framework, and its overall effectiveness, is dependent on the current need of off-shore centres to have access to the US financial market.

The same objective is being pursued at the international level where the FATF and the Basel Committee have expressed concerns about the intermediary role played by correspondent banks in international payments, given the high risks for credit institutions of being involved into money laundering and terrorist financing transactions, especially if the respondent bank itself acts as correspondent bank of other credit institutions.[95] Consistent with this, the revised version of the Forty Recommendations of June 2003 fills the gap of the previous edition by imposing special obligations with regard to correspondent accounts. In accordance with the analysis and suggestions formulated by the Basel Committee in the report on Customer Due Diligence for Banks, the new text of Recommendation 7 requires enhanced due diligence scrutiny by correspondent banks in respect of the respondent bank's ownership, business, supervision, customer due diligence procedures and the legal environment in which the foreign bank operates, with specific attention to the anti-money laundering framework.

E. Further Recent Initiatives to Protect the Financial System

Anti-money laundering regimes and obligations have so far primarily affected credit institutions, given that they are the natural gateway to inject dirty money into the legitimate economy. Practice has shown however that in addition to credit institutions, financial entities such as securities dealers

[94] See 18 US Code, s 1956 (Section 317 of the USA PATRIOT Act, *Long-arm jurisdiction over foreign money launderers*. Criticism against this aggressive extraterritoriality has been expressed by Norton, H Shams *Money Laundering Law and Terrorist Financing: Post-Sept. 11 Responses—Let Us Step Back and Take a Deep Breath?* 36 INT'L LAWYER 103 (2002).

[95] See FATF, Review of the FATF Forty Recommendations. Consultation Paper, 30 May 2002, at 13, available at <www.fatf-gafi.org> and Basel Committee on Banking Supervision, Customer Due Diligence for Banks, Oct. 2001, at 12, available at <http://www.bis.org/bcbs/publ.htm>.

are also vulnerable and can be exploited for laundering the proceeds of crime. Although the placement stage of the proceeds of crime—the first and most delicate phase of the laundering process—is unlikely to be carried out through securities dealers, given that they are usually prevented from accepting cash, there are signs of an increasing misuse of financial intermediaries for money laundering purposes. Cases have been reported of the purchase of securities with proceeds of crime, where dealers either have accepted or have disregarded customer due diligence procedures, relying on the scrutiny already undertaken by credit institutions or other professionals which channel the funds to be invested.

To ensure a more effective enforcement of the anti-money laundering framework, the second EC Directive on money laundering has clarified that the definition of financial institutions includes insurance companies, investment firms and collective investment undertakings.[96] This implies the fulfillment of customer due diligence obligations consisting in the implementation of the 'KYC' principle requiring the identification of the individual customer or of the beneficial owner, 'in the event of doubt as to whether the customers are acting on their own behalf or whether it is certain that they are not acting on their own behalf'.[97]

Besides the hypothesis of laundering of proceeds of crime generated *outside* the capital market, the case of laundering of proceeds of crime generated *within* the securities market (through insider trading, market manipulation and other practices) should also be taken into account, in the light of the findings of connections between abusive market practices and the financing of terrorism.

It is worth noting that the recently adopted EC Directive on market abuse addresses this typology, confirming the heightened awareness of the dangers that criminal finance (and its links to terrorism) may create to the integrity of the financial system. By explicitly referring to the events of 11 September, it expands the traditional understanding of 'inside information' beyond the existence of a fiduciary relationship between the insider and issuer whose financial instruments are traded, to include information acquired by virtue of criminal activities.[98] In doing so, insider dealing committed on the basis of criminal information may become a predicate offence for the purposes of application of the anti-money laundering legislation.

The attractiveness of bringing securities dealers and other non-financial institutions within the scope of application of anti-money laundering

[96] See Art 1(A) and (B) of Directive 91/308/EEC as replaced by Directive 2001/97/EC.

[97] See Art 3, para 7 of 91/308/EEC Directive as replace by Directive 2001/97/EC.

[98] See Art 2(1)(d) as well as recital n 14 of the Directive/2003/6/EC of the European Parliament and of the Council on insider dealing and market manipulation (market abuse) of 28 Jan 2003, in OJ Eur Comm L 96 of 12 Apr 2003, at 16.

schemes, besides pursuing the general interest of curbing financial crime, responds to the special need of preserving the integrity of capital markets. On the assumption that the use of funds of illegal origin in capital markets is a threat to the efficient course of transactions and to the soundness of the financial system, several international institutions have taken steps to avoid any contamination with proceeds of crime. It is acknowledged that money laundering affects the efficient allocation of resources, impacts on exchange rates and impinges on the quality of the assets managed by financial institutions.[99] A financial institution's excessive exposure against subjects involved in criminal activities heightens the risks usually managed by banks, such as reputation, concentration and legal risks. This may pose a threat to the stability of the institution and, by contagion, to the whole system. The awareness of the negative consequences to the integrity of the financial system of the contamination of the legitimate economy with the criminal finance, has induced the IMF to include in the assessment of a country's economy, conducted within the Financial Sector Assessment Program (FSAP), a section dealing with the anti-money laundering framework, considered one of the relevant parameters in the assessment of the condition of a nation's economy.[100] It is worth noting that after the events of 11 September, this part comprises an assessment of measures to combat the financing of terrorism.[101]

Concerns relating to the 'contamination' of the financial system are not confined to the realm of legislation, but are shared by actors in the financial arena. The 'Anti-money laundering guidance notes for insurance supervisors & insurance entities' issued by the International Association of Insurance Supervisors (IAIS) in January 2002,[102] the 'Customer due diligence for banks' published by the Basel Committee on Banking Supervision on October 2001,[103] the Wolfsberg Statement on the 'Suppression of the Financing of Terrorism'[104] as well as the International Organization of

[99] Adverse effects of money laundering on national economies at the national level have been identified in: 'changes in demand for money, exchange and interest rate volatility; heightened risk of asset quality for financial institutions; adverse effects on tax collections and fiscal policy projections; contamination effects on particular transactions or sectors and behavioural expectations of market actors; asset price bubbles etc. . .,' see D Jayasuriya *Money Laundering and Terrorism Financing: The Role of Capital Markets Regulator*, 5 JOURN MONEY LAUNDERING CONTROL 30, at 32 (2002); see also A Buzelay 'Secret Bancaire, Évasion Fiscale et Blanchiment de l'Argent en Europe', *Revue Mar.é Commun et de l'Union européenne* 664 (2001).

[100] Details on the initiative are available at <http://www.imf.org/external/np/fsap/fsap.asp>.

[101] See IMF, 'Intensified Work on Anti-Money Laundering and Combating Financing of Terrorism. Joint Progress Report on the Work of the IMF and World Bank', of 17 Apr 2002, available at http://www.imf.org/external/np/fsap/fsap.asp

[102] Available at <http://www.iaisweb.org/1/pasc.html>.

[103] Available at <http://www.bis.org/bcbs/publ.htm>.

[104] Available at <http://www.wolfsberg-principles.com/wolfsberg_Statement.html>. The Wolfsberg Group consists of 11 leading international banks and became known when they

Securities Commissions' (IOSCO) Resolution on Money laundering of 1992[105] are evidence of the rising concern for the preservation of the integrity of the financial system. These documents, wrapped up in a soft law format, testify to a sort of self-consciousness by the relevant actors of the gravity of the issue and provide a spontaneous and trans-national response to avert the threat. In this regard, the KYC principle is unanimously recognized as having a pivotal role, whose importance has been further underscored in the aftermath of 11 September.[106] Indeed the apparent lawful nature, of the transactions carried out to finance terrorist activities, make it difficult for financial institutions to identify them. It may happen that a cross-check of the customer's identity with that of criminals does not reveal any connection with terrorist activities. This fact, however, should not discourage the assumption of obligations by financial institutions, since the full implementation of the KYC principle, by providing pieces of information, is helpful to uncover links with terrorism. The possession of a high number of pieces of information has been repetitively stressed by the FATF as a critical element to the fight against the financing of terrorism; once collected and matched by the competent authorities; the data may be useful to reconstruct suspicious transactions and to establish relations with terrorism.[107]

F. *Prevention of Terrorist Acts and the Critical Role of International Administrative Cooperation*

Obviously this task can be best performed if the relevant information is not kept isolated but is shared among the competent authorities involved, who are thus provided with a large number of pieces in order to solve the puzzle. In the light of the trans-national character of terrorist financing, it is crucial that information-sharing mechanisms be set up both at the national (intra-agency) and international level. Indisputably, the need for reinforced international cooperation is the dominant theme of the war on terrorism.

agreed to a set of global anti-money laundering guidelines for international private banks in Oct 2000; see M Pieth and G Aiolfi *The Private Sector Becomes Active: The Wolfsberg Process*, 10 JOURN FIN CRIME 359 (2003).

105 Available at <http://www.iosco.org/resolutions/index.html>.

106 Initiatives for an enhanced due diligence are also being undertaken at the national level in highly exposed countries such as Switzerland, see EHG Hüpke *Keeping Dirty Money and Terrorist Funds Away: the Proposed Money Laundering Regulation of the Swiss Federal Banking Commission*, 10 JOURN FINANCIAL REGULATION AND COMPLIANCE 317 (2002); see also D Mulligan *Know Your Customer Regulations and the International Banking System: Towards a General Self-Regulatory Regime*, 22 FORDHAM INT'L LAW J 2324 (1999).

107 In this regard see remarks laid down by the FATF in its 'Guidance for Financial Institutions in Detecting Terrorist Financing', of 24 Apr 2002, available at <www.fatf-gafi.org>.

Calls for coordinated efforts and enhanced international cooperation are contained in UN Security Resolution 1373, and have been subsequently reiterated by FATF Special Recommendation V that urges each country 'to afford another country . . . the greatest possible measure of assistance in connection with criminal, civil enforcement and administrative investigations, inquiries and proceedings'.

The policy of prevention rather than exclusively of repression of acts of terrorism has emphasized the need of modern forms of cooperation better suited to identify and to curb typologies of financing of terrorism. Therefore, apart from and alternatively to traditional modalities of international cooperation in criminal matters, consisting of judicial assistance in the course of pending criminal proceedings, the reinforcement of administrative cooperation is a more appropriate manner in which to deal with the financing of terrorism, in particular at the ex ante, intelligence stage. This form of cooperation, traditionally developed in the field of international taxation,[108] is executed between administrative authorities[109] and is usually characterized by the goal of preventing administrative violations as well as by the urgency of the request. Whereas international judicial cooperation is directed at the gathering of evidence and is carried out through formalized and lengthy procedures, regulated by domestic law or bilateral MLATs, international administrative assistance is usually conducted within informal practices established in Memoranda of Understanding (MOUs). These are non-legally binding arrangements designed to facilitate the cooperation and exchange of information between administrative/regulatory agencies. Rather than purporting to override other channels of international collaboration, such as international judicial assistance, they aim at complementing these formalized manners of cooperation and, by revealing a mutual understanding, they seek to foster relations between correspondent administrative authorities.

Undoubtedly, the reliance on informal and flexible procedures which ensure an expedited exchange of information, makes administrative cooperation better fitted for reconstructing patterns of money laundering and for this reason has received significant support by UN Security Council

[108] Traditional lack of extraterritorial enforcement of tax laws has made resort to exchange of information between competent tax authorities a valuable tool for filling gaps in their respective data records, see M Udina *Il diritto internazionale tributario* (Cedam Padova 1949) 248; and recently, P Schlosser *Jurisdiction and International Judicial and Administrative Cooperation* (2000) 284 COLLECTED COURSES 333 et seq.

[109] On the different forms that international administrative cooperation may take, see G Biscottini *Diritto Amministrativo Internazionale, t. I, La rilevanza degli atti amministrativi stranieri* (Cedam Padova 1964) 153, spec 155, where the author underlines the fact that direct active cooperation between foreign administrative authorities is typical of cases of intense relationships, and of the need arising in special cases to take immediate action; more recently, see T Amy *L'entraide administrative en matière bancaire, boursière et financière* (Lausanne 1998) 203 et seq, spec 566.

Resolution 1373, as well as by the FATF in Special Recommendation V, where express reference is made to the enhancement of sharing of information mechanisms. Intensification of information-sharing mechanisms, as a strategic tool for the prevention of terrorist financing, was already forcefully stated in the New York Convention. For this purpose, States Parties are called upon to set up appropriate measures to establish channels of communication between agencies and services and to cooperate with one another in conducting inquiries.

Arrangements for the sharing of information are not a novelty but are already in place within the money laundering context and are carried out by the respective national Financial Intelligence Units (FIUs).[110] These are central national agencies with expertise in both criminal and financial law, receiving information such as data on suspicious transactions or customers directly from financial institutions, in order 'to collect, analyse and disseminate to the competent authorities such disclosures of financial information'.[111] Where instituted under the form of administrative—rather than judicial—agencies, FIUs are also the 'centre of gravity' of international information sharing with the reciprocal foreign FIUs; to this end, since 1995, FIUs have begun to coordinate their work in an informal organization known as the Egmont Group, with a view to improving mechanisms for the sharing of information. Mindful of the critical importance that exchange of data has in the fight against financial criminality and thus of a need for developed cooperation, the Egmont Group agreed in June 2001 on a set of principles to be taken as a reference point in the sharing of information. The document stresses the importance of overcoming national obstacles in order to allow FIUs to freely exchange information on the basis of reciprocity and mutual trust, with the limitation that the information so acquired may not be transferred to a third party or be used in an administrative, investigative prosecutorial or judicial purpose without the prior consent of the FIU that disclosed the information.[112]

The pivotal role of reinforced international cooperation, especially in the form of information sharing, has been addressed also by international

[110] The text of both Directive 91/308/EEC (Art 6) and of the New York Convention may be ambiguous in this respect in that they make a general reference to the obligation to report to the 'competent authorities' without any additional specification.

[111] According to the definition adopted by the Egmont Group at the plenary meeting held in Rome on 21–22 Nov 1996. References are available at <http://www.fatf-gafi.org/pdf/EGstat-200106_en.pdf>; on FIUs see, extensively G Steessens *Money Laundering. A New International Law Enforcement Model* (CUP Cambridge 1999) 183–99.

[112] See Egmont Group, ′Principles for Information Exchange Between Financial Intelligence Units for Money Laundering Cases, adopted at The Hague, 13 June 2001'; *available at* <http://www.fatf-gafi.org/pdf/EGstat-200106_en.pdf>. On the actual operation of FIUs and on the advantages of such administrative cooperation within the anti-money laundering framework, see G Steessens *Money Laundering. A New International Law Enforcement Model* (CUP Cambridge 1999) 269 ff.

financial bodies. Despite the fact that these kinds of issues do not fall within their ordinary fields of competence, the magnitude of the phenomenon of international terrorism and the threat it poses to financial stability,[113] strengthened the resolve of such institutions to react, thus speeding up the adoption of cooperative measures. Particularly relevant is the Multilateral Memorandum of Understanding concerning Consultation and Cooperation and the Exchange of Information adopted by IOSCO on May 2002, where explicit reference is made to the need for enhanced coordination following the 11 September attacks.[114] This is not an isolated voice, however. The Basel Committee, in its 'Sharing of financial records between jurisdictions in connection with the fight against terrorist financing' adopted in April 2002, observed that an increased cross-border sharing of information, in particular between home and host supervisors, is helpful to control the reputation and legal risks to which banks may be exposed.[115] Provisions for an enhanced cooperation among regulatory agencies in the form of information-sharing and investigation activities are contained also in the EC Directive on market abuse, taking into account the increase in cross-border trading.[116]

Mechanisms of exchange of information for supervisory purposes are not a direct consequence of the events of 11 September, being already in place before. The initiatives undertaken in the aftermath of 11 September do not purport to engage in a front-line fight against the financing of terrorism; they are however worth mentioning in that they constitute evidence of the pervasiveness of the threats of financial criminality and the need of multiple coordinated efforts to overcome the magnitude and the ramifications of such a phenomenon.[117]

V. CONCLUSION

The several initiatives undertaken to counter the financing of terrorism which have been outlined in this paper have touched upon some of the distinctive traits of today's international law, and provide an interesting portrait of the international legal system.[118]

[113] For a review of the regulators' activity in the days immediately following Sept 11th, see MI Steinberg, *The SEC and the Securities Industry Respond to Sept. 11*, 36 INT'L LAWYER 131 (2002).

[114] *Available at* <www.iosco.org>.

[115] *Available at* <http://www.bis.org/bcbs/publ.htm>.

[116] See preamble 40, and Art 16 of the EC Directive n 2003/6.

[117] For an *excursus* see FFF Friedman, E Jacobs and SC Macel IV, *Taking Stock of Information Sharing in Securities Enforcement Matters* 10 JOURN FIN CRIME 37 (2002); CAA Greene *International Securities Law Enforcement: Recent Advances in Assistance and Cooperation*, 27 VAND J TRANSNAT'L L 635 1994).

[118] The literature on the transformation recently undergone by the international legal system

From a normative standpoint, a significant feature is the proliferation of norms which have been passed after the events of 11 September. The multiplicity of sources analysed in the paper—ie UN Security Council Resolutions, European Union Directives and Regulations, ratification of the New York Convention, standards, statements and principles, to cite a few—are evidence of such an approach. This varied normative production induces reflection regarding the dynamic dimension of the international legal system. These reflections concern both the multiplicity of actors involved in the rule-making process as well as the rule-making process itself. Indeed, numerous actors with a different legal nature have taken part in this development, ranging from the UN Security Council, regional intergovernmental organizations such as the European Union, States (either by ratifying international treaties such as the New York Convention, or by implementing abovenational measures) as well as other actors with a particular expertise, such as the FATF, an intergovernmental body, and other informal fora like the Basel Committee on Banking Supervision, the IOSCO, the IAIS, the Wolfsberg Group and the Egmont Group. The variety of the legal nature of the actors is also reflected in the different typologies of sources adopted such as formally enacted provisions which coexist with informal rules/standards, statements, principles, and MOUs. Regardless of any deference to the classical hierarchy of international law sources, soft law is a reference as much as hard law.

This apparently confused and a systematic way of proceeding actually reveals a pragmatic approach to the common goal of countering the financing of terrorism; in working towards this goal, the purpose of the disparate actors and rules is unified. Such community of intents is reflected in the intensification of international cooperation, which constitutes one of the most distinctive facets of the reaction to the attack on the Twin Towers. The variety of actors involved in the collaborative efforts, and the search for informal and flexible schemes, better suited to the prevention of terror crimes, testify to the solidarity of the international community to thwart this new challenge.[119]

is extensive; without pretension of being exhaustive see G Abi-Saab 'Cours général de droit international' (1997) *Rec Cours* vol 207; R Higgins *Problems & Process. International Law and How We Use It* (Clarendon Press Oxford 1994); B Conforti *International Law and the Role of Domestic Legal Systems* (Martinus Nijhoff Publishers Dordrecht 1993); A Cassese *International law* (OUP Oxford 2001).

[119] Inter-State cooperation has since long envisaged as the sole instrument against transnational criminality and the threats it poses to the international community in the light of the magnitude of its structure, its means and the volume of money controlled world-wide; particularly telling in this regard are the considerations expressed by R Quadri who observed that '[l]e organizzazioni internazionali di malfattori necessariamente dispongono di mezzi superiori per l'attuazione dei loro propositi criminosi e colpiscono indifferentemente, a seconda delle occasioni, la sfera particolare di qualunque Stato; esse costituiscono pertanto un pericolo o

Having said this, it is legitimate to wonder to what extent this pragmatic approach can be effectively realized. It can correctly be objected that the adoption of rules is not a good thing per se, and that the emphasis should rather be shifted to their actual enforcement, rightly the central issue of this Symposium.

The focus on the intensification of international cooperation, including information-sharing, is an encouraging sign of the increased international community's sensitivity for the effectiveness of international law norms. However, there are gaps that have still to be filled. Divergences in implementation and application which may stem from the ambiguous content of the relevant norms—for example, the definition of 'financing of terrorism' or of 'terrorism' itself—and the differing levels of sophistication of domestic legal systems challenge the effectiveness of the fight against the financing of terrorism. The international initiatives risk being a suitable remedy only for countries with high quality financial systems and may seem unrealistic when addressed to developing countries that are poor in technology and financial culture and that have unsatisfactory law enforcement structures, The existence of an appropriate legal framework is just one piece of the puzzle and absent a consistent support in technological development, financial training and belowstructures the provisions may appear to be wishful thinking.

male internazionale di fronte al quale solo la solidarietà degli Stati può apportare un rimedio adeguato', R Quadri *Diritto penale internazionale* (Padova Cedam 1944) 41.

NATIONAL TREATMENT IN FINANCIAL SERVICES IN THE CONTEXT OF THE GATS/WTO

WEI WANG*

CHAPTER OUTLINE

I. INTRODUCTION

National treatment is one of the two aspects of non-discriminatory treatment.[1] The other is most-favoured-nation treatment (hereinafter referred to as MFN treatment). The purpose of MFN treatment is to ensure equal

* Wei Wong is a Counsel at Jiangsu Jinda Firm PRC; a member of the Chinese Bar Association. He has served as a legal advisor to a number of Chinese import and export corporations and as a Consultant of the Psion Development Bank. He is currently the John and Joan Jackson Research Scholar at the Centre for Commercial Law Studies, University of London.

[1] For the advantages of non-discrimination for world economy, see *Non-Discrimination: Most-Favoured-Nation Treatment and National Treatment*, WT/WGTI/W/118, at 3–4, 4 June 2002.

competition opportunities provided by one country among other different countries. The fundamental purpose of national treatment is to ensure equal treatment between a host country and foreign countries. Schwarzenberger called MFN 'foreign parity', and national treatment 'inland parity'.[2] National treatment does not exclusively pertain to world trade, or the World Trade Organization (WTO). It exists in many areas, such as trade, investment,[3] patent law or copyright law,[4] even in criminal law.[5] However, it must be pointed out that there is no rule of customary international law requiring a host country to grant national treatment to foreign investors.[6] National treatment, from the perspective of international trade, is an obligation based on a bilateral treaty, regional treaty, multilateral treaty, or national law. This paper focuses on national treatment in financial services in the context of the multilateral trade agreement—the General Agreement on Trade in Services (GATS). Section I is the overview of national treatment for trade in goods under the General Agreement on Tariffs and Trade (GATT). Section II analyses national treatment for trade in services under the GATS, especially the relationship between market access and national treatment. Section III discusses national treatment in financial services. Section IV analyses the exceptions to national treatment obligations in financial services. Section V is the conclusion.

II. OVERVIEW OF NATIONAL TREATMENT UNDER THE GATT/WHO

Under the framework of the WTO, national treatment spreads to three main areas; trade in goods (Article III of the GATT 1994, Article 2 of the Trade-Related Investment Measures), trade in services (Article XVII of the GATS) and trade-related intellectual property rights (Article 3 of the TRIPS). Moreover, there is also a national treatment article in one of the plurilateral agreements, the Government Procurement Agreement (Article III).

Obviously GATT Article III is in the scope of trade in goods, irrelevant to services. However, it is necessary to study GATT Article III before trying

[2] Georg Schwarzenberger *International Law and Order* 157 (Stevens & Sons 1971).

[3] Thomas W Waelde *A Requiem for the 'New International Economic Order': the Rise and Fall of Paradigms in International Economic Law and a Post-Mortem with Timeless Significance*,' in Liber Amicorum: Professor Ignaz Seidl-Hiohenveldern, in honour of his 80th birthday792 (Gerhard Hafner et al (eds), Kluwer Law Int'l 1998) (pointing out that national treatment is referred to in 'all current influential international and most national instruments of foreign investment policy').

[4] See Art II of Paris Convention for the Protection of Industrial Property, 1883.

[5] John H Jackson, The World Trading System: Law and Policy of International Economic Relations 213 (2nd edn MIT Press 1997).

[6] Fiona Beveridge *The Treatment and Taxation of Foreign Investment Under International Law: Towards International Disciplines* (Manchester University Press 2000) 11.

to touch upon the rules of national treatment in services because the GATT is the best background of the GATS, and 'the GATS is broadly modeled on the GATT'.[7] In the very beginning of the Uruguay Round negotiation, some countries were of the opinion that national treatment under the GATT could provide 'a useful starting point' for the incorporation of this concept in the agreement on services.[8]

Paragraph 1 of GATT article III is a general national treatment rule on trade in goods.[9] It is to prevent any contracting party from protecting domestic production by applying discriminate internal taxes, other internal charges, laws, regulations and other relevant requirements. In *Japan—Alcoholic Beverages*, the Appellate Body Stated that 'Article III:1 articulates a general principle' which 'informs the rest of Article III.'[10]

Paragraphs 2 and 3 of GATT Article III are the detailed rules about internal taxes or other internal charges.[11] The first sentence of GATT Article III:2 contains a very important definition, 'like products', which determines the scope of GATT Article IIIIn of the Report of the Working Party on Border Tax Adjustments, 'like products' should be decided on a case-by-case basis.[12]

With regard to the second sentence of Article III:2, there is a special note in Annex I of the GATT 1947 with the term of 'directly competitive or substitutable products'.[13] In *Japan—Alcoholic Beverages*, the Appellate

[7] Philip Ruttley, 'Financial Service and the General Agreement on Trade in Services', in *Liberalisation and Protectionism in the World Trading System* 184 (Philip Ruttley and Iain MacVay et al (eds), Cameron May 1999). See also Ernst-Ulrich Petersmann, 'The GATT/WHO Dispute Settlement System: International Law', *International Organizations and Dispute Settlement* 210 (Kluwer Law International 1997).

[8] Note on the Meeting of 15–17 Sept 1987, ¶ 17, MTN.GNS/10, 15 Oct 1987.

[9] GATT Art III:1 reads:

'The contracting parties recognize that internal taxes and other internal charges, and laws, regulations and requirements affecting the internal sale, offering for sale, purchase, transportation, distribution or use of products, and internal quantitative regulations requiring the mixture, processing or use of products in specified amounts or proportions, should not be applied to imported or domestic products so as to afford protection to domestic production.'

[10] *Japan—Alcoholic Beverages*, Report of the Appellate Body, WT/DS8/AB/R, WT/DS10/AB/R, WT/DS11/AB/R, Section G, adopted on 1 Nov 1996.

[11] GATT Art III:2 reads as follows:

'The products of the territory of any contracting party imported into the territory of any other contracting party shall not be subject, directly or indirectly, to internal taxes or other internal charges of any kind in excess of those applied, directly or indirectly, to like domestic products. Moreover, no contracting party shall otherwise apply internal taxes or other internal charges to imported or domestic products in a manner contrary to the principles set forth in paragraph 1.'

[12] Report of the Working Party on Border Tax Adjustments, adopted on 2 Dec 1970, BISD 18S/97, 102, ¶ 18. This practice under the GATT 1947 was followed by WTO dispute settlement practice. See *Japan—Alcoholic Beverages*, Report of the Appellate Body, above n 10, Section H1 (a).

[13] Ad Art IIII: 2 in Annex I (Notes and Supplementary Provisions) of the GATT reads:

'A tax conforming to the requirements of the first sentence of paragraph 2 would be consid-

Body and the Panel only provided another case-by-case approach for the determination of the range of 'directly competitive or substitutable products', and some ambiguous elements, such as physical characteristics, common end-uses and tariff classifications.[14]

Paragraph 4 is more important than any other paragraphs of GATT Article III for the purpose of establishing the background and terminology of national treatment of the GATS. It stipulates that the products imported shall be accorded *treatment no less favorable* than that accorded to like products in respect of *all laws, regulations and requirements.*[15]

Compared with paragraph 1 of Article XVII of the GATS, one can easily find that the two paragraphs are similar to each other in structure.[16] Both of them use the words 'treatment no less favorable'.[17] 'No less favorable treatment does not necessarily mean the same treatment'.[18] In *US—Section 337 of the Tariff Act of 1930*, the GATT panel took account of 'effective equality of opportunities' in respect of the application of laws, regulations and requirements, as a key test to analyse 'treatment no less favorable'.[19] Moreover, this test was adopted by a WTO panel in the report of *US—Gasoline*, the first panel report under the WTO dispute settlement mechanism, indicating that the WTO practice has confirmed the 'effective equality of opportunities' test, in spite of lacking further details.[20]

ered to be inconsistent with the provisions of the second sentence only in cases where competition was involved between, on the one hand, the taxed product and, on the other hand, a *directly competitive or substitutable product* which was not similarly taxed.' (emphasis added)

[14] See *Japan—Alcoholic Beverages*, Report of the Panel, WT/DS8/R, WT/DS/S10/R, WT/DS/S11/R, ¶ 6.22 (The panel held that 'the decisive criterion in order to determine whether two products are directly competitive or substitutable is whether they have common end-uses, inter alia, as shown by elasticity of substitution.' ¶ 6.22.); See also *Japan—Alcoholic Beverages*, Report of the Appellate Body, above n 10, Section H 2 (a).

[15] The first sentence of GATT Art III:4 reads:

'The products of the territory of any contracting party imported into the territory of any other contracting party shall be accorded treatment no less favourable than that accorded to like products of national origin in respect of all laws, regulations and requirements affecting their internal sale, offering for sale, purchase, transportation, distribution or use.'

[16] GATS Art XVII:1 reads:

'In the sectors inscribed in its Schedule, and subject to any conditions and qualifications set out therein, each Member shall accord to services and service suppliers of any other Member, in respect of all measures affecting the supply of services, treatment no less favorable than that it accords to its own like services and service suppliers.'

[17] EC-*Regime for the Importation, Sale and Distribution of Bananas*, Panel Report, WT/DS27/R/USA, WT/DS27/R/MEX, WT/DS27/R/ECU, ¶ 7.302 (The Panel pointed out that the formulation of Art XVII of the GATS derives from the 'treatment no less favourable' standard of the GATT national treatment provisions in Article III of the GATT).

[18] Jon R Johnson *International Trade Law* 59 (Irwin Law 1998).

[19] *US—Section 337 of the Tariff Act of 1930*, adopted on 7 Nov 1986, BISD 36S/345, 386, ¶ 5.11.

[20] *US—Standards for Reformulated and Conventional Gasoline*, Panel Report , WT/DS2/R, ¶ 6.10.

III. NATIONAL TREATMENT UNDER THE GATS/WHO

A. *Negotiation History of National Treatment for Trade in Services*

The history of national treatment dates back to 'earlier centuries'.[21] However, in the field of trade in services, national treatment is still a new topic. In the middle of 1980s, the United States called for negotiation of a framework of rules for trade in services comparable to GATT rules for trade in goods, including, inter alia, national treatment principle.[22] In 1986, an agreement was reached to negotiate services at Punta de Este,[23] and service negotiations became part of the role of the Trade Negotiations Committee, which was responsible for conducting the negotiations in the Uruguay Round.[24] Negotiating countries in the Uruguay Round knew that 'it was worth trying to examine how far these principles (including national treatment) could be applied to services'.[25] Although some countries thought national treatment was 'at the heart of the service negotiations',[26] the negotiation of national treatment for trade in services, like other services issues, was not smooth because some countries believed that national treatment might be 'more difficult to apply to services than to goods'.[27] One country even thought that the concept of national treatment was the most complex in the negotiations.[28] It was the US that made the first proposal to include national treatment as a fundamental element for a framework agreement on trade in services in October 1987.[29] The Montreal agreement made at the mid-term review meeting of the Uruguay Round in December 1988 included a list of principles applicable to trade in services, such as transparency, market access, national treatment, etc which was what the US

[21] John H Jackson, above n 5, at 213.

[22] See Jack W Flader, Jr *A Call For a General Agreement on Trade in Services*, 3 TRANSNAT'L LAW 661, 663 (1990) (pointing out that the main reason for the US' position to promote services negotiations was the value of the trade in services in the US).

[23] See Ministerial Declaration on the Uruguay Round: Declaration of 20 Sept 1986, Part II: Negotiations on Trade in Services. BISD, 33rd Supplement, Geneva, June 1987, at 28. See also John Croome, *Reshaping the World Trading System: a History of the Uruguay Round* 102 (2nd edn Kluwer Law International 1999).

[24] During the whole Uruguay Round negotiations, the goods negotiations and services negotiations were separated. The former was guided by Group of Negotiations on Goods (GNG), and the latter was guided by Group of Negotiations on Services (GNS). See Ministerial Declaration on the Uruguay Round: Declaration of 20 Sept 1986, at 27–28, Basic Instruments and Selected Documents, Thirty-third Supplement, Geneva, June 1987. See also Croome, ibid, at 25.

[25] MTN.GNS/7, ¶ 29, Note on the Meeting of 23–25 Feb. 1987, 20 Mar 1987.

[26] Note on the Meeting of 17–20 May 1988, ¶ 28 & 40, MTN.GNS/15, 14 June 1988.

[27] Croome, above n 23, at 105.

[28] See the opinion of the representative of India included in the Note on the Meeting of 17–21 July 1989, ¶ 212, MTN.GNS/24, Aug 1989.

[29] Croome, above n 23, at 107.

wanted.[30] In the Montreal Declaration, there was a preliminary definition of national treatment for trade in services:

When accorded in conformity with other provisions of the multilateral framework, it is understood that national treatment means that the services exports and/or exporters of any signatory are accorded in the market of any other signatory, in respect of all laws, regulations and administrative practices, treatment 'no less favorable' than that accorded domestic services or services providers in the same market.[31]

In July 1990, the Chairman of the Group of Negotiations on Services (hereinafter referred to as GNS) issued the Draft Multilateral Framework for Trade in Services (hereinafter referred to as Chairman's July Text),[32] which included a national treatment article, numbered XVII. It Stated as follows:

In conformity with other relevant provisions of the framework, and as set out in their appropriate schedules, parties shall grant to services and service providers of other parties, in the application of all laws, regulations, administrative practices, and decisions of general application, treatment no less favorable than that accorded to like domestic services or service providers in like circumstances.

When necessary, the treatment a signatory accords to services or service providers of another signatory may be different from the treatment accorded to like domestic services or domestic providers of like services, as long as the treatment is equivalent in effect to the treatment accorded by the signatory to domestic providers in like circumstances.

The provisions of the framework on national treatment shall not apply to laws, regulations or requirements governing the procurement by governmental agencies of services purchased for governmental purposes and not with a view to use in production of services for commercial sale.

The provisions of the framework on national treatment shall not prevent the payment of subsidies or granting of incentives exclusively to domestic service providers.

However, the Chairman's July text did not provide a complete agreement acceptable by contracting parties,[33] so in December 1990, the GNS Chairman released another draft text at Brussels, titled Draft Final Act Embodying the Result of the Uruguay Round of Multilateral Trade Negotiations (hereinafter referred to as Chairman's December Text).[34] In

[30] Fred Lazar *Services and the GATT: US Motives and a Blueprint for Negotiation*, 24 JWT 135 (1990).

[31] Part II:7(c) of the Ministerial Declaration, MTN.TNC/8, from THE GATT URUGUAY ROUND, A NEGOTIATING HISTORY (1986–1992), VOLUME III: DOCUMENT 62 (Terence P. Stewart ed., Kluwer Law and Taxation Publishers 1993).

[32] GATT, MTN.GNS/35 (23 July 1990).

[33] Stewart above n 31, at 2388.

[34] GATT, MTN/TNC/W/35/Rev 1 (3 Dec 1990) Annex II.

this text, the provision of national treatment, still Article XVII, read as follows:

In conformity with other relevant provisions of this Agreement, and in accordance with the conditions and qualifications set out in its schedule, each Party shall accord to services and service providers of other Parties, in respect of all measures affecting the supply of services, treatment no less favorable than that accorded to like domestic services or providers of like services.

[The treatment a Party accords to services and service providers of other Parties shall be considered to be no less favorable within the meaning of paragraph 1 if it accords to the services or service providers of other Parties opportunities to [compete] [supply services] that are no less favorable than those accorded to like domestic services or providers of like services.][35]

However, due to the deadlock over other issues, the negotiation on December 1990 collapsed and so did the Chairman's December text.[36]

According to the initial position of the US, national treatment would have to be a general obligation.[37] Even in the period of the Montreal mid-term review, the USTR still insisted that national treatment be one of the four basic principles governing trade in services,[38] despite opposition from the European Communities (hereinafter referred to as the EC) The EC tended to regard national treatment in services as a soft obligation, instead of a binding general obligation as insisted upon by the US.[39] As far as the developing countries were concerned, a general obligation of national treatment in services trade was unacceptable.[40] For example, Brazil directly pointed out that 'developing countries should not be expected to undertake the same level of market access or national treatment commitments as developed countries.'[41] In the end, the view of the EC and the developing countries prevailed, so the national treatment obligation in the final agreement was not designed as a general principle.[42]

[35] The bracket indicated that portion was especially controversial.

[36] See Stewart (ed), above n 31, at 2395.

[37] Mary E Footer *The International Regulation of Trade in Services Following Completion of the Uruguay Round*, 29 INT'L LAW 453, 456 (1995).

[38] Ibid.

[39] On the meeting of 1989, the representative of the EC Stated: 'National treatment could apply progressively in some cases and this application could vary from sector to sector and from country to country, depending on the regulatory structure.' Note on the Meeting of 17–21 July 1989, ¶ 210, MTN.GNS/24, Aug 1989. For further information, see Footer, ibid, at 458; See also JR Flader, above n 22, at 675.

[40] Bernard Hoekman *Developing Countries and the Uruguay Round: Negotiating on Servies* 5 (World Bank Policy Research Working Paper No 1220, 1993). See Footer at 460. See also Dilip K Das *Trade in Financial Services and the Role of the GATS: Against the Backdrop of the Asian Financial Crises*, 32 JWT 79, 101 (1998).

[41] Note on the Meeting of 17–21 July 1989, ¶ 214, MTN.GNS/24, Aug 1989. In Indian view, the negotiation on national treatment should consider the different levels of economic development of different countries. See also this Note, ¶ 212.

[42] It is worth noting that not everyone takes this view. For example, in Philip Ruttley's opin-

On 20 December 1991, Arthur Dunkel, the Secretary General of GATT at the time, released a 'final draft act', which was informally referred to as the 'Dunkel Draft'. In the 'Dunkel Draft', the GATS section contained an article, specifically dealing with national treatment, which constituted a blueprint for the final national treatment article, GATS Article XVII.[43] The differences between Article XVII of the GATS in the Dunkel Draft and of the official GATS are very subtle. In Dunkel Draft, GATS Article XVII reads:

> 1. In the sectors *or sub-sectors* inscribed in its Schedule of Commitment, and subject to any conditions and qualifications set out therein, each *Party* shall accord to services and service *providers* of any other *Party*, in respect of all measures affecting the supply of services, treatment no less favorable than that it accords to its own like services and service *providers.** (* Commitments assumed under this Article shall not be construed to require any *Party* to compensate for any inherent competitive disadvantages which result from the foreign character of the relevant services or service *providers.*)
> 2. A *Party* may meet the requirement of paragraph 1 by according to services and service *providers* of *other Parties*, either formally identical treatment or formally different treatment to that it accords to its own like services and service *providers.*
> 3. Formally identical or formally different treatment shall be considered to be less favorable if it modifies the conditions of competition in favor of services or service *providers* of the *Party* compared to like services or service *providers* of another *Party.*

In December 1993, the Uruguay Round ended with a series of agreements including the GATS, which included Article XVII. In January 1995, the GATS and other Uruguay Round agreements became effective. From that point on, the notion of national treatment has been applicable to trade in services.

ion, national treatment obligation is a general obligation set out by the GATS, as well as MFN treatment, transparency, mutual recognition, rules governing monopolies and other business practices restraining competitions. Philip Ruttley, 'Financial Service and the General Agreement on Trade in Services', in *Liberalisation and Protectionism in the World Trading System* 186 (Philip Ruttley and Iain MacVay et al (eds), Cameron May 1999). In China, some scholars also think that national treatment is one of the basic principles in the GATS. See Chen Xianmin, *Jiedu Fuwu Maoyi Zhongxieding de Jiben Yuanze (Understanding the basic Principles of GATS),* 7 Faxue (Law Science) 98 (2003). See also Zhou Qing, *Jiaru WTO dui Zhongguo Shangye Yinhang de Yingxiang he Duice (The Impact and Countermeasures of China's Commercial Banks after Entry to the WTO),* 10 *Jinrong yu Baoxian* (Finance and Insurance) 42 (2000).

43 See MTN.TNC/W/FA, 'Dunkel Draft' from the GATT Secretariat, collected and edited by the Institute for International Legal Information, 1992, William S Hein & Co, Inc (The different terms from official GATS Article XVII are in italics).

B. Position of National Treatment in the Gats

The GATS is composed of three pillars.

The first pillar is the main text of the Agreement (The GATS), including six Parts (29 articles, in addition to 3 *bis* articles).

Part I Scope and Definition[44]
Art II General Obligations and Disciplines[45]
Part III Specific Commitments[46]
Part IV Progressive Liberalization[47]
Part V Institutional Provisions[48]
Part VI Final Provisions[49]

The second pillar contains eight Annexes, which are also an integral part of the GATS.[50]

Annex on Article II Exemptions
Annex on Movement of Natural Persons Supplying Services under the Agreement
Annex on Air Transport Services
Annex on Financial Services
Second Annex on Financial Services
Annex on Negotiations on Maritime Transport Services
Annex on Telecommunications
Annex on Negotiations on Basic Telecommunications.

The third pillar contains schedules of specific commitments and Lists of Article II Exemptions provided by Members. Schedules of specific commitments include WTO Members' commitments on market access, national treatment and addition commitments, which are annexed to and part of the GATS.[51] The relationship between the framework agreement and schedules of specific commitments is deemed as that of bones and flesh by Kevin C Kennedy.[52] Lists of Article II Exemptions (MFN exemptions) provided by

[44] Part I only includes Ar I (Scope and Definition).

[45] Part II covers from Art II (Most-Favoured-Nation Treatment) to Art XV (Subsidies).

[46] Part III contains three articles, ie Art XVI (Market Access), Art XVII (National Treatment) and Art XVIII (Additional Commitments).

[47] Part IV also has three articles, including Art XIX (Negotiation of Specific Commitments), Art XX (Schedules of Specific Commitments) and Art XXI (Modification of Schedules).

[48] Part V concludes five articles, from Art XXII (Consultation) to Art XXVI (Relationship with Other International Organizations).

[49] Part VI has three articles, Art XXVII (Denial of Benefits), Art XXVIII (Definitions) and Art XXIX (Annexes).

[50] GATS Art XXIX: 'The Annexes to this Agreement are an integral part of this Agreement.'

[51] GATS Art XX:3.

[52] See Kevin C Kennedy *A WTO Agreement on Investment: A Solution in Search of a Problem?*, 24 U PA J INT'L ECON L 110 (2003).

Members are part of Annex on Article II Exemptions, also an integral part of the GATS.[53]

Additionally, there are eight Ministerial Decisions related to the GATS, and one Understanding, but none of them is an integral part of the GATS.[54]

Structurally, the national treatment clause is placed in Part III (Specific Commitments) of the GATS, which implies that national treatment is different from most-favored-nation treatment and transparency. The latter are covered in Part II of the GATS, as general obligations and principles applicable to almost all service sectors. Part III contains three articles, of which national treatment is contained in Article XVII.[55] GATS Aritcle XVII, however, is not the exclusive realm of national treatment in services trade. In fact, national treatment runs through all of the three parts of the GATS. For example, in order to know the real meaning of national treatment for a Member, it is essential to go through the schedule of specific commitments of that Member, particularly the column of limitation on national treatment.

C. Descriptive Analysis of Gats Article XVII

GATS Article XVII ('National Treatment') reads as follows:

> 1. In the sectors inscribed in its Schedule, and subject to any conditions and qualifications set out therein, each Member shall accord to services and service suppliers of any other Member, in respect of all measures affecting the supply of services, treatment no less favorable than that it accords to its own like services and service suppliers.[56]

[53] See Annex on Art II Exemptions.

[54] Compared to the unclear status of decisions under the GATS, the decisions under that GATT have guiding effect. WTO Agreement Art XVI reads: 'the WTO shall be *guided* by the *decisions*, procedures and customary practices followed by the CONTRACTING PARTIES to *GATT 1947* and the bodies established *in the framework of GATT 1947*.' (Emphases added) WTO Agreement does not mention those decisions related to the GATS or their legal status. It is difficult to understand why WTO Agreement ignored the decision related to the GATS. WTO Agreement Art II: 2 States: 'the agreements and associated legal documents included in Annexes 1, 2 and 3 are integral parts of this Agreement, binding on all Members.' Therefore, only agreements and legal documents *included in Annexes* of the WTO Agreement are considered to be part of it and have binding force. GATS is included in Annex 1B, so it is part of the WTO Agreement and has binding force, but all of the eight decisions related to the GATS and the Understanding are not included in the Annexes.

[55] Art XVIII (Additional Commitments) is beyond the reach of this paper because additional commitments are related to measures not subject to market access or national treatment obligation. See the first sentence of GATS Art XVIII.

[56] Specific commitments assumed under this Article shall not be construed to require any Member to compensate for any inherent competitive disadvantages which result from the foreign character of the relevant services or service suppliers. (Original footnote of Art XVII: 1.)

2. A Member may meet the requirement of paragraph 1 by according to services and service suppliers of any other Member, either formally identical treatment or formally different treatment to that it accords to its own like services and service suppliers.
3. Formally identical or formally different treatment shall be considered to be less favorable if it modifies the conditions of competition in favor of services or service suppliers of the Member compared to like services or service suppliers of any other Member.

Paragraph 1 is the key rule of national treatment in service trade.

First, the scope of national treatment is limited in those sectors inscribed in each Member's Schedule. This means that national treatment is not applicable to the service sectors not covered by a Member's Schedule, which means one Member of the WTO may take discriminative measures against services and service suppliers of any other Member in those reserved sectors, without violation of the national treatment rule embodied in GATS Article XVII. This reservation on national treatment came from the Uruguay Round negotiations on trade in services, at the behest of developing countries. In this regard, Peru's view could be the representative view of developing countries: 'National treatment can be interpreted as an objective to be attained in the short, medium and ling-term, *sector by sector*, activity by activity, depending on the coverage and the commitments deriving from the final framework agreement.'[57] This 'bottom-up' approach provides more flexibility for Members, especially for developing countries, to protect specific domestic services and service suppliers.

Secondly, even for those sectors inscribed in each Member's Schedule, national treatment is not necessarily or fully applicable because national treatment may be limited through '*any conditions and qualifications*' set out in its Schedule.

Thirdly, the beneficiaries of national treatment are both *services* and *service suppliers* originated from or related to any other Member. 'Service' is defined by Article I(1)(3)(b). 'Service includes any service in any sector except services supplied in the exercise of government authority.'[58] 'Service supplier' means any *person* that supplies a service,[59] while 'person' is a legal term that is defined as either a natural person or a juridical person.[60] However, one of the loopholes of the GATS definitions is that 'service suppliers' under GATS Article XXVIII (g), do not clearly include branches or representative offices because they are not juridical persons. In order to

[57] MTN.GNS/24, ¶¶ 202, 205.

[58] GATS Art I (1) (3) (c) States: 'a service supplied in the exercise of governmental authority' means any service which is supplied neither on a commercial basis nor in competition with one or more service supplies.

[59] GATS Art XXVIII (g).

[60] GATS Art XXVIII (j).

elucidate this issue, under the advice of the Secretariat of the GATT, an interpretative note was added to the GATS, which subjected branches and representative offices to part of the service suppliers.[61]

Fourthly, the measures related to national treatment are 'all measures affecting the supply of services'. 'Measure' means any measure by a Member, whether in the form of a law, regulation, rule, procedure, decision, administrative action, or any other form.[62] 'Supply of services' can be defined by the definition of 'supply of a service', which includes the production, distribution, marketing, sale and delivery of a service.[63]

Fifthly, the comparable domestic counterparts of beneficiaries of national treatment are a Member's own 'like services and service suppliers'. However, the GATS articles do not provide any clear standard of likeness between services and service suppliers of one Member and those of another.[64] It is argued by some that like services and service suppliers cover 'directly competitive or substitutable' (DCS) services and services suppliers.[65] It is also difficult to understand the relationships between like services and like service suppliers. In the *EC—Bananas III* case, the Panel's view is 'to the extent that entities provide these like services, they are like service suppliers'.[66] This view almost equates services and service suppliers, so it was criticized as 'an exceedingly broad notion'.[67] In fact, 'like services and service supplier' is not a pure legal issue, but an issue mixed with both rules

[61] Footnote 12 of the GATS States: 'Where the service is not supplied directly by a juridical person but through other forms of commercial presence such as a branch or a representative office, the service supplier (ie the juridical person) shall, nonetheless, through such presence be accorded the treatment provided for service suppliers under the Agreement. Such treatment shall be extended to the presence through which the service is supplied and need not be extended to any other parts of the supplier located outside the territory where the service is supplied.' For the history of such interpretative note, see MTN.GNS/W/176, 26 Oct 1993.

[62] GATS Art XXVIII (a).

[63] GATS Art XXVIII (b).

[64] The notion of 'likeness' is a hard question in the history of GATT. The 1970 *Working Party Report on Border Tax Adjustments* States:

'With regard to the interpretation of the term 'like or similar products'. . . The Working Party concluded that problems arising from the interpretation of the terms should be examined *on a case-by-case basis*. This would allow a fair assessment in each case of the different elements that constitute a 'similar' product. Some criteria were suggested for determining, on a case-by-case basis, whether a product is 'similar': the product's end-uses in a given market; consumers' tastes and habits, which change from country to country; the product's properties, nature and quality.' Above n 12.

[65] See Patros C Mavroidis *Like Products: Some Thoughts at the Positive and Normative Level, in Regulatory Barriers and the Principle of Non-Discrimination in World Trade Law* 125, 126–7 (Thomas Cottier and Petros C Mavroidis (eds), University of Michigan Press 2002).

[66] See Panel Report on *EC—Regime for the Importation, Sale and Distribution of Bananas*, adopted by the Dispute Settlement Body on 25 Sept 1997 as modified by the Appellate Body Report, see above n 17, ¶ 7.322.

[67] Werner Zdouc *WTO Dispute Settlement Practice Relationg to the GATS*, 2 JIEL 295, 332 (1999).

and facts. In the case of *Canada—Certain Measures Concerning Periodicals*, the Appellate Body stated that, 'the determination of whether imported and domestic products are 'like products' is a process by which legal rules have to be applied to facts.'[68] If this conclusion is also applicable to the GATS, then the consequence is that the 'likeness' issue in the GATS must be construed on case-by-case basis.

The notion of 'treatment no less favorable' is interpreted by paragraphs 2 and 3 of Article XVII.[69] Just as the text of paragraph 1 of Article XVII mirrors Article III of the GATT, the text of paragraphs 2 and 3 of Article XVII is modeled after two Panel reports related to Article III of the GATT.[70] One is *US—Section 337* in which the Panel used the words 'formally identical',[71] and the other is *Italian—Agricultural Machinery* in which the Panel used the words 'modify the conditions of competition'.[72] GATS Article XVII covers both de jure and de facto inconsistency,[73] as does GATT Article III:4 This conclusion resulted from the Uruguay round negotiations. In the beginning of the negotiations, there were three options. Option one was the traditional definition of national treatment, which tended to be de jure. Option two was the equality of competitive opportunities. Option three was that of equivalent treatment.[74] Japan and Korea were of the view that only de jure (traditional national treatment) should be applied.[75] The EC, Switzerland, Canada and the US supported option two that national treatment should 'go beyond de jure' and guarantee equality of competitive opportunities.[76]

De jure discrimination is easily identified through comparison of treatments between domestic and foreign services or service suppliers. The issue arises in *de facto* discrimination. According to paragraph 2 of Article XVII, formally identical treatment might result in 'less favorable treatment', ie de facto discrimination, whereas formally different treatment can result in 'no less favorable treatment'. Therefore, the possible permutations include:

[68] Appellate Body Report, *Canada—Certain Measures Concerning Periodicals*, WT/DS31/AB/R, 30 June 1997, s V (A).

[69] In the view of the Panel of the *Banana* case, paras 2 and 3 of Art XVII do not impose new obligations on Members additional to those contained in para 1. See Panel Report on *EC—Regime for the Importation, Sale and Distribution of Bananas*, above n 17, ¶ 7.301.

[70] Werner Zdouc, above n 66, at 335. See also Aaditya Mattoo *National Treatment in the GATS, Corner-stone or Pandora's Box*? 31 JWT 107, 123 (1997). Some scholars even State that GATS Art XVII:3 'is inspired by the GATT case law'. See Mitsuo Matsushita, Thomas J Schoenbaum and Petros C Mavroidis *The World Trade Organization, Law, Practice, and Policy* 248 (OUP Oxford 2003).

[71] *US—Section 337 of the Tariff Act of 1930*, above n 19, ¶ 5.11

[72] *Italian-Discrimination of Imported Agricultural Machinery*, L/833, ¶ 12, 60–4, BISD 7S, adopted on 23 Oct 1958.

[73] ibid.

[74] For the three options, see MTN.GNS/FIN/1, ¶ 44, 5 July 1990.

[75] See ibid, ¶¶ 46, 49, 5 July 1990. See also MTN/GNS/FIN/2, ¶ 32, 10 Aug 1990.

[76] See ibid, MTN.GNS/FIN/1, ¶¶ 45, 57, 58, 59, 5 July 1990. See also ibid, MTN/GNS/FIN/2, ¶¶ 18, 33, 58.

- formally identical treatment results in no less favorable treatment;
- formally identical treatment results in less favorable treatment;
- formally different treatment results in no less favorable treatment;
- formally different treatment results in less favorable treatment.

In the four permutations, (a) and (c) are compatible with national treatment rule of GATS, but (b) and (d) run counter to it.

There is an interesting problem here as to which party has the burden of proof under these possible permutations. With respect to item (b), it seems that the complaining party, usually a foreign country who claims its services or services suppliers are discriminated against by a host country, should take the burden of proof to show that 'formally identical treatment results in less favorable treatment'. On the other hand, with respect to item (c), it seems more reasonable that the defendant party, ie the host country, should have the burden to prove that, in spite of such differences, 'formally different treatment results in no less favourable treatment', which is also the view of the GATT Panel in *US—Section 337*.[77]

Paragraph 3 of Article XVII goes further to try to provide a criterion to determine what measures will accord 'less favourable' treatment to foreign services or service suppliers. The criterion is whether the formally identical or formally different treatment 'modifies the conditions of competition'.[78] However, the notion of 'modification of the conditions of competition' is as vague as the notion of 'like services and service suppliers',[79] all of which may be the focus of disputes in future cases related to the GATS, under the WTO dispute settlement mechanism, and it is predictable that most of disputes will focus on formally identical laws and regulations. In fact, the new concept of 'modification of conditions of competition' or its predecessor 'equality of competitive opportunities' was intentionally left for the dispute settlement mechanism to interpret.[80]

[77] *US—Section 337 of the Tariff Act of 1930*, above n 19, ¶ 5.11. See also Most-Favoured-Nation Treatment and Non-Discrimination under the General Agreement on Tariffs and Trade, Note by the Secretariat, MTN.GNS/W/103, at 3, 12 June 1990.

[78] It is worth noting that NAFTA also uses the similar standard, ie 'equal competitive opportunities' to determine whether the treatment is less favourable in financial services. NAFTA Art 1405(5) reads as follows:

'A Party's treatment of financial institutions and cross-border financial service providers of another Party, whether *different or identical* to that accorded to its own institutions or providers in like circumstances, is consistent with paragraphs 1 through 3 if the treatment affords *equal competitive opportunities*.' (emphasis added)

[79] In Hudec's view, the text of GATS Article XVII:3 introduces an economic analysis of the competitive impact of the regulation in question, see Robert E. Hudec, 'GATT/WTO Constraints on National Regulations: Requiem for an "Aim and Effects" Test', in Essays on the Nature of International Law 359, 382 (Cameron May 1999) (Originally published in 32 INT'L LAW 619–49, 1998).

[80] See the Statement of the representative of the US, MTN.GNS/FIN/1, ¶ 59, 5 July 1990.

Moreover, 'no less favourable' treatment in the GATS implies that foreign services and service suppliers could be accorded more favorable treatment than that accorded to domestic services and service suppliers by a Member. From this perspective, 'no less favourable' is more favourable than 'the same' or 'as favourable as' for foreign services and service suppliers.

D. The Relationship Between Market Access and National Treatment Under the Gats

One of the characteristics of national treatment clause, in the context of GATS, is its complicated relationship with the market access clause. It is a common misunderstanding that national treatment obligation and market access obligation function at different stages.[81] This misunderstanding stems from the fact, that in the context trade in goods, market access and national treatment can be easily separated from each other through tariffs and other border measures. However, this separation is not the case in trade in services. During the Uruguay Round negotiations, the representative of Australia noted that 'the concepts of market access and national treatment seemed to merge. . .' and 'if reservations were allowed on both market access and national treatment, drawing the line between the market access conditions and national treatment conditions might be difficult'.[82] For this reason, it is necessary to understand market access in order to understand the national treatment obligations in the context of the GATS.

1. Market Access under the GATS

The market access obligation is clearly identified by the GATS, though it cannot be found in the GATT.[83] It is set forth in Article XVI of GATS. The provision reads as follows:

1. With respect to market access through the modes of supply identified in Article I, each Member shall accord services and service suppliers of any other Member treatment no less favorable than that provided for under the terms, limitations and conditions agreed and specified in its Schedule.*

[81] Eg, Mary E Footer thought that national treatment obligation comes into play after market access has been granted. See Footer, above n 37, at 472.

[82] MTN.GNS/FIN/1, ¶ 52, 5 July 1990.

[83] Bernard Hoekman, 'Assessing the General Agreement on Trade in Services', in *The Uruguay Round and the Developing Countries* 93 (Will Martin et al eds, Cambridge: CUP 1996).

* If a Member undertakes a market-access commitment in relation to the supply of a service through the mode of supply referred to in subparagraph 2(a) of Article I and if the cross-border

2. In sectors where market-access commitments are undertaken, the measures which a Member shall not maintain or adopt either on the basis of a regional subdivision or on the basis of its entire territory, unless otherwise specified in its Schedule, are defined as:
   (a) limitations on the number of service suppliers whether in the form of numerical quotas, monopolies, exclusive service suppliers or the requirements of an economic needs test;
   (b) limitations on the total value of service transactions or assets in the form of numerical quotas or the requirement of an economic needs test;
   (c) limitations on the total number of service operations or on the total quantity of service output expressed in terms of designated numerical units in the form of quotas or the requirement of an economic needs test;**
   (d) limitations on the total number of natural persons that may be employed in a particular service sector or that a service supplier may employ and who are necessary for, and directly related to, the supply of a specific service in the form of numerical quotas or the requirement of an economic needs test;
   (e) measures which restrict or require specific types of legal entity or joint venture through which a service supplier may supply a service; and
   (f) limitations on the participation of foreign capital in terms of maximum percentage limit on foreign shareholding or the total value of individual or aggregate foreign investment.

From the structure of the GATS, market access and national treatment are in the same part of the GATS, ie Part III (specific commitments), which means that market access is not a general obligation under the GATS. Hoekman suggests that the introduction of a market access commitment reflects a characteristic of service markets in which 'their contestability is frequently restricted by nondiscriminatory measures.[84]

In each Member's Schedule, there are four columns: sector column, market access column, national treatment column and additional commit-

movement of capital is an essential part of the service itself, that Member is thereby committed to allow such movement of capital. If a Member undertakes a market-access commitment in relation to the supply of a service through the mode of supply referred to in subparagraph 2(c) of Art I, it is thereby committed to allow related transfers of capital into its territory. (footnote in the original text of Article XVI)

** Subparagraph 2(c) does not cover measures of a Member which limit inputs for the supply of services. (footnote in the original text of Article XVI).

[84] Hoekman, ibid, at 95.

ments column.[85] On the one hand, any sector or sub-sector that a Member agrees to open shall be inscribed in the sector column. In other words, if a sector or sub-sector does not appear in the Schedule, it will be presumed that the Member does not open the sector or sub-sector. This approach is called positive approach, or 'bottom-up' approach.[86] On the other hand, any limitation on market access and national treatment with respect to a specific sector or sub-sector should be inscribed in the corresponding columns, in addition to the horizontal commitment applying to trade in services in all scheduled services sectors unless otherwise specified.[87] Otherwise, it will be deemed that there is no limitation on market access or national treatment for the sector or sub-sector. Such approach is called negative approach, or 'top-down approach'. [88] A Schedule is the combination of positive approach and negative approach, called the hybrid approach.[89] For each sector or sub-sector, the limitation shall be expressed in order of four modes of supply, ie cross border supply, consumption abroad, commercial presence, and presence of natural persons.[90]

From the table, it seems that market access column and national treatment column are separate and independent from each other. In reality though, they are so connected and intertwined that they result in the most perplexing, elusive problem relating to GATS commitments, which is the contentious paragraph 2 of Article XX of the GATS.

2. *GATS Article XX:2*

Paragraph 2 of GATS Article XX provides: 'Measures inconsistent with both Articles XVI and XVII shall be inscribed in the column relating to Article XVI. In this case the inscription will be considered to provide a

[85] The column of 'additional commitments' does not belong to or overlap with market access and national treatment columns. GATS Article XVIII States: 'Members may negotiate commitments with respect to measures affecting trade in services *not subject to scheduling under Articles XVI or XVII*, including those regarding qualifications, standards or licensing matters. Such commitments shall be inscribed in a Member's Schedule.' (emphasis added)

[86] See above n 1, at 4.

[87] GATS Art XX: 1.

[88] See above n 1.

[89] This hybrid approach, especially the positive approach for service sectors and sub-sectors is criticized by some scholars as one of the weaknesses of the GATS, eg see Das, above n 40, at 100–1.

[90] The four modes of supply are from the definition of 'trade in services'. GATS Art I:2 reads as follows:

'For the purposes of this Agreement, trade in services is defined as the supply of a service: (a) from the territory of one Member into the territory of any other Member; (b) in the territory of one Member to the service consumer of any other Member; (c) by a service supplier of one Member, through commercial presence in the territory of any other Member; (d) by a service supplier of one Member, through presence of natural persons of a Member in the territory of any other Member.'

condition or qualification to Article XVII as well.' This means that, at least sometimes, some limitation measures inscribed in the market access column are also limitation measures in the national treatment column. The reason for such overlaps is that 'market access restrictions in the form of limitations or conditions on modes of supply are likely to violate national treatment for these modes as well.'[91] However, the GATS does not state which measures or what kinds of measures entered in market access column are also regarded as limitation measures in national treatment column. Logically, there are four possibilities:

(1) While there is no limitation entered into the national treatment column, there may still exist some limitations on national treatment inscribed in the market access column;
(2) While there are some limitations entered in the national treatment column, there may exist more limitations on national treatment inscribed in the market access column;
(3) While there are some limitations entered in the national treatment column, there are no more limitation on national treatment from market access column;
(4) While there is no limitation entered in the national treatment column, there is also no limitation on national treatment in market access column. In this case, there is no limitation on national treatment in either column.

Of the four possibilities, the last one is the simplest, and causes no problem, because it embodies the openness and liberalization of the service sector to the greatest extent. All problems originate from the other three circumstances except. In order to solve this problem, it is necessary to make two preliminary questions as clear as possible.

The first preliminary question is how many possible limitation measures there are in a market access column. According to paragraph 2 of Article XVI of the GATS, unless otherwise specified in its Schedule, a Member may list as many as six limitation measures in its market access column, including:

- limitations on the number of service suppliers;
- limitations on the total value of service transactions or asset;
- limitations on the total number of service operations or the quantity of service output;
- limitations on the total number of natural persons;
- limitations on the types of legal entity or joint venture;
- limitations on the maximum percentage of foreign shareholding or the total value of foreign investment.

[91] Bernard Hoekman, *Market Access Through Multilateral Agreement: From Goods to Services*, 15 The World Economy 707, 720 (1992).

Furthermore, according to *the Guidelines for the Scheduling of Specific Commitments under the GATS: Explanatory Note* (hereinafter referred to as 2001 Explanatory Note), adopted by the Council for Trade in Services on 23 March 2001, the list is exhaustive.[92] *Scheduling of Initial Commitments in Trade in Services: Explanatory Note* (hereinafter referred to as 1993 Explanatory Note) circulated during the Uruguay Round negotiations (on 3 September 1993) has a similar Statement.[93] Usually a Member only inscribes some of the six types of limitation measures in market access column.

The second preliminary question is how many possible limitation measures there are in national treatment column. Contrary to Article XVI, Article XVII of the GATS does not make an exhaustive list of limitation measures on national treatment.[94] This fact adds to the difficulty in distinguishing market access and national treatment limitation measures. Article XVII: 1 uses the phrase 'all measures affecting the supply of services', and there is not limitation on the scope of 'all measures'. Moreover, paragraph 1 of Article XX is of little help to elucidate Article XX:2 because Article XX:1 uses the words '*terms, limitations and conditions*' for market access, and uses the similar words '*conditions and qualifications*' for national treatment.[95] As to what the difference is between 'terms, limitations and conditions' and 'conditions and qualifications', there is no clear answer from the text of the GATS.

3. *The Scope of National Treatment Obligations under GATS XVII*

The next question that arises is which of the above six limitations on market access may also be regarded as limitations on national treatment? According to GATT Article III (1), national treatment obligation is on '*internal* taxes, and other *internal* charges, and laws, regulations and requirements affecting the *internal* sale, offering for sale, purchase, transportation, distribution or use of products, and *internal* quantitative regulations requiring the mixture, processing or use of products'; therefore, limitation measures on national treatment in the context of the GATT are all post-entry measures. The pre-entry measures are mainly subject to GATT Article II, 'Schedules of Concessions', and Article XI, 'General

[92] See 2001 Explanatory Note, ¶ 8, S/L/92. In Hoekman's view, the exhaustive list weakens the scope of market access obligation because it does not cover other measures that have similar effects like the six kinds of measures. See Hoekman, above n 82, at 112.

[93] See 1993 Explanatory Note, ¶ 4, MTN.GNS/W/164.

[94] The Secretariat of the WTO had prepared an illustrative list of national treatment restrictions, see JOB No 3086. However, such list is only of purely illustrative nature. See Report of the Meeting Held on 23 and 24 May 2000, Note by the Secretariat, ¶ 14, S/CSC/M/15, 29 June 2000.

[95] GATS Art XX: 1(a)(b).

Elimination of Quantitative Restrictions'.[96] There is no overlap relationship between GATT Article III and Article II or Article XI, for the reason that they are separated through pre-entry or post-entry standard. Only after crossing the border of a Member can a product be entitled to national treatment. Therefore, the GATT experience does not provide a clue to the overlap problem between market access limitations and national treatment limitations under the GATS.

However, it may be possible for the post-entry standard is to be introduced to the GATS. If so, all market access limitations would be directed against services or service suppliers before they enter the domestic market. In other words, all national treatment limitations would be merely applicable after services or service suppliers enter the domestic market. Unfortunately, this post-entry standard is oversimplified in the context of the GATS. As acknowledged by the WTO Committee on Specific Commitments, in the six exhaustive categories of market access limitations, there are some restrictions with post-entry effect, such as XVI:2 (b), 'limitations on the total value of service transactions or asset', and XVI:2 (c), 'limitations on the total number of service operations or the quantity of service output'.[97] Therefore, post-entry standard cannot demarcate market access obligation and national treatment obligation under the GATS.

This article suggests that a *discrimination standard* should be introduced in order to identify which limitation measures in market access column overlap with limitation measures in national treatment column. If a market access limitation measure is also discriminatory, de jure or de facto, it will be regarded as a national treatment limitation measure as well. The 2001 Explanatory Note provides: '[I]n accordance with Article XX:2, *any discriminatory* measure scheduled in the market access column is also to be regarded as scheduled under Article XVII and subject to the provisions of that Article.'[98] The word 'any' implies that all six, limitation measures listed in Article XVI (2), can be regarded as national treatment limitation measures, provided that they are discriminatory. If a measure scheduled in market access column is non-discriminatory, then it is only a pure market access limitation measure, without any relationship with national treatment. To some extent, *discrimination standard* will strengthen the power of

[96] Mattoo, above n 69, at 112.

[97] Revision of Scheduling Guidelines, Note by Secretariat, MTN.GNS/W/164 and 164/Add.1, S/CSC/W/19, Committee on Specific Commitments, 5 Mar 1999.

[98] Above n 91, ¶ 18. This sentence is almost the same with that of the 1993 Explanatory Note. The 1993 Explanatory Note (¶ 11) States: 'in accordance with the footnotes to Article XVI:2 and Article XX:2, any discriminatory measure scheduled in the market access column is also to be regarded as scheduled under Article XVII and subject to the provisions of that Article.' Although 'Introduction' of the Explanatory Note (both in 1993 and in 2001) States that it should not be considered as a legal interpretation of the GATS, it is very helpful to understand the views from the WTO, especially from the Council for Trade in Services.

Article XVII so that it may become a long-arm article and reduce the distinction between Article XVI and Article XVII.

In comparison with 1993 Explanatory Note, the 2001 Explanatory Note States that when measures inconsistent with both Articles XVI and XVII are inscribed in the column related to Article XVI, Members *could* indicate that this is the case (eg by stating 'also limits national treatment' in the market access column).[99] The effect of this advice is restrained by the fact that the 2001 Explanatory Note 'shall be applicable as of the date of their adoption', and 'schedules in force prior to the date of this document' should be understand to have been drafted according to the 1993 Explanatory Note and its addendum.[100] Consequently, 2001 Explanatory Note has no retroactive effect, so the question of overlap and separation of Article XVI and XVII still remains, especially for those commitment schedules achieved before 2001. Even for new schedules, if some Members fail to indicate the above words in the market access column (in fact, Members have no legal obligation to implement 2001 Explanatory Note), the question still remains, and the answer to this question, is probably to make a distinction between limitation measures in the two columns or to find out an overlap between those measures based on the *discrimination standard*.

With regard to the six limitation measures listed by XVI:2, most of them belong to quantitative measures, including sub-paragraphs (a) (b) (c) (d) and (f).[101] According to the discrimination standard, the quantitative measures are not market access measures per se, depending on whether they are discriminatory. Mattoo even views the sub-paragraph (f), limitations on the participation of foreign capital, as measures, which 'in any case', are inconsistent with national treatment.[102] Potentially and theoretically, for a Member's Schedule, the more limitations there are in the column of market access limitations, the more limitations there may be in the column of national treatment limitations, even under the extreme circumstance that there is not any limitation inscribed in the column of national treatment limitations.

The discrimination standard to distinguish Article XVI and XVII seems not as clear as the post-entry standard, but it may be the standard compatible with Article XX:2 because Article XX:2 does not use the words 'Post-entry measures', but the word 'Measures' instead as a consequence of the

[99] Above n 91, ¶ 18.

[100] ibid n 1.

[101] Subparagraph (e) is related to the measures which restrict or require specific types of legal entity or joint venture. 1993 Explanatory Note and 2001 Explanatory Note classify subparagraphs (a) to (d) into quantitative restrictions, not including (e) and (f). The author view is that subparagraph (f) is about the maximum percentage limit on foreign shareholding or the total value of individual or aggregate foreign investment, so it ca be classified into quantitative restrictions also.

[102] Mattoo, above n 69, at 116.

discrimination standard, regardless of pre-entry or post-entry, national treatment restrictions will affect the establishment of commercial presence and those activities after establishment. For example, in the context of approval and licensing requirements for the establishment of a foreign bank's branch in China, if the requirements are discriminatory between foreign banks and Chinese domestic banks, those requirements must be scheduled in the column of national treatment limitations. Otherwise such differential requirements are in violation of national treatment obligation under the GATS. If the approval and licensing requirements contain the six kinds of limitation measures in GATS XVI:2, regardless of whether the requirements are discriminatory or not, they should be scheduled in the column of market access limitations. Otherwise the requirements are in violation of market access commitments.[103]

Why is it so important to precisely set out the domains of national treatment limitation measures under GATS Article XVII? Because, only after finding the complete limitations measures on national treatment, is it then possible to determine the real domains of national treatment obligations. Otherwise, national treatment obligations, as well as GATS Article XVII, would be uncertain and unpredictable.

However, knowing what is not in the domain of GATS national treatment obligations is just the first step in determining its real domain. There are other necessary steps to be taken in order to interpret the real meaning of GATS XVII and understand the domain of national treatment obligations under the GATS. If the domain of national treatment obligations on a service sector is broad, then scope of liberalization of the service sector is also broad. Since the domain may be divided by the period of time, ie pre-entry and post-entry, this issue could be simplified as the following question:

> If a Member takes a measure (not inscribed in either the market access limitation column or the national treatment limitation column) affecting the supply of services during the period of the establishment of a commercial presence, before the establishment of the commercial presence, is it in violation of national treatment obligation under GATS Article XVII? In other words, are national treatment obligations binding on post-entry measures only, or on both post-entry and pre-entry measures?

In order to answer the above question, one must resort to the GATS articles first. GATS Article XVII :1 States: '. . .[E]ach Member shall accord to services and service suppliers of any other Member, in respect of all measures affecting the supply of services, treatment no less favorable than that it accords to its own like services and service suppliers.' For the text of GATS Article XVII :1, it is unclear whether or not '*all measures*' include pre-entry and post-entry measures or just post-entry measures.

[103] See above n 91, ¶ 10.

Since Article XX:2 has connected market access limitation measures and national treatment measures, via the discrimination standard, it establishes, as discussed above in detail, that any limitation measure taken at the stage of market access could be regarded as a limitation measure of national treatment. This conclusion implies that national treatment obligations could apply throughout all stages of the supply of services.

Moreover, in GATS Article XVII :1, the ordinary meaning of '*affecting* the supply of services' is also important to determine the scope of national treatment obligations. In the EC-*Bananas III* case, the Panel pointed out:

> T]he drafters [of the GATS] consciously adopted the terms 'affecting' and 'supply of a service' to ensure that the disciplines of the GATS would cover any measure bearing upon conditions of competition in supply of a service, regardless of whether the measure directly govern or indirectly affects the supply of the service.[104]

The Appellate Body in this case supported the Panel's opinion and further held:

> In our view, the use of the term 'affecting' reflects the intent of the drafters to give a broad reach to the GATS. The ordinary meaning of the word 'affecting' implies a measure that has 'an effect on,' which indicates a broad scope of application. This interpretation is further reinforced by the conclusions of previous Panels that the term 'affecting' in the context of Article III of the GATT is wider in scope than such terms as 'regulating' or 'governing'.[105] (Emphasis added)

In addition, the Appellate Body also agreed with the Panel's conclusion that GATS Article XXVIII(c) does not 'narrow the meaning of the term "affecting" to "in respect of".'[106] In the case of *Canada—Certain Measures Affecting the Automotive Industry*, the Panel reiterated that GATS Article I does not *a priori* exclude any measure from the scope of application of the GATS.[107]

[104] Panel Report on *EC—Regime for the Importation, Sale and Distribution of Bananas*, above n 17, ¶ 7.281.

[105] Appellate Body Report on *EC—Regime for the Importation, Sale and Distribution of Bananas*, WT/DS27/AB/R, ¶ 220, 9 Sept 1997.

[106] ibid GATS Art XXVIII (c) States:

'[For the purpose of this Agreement] 'measures by Members *affecting* trade in services' include measures *in respect of* (i) the purchase, payment or use of a service; (ii) the access to and use of, in connection with the supply of a service, services which are required by those Members to be offered to the public generally; (iii) the presence, including commercial presence, of persons of a Member for the supply of a service in the territory of another Member.' (emphasis added)

[107] Panel Report *Canada—Certain Measures Affecting the Automotive Industry*, WT/DS139/R, WT/DS142/R, ¶ 10.234, 11 Feb 2000. The Panel further Stated:

'The determination of whether a measure affects trade in services cannot be done in abstract terms in isolation from examining whether the effect of such a measure is consistent with the Member's obligations and commitments under the GATS. In this case, the determination of whether . . . measures affecting trade in services within the meaning of Article I of the GATS should be done *on the basis of the determination of whether these measures constitute less*

Summing up, the above interpretations about the scope of 'measures' in the GATS all support the conclusion that the notion of 'measures' in the GATS is not a narrow one, but a broad one. In accordance with Vienna Convention Article 31:3 (b), and WTO practice, a WTO dispute settlement mechanism, could be a source of interpretation for the WTO agreements.[108]

Therefore, the ordinary meaning of Article XVII, 'all measures affecting the supply of services' should include any measure that may affect the supply of services, no matter what kind of service is supplied, or at what stage the services is supplied. Thus, national treatment obligations under the GATS are binding on both pre-entry and post-entry measures.[109]

One argument against this broad national treatment obligation is that it would reduce the meaning or effect of GATS Article XVI, and make this Article 'address primarily non-discriminatory market access restrictions'.[110] But in fact, a broad national treatment interpretation is not incompatible with discriminatory market access restrictions. If market access restrictions can be divided into 'discriminatory' and 'non-discriminatory' measures, then those discriminatory measures are national treatment limitations, *as well as market access limitations*. It is possible that some market access measures are discriminatory in the nature, like limitations on the participation of foreign capital, but it does not mean that they are not in violation of market access obligations just because they are in violation of national treatment obligations under Article XVII. The presumption of Article XX:2 is that a limitation measure may be 'inconsistent with *both Article XVI and XVII*'. It does not mean that, if a limitation measure is inconsistent with Article XVII, it will not fall into Article XVI as well. Indeed, a broad national treatment interpretation could serve to increase the applicable scope of Article XVII, and not decrease the scope of Article XVI. If a

favourable treatment for the services and service suppliers of . . . other Members as compared to domestic ones (Article XVII).'

However, this interpretation was overruled by the Appellate Body. The Appellate Body Stated: 'the fundamental structure and logic of Article I:1, in relation to the rest of the GATS, require that determination of whether a measure is, in fact, covered by the GATS must be made *before* the consistency of that measure with any substantive obligation of the GATS can be assessed.' In the Appellate Body's view, the Panel erred in its interpretation approach at this point. In my opinion, the Appellate Body is right because whether a measure is within the scope of the GATS should be decided before determining whether a measure is inconsistent with the obligation of the GATS. The opposite direction is like putting the cart before the horse.

108 Vienna Convention Art 31:3 States: 'There shall be taken into account, together with the context . . . (b) any subsequent practice in the application of the treaty which establishes the agreement of the parties regarding its interpretation.'

109 In fact, the extension of national treatment from post-entry to pre-entry is a 'revolution' for many countries. See National Treatment, UNCTAD Series, at 4, UNCTAD/ITE/IIT/11 (Vol IV), United Nations, New York and Geneva, 1999.

110 See Mattoo, above n 69, at 116.

Member's measure is not inconsistent with both market access commitments and national treatment commitments, another Member may complain against it based on both Article XVII and XVI.

On the other hand, a broad national treatment concept does not suggest that the national treatment obligations under the GATS are all-inclusive. In *Canada—Automotive* case, Canada argued that the fact that the scope of the GATS is broad does not mean that it is unlimited.[111] After all, the discrimination standard is neither a non-standard, nor a discriminatory standard. It is a standard, and a relatively fair one at that, which could reinforce the process of liberalization of trade in services.[112]

Some argue that the best way to avoid this confusion is to separate the scope of Article XVI and XVII and make them 'mutually exclusive'.[113] However, separating market access and national treatment can be very difficult. It is an undisputed fact that some market access measures are also discriminatory in nature, so they may be inconsistent with both market access obligation and national treatment obligation. How to classify those measures is the key to resolve the issue of Article XVI and XVII. A simple, arbitrary separation like so-called 'mutually exclusive' way is not a reasonable approach.

Another idea is to merge market access with national treatment, and mix the limitations into national treatment column in the Schedule. But as Hoekman argued, the problem is that some quantitative limitations are nondiscriminatory and are thus not possible to be classified into national treatment limitations,[114] so this sort of merger is not feasible.

IV. NATIONAL TREATMENT IN FINANCIAL SERVICES

A. Legal Structure of Financial Services Documents under the Gats/WTO

1. Annex on Financial Services

The Annex on Financial Services is one of the eight Annexes to the main text of the GATS, which are an integral part of the GATS.[115] Both the GATS and the Annex on Financial Services are applicable to each WTO

[111] Panel Report, *Canada—Certain Measures Affecting the Automotive Industry*, ¶ 6.735, WT/DS139/R, WT/DS142/R, 11 Feb 2000.

[112] Mattoo uses the words 'strong national treatment', not 'discrimination standard' used by this paper. See Mattoo, above n 69, at 115.

[113] See Julian Arkell *The General Agreement on Trade in Services: A Review of its Textual Clarity and Consistency*, 27 The Geneva Papers on Risks and Insurance 337, 346 (2002).

[114] See Bernard Hoekman *Market Access Through Multilateral Agreement: From Goods to Services*, 15 The World Economy 707, 720 (1992).

[115] GATS Art XXIX.

Member.[116] The Annex on Financial Services contains five paragraphs. Paragraph 1 is 'Scope and Definition', further interpreting GATS Article I in the context of financial services. Paragraph 2 is 'Domestic Regulation', and its counterpart in the GATS is GATS Article VI. Paragraph 3 is 'Recognition', which is the application of GATS Article VII in financial services. Paragraph 4 is 'Dispute Settlement', providing that panels for disputes on financial matters shall have the necessary expertise relevant to the specific service at issue in the dispute. Paragraph 5, 'Definitions', includes three definitions: 'financial service', 'financial service supplier', and 'public entity'.

2. *Second Annex on Financial Services*

Contrary to the Annex on Financial Services, the Second Annex on Financial Services is not relevant to the substantive obligations or rules respecting financial services. Rather, it only concerns the procedures for further negotiations on financial services commitments, leading to the 1995 interim agreement. It is now merely of historical interest.

3. *Understanding on Commitments in Financial Services*

There are four parts in the Understanding on Commitments in Financial Services (the Understanding). Part A is 'Standstill'; Part B is 'Market Access';[117] Part C is 'National Treatment'; Part D is 'Definitions'.

One of the questions relevant to this paper is the legal status of the Understanding. According to the Final Act, the Understanding is an integral part of it. However, because the Understanding requires a higher degree of financial service liberalization than the GATS itself does,[118] it is impossible to be accepted as an integral part of the GATS by consensus. Thus, the Understanding is only binding on those 'interested members' who have inscribed this Understanding in their Schedules subject to conditions and qualifications.[119] In other words, the legal status of the Understanding depends on a Member's voluntary act. If a Member inscribes the

[116] See *Mexico—Measures Affecting Telecommunications Services*, Report of the Panel, WT/DS204/R, ¶ 7.4, 2 Apr 2004. In this case, one of three claims made by the United States was that Mexico's telecommunication measures were inconsistent with the Annex on Telecommunications. See ¶ 3.1 (c).

[117] Part B includes eight paragraphs: Monopoly Rights; Financial Services Purchased by Public Entities; Cross-border Trade; Commercial Presence; New Financial Services; Transfer of Information and Processing of Information; Temporary Entry of Personnel; Non-discriminatory Measures.

[118] Pierre Sauvé *Assessing the General Agreement on Trade in Services: Half-Full or Half-Empty*? 29 JWT 125, 135 (1995).

[119] See the Understanding.

Understanding in its Schedule, it is binding on the Member, and all other WTO Members can obtain the benefits of the Understanding through the MFN treatment. For example, in the head note of Japan's Schedule of Specific Commitments (Financial services sector), there is a special Statement:

> In addition to Part III of this agreement (the GATS) and the Annex on Financial Services, Japan undertakes its specific commitments with respect to Financial Services under this Agreement in accordance with the Understanding on Commitments in Financial Services. Thus, the obligations under the Understanding are incurred in the sectors of Financial Services additionally to those covered by the provisions of Part III of this Agreement and the Annex on Financial Services.[120] (Emphasis added)

In the US Schedule of Specific Commitments (Financial services sector), there is a similar Statement.[121] Generally, the 'Interested Members' are members of the Organization for Economic Cooperation and Development (OECD).[122] China, however, has not made such Statement in its Schedule, so it is not bound by it.

4. *Second Protocol to the GATS*

The Second Protocol to the GATS is the main document of the 1995 interim agreement. Its function was to replace the old schedules of specific commitments and lists of MFN exemptions made at the end of the Uruguay Round with the new ones made in July 1995. Because it was only related to the specific commitments and MFN exemptions, the Second Protocol to the GATS does not generally relate to other respects of financial services.

5. *Fifth Protocol to the GATS*

On 12 December 1997, the negotiators concluded a new agreement, the so-called financial service agreement. In contrast to the financial services commitments undertaken in the Uruguay Round and in the 1995 interim agreement, the commitments undertaken in this 1997 financial agreement by the WTO Members are not temporary, but permanent, until the WTO Members conclude a new agreement through negotiations.

[120] See Japan Schedule of Specific Commitments, Supplements 3, GATS/SC/46/Suppl 3, 26 Feb 1998.

[121] See US of America Schedule of Specific Commitments, Supplements 3, GATS/SC/90/Suppl 3, 26 Feb 1998.

[122] Eric H. Leroux *Trade in Financial Services under the World Trade Organization*, 36 JWT 413, 433 (2002). See also Pierre Sauvé, 'Financial Services and the WTO: What Next?' in *Trade Rules Behind Borders: Essays on Services, Investment and the New Trade Agenda* 131, 160 (Cameron May 2003) (pointing out that no developing country has based its financial market on the Understanding).

The 1997 financial service agreement contains three legal documents: (a) Fifth Protocol to the GATS;[123] (b) Decision Adopting the Fifth Protocol to the GATS;[124] (c) Decision of December 1997 on Commitments in Financial services.[125] The most important clause in the Fifth Protocol to the GATS is paragraph 1:

> A Schedule of Specific Commitments and a List of Exemptions from Article II concerning financial services annexed to this Protocol relating to a Member shall, upon the entry into force of this Protocol for that Member, replace the financial services sections of the Schedule of Specific Commitments and the List of Article II Exemptions of that Member.

Thus, all Members acceding to the 1997 financial agreement annexed their schedules of specific commitments and lists of MFN exemptions to the Fifth Protocol to the GATS, and consequently, these commitments and lists became part of the contents under the framework of the GATS. The Fifth Protocol to the GATS became effective on 1 March 1999. The legal significance of the fifth protocol is that it improved commitments regarding market access and national treatment, and reduced the scope of MFN exemptions.[126]

6. *Decisions*

In the Final Act, there are eight ministerial decisions with respect to the GATS, one of which is the Decision on Financial Services.[127] Nevertheless, unlike the Annexes to the GATS, none of the decisions form part of the GATS. The Decision on Financial services was a procedural document to be used for further negotiation on financial services within six months after the establishment of the WTO. Since the conclusion of the 1995 interim agreement, the Decision on Financial Services has only historical value. Additionally, the Council for Trade in Services (CTS) has adopted many decisions on financial services, but all are on the subject of procedures for negotiations or the acceptance of protocols.[128]

[123] S/L/45.

[124] S/L/44.

[125] S/L/50. Decision of Dec 1997 on Commitments in Financial services was not enforced because its application requirement was that the Fifth Protocol to the GATS did not enter into force.

[126] Roger Kampf *Financial Services in the WTO: Third Time Lucky*, 4 INT'L TLR 111, 112 (1998).

[127] Others include: Decision on Institutional Arrangements for the GATS; Decision on Certain Dispute Settlement Procedures for the GATS; Decision on Trade in Services and the Environment; Decision on Negotiations on Movement of Natural Persons; Decision on Negotiations on Basic Telecommunications; Decision on Professional Services.

[128] The decisions adopted by CTS with respect to financial services include the followings: Second Decision on Financial Services (adopted on 21 July 1995),Decision on Commitments in Financial Services (adopted on 21 July 1995), Decision Adopting the Second Protocol to the

Last but not least, under the framework of the WTO, the dispute settlement mechanism is also related to financial services. Thus the Understanding on Rules and Procedures Governing the Settlement of Disputes (herein after referred to as the DSU) is generally applicable to financial services disputes, supplemented by relevant articles in the GATS and the Annex on Financial Services.[129] According to Article 1 of the DSU, the DSU covers disputes concerning the agreements listed in Appendix 1 to the DSU and Appendix 1 (Agreements Covered by the Understanding), which include the GATS.

B. *Specific National Treatment Rules in Financial Services*

According to paragraph 5(b) of the Annex on Financial Services, a financial service supplier means 'any natural or juridical person of a Member wishing to supply or supplying financial services but the term "financial service supplier" does not include a public entity'. Compared with the definition of 'service supplier' in the GATS, the definition of 'financial service supplier' is not as restrictive. GATS Article XXVII (g) provides that 'service supplier' means any person that *supplies* a service (emphasis added), while paragraph 5(b) of thc Anncx on Financial Services uses the wording '*wishing to supply or supplying* financial services' (emphasis added). This broad definition of financial service supplier means that a person (natural person or juridical person) who has not actually supplied or does not supply financial services can still be regarded as a financial service supplier, provided that he wishes to supply financial services. This broad definition of service supplier can provide additional scope for a Member to invoke GATS Article XVII in asserting claims relating to its national treatment in financial services.

In financial services, commercial presence plays a most important role. Considering the sensitivity of cross-border transaction for the stability and safety of a domestic financial system, most WTO Members seldom make national treatment or market access commitment in this respect,[130] so commercial presence is the main mode of supply in financial services and most limitations on market access and national treatment commitments are

GATS (adopted on 21 July 1995), Decision Adopting the Fifth Protocol to the GATS (adopted on14 Nov 1997), Decision of Dec 1997 on Commitments in Financial services (adopted on 12 Dec 1997), Decision on Financial Services Negotiations (adopted on 29 May 1997), Second Decision on the Acceptance of the Fifth Protocol (adopted on 26 May 2000), Third Decision on the Acceptance of the Fifth Protocol (adopted on 1 Dec 2000).

[129] GATS Art XXII:1 states: 'The DSU shall apply to such consultation.' GATS Art XXIII:1 States: 'If any Member should consider that any other Member fails to carry our its obligations or specific commitments under this Agreement, it may with a view to reaching a mutually satisfactory resolution of the matter have recourse to the DSU.'

[130] Peter Morrison *WTO Financial Services Agreement: A Basis for Further Liberalization in 2000*, 4 INT'L TLR 188, 190 (1998).

made for this mode. Since commercial presence is naturally related to investment, national treatment in financial services under the GATS/WTO has developed into the national treatment for foreign financial investment. Therefore, financial service suppliers, to the utmost extent, are juridical persons, rather than natural persons.

As aforementioned, the Understanding is applicable only to those Members who have adhered to it in their schedules of specific commitments, such as OECD Members. The participating Member must fulfill more obligations, including, inter alia, national treatment obligation, under the Understanding than those under the GATS. Part C of the Understanding reads as follows:

> Under terms and conditions that accord national treatment, each Member shall grant to financial service suppliers of any other Member established in its territory access to payment and clearing systems operated by public entities, and to official funding and refinancing facilities available in the normal course of ordinary business. This paragraph is not intended to confer access to the Members' lender of last resort facilities.

When membership or participation in, or access to, any self-regulatory body, securities or futures exchange or market, clearing agency, or any other organization or association, is required by a Member in order for financial service suppliers of any other Member to supply financial services on an equal basis with financial service suppliers of the member, or when the Member provides directly or indirectly such entities, privileges or advantages in supplying financial services, the member shall ensure that such entities accord national treatment to financial service supplier of an other Member resident in the territory of the Member.

For a Member adhering to the Understanding, it must provide national treatment to foreign financial service suppliers 'established' or 'resident' in the territory of the host Member, including at least the following:

- access to public payment and clearing systems
- access to official funding and refinancing facilities
- access to self-regulatory bodies
- access to securities or future exchange or market
- access to clearing agency

Although these accession rights for foreign financial service suppliers, based on national treatment, are only written in the Understanding and not in the GATS or in the Annex on Financial Services, it does not means that a Member not adhering to the Understanding cannot grant those rights to foreign financial service suppliers. For example, China has not acceded to the Understanding, but China, in its Schedule of Specific Commitments, commits to allowing representative offices of foreign securities institutions to become special members of Chinese stock exchanges.

In sum, the specific commitments on national treatment in financial services are included in each Member's Schedule, which should be read in the context of the GATS Article XVI, XVII and XX:2, the Annex on Financial Services, and/or the Understanding, and should be guided by 2001 Explanatory Note.

V. EXCEPTIONS OF NATIONAL TREATMENT RELATED TO FINANCIAL SERVICES

Jackson pointed out: 'No international agreement, or domestic law for that matter, can long exist without some provisions, formal or informal, for relaxing legal norms in certain circumstances.'[131] The exception issue in financial services is outstanding. In addition to the limitations on national treatment or market access listed in the schedules of specific commitments, WTO Members also have other legal rights to turn down national treatment to foreign services or service suppliers via the exceptions under the GATS or relevant agreements. Those rights enjoyed by WTO Member to derogate from WTO obligations are contained in the articles with the nature of elasticity and function of trading off. In the case of financial services, WTO Members may take advantage of several types of exceptions to avoid fulfilling national treatment obligation under some circumstances.

A. *Gats Article XII—Balance-of-Payment Safeguard*

The most important paragraph of Article XII is paragraph 1. It reads: 'In the event of serious balance-of-payments and external financial difficulties or threat thereof, a Member may adopt or maintain restrictions on trade in services on which it has undertaken specific commitments, including on payments or transfers for transactions related to such commitments. . . .' The purpose of this article is to safeguard the balance of payments of WTO Members. Its counterpart in the GATT is GATT Article XII. According to GATS Article XII, 'in the event of balance-of-payments and external financial difficulties or threat', a Member may take measures in favour of domestic services or service suppliers, which are inconsistent with its commitments on national treatment, without violating GATS/WTO obligations.

B. *Gats Article XIII—Government Procurement*

In the discussion of the scope of national treatment obligation under the

131 John H Jackson, *World Trade and the Law of Gatt* 535 (The Bobbs-Merrill Company 1969).

GATS, it is worth noting that one kind of activities is absolutely free from GATS national treatment obligation—that is 'government procurement'.[132] The condition of exception of government procurement is that the procurement must be for governmental purposes, not for commercial purposes. For example, in the Report of the Working Party on the Accession of China, China confirmed that 'all laws, regulations and measures relating to the procurement by State-owned and State-invested enterprises of goods and services for commercial sale, production of goods and supply of services *for commercial sale*, or *for non-governmental purposes* would not be considered to be laws, regulations and measures relating to government procurement. Thus, such purchases or sales would be subject to the provision of Article II, XVI and XVII of the GATS and Article III of the GATT 1994.'[133] Furthermore, not only is the national treatment obligation irrelevant to government procurement, but also market access and MFN obligations under the GATS.

C. Gats Article XIV—General Exceptions

GATS Article XIV reads as follows:

Subject to the requirement that such measures are not applied in a manner which would constitute a means of arbitrary or unjustifiable discrimination between countries where like conditions prevail, or a disguised restriction on trade in services, nothing in this Agreement shall be construed to prevent the adoption or enforcement by any Member of measures:

(a) necessary to protect public morals or to maintain public order;*

[132] GATS Art XIII States: 'Article II, XVI and XVII shall not apply to laws, regulations or requirements governing the procurement by governmental agencies of services purchased for governmental purposes and not with a view to commercial resale or with a view to use in the supply of services for commercial sale.'

[133] See ¶ 47 of the Report of the Working Party on the Accession of China, WT/ACC/CHN/49. This paragraph has binding force; see ¶ 342 of the report.

'The public order exception may be invoked only where a genuine and sufficiently serious threat is posed to one of the fundamental interests of society.' (The original footnote)

* Measures that are aimed at ensuring the equitable or effective imposition or collection of direct taxes include measures taken by a Member under its taxation system which:

(i) apply to non-resident service suppliers in recognition of the fact that the tax obligation of non-residents is determined with respect to taxable items sourced or located in the Member's territory; or
(ii) apply to non-residents in order to ensure the imposition or collection of taxes in the Member's territory; or
(iii) apply to non-residents or residents in order to prevent the avoidance or evasion of taxes, including compliance measures; or
(iv) apply to consumers of services supplied in or from the territory of another Member in order to ensure the imposition or collection of taxes on such consumers derived from sources in the Member's territory; or
(v) distinguish service suppliers subject to tax on worldwide taxable items from other service suppliers, in recognition of the difference in the nature of the tax base between them; or

(b) necessary to protect human, animal or plant life or health;
(c) necessary to secure compliance with laws or regulations which are not inconsistent with the provisions of this Agreement including those relating to:

(i) the prevention of deceptive and fraudulent practices or to deal with the effects of a default on services contracts;
(ii) the protection of the privacy of individuals in relation to the processing and dissemination of personal data and the protection of confidentiality of individual records and accounts;
(iii) safety;

(d) inconsistent with Article XVII, provided that the difference in treatment is aimed at ensuring the equitable or effective* imposition or collection of direct taxes in respect of services or service suppliers of other Members;
(e) inconsistent with Article II, provided that the difference in treatment is the result of an agreement on the avoidance of double taxation or provisions on the avoidance of double taxation in any other international agreement or arrangement by which the Member is bound.

The counterpart of GATS Article XIV in the GATT is GATT Article XX. Since GATS Article XIV stipulates that 'nothing in this Agreement' shall prevent the adoption of the special measures necessary to protect public morals, human, animal or plant life and health, etc., national treatment obligation reflected in GATS Article XVII is without exception. The three circumstances in GATS Article XIV (a) (b) (c) cover the exceptions of national treatment obligation, as well as exceptions of other obligations under the GATS, while GATS Article XIV (d) is particularly directed against GATS Article XVII in the case of differential direct taxes measures. GATS Article XIV (e) has nothing to do with national treatment exception because it is an exception of MFN obligation.

D. Gats Article XIV BIS—Security Exceptions

GATS Article XIV BIS stipulates that a Member may deviate from its obligations under the circumstances of protecting its security interests, such as actions of provisioning a military establishment, actions relating to fissionable and fusionable materials, or actions taken in time of war, etc. Article XIV BIS also uses the wording 'nothing in this agreement', which means any obligation, definitely including national treatment obligation, under the GATS may be subject to this security exception.

(vi) determine, allocate or apportion income, profit, gain, loss, deduction or credit of resident persons or branches, or between related persons or branches of the same person, in order to safeguard the Member's tax base.

Tax terms or concepts in paragraph (d) of Article XIV and in this footnote are determined according to tax definitions and concepts, or equivalent or similar definitions and concepts, under the domestic law of the Member taking the measure. (The original footnote)'

E. Prudential Carve-Out

Given the significance of financial regulation for Members, it is viewed as necessary to have a special and clear rule relating to prudential regulation, ie paragraph 2 (a) of the Annex on Financial Services, which States as follows:

> Notwithstanding any other provisions of the Agreement, a Member shall not be prevented from taking measures for prudential reasons, including for the protection of investors, depositors, policy holders or persons to whom a fiduciary duty is owed by a financial service supplier, or to ensure the integrity and stability of the financial system. Where such measures do not conform with the provisions of the Agreement, they shall not be used as a means of avoiding the Member's commitments or obligations under the Agreement. (Emphasis added)

This rule is generally called the 'prudential carve-out'.[134] According to the prudential carve-out, a Member may take discriminatory measures against foreign financial services and financial service suppliers in order to protect domestic 'investors, depositors, policy holders. . .' or to ensure 'the integrity and stability of the financial system'. This measure was very important to the Members. In fact, some held the view that the 'inclusion of financial services in the GATS would be unacceptable without a specific exception for prudential regulation and supervision'.[135]

In contrast to the limitations listed in a Schedule, prudential measures need not be included in the Schedule as limitations because they are legal exceptions specified by paragraph 2 of the Annex on Financial Services, which are not necessarily bound by financial service commitments. However, some Members still like to list prudential measures in their Schedules. This seemingly unnecessary act, in practice, may have unexpected results. On one hand, when a dispute arises as to whether a measure is prudential or not, the Member who had listed such measure in the Schedule may rely on the listing as a defense to a possible claim. On the other, a list including broad prudential measures may frustrate other Members' arguments as to whether such a measure is prudential or not. Nevertheless, no matter how many measures have been listed in the Schedule, there may still be some prudential measures not predicted and not listed in the Schedule. Therefore, prudential carve-out is always an effective tool to evade national treatment obligations for trade in financial services under the GATS.

[134] See generally, Sydney J Key *Trade Liberalization and Prudential Regulation: the International Framework for Financial Services*, 75 INTERNATIONAL AFFAIRS 61 (1999). See also Roger Kampf *Liberalisation of Financial Services in the GATS and Domestic Regulation*, 3 INT'L TLR 155 (1997).

[135] Key ibid, at 67.

Compared to relevant exception provisions in the Annex on Telecommunications, the prudential carve-out in financial service trade is, on its face, also a lack of 'necessity test'.[136] This argument could be further enhanced by the fact that the general exceptions in GATS Article XIV do not exclude the 'necessity test', and neither do the general exceptions in GATT Article XX. In some special agreements, a necessity test, if any, is clearly identified by unambiguous words, such as 'not be more trade-restrictive than necessary',[137] or 'only to the extent necessary'.[138] However, there is no similar language in paragraph 2 of the Annex on Financial Services, [139] so it may be argued that the negotiators in the Uruguay Round, when designing prudential carve-out provision, intentionally ignored or excluded 'necessity test' or 'reasonableness test', so as to make it easy for Members to invoke this exception provision in financial service trade.

VI. CONCLUDING REMARKS

Under current GATS/WTO framework, the national treatment obligation related to services is not a general principle. This non-generality, according to some critics, reduces the value of the GATS.[140] However, it is too early to totally change the hybrid approach accepted during the Uruguay Round negotiations. A reasonable and feasible approach to reform GATS national treatment provisions is to clarify the relationship between GATS Article XVI and XVII, including, inter alia, rewriting GATS Article XX:2. This is not only a theoretical issue on the structure of GATS provisions, but it is also a practical issue directly related to the extent of national treatment commitments, as well as that of market access commitments, which together determine the scope of a Member's national treatment obligations under the GATS/WTO. This paper suggests that discrimination standard should be introduced in order to identify which limitation measures in market access column overlap with those in national treatment column. The article also argues that the national treatment obligations under the GATS are binding on both pre-entry and post-entry measures.

[136] Paragraph 5(d) of the Annex on Telecommunication States: 'Notwithstanding the preceding paragraph, a Member may take such measures as are *necessary* to ensure the security and confidentiality of messages. . .' (Emphasis added)

Paragraph 5(e) also uses the word 'necessary' to limit exception situations.

[137] Agreement on Technical Barriers to Trade, Art 2.2.

[138] Agreement on the Application of Sanitary and Phytosanitary measures, Art 2.2.

[139] It is noteworthy that the TBT and GATS VI:4 necessity test only applies to trade restrictive measures which are non-discriminatory, while GATS XIV necessity test applies to both discriminatory and non-discriminatory trade restrictive measures. See *Article VI:4 of the GATS: Disciplines on Domestic Regulation Applicable to All Services*, S/C/W/96, ¶22, 1 Mar 1999.

[140] See Das, above n 40, at 100. See also Sauvé, above n 117, at 138.

Compared with provisions of national treatment under the GATS, the national treatment obligation under the framework of financial services is more flexible due to the introduction of the ambiguous concept of prudential carve-out. It is necessary to make a clearer definition of prudential carve-out in order to make it be operational for both WTO Members when exercising domestic regulation power and WTO DSB when dealing with relevant cases. However, the ambiguity of prudential carve-out does not diminish the importance of national treatment in the area of financial services. Although the national treatment issue in financial services has not been tested so far in the WTO dispute settlement mechanism, it is necessary to make further study in this highly debated field, not only for potential WTO disputes, but also for future rounds of multilateral trade negotiations, dealing with financial services.

ARTICLES: REGIONAL AND COUNTRY COVERAGE

MERCOSUR: LESSONS FROM THE RECENT PAST: THE CASE OF FINANCIAL SERVICES

EVA HOLZ*

CHAPTER OUTLINE

* Dr Eva Holz is a Professor of Commercial Law and Banking Law at the University of the Republic of Uruguay. She has been closely involved in the reform of Uruguayan law in the areas of securitisation, trusts, investments, factoring, and corporate law. In 1998, she took office as advisor to the Minister of Economy, under contract with the United Nations Program for harmonizing regulation towards MERCOSUR integration. Dr Holz was awarded a grant by the Fulbright Foundation to conduct research on the subject of 'integration of the banking system' in the Universities of Arizona, Golden Gate, and Harvard Law School. Her work resulted in publication of a book on the above topic entitled La integracion de los sistemas bancarios. She has given courses and seminars on the securities market and banking system, as well as having written several articles and texts on the subject. Dr Holz also served as Deputy Governor at the Central Bank of Uruguay (2000–2).

Acronyms and Abbreviations

ALALC. Asociación Latino Americana de Libre Comercio (Spanish, Latin American Free Trade Association).

ALADI. Asociación Latino Americana de Integración (Spanish, Latin American Integration Association).

ALCA. Area de Libre Comercio de las Américas (Spanish, Free Trade Area of the Americas).

BCRA. Banco Central de la República Argentina (Spanish, Argentinean Central Bank).

BCU. Banco Central del Uruguay (Spanish, Uruguayan Central Bank).

BID. Banco Interamericano de Desarrollo (Spanish, Inter-American Development Bank)

BIS. Bank of International Settlements.

CARICOM. Caribbean Common Market.

CCM. Comisión de Comercio de MERCOSUR (Spanish, MERCOSUR Trade Commission).

CMC. Consejo Mercado Común. (Spanish, Common Market Council, highest MERCOSUR decision-making body).

CMN. Consejo Monetario Nacional (Portuguese, National Monetary Council). Brazil.

EU. European Union.

FCES. Foro Consultivo Económico y Social (Spanish, Economic–Social Consultative Forum).

FTAA. Free Trade Area of the Americas.

GATS. General Agreement on Trade in Services (on WTO).

GDP. Gross Domestic Product.

GMC. Grupo Mercado Común (Spanish, Common Market Group, highest MERCOSUR executive body).

IOSCO. International Organization for Securities Commissioners.

IAIS. International Association for Insurance Supervisors.

IDB. Inter-American Development Bank.

IMF. International Monetary Fund.

MERCOSUR. Mercado Común del Sur (Spanish, Common Market of the Southern Cone).

NAFTA. North American Free Trade Agreement.

SAM. Secretaría Administrativa del MERCOSUR (Spanish, MERCOSUR Administrative Secretariat).

SIB. Superintendencia de Instituciones Bancarias (Spanish, Banking Institutions Supervisor), Paraguay.

SIIF. Superintendencia de Instituciones de Intermediación Financiera (Spanish, Financial Intermediation Institutions Supervisor), Uruguay.

US. United States of America.
WB. World Bank.
WTO. World Trade Organization.

I. INTRODUCTION

This chapter analyses the MERCOSUR Agreements' perspective, especially in the area of banking and other financial services. The MERCOSUR Agreements are a framework for regional integration presently being developed in the Southern Cone of Latin America, of which the States of Argentina, Brazil, Paraguay, and Uruguay are full members.

The core issue of this chapter is to examine MERCOSUR Agreements—as they have been designed and implemented—in the light of the difficulties underscored by the liberalization and integration processes, particularly focusing on the financial sector. This chapter takes into consideration in the analysis the economic and financial crises that took place first in Brazil (1999) and then in Argentina (2000–2) and Uruguay (2002).

In view of the MERCOSUR context and its country States' current economic situation, our recommendation is that it is unwise to continue the opening-up process within the MERCOSUR framework until the macroeconomic and institutional situation of all its member countries returns to normal. It is both impossible and untimely to advance in integration stages under economically unstable conditions.

The conclusion is that the MERCOSUR framework in general terms has a positive potential and may contribute to the economic growth and well-being of the countries and societies it involves. For the further development and enhancement of its positive effects, MERCOSUR should avoid or at least mitigate the risks and difficulties involved in the opening-up processes. This general conclusion applies to, and is specially developed for, the financial sector. As a consequence of this core conclusion, we will suggest some measures to consider at the MERCOSUR level, and some concrete strategies for future negotiations regarding integration and liberalization of financial services in the context of MERCOSUR, FTAA, GATS, or other liberalization agreements involving Latin American countries.

II. MERCOSUR, ITS RELEVANCE: A GENERAL OVERVIEW

A. Integration. Liberalization of Trade

The Asuncion Treaty and the subsequent Protocols adopt and generate pragmatic structures and mechanisms. They all centre round the regulation of instruments for the progressive reduction—until its total elimination—of tariff barriers and the outright annulment of any kind of non-tariff barriers that could exist in the signatory countries.[1]

However, there is an innovative component when compared to other previous integration schemes as it establishes a process of linear, gradual and automatic reduction of tariffs while at the same time it sets the objective to establish a common external tariff and the coordination of macroeconomic policies.

In terms of the institutions and bodies, pragmatism is evident in the transitory, flexible and simple nature of the structures it creates to allow for a more fluid adaptation to existing regimes in each of the signatory countries.[2]

As a result of the previous Latin American integrationist—and not always successful—experiences, the MERCOSUR Party States did not attempt, at an initial stage, to enter more deeply into potentially conflictive aspects or areas in terms of their structure or harmonization. This is a logical attitude given the fact that, in any case, the most urgent steps relate to trade areas, facilitation for the circulation of goods between countries, reduction and elimination of trade barriers.

Despite all this, the road to trade liberalization has been paved with difficulties, which was only to be expected. It takes a long time, even among developed countries, to achieve some degree of economic convergence and simultaneously keep the path to the liberalization of trade and services. Therefore, it has not been surprising that the goals set forth in the Asunción Treaty to form a Common Market on 31 December 1994—clearly too ambitious—have been postponed formally in one instance. During the CMC meeting on 4 and 5 August 1994, it was acknowledged that the original goal would not be met. Accordingly, it was agreed to start a new convergence period as from 1 January 1995. Such agreements were reflected in a number of decisions made by the CMC (Numbers 3/94, 5/94, 6/94, 7/94, 8/94, 9/94, and 10/94) and later on in the Ouro Preto CMC meeting of 17 December 1994 and decisions adopted at such meeting. That is, in 1994 a new schedule was established and it foresaw that the Free Trade Area—not fully completed to date—would come into full force as from 1 January 2000, and the Customs Union as from 1 January 2006.[3]

[1] Asunción Treaty, signed by Argentina, Brazil, Uruguay and Paraguay on 26 Mar 1991. The Asunción Treaty went into effect on 29 Nov 1991, and on that same day was filed with ALADI as Partial Scope Economic Complementation Agreement No 18.

This first agreement for formation of a common market was supplemented by a second document, the Brasilia Protocol, signed on 17 Dec 1991, and was followed by a third document, the Ouro Preto Additional Protocol signed on 17 Dec 1994.

[2] Eva Holz, *La Integración de los Sistemas Bancarios* (Montevideo, Ed. FCU 1997).

[3] CMC Decisions (Nos 3/94, 5/94, 6/94, 7/94, 8/94, 9/94, and 10/94), and subsequently

However, this schedule has been modified again—in fact, implicitly—during 2000 and 2001 due to the Brazilian crisis and its impact on the region, with the adoption of Decisions of the MERCOSUR Re-launching Common Market Council. These Decisions cover a whole range of areas such as market access, improvement of the dispute settlement system, analysis of the structure of bodies depending on the Common Market Group and the Trade Committee, or that for the Common External Tariff etc. (Nos 22/00, 25/00, 26/00, 27/00, respectively) whose object is to analyse and solve difficulties related to the operation of MERCOSUR encountered in their respective areas of competence. Later on, Common Market Council Decision Number 7/01 postponed to different periods throughout 2001 the terms that previous Decisions related to the Re-launching of MERCOSUR had set for the year 2000. It must be pointed out that such Decisions of the MERCOSUR Re-launching Council imply a relatively positive response in view of the critical situation facing the Member countries since 1999 which brought forth serious difficulties in the implementation of the MERCOSUR Agreement.

B. *MERCOSUR: Its Negotiating Capacity in Trade Agreements*

Regardless of the ups and downs in the economic integration process of MERCOSUR, the four Party States have undoubtedly formed a somewhat coherent group, especially in terms of the consideration and negotiation with interlocutors or in terms of economic agreements at international fora. It is interesting to observe that in the different processes of economic and political analysis, regional circumstances are identified with those of MERCOSUR. In this sense, the expression is used as an equivalent of the Southern Cone area of South America. In addition, the fact that countries signing the Asuncion Treaty have sometimes joined efforts when making proposals to international interlocutors, has led to the perception of MERCOSUR as an economic and political unit. Hence, the twofold effect of generating internal cohesion and a common front before the different external interlocutors.

Concrete institutional expressions of this nature and of joint international negotiation policies are already suggested in Decision Number 32/00 of the Common Market Council, vis-à-vis MERCOSUR Foreign Relations,

the CMC meeting in Ouro Preto on 17 Dec 1994 adopted Decision No 22/94, for creation of the Common External Tariff, lists of exceptions to the CET, and lists of convergence for the capital goods, computer technology and telecommunications sectors; Decision No 23/94 on the Origin Regimen for products not included in the CET or with specific requirements, all of which are subject to the Original Regime set forth in Decision No 6/94; Decision No 24/94 on the Regime for Final Adjustment to the Customs Union; and Decision No 25/94 approving the Customs Code, the basic regulations for MERCOSUR customs territory.

which reaffirms the commitment of Party States to negotiate trade agreements jointly with third party countries or groups of countries outside the area, wherever tariff preferences are agreed. Later on, this trend is defined in Decision Number 08/01 of the same body, relative to Negotiations with Third Party Countries. In this Decision, it is resolved to accelerate bilateral negotiation processes MERCOSUR is part of, in particular the ongoing one with the European Union. The latter also includes the mandate to the Pro Tempore Presidency of MERCOSUR to convene the Consultative Council following the Agreement signed by the MERCOSUR Party States and the Government of the United States of America, in order to study the possibility of initiating bilateral negotiations under the 4 + 1 format. To this effect, a Negotiation Group has been organized and its number one priority will be the consensual definition of a common negotiation platform. The President of IDB, Dr. Enrique Iglesias, has been invited to act as Senior Advisor of the Negotiation Group.[4]

One aspect of great relevance for the continuity and success of this new role of MERCOSUR lies upon each of its Party States policies—particularly Brazil and to some extent Argentina, toward MERCOSUR and the region. By this, we refer to the importance they will attribute to MERCOSUR's best interests as a whole, especially where those interests may clash with others on the national sphere.

It must be pointed out at this stage that the fact that MERCOSUR is negotiating necessarily as a block with FTAA, US and the European Union, will constitute an element of alignment and consistency, necessary for the Regional Agreement. The joint policy of such negotiations, with developed countries as counterparts, will make it an imposition and an obligation to preserve consistent parameters that adjust to policies and macroeconomic coordination and, in addition, are consistent in setting tariffs, as an essential requisite to successful progress.

C. *Financial Globalization and Macroeconomic Strengthening*

In the light of the successive Asian, Russian and Brazilian crises, followed by the Turkish and, recently, the Argentine crisis, it becomes imperative to question whether the benefits of globalization and financial integration justify the absorption of their costs and risks, dramatically experienced by societies.

In fact, the liberalization of the circulation of goods, services and capitals generates trade growth—and as result, product growth—increasing efficiency in terms of the global location of resources and capitals which are, therefore, more efficiently used and contribute to the wellbeing and

[4] CMC Decision No 32/00, CMC Decision No 08/01.

improvement in the standards of living of many societies subject to the integration framework. In the specific sense of financial globalization, many countries in Asia and Latin America have had the possibility to modernize their industry and their economy, at least in part, due to the fact that they have had freer access to available external savings, regardless of the need to recognize the advisability of protecting their dependency on very short-term capitals.

On the other hand, the growing perception of risks—relative to crises or to a higher probability of a crisis extension—and the resulting costs to societies in terms of loss in well-being for the population, requires our profound study in order to avoid them or at least mitigate them.

Precisely, the increasing possibility of 'contagion' due to financial globalization, should not lead us to lose sight of factors inherent to each country that represent the underlying causes of their fragility in resisting external blows. This leads us inexorably to the need for macroeconomic strengthening of each one of the countries themselves, beyond integration processes, as a true way to mitigate individually the impacts of financial globalization.

Furthermore, globalization may contribute to deepening crises due to the persistent application of imbalanced macroeconomic policies. Under such circumstances, a trigger to spark off the crisis could be the investors' loss of confidence in the maintenance of policies in a given country, causing them to withdraw their investment and thus close access to international credit.

What the Asian, Russian and Brazilian crises have had in common is that—despite the fact that they responded to partially different reasons—they were generated and aggravated by persistent macroeconomic inconsistencies, due to persistence of unsustainable structural deficits and significant external debt, mostly too short-term, or any other similar deficit-financing mechanisms, without substantial corrections of the reasons generating them. It is essential that macroeconomic policies of countries lead to sustainable values in terms of deficit, debt and product growth.

III. FINANCIAL LIBERALIZATION—REFLECTIONS

A. *Macroeconomic Coordination in Regional Integration*

1. *Macroeconomic Situation in the MERCOSUR Countries 1999–2002*

Entry into effect of the MERCOSUR gave rise to a rapid and intensive increase of trade flows among the member countries. For example, Argentine exports to Brazil rose from US$1.67 billion to US$7.7 billion in 1997.[5]

[5] Holz Eva *The Impact of Financial Crises on Regional Integration Processes. The Case of*

Brazil, with a GDP of approximately 500 billion dollars has a significant influence on MERCOSUR trade. Argentina represents approximately 40 per cent of Brazilian production and the Uruguayan and Paraguayan product together do not reach 5 per cent of Brazil, which supports our statement. Additionally, this explains why Brazilian macroeconomic stability is so relevant in the region.[6] This has repercussions on the level of regional trade—which notoriously increases during periods of stability—as occurred since the implantation of the Real plan. However, in turn, it is clear that growth of trade in the region is also explained by a relatively higher level of prices in Brazil than in the rest of its trade partners and by a preferential rate of customs duties among them. All this enables us to understand that the increase of trade in the region, at least in part, took place at the expense of an increase in the Brazilian trade balance. As an example, in 1993, the Brazilian trade surplus reached 13.3 billion dollars, while in 1998 the trade deficit was over 6 billion dollars. Over this same period, Uruguayan and Argentine exports to Brazil increased by 150 per cent and 188 per cent respectively (even considering goods that are hard to place on other markets and that are exported under MERCOSUR special regimes).[7]

In this context, the exchange rate started undergoing sustained pressure as from mid-1998, when the Russian crisis broke out. This pressure caused a significant loss of reserves, linked to the evolution of the increasing fiscal deficit and the level of Government indebtedness, to which political factors were added.[8] Thus on 15 January 1999 the Central Bank of Brazil withdrew from the exchange market. Devaluation of the Real finally became stable at approximately 50 per cent, although during the last months of 2000 (and throughout 2001) it again showed an upward trend. Together with exchange measures, the Brazilian Government adopted various substantive measures in order to reduce the fiscal deficit, making it possible for the economic and financial variables to become stable during the year 2000. Thus, during 2000, industrial activities in Brazil grew approximately by 7 per cent, export of goods grew 17 per cent and imports 14.6 per cent. Inflation during the same year was almost 6 per cent. The economy stabilized and grew slightly during 2001 and 2002, inflation was kept under control, and the Real oscillated between 3 and 3.5 per U$ dollar (mostly due to political uncertainty prior to Brazilian elections which took place at the end of 2002).

the Crisis in the Brazilian Economy (1999) and MERCOSUR (paper presented at the Sixth Annual Conference of the International Law Review Association of Southern Methodist University) (27 Mar 1999).

[6] ibid.
[7] ibid.
[8] ibid.

2. *Repercussions*

The Brazilian crisis eliminated overvaluation of the Real, involving among other things, the modification of trade flow within the MERCOSUR due to a drop in exports to Brazil and an increase in Brazilian exports to the other member countries of the Agreement.[9]

These elements conspired to lessen demand for goods and services in the countries of the region, leading to a drop in production. The prices of the various goods and services also tended to drop, with both aspects leading to the consequent recessive effect. Product fell to all countries of the region (the most affected cases being that of Argentina and Uruguay with drops of 3.5 per cent in the GDP), unemployment rose substantially (14.5 per cent in Argentina, 6.3 per cent in Brazil, 11.2 per cent in Uruguay, 9 per cent in Paraguay and 10 per cent in Chile) and the rate of inflation in all the above-mentioned countries also dropped.

It is evident that the significant variation in the economic situation of the various MERCOSUR member countries, which went hand in hand with the correction of many prices of goods and services traded intra-regionally had repercussions—in an ongoing process—on the evolution of integration. However, the final results will depend significantly on the type of mechanisms used to mitigate the impact of such price changes.

3. *The impact on Argentina. Its consequences on Uruguay*

As from the recessive adjustment of 1999 which, among other consequences, led to a drop in the price of tradable goods, during the first half of 2000 an improvement in the merchandise account was observed, becoming a surplus. However, recession continued during 2000. It should also be remembered that since 1989 with the implantation of the convertibility plan, the exchange rate in Argentina was fixed, parity being established at one peso per US dollar. During 2000, unemployment rates continued to be close to 15 per cent. Although exports showed an upwards trend, the GDP dropped slightly, public income continued to fall, and in spite of the successive attempts at containing public expenditure and at increasing collecting, the deficit in public accounts continued to rise. At the end of the year, this led the Government to request financial assistance ('shielding') from the international funding bodies (International Monetary Fund) for an amount of U$39,700,000 announced at the beginning of 2001. During 2001 the situation was further complicated by the closure of foreign capital markets and deterioration of fiscal accounts, already to be observed at the beginning of the year. During March 2001, the Minister of Economy was changed

[9] ibid.

three times. The last one, Cavallo, promoted a plan to make the country's economy competitive once again, eluding more cuts in expenditure. Among the measures adopted, mention can be made of taxes on bank transactions, unilateral modification of MERCOSUR customs duties, sectoral reactivation plans with special tax treatment for sectors considered to be strategic, and the creation of a 'trade dollar' which in fact involved a change in the convertibility exchange system. He also adopted measures to improve the external debt profile. Simultaneously, in order to obtain domestic credit, he reduced the reserves of financial institutions, and modified their composition, admitting National Government obligations for the purpose of constituting the reserve. In this way, the strength of the financial system was undermined, increasing its exposure to Government risk. Halfway through the year, when the bid for domestic obligations failed, Cavallo had to admit that he did not have domestic credit, and introduced a budgetary ruling of zero deficit, also applicable to the Provinces which were temporarily authorized to finance their excess expenditure by issuing obligations with canceling power (quasi-currencies such as the LECOP and the Patacones). The debt in the Government's paying capacity and the antecedent of the 1989 Bonex Plan led to a persistent drain on the system's deposits. In this context, recession was worsened with drops in investment of over 20 per cent, notoriously lessening domestic consumption, with the consequent reduction of GDP.

Finally the economy collapsed (in December 2001) and new economic and financial rules were issued by the Government (eg Law No 25561, 7 January 2002), which were focused on employment, on reasonable income for the population and, to that end, on reducing its indebtedness with the financial system. But those rules at the same time meant the collapse of the paying system, the credit chain and the end on the confidence in Argentine financial system. Also, it destroyed the Argentine reputation in the international credit and financial markets. For instance, on 24 December 2001, the Argentine Government defaulted its debt (141 billion US dollars); the convertibility currency rule was changed (1 peso equal to 1 US dollar) and all of a sudden, a couple of days later (January 2002) the peso was worth one third of one US dollar; almost all deposits were frozen, meaning that depositors could not withdraw their savings from the banking system ('corralito'). Also in January 2002, banks had to accept that many debts named in US dollars or other strong currencies could be cancelled by paying in the Argentine devaluated currency (peso) at nominal parities (one peso one dollar, when the peso at the time was worth one third of a US dollar), but depositors had to be maintained and finally paid back in the currency of the original deposit or at a parity to be fixed by the Executive Power in order to preserve the value of the saving, which was called 'pesificación asimétrica.' These rules meant the insolvency of all financial institutions. There are estimates that during 2002, bank losses due to asset depreciation amounted to 20 billon US dollars. The above-described situation was followed by some international banks deciding (ie New Scotia bank) to quit their operations in Argentina. The subsequent economic measures applied by the new Government during the year 2002 and the first part of 2003 were unsuccessful, especially regarding the 'rebuilding' of the financial system. The IMF and other international financial organizations criticized the inconsistency of the Government's economic measures. Public debt is still in default. Since July 2002, the economy has begun its recovery, but still without the assistance of a local operating banking system: there is no domestic or international credit, and international trade is mostly financed by some international financial institutions.

The collapse of the Argentine financial system first had an impact (January 2002) on those banks operating in both countries, Argentina and Uruguay, when the restrictions imposed on operations in Argentina forced Argentine bank clients to withdraw their deposits from the Uruguayan branches of the same institutions. This initial development was soon followed by a general run of most Argentine depositors from all Uruguayan financial institutions, even from international banks, due to their fear of having their deposits frozen in Uruguay as well, in the event that similar measures to those imposed in Argentina should be adopted by the Uruguayan Government. As the Argentine crisis continued during 2002, its impact on the Uruguayan economy worsened over the same period, causing continuation of the depositors' run. In the context of currency exchange, on June 2002 Uruguay abandoned its crawling peg system, allowing the Uruguayan peso to float. In July 2002, a bank holiday was declared, four private banks were suspended (not liquidated but closed), and deposits on two seriously illiquid State-owned banks where extended for two years, to be paid in the currency in which the deposit was established. Rules for solvent banks (international banks) were not changed. There was no general freezing of deposits, or any change in the currency of deposits. From January 2002 up to July 2002, Uruguayan financial system lost over 40 per cent of its deposits. Finally, in December 2002, Law No 17613, 27 December 2002, was passed, establishing a new procedure for the liquidation of the four suspended banks, and broadening Central Bank regulatory and controlling powers over private and public financial institutions as well as on private bank shareholders, directors and managers. On the other hand, public debt was not defaulted, and in May 2003 a voluntary extension of same was agreed by international and local Uruguayan debt-holders.

4. *The Need for Macroeconomic Coordination*

The need for consistent macroeconomic policies is increased within the framework of a regional integration process. In fact, a comparison of experiences and of MERCOSUR itself reveals that macroeconomic coordination represents an unavoidable foundation to consolidate integration agreements. In the case of this region, the situation over the last few years reveals once again that the lack of close coordination among the governments of the Parties in the definition and implementation of the macroeconomic variables that simultaneously affect each and every one of them, is what has underlain all the difficulties that have been threatening the continuity of MERCOSUR since 2000.[10]

Relevant monetary, currency, and inflation policies; the situation and evolution of the balance of payments, and of balance of trade; close follow-up of these and other relevant variables in the respective economies, are some of the aspects affecting each the countries simultaneously. For this reason, all stages of macroeconomic policy implementation—from initial definition to the necessary and permanent follow-up process to monitor their evolution on a daily basis—require coordinated thought on the part of all governments in the countries undergoing integration processes.

The more the progress observed in the liberalization of the flow of trade and services due to the implementation of the integration Agreement, the more the repercussion on the rest of the Party States of maladjustments—at the level of each of the main economic variables—in any of the member countries. We can demonstrate the truth of this statement—even in the early stages of the opening-up process in MERCOSUR—by observing the adjustments that the radical change of the Brazilian foreign exchange criteria gave rise to and will still require, that led to an unforeseeable and unaligned fluctuation in the relative prices of goods and services at the level of the other MERCOSUR partners.[11]

An essential element in the improvement of coordination is to intensify the flow and quality of information that countries exchange, relative to both the public and private sectors. In addition, information transparency must be enhanced. For example, information in terms of international reserves, foreign debt—especially short-term foreign debt—and capital flows from each one of the countries. This information, together with its follow-up, will enable a more precise assessment of the situation and risks facing each of these countries and the region to be made. Enhanced-quality information will, in turn, influence the adoption of more accurate and appropriate economic measures, as it facilitates analysis and discussion on the part of the other partner countries.

[10] See above subsection III.A.1.
[11] ibid.

B. Political Commitments in the Implementation of Coordinated Macroeconomic Policies

The prevention of distortions in the macroeconomic policies of the region calls for an intensification of coordination on the part of countries and for a high level of reciprocal, political commitment. Each one of the governments is responsible not only for the sound development of the variables in its own country but also for ensuring that their own policies are not obstacles in the development of economies in the other member countries of the integration agreement. From the very outset of MERCOSUR, this commitment was taken up by the four Party States—basically in an implicit and consensual way—on the understanding that none of the signatory parties of the Asuncion Treaty would fail to comply.

However, over the last couple of years there has been enough evidence of the shortcomings of this commitment, which has not been complied with on more than one occasion since 1999. This leads us to confirm that the new integration stages within the scope of MERCOSUR will call for more formal and intense mechanisms to keep macroeconomic coordination commitments among the countries. Any breach in coordination rules should involve pertinent and detrimental consequences for the offender.

The initial steps in that direction are first suggested in Decision No 6/99 of the Common Market Council which calls for the creation of a Top Level Working Group in the sphere of the Meeting of Ministers of Economy and Presidents of Central Banks with the objective of coordinating macroeconomic policies in the Member States.[12] The fields covered are intertemporal sustainability of the countries' public and external accounts; the alternatives for macroeconomic coordination and a working programme proposal to that end; the harmonization of statistical macroeconomic and financial information and the intensification of information relative to methodological criteria used by each State to prepare their respective economic indicators. Likewise, Decision No 30/00 of the Common Market Council entrusts Ministers of Economy and Presidents of Central Banks with the preparation of harmonized statistics based on a common methodology in macroeconomic and financial services areas. Harmonization will start with the information included in the Nominal Fiscal Results and Primary Fiscal Government Result, the Governmental Net Debt and that of the Consolidated Public Sector and the level of prices. Indicators relative to fiscal aspects must be published as from September 2000. Harmonized statistics were first published on 21 October 2001.

This process must be expedited and deepened for the sake of regional economic wellbeing as well as for MERCOSUR integration perspectives.

[12] ibid.

Clear commitments must be made regarding macroeconomic variables and their convergence. Non-compliance with those commitments should cause diplomatic and/or economic penalties to the offender, which should be established according to their severity.

C. *Clear Policies in Bank Integration*

To date, MERCOSUR and its Party States have not addressed financial liberalization in depth. Apart from the mechanism implemented so far—the preparation of lists of offers and commitments for service liberalization—the fact that from the time of the subscription of the Montevideo Protocol up until now, no progress has been made in the incorporation of financial services to such lists, is remarkable. Moreover, restrictions and limitations to liberalization expressed by the countries when the initial list of commitments was prepared in the framework of the Montevideo protocol have not been altered. Let us recall that that first list simply gathered the commitments that each country already presented as a list to the WTO, with no additional considerations, even in cases where they could have been feasible without having to introduce changes at the level of national legislation (at present, as from 2001, the work of the Services Group includes the detection and incorporation to the lists of the country's commitments, non-restricted areas in terms of internal regulations and, despite this, not included in the specific commitments). We must also bear in mind that such lists of offers and commitments were created and presented under those conditions despite the fact that the information relative to the existing spaces for greater openings and liberalizations was then available, as a result of the work conducted by Sub-group IV.[13]

The lack of political will to start with the necessary liberalization to harmonize and integrate financial sectors is reaffirmed by other means with the Brazilian decision expressed at the level of Sub-group IV and included in their Minutes 1/95 of 20 October 1995, which postpones until the year 2000 consideration of attempting to harmonize in any aspect related to derogation of restrictions to access and invest in the financial sector, by companies from a MERCOSUR country in any of the other Party States.[14]

This situation clearly reflects the lack of commitment to move forward in financial integration and to reduce and finally eliminate restrictions to competition that are still present in some countries.

[13] See CMC Decision No 13/97 (Montevideo Protocol about Mercosur Commerce Services); CMC Decision No 9/98 (Financial Service and Initial List of Specific Commitments Annex); CMC Decision No 36/00 (South Africa Negotiations); see also WTO's complete text of the Final Agreement, Uruguay Round and of the General Agreement on Trade and Services (GATS).

[14] CMC Decision No 9/95.

At this point, it is relevant to stress that the opening up on the range of activities granted to bank institutions and investing regimes, which took place in the MERCOSUR countries during the 90s, was not a consequence of the Agreement. It was due to national policies of some of the Party States following international trends.

On the other hand, it is natural that at present, as the whole region and its Party States are immersed in macroeconomic crises, it is neither timely nor advisable to address a financial liberalization agenda. The macroeconomic instability that conspires against commercial integration has a stronger negative incidence in the case of financial integration due to the possible systemic and contagious repercussions in the financial systems of each country. Only when the region reaches stability will it be able to reconsider its agenda and aim at a financial opening and integration within MERCOSUR.

In due course this process should undoubtedly be approached carefully and gradually in order to avoid excesses in deregulations with prudential implications or with marked lack of protection of the weaker segments in the financial systems of each country. These elements, according to evidence, have neither been analysed nor coordinated.

D. Opportunities for Liberalization in Banking Activity

An analysis of the financial system regulations in the countries of MERCOSUR reveals that there is still plenty of room to liberalize such services, increasing competition. This declaration is especially valid in an integration context as many of the restrictions that we have referred to have a particular impact on the supply of financial services that can be developed in any MERCOSUR country and in the foreign investment (from companies in other Party States) in each one of them.

The Member countries, in general, over the last decade—and consistently as is the trend observed in the rest of Latin America—have expanded their range of activities granted to banking institutions, and have admitted in one way or another foreign investment in the sector. All this has been done regardless of the fact that, simultaneously, they have imposed stricter prudential rules to the whole of their banking system. As pointed out previously, the opening up in banking regulation and investing regime was not due to the Agreement. It was part of the national policies of some of the Party States following international trends.[15] On the contrary, many aspects of the modifications and strengthening of prudential rules imposed in each

[15] International organizations like BIS, IOSCO, IAIS, IMF, WB, IDB, and WTO foster the liberalization and opening up to foreign investment and competition in financial sectors. Some of them, on the other hand, also promote the strengthening of the prudential requisites (BIS, IMF, WB, IDB).

of the Party States were due to a coordinated policy decided at MERCOSUR level.[16]

Nevertheless, if we compare these advances with the general international trend we may conclude that there is still ample room for opening up in the banking industry. In addition, the levels of liberalization admitted by each one of the Party States are diverse. This may potentially have repercussions in the sense of creating uneven conditions for competition in the sector. For example, in terms of the banking activity, the MERCOSUR countries, in general, do not admit universal banks, meaning that banking institutions cannot normally provide all the range of financial services, operate as securities agents, or render any other services related to the capital market. Neither can they perform activities related to insurance. On the other hand, there is some margin to make the investment scheme of banking institutions more flexible, enabling them to invest in the capital market sector and in non-financial institutions, allowing for the establishment of financial and insurance clusters, and by more freely accepting foreign investment in the sector.

Another parallel phenomenon is observed in the sense that there are also areas where liberalization might be possible—as there are no regulatory obstacles preventing this—but, nevertheless, countries neither offer nor commit greater openings in the framework of negotiations of the Montevideo Protocol and the Financial Services Annex. For example, this is perceived in the areas of trans-boundary supply and foreign consumption of insurance and banking services, where none of the countries has consolidated their offers. Another example can be the horizontal commitments of Brazil, applicable to insurance and banking services, relative to foreign investment or to the limitation in the employment of foreign staff that exceed the existing constitutional and legal restrictions.[17]

The above observations do not mean that countries should attempt the maximum level of opening that is possible in their financial services to achieve integration. However, they will duly require a common approach

[16] All the MERCOSUR countries have adopted requirements for credit risk-weighted capital of at least 10 per cent of the assets. Another valuable example is that, on the basis of the Subgroup's policy harmonization efforts regarding prevention and struggle against legitimization of assets from illegal activities, set out in Recommendation No 01/00 submitted to the Common Market Group, this body adopted Resolution No 53/00 regarding 'Minimum Regulation Standards to be adopted by Central Banks for the prevention and repression of money laundering.' In turn, this Resolution gave rise to Common Market Council Decision No 40/00 adopting the 'Cupertino Convention among Central Banks in the Party States to the MERCOSUR, for the prevention and repression of procedures aiming at the legitimization of assets from illegal activities.' Also, by Common Market Group Resolution No 20/01 it was stipulated that the Party States should adopt the information transparency rules recommended by the Basle Committee before 31 Dec 2005.

[17] See above n 13.

strategy, to move ahead with caution—but not indiscriminately—to attain liberalization stages that are in themselves balanced in order to avoid competitive distortions among the integrated countries. This harmonization is essential so that, when the access of financial institutions to other MERCOSUR countries—that are not the country of origin—starts to be liberalized, the institutions' trend to establish themselves or to provide financial services from one country and not from others—caused by a difference in the schemes related to activities and investment allowed in the banking sector—can be avoided.

For example, Paraguay today is the only MERCOSUR country that completely and clearly allows universal banks. In full integration contexts where the rest of the countries do not admit this broad activity to their financial systems, we would probably observe that all banks in the region would settle in Paraguay in order to take advantage of the greater business opportunities that the universal activity grants them. Additionally, from the Paraguayan subsidiary or branch they could offer such services to their customers throughout the region. Likewise, if Brazil maintains its present restrictive foreign investment scheme in the banking sector, in an integration context we would observe that international and regional banks would settle in any other MERCOSUR country to provide all banking services to their Brazilian customers through that branch and to request their being acknowledged as an institution installed within MERCOSUR to provide services to the Federative Republic of Brazil.

Along this road to liberalization, and in order to mitigate the impact of the opening up and increased competition, it may be temporarily necessary for some of the Governments to protect certain key areas in banking services. For example, it may be temporarily wise not to dismantle the totality of benefits or protection to sectors such as local banking or to certain institutions that have social objectives. These partial policies reduce the more potentially negative impacts of integration and can be appropriate instruments for the gradual opening of the markets.

The greater competition, resulting from the opening and a certain level of deregulation, may cause a trend towards banking concentration and consolidation, at least in the short run, as part of the possible strategies of the financial institutions to reduce the effects of the growing presence of new competitors. In any case, facilitating market access that adds to the general phenomena of globalization and internationalization can alleviate the trend towards concentration. On the other hand, a certain consolidation of the banking sector may constitute an institutional strengthening factor, a very necessary factor to preserve the solvency of the system in a more competitive and deregulated environment.

E. Liberalization Mechanisms

Another aspect to be considered involves the instruments specifically used to integrate MERCOSUR financial sectors as it clearly conveys the influence and solutions of the GATS Agreement of the World Trade Organization. In the light of results attained, this strategy so far has not been able to meet the expectations of its supporters.

The approach and concrete solutions to integrate services as set out in the Montevideo Protocol are very similar to those of the General Agreement on Trade and Services of the WTO,[18] with the exception that in the former the most-favoured nation clause has no limitations, while it does have limitations in the WTO Agreement. This analogy is once again observed in the Annex to Financial Services in the Montevideo Protocol, which includes the solutions of Annex to Financial Services of the General Agreement on Trade and Services of the WTO. Moreover, CMC Decision No 36/00 adopts the GATS services classification of the World Trade Organization to classify services within the scope of MERCOSUR.

In short, the instrument used by MERCOSUR to approach liberalization of trade in services has been that of a trade agreement with the aim, as is the case of the Agreement on Trade and Services of the WTO, of creating a Free Trade Area. This is a very different approach from the one used by the European Union towards the creation of a Common Market. We have explained at length the reasons why the MERCOSUR Member countries have adopted this approach instead of favouring solutions more similar to those adopted by the European Union.

Another element adding to the complexity of the mechanism under study lies in the fact that the liberalization resulting from the preparation of banking service lists with a high degree of disaggregation, makes the opening and the negotiation of offers and commitments therein included very fragmented and complex. It is very difficult to compare offers by analysing their equivalences.[19]

On the other hand, a different and necessary approach to the study of the process towards financial integration can be obtained by comparing the existing regulatory restrictions in the national schemes to the commitments and offers in each country within the framework of the Montevideo Protocol at the different negotiation rounds conducted by the Services Group. Since the signing of the Montevideo Protocol, the approach to the negotiation for the opening of services was the definition of the areas of service where each country prepared at a later stage, individually and freely, its own list of offers and commitments. Moreover, this led each country to propose offers and commitments at the MERCOSUR, analogous to those

[18] See above n 13. [19] ibid.

that it had previously presented at the WTO. This situation remains unchanged at present and in spite of the fact that there are areas where liberalization would be possible—there being no regulatory obstacles to prevent it—the countries, notwithstanding, neither offer nor promise a greater opening within the framework of the Montevideo Protocol and the Annex to Financial Services. An example of this is perceived in the area of trans-boundary supply and foreign consumption of banking and insurance services, where none of the countries has consolidated its offer.[20]

Another aspect to be stressed up, linked to the latter, is the need to deepen and systematize the coordination between the MERCOSUR bodies in charge of the harmonization process (Sub Group IV) and the liberalization negotiations (Services Group). Better coordination would give the Services Group necessary tools—up-to-date information—to put adequate pressure on the representatives of the Member countries to improve their offers and deepen their commitments during the liberalization negotiations.

Therefore, in view of the points raised, and the evolution that bank integration has achieved over the years, it may be said that it would be advisable to rethink whether this strategy is in fact the best one to address and implement the aforementioned integration process. We would suggest at least inverting the concept of the lists of offers and commitments and instead gradually liberalizing the universe of services—in a similar way to goods liberalization—with the exceptions stated by each country in the list corresponding to the nature of service involved.

IV. PRUDENTIAL REQUISITES IN LIBERALIZATION AND GREATER COMPETITION

In terms of prudential rules, the MERCOSUR countries have made efforts—even today—to harmonize and approach solutions. In addition, that coordination has been oriented towards increasing the requirements by adapting to, and in some cases exceeding, international recommendations. For example, only Argentina considers capital requirements on the basis of market risk; in Paraguay basic capital and supplementary capital are not separated even though all the capital components suggested by Basle are contemplated in its regulations. It should also be noted that asymmetries existing in credit risk asset weighting have not been updated at the present time.

The policy adopted at MERCOSUR level to strengthen prudential rules in each Member Country does not mean that all difficulties and asymmetries have been solved. For example, all MERCOSUR countries maintain minimal net worth requisites during the operation of the financial institu-

[20] ibid.

tions, whose amounts are calculated, in general, following the recommendations of the Basle Committee (relation between the capital or computable net worth items and risk-weighted assets). However, the content of such demand is diverse and its comparative analysis is difficult. Also, if we compare the application of the recommendations of the Basle Committee in the four countries, we can observe that even when all of them apply the recommendations, capital composition is not equal and asset weighting varies from country to country.[21] Thus, Argentina requires a minimal proportion whose range depends on the goods under consideration, of 8 per cent capital in terms of the assets weighted by risk. Brazil, Uruguay and Paraguay require 10 per cent, though the latter's Central Bank is entitled to increase that minimal proportion up to 12 per cent. Furthermore, the differentiation between basic and supplementary capital (Tier 1 and 2 of the Basel Committee), is not present in the Paraguayan standards.[22]

Additionally, in the rest of MERCOSUR countries the items admitted in one or the other, and their consideration, maintain certain differences. For instance, when computing inflation, when revaluating goods, in the admission and treatment of subordinate debt, etc. Differences are also noticeable in the way each country weights its assets against risk, to apply the requirements of capital on this. This leads us to consider whether in order to strengthen national financial systems and their integration potential, some of the remaining asymmetries become significant. So far, we can attest that beyond some difficulties when interpreting or comparing the requirements in each country, it is essential that all of them regulate and implement the Basle recommendations in full, in relation to the composition of capital and its amount, by weighting it in terms of the different risks the institution may have to face.

Precisely in view of a liberalization and deregulation context—so characteristic of integration—it is imperative to preserve and to strengthen the soundness of banking systems for the sake of financial stability. No models exist that may be transplanted in terms of prudential regulations. Similarly, control must respond to the new and more deregulated framework and this requires training and experience, implying a certain amount of application time.

The special importance of domestic financial systems, which is intensified in a potential integration context, lies in its close impact on the macroeconomic variables and in the ease with which the difficulties of this sector

[21] Argentina: Law No 21526, 14 Feb 1977, Communications A Nos. 2470, 2754, 2970, 2753, 2774, 3007, 3022, 3959 and B No 4489; Brazil: Lei No 4.595, de 31 de dezembro de 1964, and Resolutions BCB Nos 2099, 2122, 2212, 2309, 2606, and 2607; Paraguay: Law No 861; 12 July 1996; Uruguay: Law-Decree No 15.322, 17 Sept 1982, Law No 16327, 11 Nov 1992, Decree No 614, 11 Dec 1992, and Circulars Nos 1613, 1721, and 1847.

[22] ibid.

can be transmitted to the other countries of the region, and even to the rest of the world, through payment systems, and inter-banking credits and deposits.

Thus, it is necessary to balance the opening of the banking sector and the preservation of its soundness. There are no recipes to accomplish this. There are institutional factors, aspects related to pre-existing regulations and even elements relative to the circumstantial situation of the banking sectors, which have a direct influence on the rhythm and degree of liberalization and, therefore, on the subsequent cautionary adjustments.

Whereas deregulation can generate a certain idle capacity in the banking sector, this can be a transitory factor of financial fragility. The new context for greater openness, which enables new types of business and opportunities to financial stakeholders, simultaneously requires new rules that are clear and intense, which adjust the focus and objective of the standards to the new reality of the sector and the mobility of operators. It is necessary to give support to the development of a banking sector which is adequately capitalized, has good liquidity and management and which can correctly balance risk and profitability. This, in turn, also implies fluid and transparent information and a correct regulation and prudential control. This requires training and adjustments in control and regulations that help keep pace with economic agents. It also implies more emphasis on, for example, internal banking management systems, risk management, internal control, stronger implementation of international standards in terms of accounting, auditing, etc. It is important to develop sound commercial practices and, simultaneously, facilitate the differentiation between debtors, even before international credit markets which—as investors and lending institutions—will look closely at all improvements and modifications that may be introduced in this group of emerging countries. All of this should be done without completely drowning the benefits sought by liberalizing the banking sector—this may easily happen if the opening is either very sudden or excessive.

V. MERCOSUR: STRATEGIES FOR FUTURE NEGOTIATIONS WITH THIRD PARTIES ON FINANCIAL AREAS

A. Location

In the scope of negotiations related to trade liberalization agreements, MERCOSUR as a political factor could become very relevant if it established strategies oriented to strengthen and develop its activity sectors. In all cases, we refer to negotiations or agreements regarding the opening up of the economies or the financial sectors of the MERCOSUR countries to be actually implemented only after the macroeconomic and institutional situation of all its member countries returns to normal. In relation to said future negotiations and or agreements, our comments will focus on the use of the political capacity of MERCOSUR in the stable and solid growth of banking institutions and activities throughout the region. On the other hand and at the same time, the joint negotiation policy of such negotiations, with developed countries as counterparts, will benefit and help the implementation of MERCOSUR integration process. Negotiations with developed countries will make it an imposition and an obligation for MERCOSUR to preserve consistent parameters that adjust to the policies and macroeconomic coordination and, in addition, to be consistent in setting tariffs, as an essential requisite to advance them successfully.

In this regard, and as a means to approach a feasible strategy, we must bear in mind that the trend of international organizations vis-à-vis the liberalization of financial markets and the simultaneous strengthening of prudential standards will maintain its influence in the whole of Latin America and, within this hemisphere, in the MERCOSUR countries.[23] Let us recall that, even when reforms introduced in the MERCOSUR countries in the nineties expanded the activities permitted to the banking institutions and made pre-existing restrictions for foreign investment in the sector more flexible, there are still significant margins for a possible liberalization. Stricter prudential rules and standards must necessarily be implemented to accompany the liberalization process, as was the case in the 1990s.

On the other hand, in order to prepare a strategy to negotiate new trade agreements, especially those relative to accessing markets to supply financial services, some elements relative to the banking sector should be borne in mind:

In order to compete successfully in the context of global financial markets (electronic banking, merged capital markets) considerable investment must be made in technological development.

Competition in the global financial sector implies that smaller institutions will not be able to survive due to their more limited range of supply of services and proportionally higher fixed costs when compared to larger enterprises. Customers, even investors and consumers, will be attracted to lower prices in services rendered, easier access (via home computer or at the supermarket) to any financial service they want, which will be offered mostly by the largest institutions.

Some local Latin American financial institutions, mainly Chilean and Brazilian ones, have started to develop strategies and to invest in order to position themselves in this new context. They are incorporating cutting-edge technology, they are undergoing reengineering, and they are acquiring smaller financial institutions both in their countries of origin as well as in

[23] See above subsection III.D.

third party countries. Their core assets are the know-how they develop, based on the best technology and their management models which enable them to offer a wide range of financial services in any market globally.

The MERCOSUR countries, with the exception of Brazil, so far have made their schemes more flexible to admit foreign investment unilaterally in the banking sector and this has not granted them returns in terms of accessing other markets. In addition, this could imply a specific difficulty to local financial clusters that might require the support of joint governmental policies to overcome the barriers that block their access to other countries when trying to render financial services. A similar analysis may be conducted in terms of the possibility of encouraging and strengthening regional financial clusters. The latter, on the other hand, may become a useful tool to mitigate the trend of financial concentration in the largest multinationals that have recently generated uncertainty as to the soundness of their policies when countries and regions where they have established get into critical situations.

B. Context and Strategies

MERCOSUR should focus their external negotiations in an attempt to neutralize or mitigate the trend towards direct liberalization spurred by international organizations and by the majority of countries in the developed world,[24] by granting the financial institutions of its Member States at least gradual concessions to allow them access—restricted today—to provide financial services in foreign markets.

These aspects are essential so that MERCOSUR Party States may obtain greater benefits in such negotiations and the latter do not result in mere openings of economies to the trade flows coming from third countries. This bears special significance in the light of the potential growth of the banking sector in the MERCOSUR countries. The direction that negotiations take in the international arena may define how and who will be able to develop this potential for expansion.

The General Agreement on Trade and Services of the World Trade Organization and the Basle Committee are and will be factors of great influence on the banking regulations of MERCOSUR countries, and on Latin America in general.[25] The first emphasizes liberalization and the second the strengthening of prudential standards in the banking sector. Recently, recommendations of the World Bank, the International Monetary Fund and the Inter-American Development Bank have been contributing to both trends—greater opening and increased prudential requirements in the financial activity.

[24] ibid. [25] ibid.

The four MERCOSUR countries have signed the General Agreement on Trade and Services of the World Trade Organization which promotes competition in the financial sectors by avoiding anti-competitive practices in those institutions and a greater efficiency in the allocation of resources and services of the financial industry. These concepts are being implemented in different ways by each country: Argentina first and in greater depth and, recently, Brazil, has privatized several federal banks.[26] In addition, they have dismantled pre-existing monopolies in the banking activity. This has all been done without designing or foreseeing a common strategy in the framework of the World Trade Organization. This should be corrected. Furthermore, the United States of America and some other countries such as the United Kingdom and Germany have been negotiating directly with some of the countries, mainly with Brazil and Argentina, to open financial markets. In the context of these bilateral negotiations, it is easy for any of the developed countries to preclude the access of MERCOSUR entities to their own market, for example, by stating the exception to prudential standards accepted by the General Agreement on Trade and Services of the GATS. This circumstance would hardly take place during a joint negotiation by the block, due to the greater power of the group.

In terms of fundamental aspects, the MERCOSUR countries benefited from the adjustments they introduced to their financial systems between 1980 and the late 1990s. Privatization, mergers, readjustments and banking modernization have produced positive effects. On the other hand, the lack of common strategies at the level of MERCOSUR, vis-à-vis an opening in foreign investment in the banking sector, may have a negative influence in the development of local financial institutions. These institutions may require consistent governmental policies to overcome the barriers that prevent foreign institutions from operating in some countries. It would be recommendable to help local institutions to face the growing trend towards concentration around international financial conglomerates. It is true that the latter contribute investment, business expertise, technology and innovation. However, excessive concentration may lead—in case of a crisis of one or any of these international institutions—to dramatic consequences at the global level, especially in countries where their presence is more relevant. It may also contribute to make capital flows more volatile—and, in consequence, may cause restrictions in domestic credit, in so far as multinational financial institutions move their resources from one region to another extremely quickly, following decisions of their headquarters in response to changing circumstances and better business opportunities. Accordingly, we must point out and bear in mind that the new Basle capital rules—that will come into force in a couple of years—will probably bring about a reduction

[26] ibid.

of investment on the part of international banks or financial conglomerates in the region. Therefore, the generation of strategies to strengthen and develop negotiation opportunities for regional entities –even including clusters—may represent an efficient way to really preserve competition in the local markets, avoiding—or at least, mitigating—an excessive concentration in financial oligopolies and, simultaneously, diminishing the risks of a potentially greater volatility of capital flows or of a potential crisis at the level of any financial institution operating in a highly concentrated market.

BIBLIOGRAPHY

A. REGULATION

A.1. INTERNATIONAL REGULATION

ALCA (FTAA)

—America's Meeting—Miami Principles Declaration—December 1994.

—ALCA Ministerial Meetings Joint Declarations.

—First Trade Ministerial Meeting—Denver, EE.UU.—30 June 1995. Joint Declaration

—Second Trade Ministerial Meeting—Cartagena, Colombia—21 March 1996. Joint Declaration.

—Third Trade Ministerial Meeting—Belo Horizonte, Brasil—16 May 1997. Joint Declaration.

—Forth Trade Ministerial Meeting—San José, Costa Rica—19 March 1998. Joint Declaration.

—Fifth Trade Ministerial Meeting—Toronto, Canadá—4 November 1998. Joint Declaration.

—Sixth Trade Ministerial Meeting—Buenos Aires, Argentina—7 April 2001. Joint Declaration.

—ALCA Agreement Draft April 2001.

MERCOSUR

(a) Decisions of Common Market Council (CMC Decisions):

—Decision No 8/93—17 January 1994—Capital Markets minimum regulation.

—Decision No 10/93—17 January 1994—Adoption of Basel Rules.

—Decision No 13/97—15 December 1997—Montevideo Protocol about Mercosur Commerce Services.

—Decision No 9/98—23–24 July 1998—Montevideo Protocol about Mercosur Commerce Services—Specific sectorial rules attachments and initial commitments lists.

—Decision No 12/98—July 23–24, 1998—Montevideo Protocol—about Mercosur Commerce Services.

—Decision No 1/00—30 June 2000—First round Negotiation for specific commitments in services.
—Decision No 3/00—30 June 2000—Mercosur origin regulation.
—Decision No 6/00—30 June 2000—General plan of reciprocal cooperation and coordination for regional safety regarding child traffic.
—Decison No 8/00—30 June 2000—General plan of reciprocal cooperation and coordination for regional safety regarding financial and economic crimes among Mercosur States.
—Decision No 14/00—30 June 2000—Neighboring Traffic Regulation among Mercosur states.
—Decision No 18/00—30 June 2000—Definition and configuration of safety information exchange system among Mercosur states.
—Decision No 22/00—30 June 2000—Market access.
—Decision No 24/00—30 June 2000—Mercosur Administrative Secretary.
—Decision No 25/00—30 June 2000—Improvement of Brasilia's dispute settlement system Protocol.
—Decision No 26/00, 30 June 2000—Analysis of Common Market Group and Commerce Commission subordinated bodies.
— Decision No 27/00, 30 June 2000—External Common Tariff.
—Decision No 28/00, 30 June 2000—Commercial and competition defense.
—Decision No 29/00, 30 June 2000—Defense rules against subsidies granted by non Mercosur countries.
—Decision No 30/00, 30 June 2000—Macroeconomic Coordination.
—Decision No 31/00, 30 June 2000—Inversions, production and exportation incentives, including Free Trade Zone, Temporary Admission and other special systems.
—Decision No 32/00, 30 June 2000—External Relationship.
—Decision No 36/00, 30 June 2000—South Africa Negotiations.
—Decision No 37/00, 30 June 2000—Mexican Negotiations.
—Decision No 40/00, 14–15 Dec 2000—Cooperation Agreement between Mercosur Centrals Banks for prevention and repression of money laundering operations.
—Decision No 51/00, 14–15 Dec 2000—Global Preferences System.
—Decision No 53/00, 14–15 Dec 2000—Administrative Cooperation Agreement—Mercosur Aladi General Secretay.
—Decision No 56/00, 14–15 Dec 2000—Second Round Negotiation for specific commitments in services.
—Decision No 57/00, 14–15 Dec 2000—Markets access.
—Decision No 64/00, 14–15 Dec 2000—Commerce and competition defense.
—Decision No 65/00, 14–15 Dec 2000—Improvement of dispute settlement system.

—Decision No 67/00, 14–15 Dec 2000—External common tariff.
—Decision No 69/00, 14–15 Dec 2000—Special importation customs rules.
—Decision No 70/00, 14–15 Dec 2000—Mercosur automotive policy.
—Decision No 03/01, 22 June 2001—Mercosur action program against illicit activities in international commerce.
—Decision No 04/01, 22 June 2001—Mercosur automotive policy.
—Decision No 05/01, 22 June 2001—High level group for the examination of consistency and dispersion of external common tariff.
—Decision No 07/01, 22 June 2001—Timetable adjustment for Mercosur relaunching program.
—Decision No 08/01, 22 June 2001—Mercosur and third countries negotiations.

(b) Common Market Group Resolutions:
—Resolution No 62/97, 13 December 1997—General conditions of civil responsibility in transportation insurance.
—Resolution No 63/99, 27–29 September 1999—Compulsory civil responsability insurance for some cases in international trips—damages caused to objects or persons not transportated.
—Resolution No 3/00, 4–5 April 2000—Modification of Mercosur common nomenclature and its corresponding AEC.
—Resolution No 36/00, 26–28 June 2000—Deepening of specific commitments in services.
—Resolution No 43/00, 26–28 June 2000—Ad hoc Group for electronic commerce Group Ad Hoc.
—Resolution No 44/00, 26–28 June 2000—Ad hoc Group for public works or services concessions creation.
—Resolution No 76/00, 5–7 Dec 2000—Deepening liberalization commitments in services 'III Round Negotiation for specific commitments in services'.
—Resolution No 01/01, 28–29 March 2001—Decision Project 'Exceptional Rules in Tariffs'.
—Resolution No 25/01, 12–13 June 2001—Modification of Common External Tariff.

(c) Subgroup No 4 Acts:
—Act No 1/95—First Meeting, Oct 1995.
—Act No 2/96—Second Meeting, 8–10 Apr 1996.
—Special Meeting Act, 7–9 Aug 1996—(Chart of account).
—Brazil report on Financial Affairs Negotiations evolution (Brazil, October 1996).
—Third Act Meeting, 6–8 Nov 1996.
—Fourth Act Meeting, 28–29 Aug 1997.
—Fifth Act Meeting, 17–18 Nov 1997.
—Sixth Act Meeting—First of 1998, 4–6 May 1998.

—Seventh Act Paraguay Meeting, 17–18 May 1999.
—Eighth Act Montevideo Meeting, 20–21 Oct 1999.
—Ninth Act Montevideo Meeting, 20–22 Oct 1999.
—Tenth Act Argentina Meeting, 26–28 Apr 2000.
—Eleventh Act Recife Meeting, 25–27 Oct 2000.
—Twelfth Act Paraguay Meeting, 9–11 May 2001.
Common Market Group Acts:
—Act No 01/01—Extraordinary Meeting, 28–29 Mar (Asunción).
Common Market Council Act:
—Act No 01/01—2nd Extraordinary Meeting in Buenos Aires 7 April 2001.
OMC (WTO)
—Sectorial Specific Commitment List
—Legal Text: WTO Agreement.
—Uruguayan Round Final Act Summary.
—Uruguayan Round Final Act Full Text.
—Annex 1B: General Agreement in Services.
—Financial Services Decision.

A. 2 NATIONAL REGULATION

ARGENTINA
(a) Banking regulation:
—Law No 21526, 14 Feb 1977, modified by Laws Nos 22.871, 8 Aug 1983, 23.267, 1 Sept 1989; and 22144, 23 Sept 1992; Decree Nos 1860, 13 Oct 1992, 1887, 15 Oct 1992, 146/94, 21 Feb 1994, 290, 27 Feb 1995, Laws No 24.485, 5 April 1995, and 24.627, 11 Feb 1996.
—Central Bank of Argentina Statute, Law No 24144, 23 September 1992, Decree No 1860, 13 Oct 1992, and Decree No 1887, 22 Oct of 1992).
—Communication A 2729, 6 July 1998.
—Communication A 2840, 13 Jan 1999.
—Communication A 2893, 31 Mar 1999.
—Communication A 2935, 25 June 1999.
—Communication A 2936, 25 June 1999.
—Communication A 2937, 25 June 1999.
—Communication A 2950, 16 July 1999.
—Communication A 2970, 11 Aug 1999.
—Communication A 3028, 2 Dec 1999.
—Communication A 3128, 30 June 2000.
—Communication A 3278, 1 June 2001.
—Communication A 3307, 31 July 2001.
—Communication A 3314, 6 Aug 2001.
(b) Capital markets:

—Law No 17811, 22 July 1968, modified many times, last modification: Law No 24241, 13 Oct 1993.

(c) Insurance:

—Insurance Law No 17.418, in force since 1 July 1968.

—Insurance and reinsurance activity law No 20.091 in force since 1 July 1973, modified by law No 24241, dated 19 Oct 1993.

—Regulation of Insurance Advisor Producer Activity Law No 22400, in force since 17 Aug 1981.

—Resolution No 25565, in force since 1 Apr 1998.

BRASIL

(a) Banking regulation:

—Law No 4.595, de 31 de dezembro de 1964 (31 Dec 1964).

—Law No 4.728, de 14 de julho de 1965, regulating the access of foreign institutions to national financial system (14 July 1965).

—Resolution No 1.524, 17 Aug 1994.

—Resolution No 2.099, 17 Aug 1994.

—Resolution No 2.193, 31 Aug 1995.

—Resolution No 2.197, 30 Aug 1995.

—Resolution No 2.211, 20 Nov 1995.

—Resolution No 2.212, 20 Nov 1995.

—Resolution No 2.267, 29 Mar 1996.

—Resolution No 2.474, 27 Mar 1998.

—Resolution No 2.543, 26 Aug 1998.

—Resolution No 2.606, 27 May 1999.

—Resolution No 2.607, 27 May 1999.

—Resolution No 2682, 22 Dec 1999.

—Resolution No 2.692, 1 Mar 2000.

—Resolution No 2.724 1 June 2000.

—Resolution No 2.977 6 April 2000.

(b) Capital Markets:

—Law No 6.385, 7 Dec 1976—regulates Capital Markets and the Securities Commission.

—Law No 6.404, 1976—regulates Corporations.

—Law No 9.457, 5 May 1997, modifies laws No 6.385 and No 6.404.

—Resolution No 1656, 26 Oct 1989.

(c) Insurance:

Law-Decree No 73, 21 Nov 1966.

CHILE

(a) Banking regulation:

—Banking Law No 19.528, 4 Nov 1997.

(b) Capital markets:

—Law No 18.045, 22 Oct 1981. The law has been modified in many opportunities, last modification: Law No 19601, 18 Jan 1999.

PARAGUAY

(a) Banking regulation:

—Law No 861/96, 12 July 1996.

—Decree No 18/52.

—Law-Decree No 18, 25 Mar 1952—creates the Central Bank of Paraguay.

(b) Capital markets:

—Law No 1284/98, 4 Aug 1999.

(c) Insurance:

Insurance and Reinsurance Law, Law No 827, 12 Feb 1996.

URUGUAY

(a) Banking regulation:

—Law-Decree No 15.322, 17 Sept 1982—regulates the Financial Intermediation System

—Law No 16.327, 11 Nov 1992 which reforms the last.

—Decree No 614/92, 11 Dec 1992, reglamentary of Law 16.327.

—Central Bank of Uruguay Statute, Law No 16696, 30 Mar 1995.

(b) Capital markets:

—Law No 16749, 30 May 1996.

—Law No 16774, 27 Sept 1996

—Decree 344/96, 28 Aug 1996.

—Law No 17202, 24 Sept 1999.

(c) Insurance

—Law No 16.426, 21 Oct 1993.

—Financial Intermediation Laws No 15.322, 17 Sept 1982 and 16.327, 11 Nov 1992, which apply by referral of Sec. 5 of Law No16.426.

—Decree No 354/94, 17 Aug 1994.

B. DOCTRINE

B.1 BOOKS

Abreu, Bonilla 'Mercosur e integración', Montevideo, 1991, 2th Edición.

Aguinis, Ana María 'Empresas e inversiones en el MERCOSUR', Argentina 1994.

Aguirre, Ernesto and Norton, Joseph 'Reform of Latin American Banking Systems. National and International Perspectives.' Kluwer Law International (International Economic Development Law, Vol 11), 2000.

Andenas and Kenyon Scade 'EC Financial Markets Regulation & Company Law' (1993).

Babace Héctor 'La libre circulación de los trabajadores en el MERCOSUR', Estudios multidisciplinarios sobre el MERCOSUR

Bicker, Lyn 'Private Banking in Europe', USA, United Kingdom, 1996.

De Mello, Xavier 'El MERCOSUR después de Ouro Preto', Montevideo 1995.

Dermine ' European Banking in the 1990s' (1990).

Di Biase, Héctor N 'El Mercosur después de Ouro Preto', Montevideo 1995.

Durán, Augusto (coordinador) 'El MERCOSUR después de Ouro Preto. Aspectos jurídicos', Montevideo 1995.

Esteva, Eduardo G 'El Mercosur después de Ouro Preto', Montevideo 1995.

Fry, Maxwell Publ. Info. 'Central Banking in Developing Countries: Objectives, Activities, and Independence' USA, United Kingdom, 1996.

Gaggero, E 'Armonización de las legislaciones sobre transporte en el MERCOSUR', en Estudios multidisciplinarios sobre el MERCOSUR, Montevideo 1995).

Gamio, José Ma 'El Mercosur después de Ouro Preto', Montevideo 1995.

Gavalde and Soufflet 'Les Institutions' France (1990), 'Droit Bancaire' France (1992).

Goodhart 'The Central Bank and the Financial System' (US 1995).

Gruson, Michael and Reisner 'Regulation of foreign banks: United States and International', USA 1995.

Hablutzel, Philip N 'International Banking Law' Vol 1, 1994 New York.

Holz, Eva La integración de los sistemas bancarios, Ed. FCU, Montevideo, 1997.

Hopt and Wymeersch 'European Company and Financial Law', 1991.

Klein, Dietmar 'The Banking Systems of the EU Member States', United Kingdom, 1995.

Kluver 'Banking and EC Law: Commentary' (1992).

Margariños, Gustavo 'Uruguay en el Mercosur', Montevideo 1991.

Moreiro González, Carlos Javier 'Banking in Europe after 1992' (US 1993).

Opertti, Didier 'El Mercosur después de Ouro Preto', Montevideo 1995.

Prentice 'EEC Directives on Company Law Financial Markets' (1991).

Reinicke Wolfgang 'Banking, Politics and Global Finance. American Commercial Banks and Regulatory Change, 1980–1990', 1995.

Schneider, Hellwig, Kingsman 'The German Banking System' 4th edn Germany (1986).

Villegas, Carlos Gilberto 'Compendio jurídico, técnico y práctico de la actividad bancaria', Buenos Aires 1989, 2a. Reimpresión.

Wright 'Industrial and Banking privatization in Western Europe: Some public policy paradoxes', Italia (1995).

B.2 OTHER PUBLICATIONS

Alford, Duncan ' Basle Comitee International Capital Adequacy Standards: Analysis . . .', 10 Dick J Int Law 189 (1992). 'Basle Comittee Minimun Standards', 26 Geo Wash J Int L & Econ 241 (1992).

Arellano, Félix 'La relación entre el Multilateralismo y el Regionalismo:

Algunas reflexiones sobre sus implicaciones para los países en desarrollo', in Regional Meeting UNCTAD/PNUD/CEPAL with collaboration of LATN, Santiago de Chile, 4–5 Nov1999.

Cull, Robert 'The Effect of Foreign Entry on Argentina's Domestic Banking Sector', for World Bank and WTO Conference 'Liberalisation and Internationalisation of Financial Services', 10 May 1999.

Devlin, Estevadeordal, Garay 'The FTAA: Some Longer Term Issues' IADB, INTAL/ITD, August 1999, Occasional Paper 5.

François Joseph, and Schuknecht Ludger 'Trade in Financial Services: Procompetitive Effects and Growth Performance', for World Bank and WTO Conference 'Liberalisation and Internationalisation of Financial Services', 10 May 1999.

Gardener, Molyneux, Moore, and Winters 'The impact of the Single Market Programme on EU Banking', Institute of European Finance, for World Bank and WTO Conference 'Liberalisation and Internationalisation of Financial Services', 10 May 1999.

Garza Miguel Angel 'The Mexican Financial System Towards the Next Century', for 6th Annual Conference of the International Law Review Association of Southern Methodist University, Dallas, 29 March 1999.

Granados, Jaime 'El ALCA y la OMC: Especulaciones en torno a su interacción' IADB, INTAL/ITD, August 1999, Occasional Paper 4.

Hablutzel, Philip N 'British Banks Role in United Kingdom'. 68 Chi Kent L Rev 365 (1992).

Hindley, Brian 'Internationalisation of Financial Services: A Trade Policy Perspective', for World Bank and WTO Conference 'Liberalisation and Internationalisation of Financial Services', 10 May 1999.

Holz, Eva 'The impact of Financial Crises on Regional Integration Processes. The Case of the Crisis in the Brazilian Economy (1999) and MERCOSUR' (paper presented at the Sixth Annual Conference of the International Law Review Association of Southern Methodist University) (27 Mar 1999).

Kaji, Gautam 'The Internationalisation of Financial Services: Not Just Another Sector' An Issues Note for the Ministerial Workshop, WB, 1997 Annual Meeting WB/IMF, 25 September.

Kono, M et al 1997 'Opening Markets in Financial Services and the Role of the WTO', Geneva, WTO, Special Study 1.

Miller, Eric 'Financial Services in the Trading System: Progress and Prospects' IADB, INTAL/ITD, July 1999, Occasional Paper 4.

Norton, Joseph 'The Development of Public Financial Law: a "New Financial Arquitecture"?, for 6th Annual Conference of the International Law Review Association of Southern Methodist University, Dallas, 27 March 1999.

OECD Publications and Information Center, 'The New Financial

LandScape: Foreces Shapint the Revolution in Banking, Risk Managment and Capital Markets', Fr 1005.

O'Keefe, John 'Risk based capital standards for banks. Improvements in Letter of Credit Update, December 1995.

Scott, Hal 'Competitive implications of the Basle Capital Accord' in Saint Luis University Law Journal VII International Conference of the Academy of Commercial & Consumer Law, Vol 39, No 3 spring 1995).

Steinberg Marc 'Legal Reform and the Importance of Robust Securities Markets' for 6th Annual Conference of the International Law Review Association of Southern Methodist University, Dallas, 27 March 1999.

Tórtora, Manuela 'The Asian Crisis: Impact on Mexico and Latin America', for 6th Annual Conference of the International Law Review Association of Southern Methodist University, Dallas, 27 March 1999.

Van Empel and Mörner 'Financial Services and Regional Integration', for World Bank and WTO Conference 'Liberalisation and Internationalisation of Financial Services', 10 May 1999.

Ventura, Días Vivianne and team, International Trade Unit from International trade and development financing divisions, UN, CEPAL/ECLAC, 'América Latina en la agenda de transformaciones estructurales de la Unión Europea', Santiago de Chile, July 1999 (Temas de coyuntura)

Vives Xavier 'Competition and Regulation in European Banking', for World Bank and WTO Conference 'Liberalisation and Internationalisation of Financial Services', 10 May 1999.

Ying Qian, 30 April 1999 'Financial Services Liberalisation and GATS. The Commitments Under de General Agreement on Trade in Services at the World Trade Organization', for World Bank and WTO Conference 'Liberalisation and Internationalisation of Financial Services', 10 May 1999.

REGULATORY JURISDICTION AND THE COUNTRY OF ORIGIN PRINCIPLE IN THE FINANCIAL SERVICES SECTOR AFTER THE E-COMMERCE DIRECTIVE

IRENE TAGLIAMONTE*

CHAPTER OUTLINE

I. INTRODUCTION

The advent of the Internet as a mechanism of global communication has raised new challenges for existing financial laws and regulations by reason of its purely virtual geography. Any on-line transaction, even though it appears to take place between actors in the same jurisdiction, normally involves international factors and may therefore potentially result in an application of more than one legal system.

This essay is intended to focus on the Community efforts regarding distribution of regulatory jurisdiction among Member States in connection with the offering and supplying of financial services via the Internet. This

* Post-graduate research law student, London School of Economics and Political Science.

problem is particularly important, since the financial sector is one of the most heavily regulated areas of commercial activity.

This paper addresses the difficulties in adapting the principles of jurisdiction and the criteria of localization to the on-line environment, traditionally applied to the off-line financial sector. The peculiarity of the approach rests on the adoption of an international law perspective.

The essay has been structured into two sections.

The first section concerns the general division of national responsibilities in the Financial Directives[1] with respect to the off-line world. In particular, the country of origin/mutual recognition scheme is analysed in the light of the general principles of jurisdiction of international law, with a view of pointing out its meaning, scope and operation.

For this purpose, reference is also made to the Commission interpretative initiatives aimed at clarifying the resulting complex legal scenario. In addition, the interaction of the country of origin as a public law principle with the private law area is considered, so as to assess how connecting factors used for private international law purposes have been proposed to determine the applicability of regulatory rules. Conversely, this paper will also address how regulatory principles of community legislation impact the operation of the conflict of law rules.

The second section is envisaged to examine the extent of which the community principles allocating regulatory jurisdiction have changed as a consequence of the entrance into force of the E-Commerce Directive (ECD).[2] Thus, the new regime provided for Internet-based activities is outlined and compared to the one encompassed under the Financial Directives. Its relationship with private international law is also analysed, to assess whether the country of origin provided for under the ECD constitutes a conflicts rule.

Moreover, relevance is given to the recent international initiatives to promote co-ordination of national jurisdictions through the introduction of a targeted-based approach. A role of this internationally developed solution within the framework of the ECD is proposed in order to benefit, at least in crucial areas, of a partial alignment between regulatory, civil and court jurisdiction.

Finally, it should be underlined that, given the different approaches endorsed under the several instruments, which impact the subject under examination, the resulting regime shows an extraordinary level of intricacy.

[1] The paper focuses to the Second Banking Co-ordination Directive ('2BCD') No 89/646 (1986)OJL386/1 as amended by Directives (i) 92/30(1992)OJL110/52 and (ii) 95/26(1995)OJL168/7, the Investment Services Directive ('ISD') No93/22(1993)OJL141/27 as amended by Directive 95/26(1995)OJL168/7, hereinafter collectively referred to as the 'Financial Directive'.

[2] European Parliament and Council Directive on Certain Legal Aspects of Electronic Commerce in the Internal Market, COM(1998) 586 Final-98/03125(COD), adopted 13 Dec 1999.

This multiform ongoing scenario gives rise to interesting problems of interpretation and coordination of the various applicable rules into a consistent legal system. Therefore, this paper primarily attempts to suggest—when feasible—how consistency might be increased, as well as to outline those areas still riddled with legal uncertainty.[3]

II. GENERAL ISSUES OF JURISDICTION IN THE FINANCIAL SERVICES SECTOR

A. Introductory Remarks

1. General Principles of Jurisdiction under International Law

Historically, the concept of State jurisdiction derives from the relatively recent Westphalian model of public international order, as shaped upon the principles of sovereignty and equality of States. In this context, States—as independent and supreme entities within the boundaries of their own territory—emerged as sovereign actors in an international system based on formally horizontal relationships.

The concept of jurisdiction is the other side of the coin of the sovereignty principle. It expresses in legal terms both a power and a duty of a State: the power to regulate, judge and enforce within its own territory and the duty not to intervene into other sovereign States' domestic affairs.

Although jurisdiction is closely linked to the notions of sovereignty and territoriality,[4] the principle of extraterritorial jurisdiction is nonetheless recognised under international law in so far as its application is balanced against the interests of international comity.[5]

Jurisdiction is therefore intended both to justify and self-limit the assertion of governmental authority. Accordingly, as a general term, it refers to the legitimate scope of the legislative, judicial and executive powers, which in turn give rise to the three kinds of jurisdiction: prescriptive (or regulatory) jurisdiction, adjudicatory jurisdiction and enforcement jurisdiction.

As to the jurisdiction to prescribe, on which the present essay is intended to focus,[6] it reflects the ability of a State to issue and apply its substantive (private or public) laws to persons and situations. According to international law, traditional principles supporting assertion of prescriptive jurisdiction are based on the notion of nationality and that of territoriality.[7]

[3] How far this attempt will be achieved, only the reader will judge.

[4] CONFORTI (23), 133.

[5] On the extraterritoriality, see WESTBROOK (94), 71 et seq.

[6] However, given the inter-dependence of the above-mentioned kinds of jurisdiction, references may be incidentally made to the other categories.

[7] Additional principles of jurisdiction, which have no relevance in the contest of this essay and therefore will be not analysed herein, are the so-called 'protective jurisdiction (power to punish a limited number of offences directed against the integrity or the security of a State) and the universal jurisdiction (over international crimes, for instance piracy).'

The nationality principle justifies assertion of control over conduct of nationals (natural as well legal persons), wherever they are. Nationality may be the basis for a country to prescribe—although it may not be able to enforce its law—over nationals in another country's jurisdiction. In civil and commercial matters, prescriptive jurisdiction is commonly determined on the basis of the principle of establishment or domicile, which are variants of the nationality principle.

The territoriality principle confers prescriptive jurisdiction to the State in which the persons or the goods in question were situated or an event took place. Granting an exclusive power over, and within the ambit of a territory, this principle recalls the problem of localisation of persons and behaviours. Moreover, territoriality gives rise to two distinct principles of jurisdiction: subjective and objective. Subjective territoriality recognises jurisdiction over a State where acts, which originated within its territory, were completed abroad; while objective territoriality gives a state jurisdiction over acts originated abroad but completed, at least partially, in its territory.[8]

An extension of the objective territoriality principle is the so-called 'effects doctrine,' according to which a state may claim jurisdiction on the ground that an activity or a harmful event produced direct, foreseeable and substantial effects within its own territory. This principle has been the basis for US courts to apply local law in anti-trust cases and is particularly controversial as an unduly interference with third States' sovereignty.[9]

2. *Division of Prescriptive Jurisdiction Among EU Member States*

The ultimate effectiveness of the general principles of jurisdiction depends on their application within domestic legal systems. In enacting the above principles, each State delineates the scope of its legislation by reference to its frontiers, or the nationality/domicile of persons, with a view to respect the comity of nations and to not interfere with the legitimate affairs of other states.

Although this self-limitation of the State authority vis-à-vis equally ranked entities is a fundamental duty under international law, the decentralised nature of international relationships renders it impossible to impose it coercively and thus to reach uniformity of solutions. As a consequence of

There is an enormous literature on jurisdiction in international law. See, inter alia, Mann (61); Brownlie (10); and Bowett (9). For a brief overview on the principles of jurisdiction traditionally applied by national courts see Long (58), 502 and Campbell (13) 24.

[8] Objective territoriality was recognised by the Permanent Court of the International Justice in the *Lotus* case (1927), PCIJ, Ser A, No 10, 23. However, there is great uncertainty about the scope of the decision: see Brownlie (10) 305.

[9] On the extraterritorial application of the US as well as EU competition law *see* Jones and Sufrin (49) 1040 et seq.

this basic structure of international relations, the matter of coordination among the plurality of legal systems has been generally dealt with through national conflict of laws (or choice of law) rules.

However, the recent phenomenon of regionalization and the growing importance of international organizations have pushed towards the verticalisation of international relations, affecting the traditional notion of state sovereignty. This new environment has led to additional methods for allocating regulatory jurisdiction among states, which apply along with the traditional decentralized and horizontal approach.

The above change is wholly reflected within the EU, where the establishment by the Treaty of Rome of an internal market pursuant to the principle of free movement called for some sort of supra-national coordination of the relations between the Member States' legal systems.[10] In this respect, the allocation of prescriptive jurisdiction has been often conducted in accordance with a centralised system, in which EC law making institutions have been in charge of determining the Member States' respective responsibilities. Each Member State, in turn, has been given a more limited role of implementing the community scheme in its internal legal system. In particular, member states are required to issue rules whose content and scope of application shall be consistent with the division of tasks provided at the community level.

B. Allocation of Regulatory Jurisdiction in the Financial Sector

1. Country of Origin, Mutual Recognition and Single Licence

In the ambit of the financial sector,[11] the allocation of prescriptive jurisdiction has been achieved with a view to increasing liberalisation and improving the functioning of the internal market in financial services.

As the financial sector is traditionally one of the most strictly regulated of the economy, the liberalisation proved to be very complicated.[12] Notwithstanding the basic freedoms under the original EEC Treaty,[13] Member States retained the power to apply national provisions limiting the free flow of financial services on the grounds of (legitimate) considerations of the general good,[14] especially in matters of consumer protection. As a

[10] BOGGIANO (8), 70 et seq.

[11] This essay focuses on the banking and investments services areas.

[12] On the process of liberalization of the financial sector see ANDENAS (5) and DALHUISEN (29) 795; CRANSTON and HADJIEMMANUIL (26 344 et seq; DERMINE (33) 103 et seq; DASSESE (30) 17 et seq.

[13] Art 43 and 49 (ex Arts 52 and 59) of the Treaty.

[14] Case 205/84, *Commission v Germany* (1986) ECR 3755; Case C-55/94 *Reinhard Gerard v Consiglio dell'Ordine degli Avvocati e Procuratori di Milano* (1995) ECR I-4165; Case C-362/88, *GB-Inno-BMV* (1990) ECR I-667; Case C-101/94 *Commission v Italy* (1996) ECR 2691.

reaction against the overly ambitious initial approach towards full harmonisation, the Commission announced in the White Paper of June 1985 the completion of the internal market and a 'new' strategy aimed at alleviating the burden of financial institutions operating across borders under a plurality of regimes.

On prudential matters, this strategy was implemented on the basis of the guiding principles of mutual recognition upon provision of minimum harmonised rules and of the country of origin (or home country control).[15]

According to the home country control, the primary responsibility for prudential regulation, supervision and enforcement has been granted to the Member State where the true head/registered office of the financial institution is located (home country).

Moreover, the mutual recognition requires member states not to impede cross-border provision of services insofar as compliance with the home state rules is assured. Thus, the principle imposes on member states a negative duty of refraining from applying their own regulations to foreign EU institutions operating on their territory. The principle rests on the notion of equivalence among national legislation and, accordingly, it has to be developed hand in hand with progressive harmonisation of substantive domestic rules.

In practice, the principle of mutual recognition operates in practice through the single licence mechanism. Once a financial undertaking has been granted by its home regulator the authorisation (so-called passport or licence) to carry out certain listed activities, it is allowed -upon completion of a notification procedure- to freely export these activities to other Member States without any need for further authorization by setting up branches or by carrying on services with no permanent presence there.[16]

Therefore, the host State must recognize the authorization granted by the competent authority in the home State, irrespective of whether the authorisation actually meets the requirements in the host State's legislation. It follows that the system of mutual recognition tends to expand the role of the home State[17] by allowing extra-territorial application of its public law rules.

In compliance with the traditional theory of comity, the extension of the home state jurisdiction has been counterbalanced by building (ie the State within the territory of which the service is provided) safeguards for the host

[15] On the issue, see inter alia CREMONA (27), CRANSTON and HADJIEMMANUIL (26) 342, O'NEILL (72) 189 et seq; NIELSEN (67); LOMNICKA (55); MOHAMED (64); FERRARINI (37) 1283, 1970–1300.

[16] 2BCD Art 18 and ISD Art 14. Please note that the passport does not extent to permitting the establishment of a subsidiary, the set-up of which shall therefore occur upon local authorization.

[17] NIELSEN (67) 159–60.

country in areas where the current low level of harmonization renders the application of the sole home state rules throughout the community inappropriate. This is the case in matter of advertising, where both the 2BCD and the ISD grant to the host State the power to regulate its content and form in the interest of the general good.[18]

However, except for advertising, the provisions relating to these safeguards and, thus, to the role of the host State under the 2BCD seem to differ, to a certain extent, from those under the ISD. In fact, while the 2BCD focuses merely on prudential matters and does not make explicit reference to the rules governing the conduct of credit institutions, the ISD deals directly with this area. In particular, it indicates positively the host country as the State primarily in charge of regulating and supervising the conduct of business in its territory.[19] In contrast, safeguards under the 2BCD are provided only in terms of limited restrictions that the host State is admitted to apply, insofar as the cross-border provision of services conflicts with those national provisions adopted in the interest of general good.[20]

Nonetheless, host States have invoked their powers to impose national measures under the 2BCD in connection with conduct of business rules, investor protection and market organization, ie precisely in the same fields expressly referred by the ISD to the competence of the host State.[21] Therefore, it is true that with respect to both the ISD and 2BCD, the allocation of tasks between home/host countries follows the distinction between those rules relating to the structure and the organisation of the undertaking and those regulating the financial products and the relationships of the financial institution with its clients.

Thus, the country of origin scheme in the financial services sector is based on the separation between *prudential and transaction supervision*. The former consisting of the home State power of ruling and controlling compliance with the conditions for the initial and continuing permission to operate, and *the latter* relating to the host State power of regulating and enforcing rules in matter of conduct, financial products and transactions to be entered into with the investors.

Finally, notice should be taken that the community allocation of regulatory jurisdiction between home country and host country results respectively

[18] 2BCD Art 21(11); ISD Art 13.

[19] ISD Art 11(2).

[20] 2BCD Arts 19(4), 21(5). Note that, conversely, no reference is made under the ISD to the concept of general good. I maintain herein that the general obligation of interpreting national and community law in accordance with the Treaty, and therefore to the free movement principles, leads to the introduction of the general good test also in the ISD. See, inter alia, THORKILDSENN (90) 102–8 WOUTERS (97) 302–3 and TISON(91) 33 et seq.

[21] Although responsibilities among Member States are diversified, the resulting regime still requires close collaboration between national authorities regarding the supervision of the institution operating across borders. See Arts 7, 14 (1) and 15(2) 2BCD and Art 23 ISD.

from the application of the nationality principle and the (objective) territoriality principle. More precisely, as far as the former is concerned, the connecting factor granting general governance on the service provider is the place where the office of the financial undertaking is located. On the other hand, the role of the host State depends on whether an activity has been carried out within its territory. As a consequence, the community allocation of jurisdiction has indirectly reinforced the importance of territoriality in the financial sector among Member States.

Within this legal framework, the assessment of the host state's responsibility presupposes the prior solution of the problem of localising financial activities. This circumstance, however, opens complex jurisdictional issues as long as the extent to which a service provider enters the competence of the host country is a matter of degree, particularly when neither the service provider nor the receiver moves across borders, but only the services themselves are cross-border.

2. *The Harmonization of Minimal Legal Standards*

The country of origin/mutual recognition mechanism presupposes competition among home country regulatory rules operating side-by-side, depending on the origin of the service provider involved. The risk under this scheme is that national authorities are encouraged to lower their regulatory standards in order to attract financial activity in their own territory. Therefore, the operation of the principle calls for the introduction of harmonization of national rules, with the purpose of avoiding those least regulated financial firms gaining competitive advantages in the single market.[22]

In the financial sector, this process of harmonization has been introduced by requiring Member States to implement certain 'minimum' standards, which can be replaced by stricter national requirements in so far as it would not unreasonably impede the internal market's proper functioning.[23] The current status is characterised by a harmonized legal framework as long as authorisation and prudential requirements are concerned, especially in the matter of capital standards. The detailed level of legal convergence achieved in such a field allows full application of the country of origin principle.

On the other hand, national conduct of business rules, which fall within the competence of the host state in so far as they are drawn up in the interest of the general good, are currently divergent throughout the community. As a consequence, a firm willing to offer or provide services across borders must comply with different requirements across the European Union. The

[22] On the process of harmonization in the financial field, *see* particularly KÖNDGEN (53), CRUICKSHANK (28), and AVGOULEAS (6).

[23] However there are still strong disincentives of applying higher standards, LOMNIKA (55) 326.

content of the above requirements vary considerably from one country to another and from one service to another,[24] so that it may result in market segmentation.

The lack of harmonization is particularly critical in matters of consumer legislation, where the tension between the aim of removing restrictions within the single market and the imperative of investor protection gives rise to conflicts among different policies.[25] In this respect, the community legislator seems to have posed limited attention to the importance of assuring an ordered set of rules capable of properly defending investors' interests.[26] On the contrary, since only specific aspects—for instance unfair contract terms, distance selling and consumer credit—are regulated, no comprehensive approach currently exists. Moreover, the complexity of the resulting legal framework gives rise to delicate problems of coordination among the various EU instruments.[27]

Accordingly, even if the regulation of cross-border provision of financial services can cope with the negative effects of legal barriers in terms of legislative segmentation, it shall concurrently take into consideration the need of excluding from the application of home country principle those fields which have not yet been sufficiently harmonized.

3. *Country of Origin and Private International Law: an Open Issue*

The country of origin principle constitutes a criterion of demarcation of competences among national authorities. Accordingly, it pertains to the public law sphere of the community legislation.

Nonetheless, it should be considered that the host state restrictions allowed therein are enacted internally as substantive rules, which may have different legal status. In fact, restrictive measures may play the dual function of public law provisions for supervisory purposes and private law duties owed to investors.[28] In other words, restrictions may take the form of supervisory rules, as well as of obligations applicable both in tort and in contract.[29] Moreover, financial products are substantially shaped on the basis of private law provisions.

[24] Section 3 of the FSA Consultation Paper of March 2002.

[25] STUYCK (88), particularly 370, on consumer protection see also ALPA (3) and DECOCK BUNING-HONDIUS-PRINS-DEVRIES (18).

[26] CRANSTON and HADJIEMMANUIL (26) 363. It should be pointed out, however, that according to Art 129a(1) of the EC Treaty, protection of consumers remains under the responsibility of individual Member States, while any action at the community level must comply with the principle of subsidiary requirements.

[27] JOUSTRA (50) 14

[28] KÖNDGEN (53) 126. The ECJ case law also seems to confirm that restrictions may be represented by rules of both private and public law, TISON (91) 4–5.

[29] WYMEERSCH (95), particularly 36.

The scenario resulting from the community effort of 'legal engineering'[30] in the financial field is therefore a complex regime constituted by public rules having some private law implications. The overlap between the areas of public and private law has been increasing as more public laws have been superimposed on private transactions, mainly in order to strengthen investors' position.[31] This mixture of rules renders it particularly interesting to investigate the private law consequences of the extraterritorial application of the home state legislation under the mutual recognition and, in particular, whether predominance of the home country (public) law over the host country law may be envisaged also with respect of rules pertaining to the private law sphere.

In principle, in the absence of specific community conflict rules with respect to most financial contracts,[32] the cross border provision of financial services is subject to the interplay of directly applicable Treaty provisions (freedoms of movement), directives having possible impact on conflict of laws (Financial Directives), conflict rules under the Rome Convention[33] and national conflict rules.[34] Therefore, the financial services sector offers an excellent illustration of the issue of the implications of the country of origin rule—and, in general, of the principle of mutual recognition under the Treaty freedoms as interpreted by the ECJ—on the traditional techniques for the solution of conflicts of laws.

Nevertheless, it should be pointed out in such respect that, although both sets of rules deal with the same problem of solving conflicts among a plurality of jurisdictions potentially interested in regulating a trans-national situation, the 'technical' response given by the one is different from the other. In particular, while the choice of law rules provide connecting factors aimed at identifying the applicable legal system, in principle no applicable law is expressly indicated at the community level. Rather, only the competent authority and the relevant responsibilities are delineated.

Nevertheless, in private law, one can argue that an implicit choice of law rule is to be inferred in order to achieve the goal of allocating regulatory

30 CRANSTON (25) 45–6.

31 This is true especially in relation to investment services. In fact ISD Art 11(1) sets forth regulatory principles attaining to the relationship between the financial undertaking and its clients which are nothing else than a specification of private obligations arising from agency contracts. However, transforming these duties of a contractual or pre-contractual nature in public-law obligations ensures them not to be contracted out. In addition, any misconduct of financial firms makes available a supplementary mean of enforcement by the supervisory authority. See KÖNDGEN (53) 116–17 and CRANSTON (25) 60–3.

32 Insurance contracts, in connection of which specific conflicts rules are indicated, constitute an exception.

33 Since the financial services are provided on a contractual basis, the law applicable is to be determined in accordance with Convention on the law applicable to contractual obligations (1980) OJL266/1 (the 'Rome Convention').

34 On private international law see DICEY and MORRIS (34) and DICKIE (35).

jurisdiction in accordance with the home country priority principle. More precisely, it is not unreasonable to envisage an implicit conflict rules imposing the application of the home country legislation on the private law aspects concerning the supply of financial products.[35] Given the above, it is no wonder that the evaluation of the extent of the private international law provisions of a Member State, and how they are affected by the precedence of the home country law in the financial sector, is an issue that remains highly debated among scholars.[36]

The topic is particularly interesting in understanding the potential consequences when the outcome of the national choice of law rules provokes restrictions to the right of the financial firms to provide services '*in the same manner as in their home country*'. This may be the case, for instance in contract law, when conflicts rules allow application of national provisions by reason of their mandatory character or on the grounds of public policy.[37] Similarly, with respect of rules of market behaviour, such as those in matter of unfair competition or advertising, the applicable law is often that of the market on which the behaviour produces significant effects.[38] In these situations, it cannot be excluded that the national rules applicable pursuant the private international law could constitute a barrier to intra-community trade.[39]

However, even considering the risks under these possible conflicting results, one cannot deduce an implicit private rule of choice of law from a public law principle aimed at distributing regulatory tasks. From a public law perspective, the rule under the country of origin/mutual recognition scheme produces the 'positive' effect of allocating regulatory jurisdiction among Member States, while in the field of private law, it merely imposes the 'negative' duty on Member States to not introduce restrictions to the internal market, unless they are legitimate on the grounds of the general good.[40] Attributing the principle of the home country priority in public law of a much more pervasive role as indicative of the private law applicable to a cross-border transaction is therefore a hardly justifiable jump in logic.

35 Carbone and Munari (14) 330–3.

36 Some authors argue that the freedom to provide services contains a conflicts rule itself, others sustain that the free movement would render applicable the law most favourable to the service provider (*favor offerentis* principle). An opposite doctrine holds the theory of 'indifference,' according to which no preference for the home or for the host State law may be inferred from the community provisions under examination. Finally, there are 'middle theories' in favour of an impact of the community legislation on the national conflicts rules in term of subjecting the latter to a 'legitimacy pressure' (ie conflict rules shall comply with the community justification and the proportionality test). See Wouters 284 et seq and Tison 39 et seq.

37 Rome Convention Arts 3.3, 5.2, 7 and 16.

38 Tison (91) 41.

39 Van Gerven and Wouters (92) 43 et seq.

40 A similar reasoning in Tison (91) 40 and Carbone and Munari (14), 330–1.

Rather, the correct approach in dealing with the issue of the actual implications of the country of origin/mutual recognition principles on the conflicts rules is that of considering the question in the light of the principle of supremacy of community legislation. This principle constitutes the pillar rule according to which conflicts between the community legal system and the laws of the Member States must be solved in favour of the prevalence of the former.[41]

According to ECJ case law,[42] this prevalence takes place with respect of all areas, including—when necessary—the national private law provisions Consequently, by virtue of the precedence of EC law, as long as a measure in force in a host State is contrary to the country of origin/mutual recognition principles, it shall be inapplicable However, this does not necessarily entail the application of the home country law in substitution of the overruled host State provisions.

Conversely, given the purely negative impact on private law of the aforementioned principles, their material effects are limited to the imposition on the Member States (including their organs, such as regulatory authorities and courts) of a duty to formulate, interpret and apply conflict rules in such a manner that their results do not constitute a restriction within the meaning of community law.[43]

In particular, the proper implementation of the Financial Directives does not necessarily require member states to replace their conflicts law with a rigid and fixed rule imposing application of the home country provisions to all the different private law aspects. This is because the application of substantive laws pertaining to a legal system different from the one of the service provider does not constitute, per se, an infringement of the 'negative' duty of not to impose restrictions on free movement. On the contrary, each host Member State shall be free to formulate whatever choice of law rule it considers appropriate, insofar as its actual application does not determine restrictions against the foreign service provider.

Should the national choice of law result in such an incompatibility, the principle of supremacy of community law would thus impose an obligation on the organs of Member States to use their margin of appreciation in interpreting the internal legislation, with a view to avoiding the conflicting result.

Moreover, even if an incompatibility is not strictly at hand, the country of origin shall nevertheless play a 'complementary' role as long as all steps of the process of applying the conflicts rules, for instance, the qualification or the selection of the proper connecting factor, should have to be carried out in the light of ensuring full operation of the community principles.

[41] LASOK and STONE (54) 19 et seq.

[42] The ECJ case law is quoted in the 2BCD Interpretative Communication (cited below) 25–6.

[43] References to doctrines employing a similar approach are in WOUTERS (97) 294 et seq.

Finally, notwithstanding the above, the substantive provisions resulting from the proper application of the choice of law rules imposes a restriction on the free movement, compatibility with the community law shall be verified on the ground of the general good justification. In case the restriction does not comply with the general good requirements, the substantive law concerned must be consequently inapplicable. Therefore, the country of origin/mutual recognition principles does not interfere on the determination of the applicable law, but only operates ex post, ie limiting the applicability of the substantive law once it has been individuated.

Accordingly, it is my belief that the freedom to provide services intervenes with national conflict rules on three levels, formulation, interpretation and application without causing, the creation of special or new private international law rules, nor a 'positive' effect on the traditional technique of determining the applicable law.

C. *The Commission's Interpretative Efforts*

1. *Freedom to Provide Services and the Interest of General Good*

In addition to the problems relating to the current legislative fragmentation, obstacles to the creation of the single market in financial services have been aggravated by the lack of legal certainty over the interpretation of basic concepts included in the Financial Directives. The above difficulties pushed the Commission to issue two interpretative communications relating to the banking and the insurance sectors.[44]

In discussing the problems associated with the 2BCD interpretation, the major contributions relate to the freedom to provide services and the interest of the general good.

The first issue faces the difficulties in drawing a demarcation between the right of establishment and the freedom to provide service.[45] The 2BCD Communication focuses specifically on the provision of services through an intermediary and through electronic machines, such as ATMs.[46] As far as the former is concerned, the Commission held that, in principle, a true

[44] Respectively, the 2BCD Communication and the Communication (2000) OJC43/5, intended to make public the attitude that the Commission would be likely adopt in the event a particular problem being brought to its attention. They are intra vires only insofar as they are limited to make explicit member states' obligations already existing under community legislation. Although not binding over the member states and the ECJ, the above instruments are intended to promote a common understanding on the 2BCD provisions and to exercise a substantial influence on the European legal operators.

[45] Since the notification procedure differs depending on whether the institution intends to set up a branch or not, the topic is crucial. See 2BCD Art 19 (branch), Art 20 (cross-border services), ISD Art 17 (branch), Art 18 (cross-border services).

[46] Please note that individual, data-processing equipment providing or receiving distance services, eg through the Internet, are however excluded from the scope of the interpretation.

independent intermediary has not to be regarded as a branch. However, if the intermediary (i) operates upon permanent mandate, (ii) is subject to the management and control of the credit institution, or (iii) has the power to commit the institution, the bank will fall within the scope of the right of establishment. In this circumstance, however, the intermediary shall not be considered as constituting a 'branch' within the meaning of the 2BCD. Moreover, the Commission suggested that electronic machines might result in the provision of services, but not the establishment of a branch, unless the machine is attached to a branch or an agency.[47]

As to the latter, the 'general good' raised an active debate within the EU about the proper scope of host state regulation, ie the limit of its prescriptive jurisdiction. The 2BCD Communication sets forth a general good test, which gives guidance over the conditions under which a credit institution may be required by the host State to comply with national restrictions. Essentially, the measures must be non-discriminatory, not falling within a harmonised area, justifiable by imperative requirements in the general interest, not duplicating the home State rule, proportionate and suitable for attaining their objective.[48] Since the uncertainties surrounding the concept present a major impediment for gaining effective advantages from the single passport, the initiative of the Commission should be welcomed. However, one should admit that the analysis carried out does not always give sufficient clarification on this vague and exclusively case law-built concept.

2. *General Good and Private International Law*

Furthermore, in view of impeding 'obstructionist' or 'protectionist' behaviours from the host State, the 2BCD Communication holds that the principle of precedence of community law implies the general good test to be applied to any restriction resulting from the application of national choice of law rules. According to the Commission's point of view, even if a conflicts rule cannot be regarded in itself as a restriction to the free movement, it might result in barriers to the internal market implementation, as long as the law thereby designated as applicable does not satisfy the general good test.[49]

Therefore, the Commission's position seems to confirm the relationship between the country of origin/mutual recognition principles and the conflict of laws rules envisaged in this contribution, in term of a possible ex post and only negative impact of the former on the process of application of the latter.

[47] Having the Commission focused the discussion only to specific aspects, various problems behind the distinction rest still unsolved, see LOMNIKA (55) 326.

[48] 2BCD Communication 20 et seq. Examples of areas reasonably covered by the general good concept are also given.

[49] 2BCD Communication 25.

3. *Localization of Off-Line Financial Activities*

Further uncertainties relating to the application of the Financial Directive lie on the *preliminary* question of localising financial activities. In fact, the operation of the country of origin regulatory scheme comes into play only when a financial service is provided or offered within the territory of a State other than the home country.[50] However, the dematerialised nature of financial services and their increasing provision in intangible form exacerbate this problem and demand specific solutions.

In the 2BCD Communication, the Commission has examined the issue in order to clarify when the prior notification requirement should be complied with. After evaluating and excluding the opportunities for a service to be located at the place of the originator of the initiative, the customer's place of residence or the place where the contract is executed, the Commission suggested a very restrictive test according to which a service should be located at the place where the characteristic performance (ie the essential supply for which the payment is due) occurs.[51] This place will normally coincide with the home Member State, rather than the country of the investors.[52]

Although the test is given to determine whether the notification procedure applies, its application has a much more pervasive impact. It also conditions the allocation of competence pursuant to the mutual recognition strategy and actually indicates which regulator is affected from time to time.

Since the approach followed by the Commission causes a financial service to be located normally within the territory of the home State, it tends to exclude any host country's power to impose restrictions under the meaning of the Financial Directives. As a consequence, the test would allow a very broad operation of the home country rule.

Moreover, it is interesting to notice that the process of localisation has been carried out by reference to a concept derived from private international law. In that contest, the notion of 'characteristic performance' is used to determine which jurisdiction is the most closely connected to a contractual relationship, with the effect of indicating the applicable law.[53] The general principle of jurisdiction applied within this legal framework is based on the domicile. Conversely, the Commission has employed the same connecting factor for regulatory purposes, in particular to allocate the host

[50] DALHUISEEN (29) 820–1 and REYNOLDS (80) 7.

[51] 2BCD Communication 6.

[52] On the implications of the Commission's approach *see* DASSESE (31) 46.

[53] Art s 3(1), 4(1), 5, 7 Rome Convention. The characteristic performance test is used only if (i) the parties has made no choice of applicable law (b) the contract is not a consumer contract (c) there are no mandatory rules on the part of a state which is connected to the transaction.

state's prescriptive jurisdiction on the different ground of the territoriality principle.

By reason of the narrow concept of territoriality employed in the test, temporary visits by representatives of the financial undertaking to a country different from the one of origin, not involving the provision of the essential banking activity, should not allow the host country to be vested by any regulatory competence.

Furthermore, the reference to the place of characteristic performance takes preliminarily activities outside the notification procedure.[54] In particular, the Commission considers outside the scope of the notification all forms of advertising, including all offers made by means of distance communication, such as post, fax or electronic mails. As no criteria for localising the mere offer of financial services are given by the 2BCD Communication, the problem of determining regulatory jurisdiction in these fields remains substantially controversial. Particularly, the Commission missed the opportunity to consider whether, and in which circumstances, advertising specifically targeted to a certain country, for example when the advertising is sent along with reply-coupons to the address of potential investors, represents evidence of the intention to pursue financial activities in a particular jurisdiction.

In light of the above, the interpretation suggested by the Commission, although constituting an incentive toward the internal market liberalisation,[55] can be criticized on the grounds that the wide extraterritorial application of the home State rules allowed therein might—in certain circumstances—excessively limit the investor protection under the host State rules. In fact, the Commission has not sufficiently addressed the risk of entailing exclusion of the host country regulatory competence (i.e. the country of the service receiver) with respect to situations in which the protection of an unsophisticated investor is extremely crucial.

This is the case, for instance, of a 'passive' consumer (ie consumer who has not taken the initiative to enter into the financial contract) that has been solicited individually and directly by the foreign supplier and at no time has entered the supplier's Member State. In the event a financial contract is entered into in such circumstances, the investor would reasonably expect a level of protection equivalent to that offered under the rulebook of its country.[56] However, given the lack of sufficient harmonization the field of financial products and conduct of business, this equivalence is not guaranteed per se. Hence, it is worthy to point out that any effort to extend the home

[54] 2BCD Communication 7.

[55] For an opinion welcoming the characteristic performance test see CRUICKSHANK (28) 131, ABRAMS (2) 248 and DASSESE (31) 54.

[56] KONDGEN (53) 126.

State control rule without taking into account the opportunity to meet legitimate consumer expectations would give raise to arbitrary consequences.

On the contrary, it should be noted that in the area of private international law, the characteristic performance test does not deprive passive consumers from the protection afforded by the country of their habitual residence.[57] It follows that the narrow application of the territoriality principle suggested by the Commission would, to a certain extent, dissociate civil and regulatory jurisdictions. However, considering that only the host state control can guarantee the application of the same provisions by both a court and a regulator in connection with a given misconduct, the opportunity of aligning them—at least in connection with passive consumers-cannot be denied.[58]

III. ALLOCATION OF REGULATORY JURISDICTION AFTER THE E-COMMERCE DIRECTIVE: THE NEW COMPLEX SCENARIO

A. The Issues Surrounding Cyber-jurisdiction

1. Adapting Traditional Principles of Jurisdiction to the Unique Features of the Internet

The localisation of financial activities is exceptionally complex when services are provided, advertised or offered through means of distant communication, ie not requiring the simultaneous physical presence of the parties. The difficulty arises when the parties concerned are located in different countries, and neither the service provider nor the customer moves. Although the transaction surely has an international or 'cross-border' dimension, no immediate connection with either country can be envisaged in view of allocating prescriptive jurisdiction.

This aspect is particularly troublesome with respect to activities carried out through the Internet, given the very unique features of this mean of distance communication. The Internet is a communication network where information and services are instantaneously accessible from any connected computer, regardless of its physical location. Thus, any on-line resource is available from everywhere. Accordingly, any reference to *cross-border* activities may sound bizarre if related to the intrinsically *borderless* nature of the web.

[57] Art 5 Rome convention according to which consumers cannot be deprived of the protection of any mandatory rules of their country of habitual residence if in that country the conclusion of the contract was preceded by a specific invitation addressed to them or by advertising, and they have taken in that country all the steps necessary to conclude the contract.

[58] In the same sense KONDGEN (53) 126.

One of the major problems arising from the geographic ambiguity of cyberspace and the public access to information available, is that on-line activities are potentially subject to the simultaneous jurisdiction of any and every state. The consequent multitude of applicable national rules evidently constitutes a major impediment to the development of e-finance. Moreover, global jurisdiction facilitates undesirable opportunities of forum shopping and regulatory arbitrage.

Certainly, the problem of overlapping applicable regulations should be dealt with consistently in international law.[59] Nonetheless, one must recognise that the traditional meaning of the comity of nations and the principles of jurisdiction hardly fit with the special character of the Internet.[60]

In fact, the typical criterion for allocating jurisdiction implies the prior localisation of persons and activities within the boundaries of either sovereign country. However, geographic location may be meaningless in the non-physical web environment, while the nationality of the actors is not necessarily ascertainable. Hence, given the irrelevance of any operational notion of 'national border', the nature of the Internet challenges the territorially-based concepts of jurisdiction and national sovereignty.

On the other hand, states cannot refrain from developing mechanisms to address the jurisdictional problems relating to the on-line activities in the light of guaranteeing judicial certainty, predictability of solutions and comity of nations. This calls for an evolutionary approach aimed at adapting—rather than revolutionizing—the traditional principles of jurisdiction to the borderless character of the means. This approach has been adopted by US courts and regulators,[61] who have developed a modified form of the objective territoriality principle in view of ensuring that the scope of prescriptive jurisdiction does not extend beyond what may be practically and legitimately enforced.[62]

In order to achieve this balance, jurisdiction on the content of the Internet has been increasingly asserted on the basis of the effects *it is intended to cause* in the territory of a state. More precisely, the new trend developed in the US applies a variant of the effects doctrine of international

[59] Reed and Hargreaves (78) 1005.

[60] Sookman (87) 53–4; Long (58) 501.

[61] Considering that US has been among the first to deal with the jurisdictional issues arising from Internet transactions, reference to the US cases is an useful indication of the direction that other countries may take. This is confirmed by the circumstance that in the course of the last few years a trend similar to that referred below has been actually adopted by a number of other regulators eg in Australia, Canada, UK, and Italy. Although highly interesting, any comparative analysis on the subject matters would transcend the scope of this essay. Fundamental contributions to this field are given by the ABA Report(4) and the 2001 IOSCO Report(48).

[62] Long (58) 505.

law,[63] excluding that the mere use or accessibility of the Internet is sufficient to satisfy the requirements for asserting jurisdiction.[64] In particular, a double test has been introduced in order to restrict claimant of jurisdiction to those Internet activities (a) producing significant effects within the state concerned and, simultaneously and (b) specifically aimed at targeting the audience in that state.[65]

This new approach involves the assessment of the intention of an Internet operator to direct the content of its website or its on-line activity to the customers of a certain jurisdiction (the so-called '*directed at*' test). Clearly, the main problem in this respect is that of determining suitable factors according to which the above assessment should be carried out.

Nevertheless, phenomena of global jurisdiction are effectively contrasted only when it is recognized that the mere maintenance of a web-site and the placement of a service in the Internet should not constitute targeting a jurisdiction. In fact, US jurisprudence has increasingly inferred the operators' intention to seek or achieve business in a jurisdiction from the steps taken to either enter or avoid the given national market.[66] For this purpose, the assessment has been made on the basis of objective criteria, such as the characteristics of the activity carried on on-line, the passive or active nature of the site and, in general, its level of interactions with the customers of the jurisdiction.

[63] The effects principle is briefly dealt with in s I para 1. The employment of a mere effects principle in the cyberspace context would lead to a dramatic multiplication of the potentially competent national jurisdictions. The drawbacks of this approach can be easily identified when considering the recent French Yahoo! Decision (*Yahoo! Inc v La Ligue Contre Le Racisme Et L'Antisémitisme* Ordinance rendered on 20 Nov 2000 in Urgency Proceedings. Court of Great Instance of Paris. See GEIST (42) 561 et seq.

[64] This trend is shared by both US regulators and courts. As to the former, *see* the SEC Interpretative Release. As to the latter, the US Constitution under the Due Process Clause of the Fifth and Fourteenth Amendments requires personal jurisdiction over non-residents to be asserted on the basis of the so-called 'minimum contact test.' In the last years, the test has been considerably developed by US courts in order to address internet-related cases. Although there has been no full consistency in the decisions, US courts seem to have increasingly adopted stricter standards. Currently, the leading case on this issue is an opinion rendered by a District Court in *Zippo Manufacturing Company v Zippo Distribution Company Inc* [952 F Supp 1119 (WD Pa1997) hereinafter the 'Zippo Case'] where a distinction has been drawn up between passive and active website. The former, characterized by information merely posted, should not allow assertion of personal jurisdiction, while the latter requires an analysis over the level of interactivity. This evolution is analysed, *inter alia,* by KIDD and DAUGHTEREY (50), 220–38; LONG (57) 504–5; Committee on international securities regulations (24) 4 et seq; REES and HARGREAVES (77) 175; MITRANI (61) 50; SOOKMAN (85) 91; GEIST (42) 577.

[65] LONG (58) 95 and LONG (56) 503–4.

[66] See, for instance, the SEC Interpretative Realise. No targeting-based approach is used, however, in connection with fraudulent or manipulative on-line activities originated in US or placed US investors at risks. In these cases, therefore, a strict effects principle is applied.

2. International Instruments: The Developing Targeted-Based Approach

The exigency to face the risk of multiple jurisdictions through a targeting-based test has been recognized also at the international level, where several organizations have issued soft-law instruments recommending uniform solutions to the jurisdictional issues of regulation over the Internet.[67] In this regard, it seems that a common regulatory approach has been promoted to restrict assertion of jurisdiction upon application of a 'direct at' test.

The OECD Consumer Protection Guidelines encapsulates this idea through the assertion, 'business should take into account the global nature of the electronic commerce and, wherever possible, should consider various *regulatory characteristics of the markets they target*'.[68] A similar recommendation is in various passages of the ABA Report where, in conducting a global study on the Internet jurisdiction, it is settled that the 'targeting' is an efficient and fairer way of making jurisdictional determinations in Cyberspace, especially in matters of consumer protection. Nonetheless, the major effort in the field of financial services is represented by the 1998 IOSCO Report,[69] where specific guidelines are given on the circumstances under which regulatory authority should be exercised over cross-border financial activities on the Internet.

Hence, in line with the recent US developments, the common approach indicated under the above recommendations recognises the necessity to employ a variant of the effects doctrine, ie the '*subjective effects principle of jurisdiction*',[70] in view of assessing the parties' intention of targeting a given jurisdiction. However, the application of this principle once again opens the issue of determining which criteria constitute evidence of this parties' intention.[71] The issue represents the very core problem of the debate considering that, as recognised in the ABA Report, in the absence of universally applicable standards for targeting assessment, the 'direct at' test would not be capable of ensuring legal certainty and foreseeability in the Internet-related framework.

A positive attempt to indicate possible solutions has been made under the 1998 IOSCO Report, which provides a list of (non-exhaustive) factors

[67] More precisely, there is actually one international forum dealing with e-commerce matters in view of producing binding (instead of soft-law) rules. I am referring to the WTO. In fact, upon EU initiative, discussions have been currently undertaken within the WTO framework in order to clarify the application of its rules to the e-commerce. See POWELL (73).

[68] See Bibliography No 68.

[69] See Bibliography No 46.

[70] LONG (57) 503.

[71] Actually, the problem is somehow similar to the one referred to in Section I in matter of promotional activities. I am referring to the issue of when promotional activities would constitute evidence of the intention to carry out business in a certain jurisdiction (and therefore give rise to the prior notification requirement). As mentioned, in the 2BCD Communication the Commission failed to take the opportunity to give clarifications.

supporting evidence that information or activities are targeted to residents of the regulator's jurisdiction (eg the language used in the communication, or the currency in which the transaction is denominated) or that the on-line activity produces a substantial effect in the jurisdiction (eg acceptance of purchases from or e-mails addressed to customers in the jurisdiction).

In addition, other factors are indicated in support of decision not to assert jurisdiction, such as the use of disclaimers and warnings or the introduction of precautions designed to prevent sales to residents in the jurisdiction. On the other hand, activities involving fraud or market manipulation should entail application of a more traditional principle of territoriality.

The approach recommended by IOSCO is therefore very similar to the one increasingly developed in the US (as well as in other) legal system(s). This constitutes a signal towards the development of a broader regulatory consensus that, in consideration of the very unique features of the Internet, is intended to limit prescriptive jurisdiction through the application of a targeting-based test. One should recognize, however that given the difficulties in assessing the characteristics associated with 'targeting', the above approach is viable only when states are willing to further cooperate on the international level in determining common objective standards.[72]

3. *The Localization of On-line Financial Activities*

In relation to the EU financial services sector, before the entrance into force of the ECD, the sole effort to address the issues of jurisdiction relating to on-line financial activities has been made by way of interpretation in the 2BCD Communication. The logical procedure followed by the Commission was based on a very traditional approach aimed at determining where online activity takes place.

In particular, regardless of the irrelevance of physical location in the Internet, the Commission applied the usual 'characteristic performance test' to on-line financial activities. On the grounds of the same narrow territoriality principle employed in the off-line environment, the Commission suggested that the place of provision of distance banking activities should not be deemed the customer's territory. Once localized within the 'boundaries' of the

[72] Another option for addressing internet-related jurisdictional problems is the unification or harmonization of rules through the promotion of global minimum legal standards. It is true, in fact, that the practical negative impacts of global jurisdiction are reduced when national laws converge. At this purpose, UNCITRAL and OECD have supported unification by drafting model laws which national states are free to introduce in their own jurisdiction. The issuance of model laws should be surely welcomed, in the light of their flexibility and adaptability to different legal traditions. However, since their application does not eliminate the basic need of private international law, model laws hardly represent a fully effective solution, unless some sort of coordination among national legal systems accompanies them. An overview of these initiatives are in DIEDRICH (36) and RAWSON (74)171.

home state, the provision of financial services through the Internet would not entail any host country competence over conduct of business. Moreover, no specific explanations have been given as to whether offering activities may constitute evidence of the intention of having business in a given jurisdiction.

It seems clear from the above that under the 2BCD Communication, the Commission failed to elaborate specific proposals in view of adapting the traditional rules of jurisdiction to the borderless nature of the mean. The solution suggested is thus highly unsatisfactory. In fact, rather than giving guidance by taking into account the special nature of the mean, the Commission merely attempted to circumvent the issue of identifying which factors should be employed for allocating cyber-jurisdiction. Conversely, it has only dealt with the aspect of physical location of financial activities, an aspect that—if is extremely problematic in the off-line environment—is essentially meaningless in the virtual geography of the Internet.

The irrelevance of the services' physical location in Cyberspace has been finally acknowledged in the contest of the ECD, the recent EU instrument intended to ensure the free movement of 'information society services'.[73] By reason of the very wide range of on-line economic activities covered, the ECD is horizontal in nature and complements—rather than substitutes- the other applicable EC specific directives, as well as the relevant implementation of national laws.[74]

The legal framework established by the ECD is based on the recognition that Internet activities are almost universally not restricted to a single territory, rather they affect a plurality of countries (namely, potentially any countries where they are accessible). This risk of multiple jurisdictions intrinsically calls for the individuation of a rule of coordination among member states' legal systems.

In the ECD architecture, this rule is represented by the internal market clause, a synthetic expression summarizing the principles of country of origin and mutual recognition upon minimum harmonization.[75] As is well known, the above principles constitute a rule for allocating regulatory juris-

[73] The 'information society services' are defined in Art 2(a) (but *see also* Recital 18) by reference to prior legislation as: 'any service normally provided for remuneration, at a distance, by electronic means and at the individual request of a recipient of services.' A part from certain named exceptions set out in Art 1(5) (not related to the financial services sector), the definition covers all form of on-line financial services, co apprising activities for which the addressee pays no remuneration (eg, on-line offers of information, as well as access and service provider services).

[74] Art 1(3).

[75] On the ECD legal framework see CALLEJA (12); RENNIE (78); MITRANI (61); MOEREL (62); SOOKMAN (85–6); WALDEN (92); DE LAS CUEVAS and ANTON (32); TARRUELLA (88); BROWNSWORD and HOWELLS (11); PEARCE and PLATTEN (72); DIEDRICH (36), FOSS and BYGRAVE (40); HORNLE (45), REED (75); REYNOLDS and SMETHURST (80); LONG (56).

diction in connection with transnational transactions. In the ambit of the ECD, the internal market clause is employed in terms of granting general governance over an on-line service provider to the member state where the provider is established.[76] Additionally, in accordance with the principle of mutual recognition, each Member State is bound, in turn, not to impose restrictions to the free movement of the on-line services, unless these can be justified under the derogation regime set forth.[77]

At first sight, the system does not seem to differ from the legal structure generally adopted in the financial services sector. In fact, as in the contest of the Financial Directives, the internal market clause allows the extra-territorial application of the home country regulatory system, upon provision of limited exceptions. Similarly, prescriptive jurisdiction is allocated to the home state on the basis of a variant of the nationality/domicile principle. In the case of the ECD, the core concept is that of establishment.

However, a very fundamental difference should be underlined between the two schemes. In particular, while in the framework of the Financial Directives the concept and the role of the 'host State' is defined on the grounds of the principle of territoriality,[78] no such principle has been applied in the contest of the ECD, where the concept of 'host State' is not even mentioned.

Furthermore, it is interesting to note that, except for the geographic notion of 'establishment' under the ECD, any reference to territorially based concepts has been accurately avoided. The rationality of this solution probably lays on the intention of the EC legislator to reduce the pervasiveness of physical borders in the ambit of Internet-based activities.

The new attitude encompassed under the ECD should be welcomed, since it finally acknowledges the de-localised nature of the Internet. In fact, in the legal framework established by the ECD, on-line activities are treated as having an *inherent transnational dimension*, regardless of their actual localisation. This is demonstrated by the fact that they call for the application of a rule to allocate prescriptive jurisdiction among member states, namely the internal market clause, which operates whenever services are offered or supplied through the Internet. In this context, the preliminary analysis of whether on-line activities have been provided across borders is no longer material. In my opinion, the irrelevance of any question of localisation rests on the peculiarity of the approach introduced by the ECD.

In the light of the above, it should be recognised that the application of the characteristic performance test to on-line activities, originally adopted by the Commission at the time of the 2BCD Communication, cannot be

[76] Art 3(1) and Recital 22.

[77] Art 3(2) and (4).

[78] 2BCD Art 1(8) ISD Art 1(7), according to which host State shall mean the Member State *in which* a service is provided (or, in case of freedom of establishment, a branch is set up).

reconciled with the approach envisaged under the ECD[79] and it should therefore be regarded as superseded by the new legal framework.[80]

However, it is worthy to note that, although the preliminary problem of physical localisation does not arise anymore, the ECD scheme nevertheless opens a new and equally thorny problem. Particularly, in lack of any 'host state' definition, no indications are given as to when a state may be regarded the recipient of a web-based activity. Nonetheless, this issue is significant enough to determine the circumstances under which a member state is allowed to impose restrictions under the ECD derogation regime.

This point is critical considering that the more a member state is legitimated to claim jurisdiction over a field subject to derogation, the more the freedom to provide services risks are hampered. Hence, the adoption of a common approach among member states aimed at restricting jurisdiction is crucial for problems of multiple jurisdictions and the lack of foresee-ability to be avoided. Therefore, it cannot be denied that the actual balance of the legal solution offered by the ECD is dependent on the proper individuation of a rule suitable to limit and thus to coordinate the power of member states to impose restrictions.

Despite the critical importance of this issue, no such rule is provided at the community level. Conversely, the ECD has not clarified the conditions under which service providers may be subjected to the regulatory jurisdiction of a state different from the one of establishment. Thus, for the time being, the proper definition of the concept of 'host State' is left fully to the law of individual Member States, whereby they so can impose compliance with certain national laws (falling within the derogation regime) even in connection with on-line services merely accessible from customers in their own territory.

This failure from the part of the EU legislator should be strongly criticised, since it risks contradicting one of the main purposes of the ECD, such as the elimination of those '*obstacles (which) arise from divergences in legislation and legal uncertainties as to which national rules apply to such services.*'[81]

Conversely, it would have been appropriate for the EU legislation to follow the general trend favourable to a target-based test. This is particularly true in the light of the fact that: 'in view of the global dimension of electronic commerce, it is, however, appropriate to ensure that the Community rules are consistent with international rules' and that: 'this

[79] I do not agree therefore with the opinion that the offer of investment services through the Internet fall outside the 2BCD and the ISD passport, as held by AVGOULEAS (6) 79.

[80] Note in fact the different approach encompassed by the Commission in the recent ECD Communication where it recognizes for instance that: 'The defining characteristic of e-commerce is its borderless nature' (4).

[81] ECD Recitals No 5 and 6.

Directive is without prejudice to the results of discussions within international organisations (amongst others WTO, OECD, UNCITRAL) on legal issues.'[82]

The ECD should have given guidance as to whether a service provider is entering the competence of a Member State. Moreover, in accordance with the common approach currently developed in the international fora, it should have defined the recipient country as the state to which the service provider intends to direct its on-line activity, insofar as that activity is capable of producing substantial effect in the jurisdiction. The good point of this definition rests also in the circumstance that, in line with the general approach encompassed under the ECD, no un-desired concepts based on strict physical territoriality would be introduced.

B. *The Country of Origin Principle after the E-Commerce Directive*

1. *The Principle of Establishment*

As mentioned, the core concept for individuating the regulatory regime applicable in connection with on-line financial activities is the geographic location of the service provider. Within the framework of the ECD, the much debated problem of determining this location in the virtual world of the Internet has been tackled by making reference to the concept of establishment elaborated by the ECJ case law.[83]

More precisely, in the ambit of the ECD scope, 'home country' means the Member State where the provider actually pursued an economic activity through a fixed establishment for an indefinite period, notwithstanding the situation of the website or service. In case of companies registered in a plurality of states, the place of establishment shall be where the service provider has its centre of activities for a particular service.[84]

The main merit of the definition of establishment under the ECD is that it clearly states the irrelevance of the place where the technology supporting the website is located or where the website is accessible.[85] Nonetheless, the gap is that no indications are given as to where a 'fixed establishment' should be located when a company has no physical office. Therefore, the

[82] ECD Recital 58.

[83] *Factortame* case, *R v Secretary of State for Transport, ex p Factortame Ltd* [1996] ECR I-1029.

[84] ECD Art 2 and Recital 19. See also Art 5(1)(b), that imposes an obligation on service providers to indicate in dealing with customers the geographic address at which the service provider is established.

[85] The definition of permanent establishment recommended by the OECD for tax purposes is partially different, since it is recognized that a website hosted on a server could be treated as a permanent establishment provided that the server is a business asset of the enterprise concerned. See OECD, para 42.3, REED (75) 1018 and CATCHPOLE (15).

centre of economic activity definition under the ECD still leaves the question of locating a 'virtual' company unanswered.[86]

Additionally, with regard to the financial services sector, the notion of establishment must be construed as taking into account the indications given by the Commission under the 2BCD Communication which mirrors the ECJ jurisprudence in the field. In essence, three requirements have been indicated for a permanent establishment to exist: (i) a management, ie the presence of staff or of an intermediary; (ii) the ability of those staff to commit the undertaking; (iii) a permanency, such the use of fixed premises or equipment for an indeterminate period or of an intermediary having a permanent mandate.[87]

Considering the concept of establishment adopted in the framework of the ECD, a problem of coordination between the principles set forth under this directive and those under the Financial Directives appear to arise. In particular, difficulties arise when different definitions of 'home State' are given. In fact, given the case of a financial undertaking having a branch in a country different from the one where the head office is located, while the ECD places the general responsibility in prudential matters on the Member State where the branch operates, the Financial Directives would refer it to the member state of the head office.

On deeper analysis, however, this divergence does not actually bring about the contradictory consequences one could at first expect. This is because the horizontal and complementary nature of the ECD requires it to be applied by Member States along with any sectoral EU legislation, ie cumulatively. Therefore, even though the ECD calls for the application of the regulatory law of a state different from the one indicated under the Financial Directives, this regulatory law will nonetheless refer the competence on prudential matter to the country where the head office is located. This result follows from the Member State of the establishment having previously implemented the division of tasks provided for under the Financial Directives in its national law, and therefore would have already referred the competence on prudential supervision over to another State.[88]

Accordingly, it is true that, as stated by the Commission in the ECD Communication: 'The e-commerce Directive does not change the existing arrangements for the prudential supervision of financial service institution. [. . .] Consequently, as a result of previous express transfers made by EU

[86] LONG (55) 331.

[87] Section I, Part C para 1. See REED (75), 1015–16; Long (55 330–1.

[88] I do not agree therefore with the ap proach of MOEREL (62) 186, according to which: 'To achieve this result (or at least to avoid any discussion in this respect), the 'single passport rule' in the banking directives should have been listed as one of the exceptions to the country-of-origin principle.'

sectoral directives, prudential control of branches remains with the 'home country' in the meaning of this sectoral directives.'[89]

2. *The Scope of Application of the 'Internal Market Clause'*

Once determined where the presence (in term of establishment) of a service provider shall be located, the internal market clause operates by:

(1) allocating on the State of the establishment (or home state) the responsibility of ensuring compliance with those national legal requirements falling within the coordinated field,[90]
(2) imposing on each Member State the duty not to restrict the on-line activities for reasons falling within the coordinated fields.[91]

The extent of the home country control is therefore determined through the notion of 'coordinated field', which covers all the 'requirements laid down in member state legal systems applicable to information society service providers or information society services, regardless of whether they are of a general nature or specifically designed for them' and it concerns both the *taking up* of the activity (ie qualifications, authorisation or notification) and the *pursuit* of it (ie the behaviour of the provider, quality or content of the service including advertising, contracts and liability of the provider).[92]

From this definition, it appears that the operation of the country of origin principle with respect to the on-line financial activities is much broader than in the contest of the off-line financial services. In fact, it extends to virtually every applicable requirement, regardless of the private or public nature of the relevant rules. Moreover, no differentiation between prudential and transactional supervision analogous to the one characterizing the division of competences in the Financial Directives is encompassed under the ECD.

Therefore, this s new legal framework introduces some inconsistencies between the two modes of trade, considering that under the ISD, the power to regulate and supervise the relationship with customers (being either consumers or *professional investors*) is granted to the host State, rather than to the state of establishment.[93] The same inconsistency occurs in matters of commercial communication and advertising, being reserved to the competence of the host state under both the ISD and the 2BCD. Therefore, as clarified by the Commission in the ECD Communication,

[89] ECD Communication 18.
[90] Art 3(1).
[91] Art 3(2).
[92] Art 2(h)(i). However, it does not cover requirements applicable to good as such, the delivery of goods, and the services not provided by electronic means. See also Recital 21.
[93] A review of the ISD provisions has been in fact undertaken in the light of securing more coherence. *See* COMM(2000) 729, 15-11-2000.

different regulatory regimes shall be applied with respect to on-line and off-line financial activities, even in the case where a financial service is provided in part off-line and in part on-line.[94]

Some limitations to the scope of the home country rule are the general exceptions listed in Annex of the ECD, a number of which are relevant in the financial services sector, namely:

(i) the advertising of collective investment scheme;
(ii) the taking up and the carrying out of life and non-life insurance business;
(iii) choice of law contractual clauses;
(iv) contractual obligations concerning consumer contracts.[95]

It should be underlined that exemptions are provided only with respect to consumer contracts and choice of law clauses. This confirms that the country of origin principle applies to all remaining private law matters. Its expanded application beyond merely regulatory requirements is the innovation provided for by the ECD in the matter of allocation of jurisdiction. As it will be dealt with in the following, while serving the purpose of increasing market integration, this extension has actually brought some confusion by reason of the immediate interaction it seems to introduce with private international law.

3. *The New Derogation Regime*

Another novelty established by the ECD is the derogation regime, which is the residual safeguard ability for member states to impose restrictions when necessary, by reason of public order, protection of public health, public security or protection of consumers (including investors).[96] The above regime differs from the one set forth under the Financial Directives much more from a procedural than from a substantial standpoint.

In fact, as the general good exemption in the financial services sector, the ECD derogation system reflects the ECJ case law on the subject and therefore requires the measures to be justified on the ground of necessity and proportionality. In addition, in conformity with the Treaty and the general indications of the ECJ, restrictions shall not be not admitted in areas

[94] ECD Communication 6.

[95] Since the above subjects represent general derogations only to the internal market clause, they do fall within the scope of the co-ordinated fields and therefore are subject to the remaining ECD provisions. Fundamental is that criminal law is not generally excluded, thus member states are allowed to apply their national criminal laws without the need of prior notification of the measures to the Commission.

[96] Art 3(4).

already subjected to harmonization and shall be consistent with the principles of non-discrimination and non-duplication.[97]

Nonetheless, the regime is novel in introducing an *ex-ante* procedure intended to limit abusive imposition by the recipient Member State of its own rules. In particular, prior to the application of the restrictive measure, any national authority shall (i) ask the home country to impose its own measures to address the misbehaviour and, only if the home country fails to act accordingly, or the measures applied is inadequate, (ii) notify the Commission of its intention to take the measure. The host Member State is allowed to legitimately apply the restriction provided only that the Commission has previously issued a decision in favour of its compatibility with the ECD requirements.[98]

Therefore, while under the Financial Directives the application of restrictions under the general good exemption can be controlled only *ex post*, upon the business subject to the burden having challenged it through the courts, the legitimacy of the ECD derogations is assessed by the Commission *ex ante,* upon prior request from the national authority concerned.

This new legal regime should be welcomed for the deterrent effect it will presumably exercise on Member States in applying measures capable of hindering the proper function of the internal market. Nevertheless, it still presents a fundamental gap. In particular, in the absence of any host country definition, no conclusive guidelines are currently given for determining the Member States' power of asserting jurisdiction in those areas on which the country of origin principle does not apply.

Currently, the Commission has undertaken a review of the national rules relating to the financial services sector on which the Member States have traditionally retained powers to assert restrictive measures, with a view of identifying which of those rules are capable to fall within the new derogation regime.[99] The above analysis would result in a list of black and white clauses aimed at securing homogeneous implementation of the ECD derogation regime. Even though not legally binding, the Commission's initiative is destined to influence appreciably the Member States' attitude to apply restrictions.

Given the current lack of criteria for a member state to claim powers with respect of legitimate restrictions, it would be appropriate for the Commission to carry on its task with a view of securing convergent approaches in such respect. In particular, the Commission should provide suggestions on how to assess the necessity and proportionality of certain

[97] Refer also to our Section I, Part B, para 1.
[98] Avoidance of the ex ante procedure is admitted only in case of urgency (Art 3(5)).
[99] ECD Communication 14.

measures in line with the current international trend favourable to the adoption of a 'direct-at' test. In my opinion, this would constitute a particularly suitable incentive towards a fairer regulatory approach for web-based activities, especially until more acceptable levels of harmonization are achieved.

4. *Private International Law Issues*

The horizontal nature and the wide scope of application of the ECD have broadened the country of origin principle much beyond its traditional extension. Once shaped the coordinated fields as including aspects of both public and private law, the EU legislator was faced with the problem of the impact of the internal market principle with the rules of private international law. This key issue was in fact raised during the negotiation of the ECD and eventually solved by expressly excluding the establishment under the ECD of additional private international law rules.[100]

Aside from this declaration of 'indifference', however, the wide application of the country of origin principle, as allowed under the ECD, surely complicates the issue. This is true considering that where a country of origin is applicable to private law subjects, it would seem to directly contain a conflict of laws rule.

In fact, the ECD is intended to deal with the problem of legislative fragmentation by enabling, in principle, 'on-line providers to supply services throughout the Union base on the rules of the Member State where they are established.'[101] As a consequence, at first sight, the application of the internal market clause to subjects pertaining to the private law sphere would result in the indication of a connecting factor (the place of establishment) individuating the legal system governing the transaction both from a public and private law perspective.

Nevertheless, as explicitly stated, the ECD calls for a different interpretation capable of excluding the introduction of additional private international law rules. This interpretation can be attained considering that, as mentioned in the previous section, the impact of the country of origin principle on private law is merely negative. Indeed, the above principle imposes duties on Member States in view of allocating regulatory jurisdiction but does not identify directly the private law applicable to the transaction. This is confirmed by the wording of Article 3(1)(2), which does not refer to an obligation on the part of the Member States to apply the law of the place of establishment. On the contrary, it just provides two sets of duties.

[100] Art 1(4) and Recital 23.
[101] ECD Communication 2. This wording may be actually misleading.

First, the country of establishment is required to ensure compliance with the applicable national provisions when they fall within the coordinated field. Nothing in this statement impedes the operation of the traditional technique for determining which national private law is applicable, namely the conflict of laws rules.

Secondly, Member States are demanded not to impose restrictions on free movement. In the private law field, this means that national supervisory and jurisdictional organs shall not admit whatever restrictive provisions (whether or not pertaining to their own national legal system) applicable pursuant to the national conflicts rules, unless justifiable under the derogation regime.

Therefore, far from imposing the application of the home country legislation, the ECD only requires member states to admit free provision of online services under the mutual recognition regime once compliance with the home country regulatory provisions is ensured. Hence, while in the public law area the country of origin distributes supervisory and regulatory tasks among member states, in the private law area it really operates *ex post*—just as, using a private international law concept, an *ordre public* rule—in such a way as inhibiting application of restrictive provisions previously identified by the conflicts rules.

Because of this mere negative impact, the exclusion of certain areas pertaining to private law from the operation of the internal market clause is relevant only at the level of the applicable derogation regime. In fact, since the country of origin principle does not establish an additional conflicts rule, the process for individuating the applicable law for those private law fields covered by the internal market is the same as for those excluded. However, while for the former restrictive measures are admitted on the basis of the *ex ante* procedure set forth under the ECD, for the latter the less burdensome general good test shall apply.

Thus, as a consequence of the exclusion, the difference between the legal regimes relating to consumers contract obligations and choice of law clauses on the one side and pre-contractual obligations and business-to-business transactions on the other side rests merely on the assessment of the legitimacy of restrictive measures.

Finally, additional critics against the ECD have been raised in the light of its purported inconsistency with respect to the country of destination approach adopted under the recent Brussels Regulation.[102] In particular, the Brussels Regulation allows consumers to sue in their own court of domicile subject to the provider's activity being 'direct at' that particular juris-

[102] Council Regulation (EU) No44/2001 on jurisdiction and the recognition and enforcement of judgements in civil and commercial matters, OJL12 16.01.2001.

diction.[103] In the conflict of jurisdiction, relevance is given therefore to the location of the consumer, rather than that of the supplier.

Actually, the problems concerning the relationship between the country of origin principle and the jurisdiction of courts are less evident than those relating to the conflicts rules. In fact, while the country of origin relates to the jurisdiction to prescribe, the rules under the Brussels Regulation concern the jurisdiction to adjudicate and to enforce.[104] Therefore, in no case an immediate conflicting interaction can be envisaged between the two aforementioned instruments.[105]

Nevertheless, it is true that the solution adopted under the one brings about practical consequences impacting the other. More generally, the risk is that the consistency of the resulting legal framework as a whole would be undermined whenever the adoption of opposite approaches leads to the dissociation of court jurisdiction from regulatory jurisdiction. The problem may be even aggravated when the dissociation additionally impacts civil jurisdiction.

This is in fact the scenario currently in force in the financial services sector following the entering into force of the ECD. When a dispute concerning the supplying of investment services to a consumer arises, it may happen that the court of the consumer domicile shall deal with the private law of the country contractually chosen by the parties, including the mandatory rules of the consumer's jurisdiction (insofar as the general good test is met), the provisions of the country of establishment in matter of pre-contractual issues and commercial communications and those of the country of destination (if any) applicable under the new derogation regime, the public law rules of conduct of the country of establishment and those of the country of destination, if amounting to a legitimate restriction.

Given the current divergences among EU national legal systems, the simultaneous application by a given national court of such a plurality of different laws is inevitably destined to cause serious difficulties as regards coordination and lack of predictability. Furthermore, the divergent implementation of the community directives on consumer protection[106] among Member States has increased intra-community inconsistency. The scenario is particularly blurry in a number of areas—such as the regulation of conduct of business—where the number of public laws having private law effects is increased dramatically, for the reconciliation of interacting public and private rules pertaining to different legal systems is hardly conceivable.

[103] Art 15.

[104] On the EU rules of courts jurisdiction for electronic contracts see, MITRANI (61) 51; GILLIES (42); HORNLE (44) WALDEN (92) 540; MOTION (65); ROEBUCK (81); RUSSEL (82).

[105] LOPEZ-TARRUELLA (88) 1350.

[106] On the matter, see particularly KLAUER (51) and MOLONEY (64).

Therefore, attempts to deal separately with each 'face of jurisdiction,' on the assumption that, being logically distinguishable, they do no clash, is certainly naive, especially considering the complexity of the financial services sector.

IV. CONCLUDING REMARKS

In conclusion, the entrance into force of the ECD has not changed the nature of the country of origin principle as a mere criterion of division of regulatory competences among Member States. As held in the above, in both the on-line as and the off-line financial sector, the principle does not affect the general operation of the conflict of laws rules, except for the limited extent it forbids results in contrast with the free movement of services.

Indeed, from the private law perspective, the impact of the country of origin in the financial field operates mainly at the level of the derogation regime. In fact, while the legitimacy of restrictions against on-line financial activities falling within the scope of the internal market clause has to be assessed ex ante, those against off-line activities or relating to matters exempted from the application of the internal market clause are admitted under the less stringent general good test, which conversely operates ex post.

Conversely, the impact of the ECD country of origin principle is much more pervasive in the sphere of public law, considering that all the regulatory powers pertaining to the advertising and the conduct of business areas formerly retained by the state of destination are now passed, in principle, to the competence of the country of establishment, except for those restrictions admitted under the new ex post procedure for individual exemptions.

This different operation of the internal market clause in the public and in the private law area constitutes the source of the dissociation among court, civil and regulatory jurisdiction on cross-border provision of on-line financial services. The resulting multiplication of the legal orders relevant with respect to the same transaction raises problems of reconciliation among different systems of law, which the current legal fragmentation of the financial sector renders particularly complex.

In fact, national rules of conduct and consumer protection legislation continue to be substantially different throughout the EU in term of content, legal form, sanctions and means of enforcements.[107] Moreover, as recognised by the Commission under the ECD Communication, the country of origin approach suits only in the contest of deeply harmonized areas of legislation. This is because, in absence of substantial convergence, the

[107] Avgouleas (6) 74.

extraterritorial application of the home country legislation would inevitably grant competitive advantage to those countries having less onerous legal standard and consequently give incentives to phenomena of forum shopping.

As a result, until substantial divergences in national legislations are not replaced by a much more coherent legal framework, the new derogation regime under the ECD—although more stringent that the one provided for off-line activities—is very likely to be broadly used by host States as a safeguard for asserting jurisdiction on critical areas. These exceptions to the principle of establishment are therefore destined to complicate the already confused regulatory structure for passported financial activities.[108]

The complexity of the situation is aggravated by the absence under the ECD provisions of any 'host State' definition. As a consequence, no conclusive criteria currently exist under community law as to the circumstances in which a state may legitimately claim jurisdiction on matters outside the operation of the ECD principle of establishment.

All the above jurisdictional issues should be approached once it is acknowledged that Internet-based problems should be dealt with on a global basis, thus, by taking into account the outcomes of international fora. In the web environment, where the inherently global reach always exposes on-line operators to a multiplication of potentially competent jurisdiction, special international efforts are necessary to coordinate national legal systems and, thus, to reduce uncertainty with respect to the allocation of prescriptive jurisdiction.

Certainly, the higher degree of legal convergence required for the proper operation of the country of origin principle does not allow to take the internal market approach as a model suitable at a worldwide level. Nevertheless, it would be opportune to increase consistency between the community regulatory framework and the common international trend towards a 'targeting-based' approach.

Higher consistency might be achieved through the promotion of the 'direct-at' test in the ambit of the ECD legal framework. In particular, the test might be employed in connection with the new derogation regime, in order to give guidance on the circumstances for Member States to claim jurisdiction on exempted fields. According to this solution, the State of destination should have this power only once it is proved the service provider's intention of targeting the jurisdiction concerned. The assessment over the provider's subjective intention should be based on objective criteria, in view of ensuring foresee-ability and legal certainty.

Finally, it is worth noticing that the targeted based approach fits also in the contest of private international law. In fact, the consumer protection

[108] LONG (55) 330.

provisions of both the Brussels Regulation and the Rome Convention[109] are suitable to be interpreted and applied in the light of the 'direct at' test. This solution should be certainly welcomed, considering that it would bring about the very desirable effect of realigning—at least partially—court and regulatory jurisdiction: a step towards a more predictable legal framework.

109 Particularly, Art 15 Brussels Regulation and Art 5 Rome Convention.

THE CONVERGENCE OF COMMERCIAL AND INVESTMENT BANKING UNDER THE GRAMM–LEACH–BLILEY ACT: REVISITING OLD RISKS AND FACING NEW PROBLEMS

MATTHEW J RESTREPO*

CHAPTER OUTLINE

* Mr Restrepo is a member of the law firm of Jones, Day, Reeves & Pogue, Dallas, Texas, and is a Research Fellow at the SMU Institute of International Financial, Commercial, and Technology Law.

I. INTRODUCTION

With the repeal of the Glass–Steagall Act, commercial banks can now freely affiliate with securities firms that underwrite securities. This paper will demonstrate that these commercial lending institutions are engaging in or have the ability to engage in the types of high-risk activities, associated with securities underwriting, that compelled the framers of the Glass–Steagall Act to separate commercial and investment banking in 1933. This paper will analyse and explain the severity of these risks and will recommend the promulgation of three regulations, which could substantially mitigate or completely eliminate them. Part II of this paper will trace the evolution of the relationship between commercial and investment banking from the National Banking Act to the Gramm–Leach–Bliley Act. Part III of this paper will examine the risks associated with the underwriting of both stock and bond issues, the two ways in which banks may face a two-tiered or double exposure to these risks, and the tendency of banks to expose their depositors funds to high-risk securities such as junk bonds and tech stocks. Part IV of this paper will discuss the manner in which commercial banks have used their competitive advantage over unaffiliated securities firms to become leaders in the underwriting industry, how banks may be engaging in anti-competitive activities to exploit their competitive advantages over securities firms, and the possible consequences of the oligopoly that may emerge as a result of these activities. Part V will deal with the conflicts of interests that may arise from commercial banks affiliating with underwriting firms including a bank's ability to rescue its financially distressed securities affiliate and the possibility that banks may recommend speculative securities, underwritten by their securities affiliate, to their depositors. Part VI will point out that even though these risks could be very detrimental to the safety and soundness of a commercial bank, if they came to fruition, the Promulgation of three new federal regulations, by the relevant regulatory authorities, could substantially mitigate or completely eliminate these risks. The Federal Reserve Board and the Office of the Comptroller Currency would have the ability to promulgate these regulations under their power to regulate the 'safety and soundness' of covered banking institutions.

II. THE EVOLUTION OF THE RELATIONSHIP BETWEEN COMMERCIAL AND INVESTMENT BANKING

The relationship between investment and commercial banking, in the United States, has come full circle over the past 80 years in that commercial banks were allowed to affiliate with underwriting firms under the McFadden Act, prevented from doing so under Glass–Steagall, and again allowed to do so under the Gramm–Leach–Bliley Act.

In the early part of the 20th Century, the banking industry witnessed the rise of trust companies, which were entities that not only offered traditional banking services but securities-related services, such as underwriting, as well.[1] In order to compete with these trust companies, many national banks utilized their incidental corporate powers, under the National Banking Act, to enter the securities underwriting business.[2] Congress later officially recognized the ability of national banks to affiliate with securities firms, under the McFadden Act of 1927.[3] This congressional stamp of approval, combined with the rise in stock market prices from 1927 to 1929, resulted in commercial banks becoming very active in the securities market.[4] In 1929, the stock market crashed, and by 1933 11,000 banks had failed or were forced to merge, thereby reducing the number of banks in the country by 40 per cent.[5] In the years prior to the passage of the Glass–Steagall Act, Senator Carter Glass had sought to prevent commercial banks from dealing in and holding corporate securities because he believed that such activities were responsible for the rampant stock market speculation that eventually lead to the Crash of '29, bank failures, and the Great Depression.[6] His theory that securities activities, on the part of banks, lead to many bank failures, gained a great deal of acceptance in Congress after the Bank of the United States failed in 1930, presumably due to its activities with its securities affiliates.[7] Many Congressman began to suspect that the waive of bank failures that had plagued the county had been caused, at least in part, by the exposure of banks to the securities markets, both directly and indirectly through their securities affiliates. One Congressman elaborated on

[1] Christian A Johnson *Holding Credit for Hostage for Underwriting Ranson Rethinking Bank Antitying Rules* (2002) 64 UPTLR 157 163.
[2] ibid. [3] ibid. [4] ibid, at 164.
[5] George J Benston *The Separation of Commercial and Investment Bankimg* (OUP New York 1990) 1.
[6] ibid.
[7] See Johnson, above n 1, at 164.

this concern in a statement he made before the House of Representatives in 1933. In it, he said 'The outstanding development in the commercial banking system during the pre-panic period was the appearance of excessive security loans and over-investment in securities of all kinds. A very fruitful cause of bank failures within the past three years has been the fact that the funds of various institutions have been extensively tied up in long-term investments.'[8] Statements that reflected this same sentiment were made over and over again in the Congressional Sessions of 1932 and 1933. In response to these concerns, Congress passed the Banking Act of 1933, which included provisions that separated commercial and investment banking. These provisions make up what is commonly referred to as the Glass–Steagall Act.

Sections 16 and 20 of the Banking Act of 1933, specifically address the issue of commercial bank involvement in investment banking activities. Section 16 states that a national bank 'shall not underwrite any issue of securities or stock'.[9] Section 20 prevents commercial banks from affiliating with firms 'engaged principally in the issue, flotation, underwriting, public sale, or distribution of stocks, bonds, debentures notes or other securities'.[10] These regulations together acted to prevent commercial banks from underwriting most types of securities and to prevent their affiliation with investment banking firms. Section 21 of the Act, which states that any person 'engaged in the business of issuing, underwriting, selling, or distributing . . . stocks, bonds, debentures, notes, or other securities' can not engage 'to any extent whatsoever' in deposit banking',[11] prohibits investment banking firms from entering the commercial banking business. Section 16, 20, and 21, would seem to drive a permanent wedge between investment and commercial banking, but over time, federal regulators would soften these restriction, particularly those involving affiliation.

In 1987, the Federal Reserve Board approved securities activities in non-bank subsidiaries of Bank Holding Companies, subject to certain revenue limitations and firewalls.[12] This allowed commercial banks to affiliate with firms that engaged in underwriting as long as these firms were not principally engaged in bank-ineligible activities. The 'principally engaged' test was based on the revenue of the securities firm. As long as no more than a certain percentage of the firm's revenue was derived from bank-ineligible activities, such as securities underwriting, a commercial bank was free to affiliate with them. In 1997, commercial banks acquired the ability to indi-

[8] S Rep No 77, 73 Cong, 1st Session 8.
[9] 12 USC § 24
[10] 12 USC § 377
[11] 12 USC § 378(a)(1)
[12] Heidi Mandanis Schooner and Michael Taylor *United Kingdom and United States Responses to Regulatory Challenges of Modern Financial Markets* (2003) 38 TXILJ 317, 325.

rectly participate in securities underwriting through a different type of entity, an operating subsidiary. In this controversial ruling, the office of the Comptroller of the Currency 'determined that securities activities, including the underwriting and dealing in municipal revenue and corporate bonds qualified as part of the business of banking under 12 USC § 24 (Seventh). The Comptroller further held that, if the activities were conducted out of the subsidiary, rather than the bank itself, the limitations on securities activities under Section 16 did not apply. Rather, the applicable provision was Section 20, which permitted securities activities as long as the entity in question was not principally engaged in the defined conduct.'[13] Thus the revenue based 'principally engaged' test would also apply to these operating subsidiaries. In interpreting the Bank Holding Company Act of 1956, the Federal Reserve Board originally set the revenue limitation at 5 per cent in 1987[14], but by 1999, the revenue cap had risen all the way to 25 per cent.[15] This trend of the softening of certain Glass–Steagall restrictions, by federal regulators, came to a dramatic climax in 1999, when Congress passed the Gramm–Leach–Bliley Act, which did away with Section 20 of the Banking Act of 1933. This legislation effectively opened the door to the merger of commercial and investment banking, just as the McFadden had done 72 years before.

The GLB Act repeals Section 20 of the Glass Steagall Act by amending section the Bank Holding Company Act of 1956. Section 1843(c)(8) of this act allowed a bank holding company to only acquire a firm whose acts were determined 'to be so closely related to banking as to be a proper incident thereto'.[16] The GLB Act adds Section 1843(k)(1) to the BHCA which allows a financial holding company to engage in any activity that is 'financial in nature or incidental to such financial activity'.[17] The Act then goes on to specifically list 'underwriting, dealing, in or making a market in securities as financial in nature.[18] Any bank holding company that is well-capitalized, well managed, and whose banks have a satisfactory Community Reinvestment Act rating, may become a financial holding company.[19] Once a financial holding company has been established, the commercial bank within the entity is free to affiliate with an underwriting firm, and no revenue restrictions are applicable to that firm, as they were under the Federal Reserve Board's interpretation of the BHCA. The

[13] Johnathan Macy, Geoffrey Miller, and Scott Carnell *Banking Law and Regulation* (Aspen Law and Business New York 2001) 583.

[14] Ingo Wallenborn *Competitiveness of* US *Banks After Gramm-Leach-Bliley: A Comparison Between the* US *and European Regulatory Systems* (2001) 20 ANN REV BANKING L 243, 251.

[15] See Schooner, above n 12, at 324.

[16] 12 USC § 1843 (c)(8).

[17] 12 USC § 1843(k).

[18] 12 USC § 1843(k)(4).

[19] 12 USC § 1843(l)(1).

Gramm–Leach–Bliley Act also allows a national bank that is well capitalized and well managed to control or hold an interest in a financial subsidiary if the subsidiary engages only in activities that are 'financial in nature or incidental to financial activity'.[20] Securities underwriting is included under this standard, but the financial subsidiary's assets must not exceed the lesser of 45 per cent of the assets of the parent bank or fifty billion dollars.[21]

Now that the Gramm–Leach–Bliley Act has effectively done away with the Glass–Steagall restriction that made it difficult for commercial banks to indirectly participate in securities underwriting, through affiliated securities firms, the question arises as to whether such activity could have a detrimental effect on the safety and soundness of the banks that decide to participate in the underwriting process. Congress passed the Glass–Steagall Act to address concerns about multiple high-risk endeavors of which commercial banks could or were engaging in. Banks exposure to underwriting risk, through various activities, was one of these concerns, but there were others including the risks of banks taking part in anti-competitive activities and the risks associated with the conflicts of interest that a bank's involvement in underwriting could create. All of these risky activities could potentially jeopardize the safety and soundness of a bank and the stability of the banking system as a whole, and unfortunately many banks now have the ability to engage in these activities or are currently engaging in them. If the risks associated with these endeavors were to come to fruition, for a particular bank, that bank could definitely find itself in need of a large-scale government bailout. Whether these risky activities, if undertaken by a majority of the country's banks, could lead to another banking crisis is debatable, but there is no reason for federal regulators to take this chance. Three new federal regulations need to be promulgated that restrict these high- risk activities.

III. UNDERWRITING RISKS

Now that commercial banks have the ability to affiliate with securities firms that engage in underwriting, they not only face the risks associated with underwriting stock and bond issues, but they may also face a two-tiered or double exposure to these risks.

20 12 USC § 24a.
21 12 USC § 24a(a)(2)(D).

A. *Underwriting Risks in General*

The framers of the Glass–Steagall Act recognized the inherent risks of underwriting as evidenced by this statement read aloud during the Glass Subcommittee Hearings. 'The wholesale underwriting of securities does tend at times to leave the securities affiliate with big unsold commitments that in times of rapidly declining prices, may result in large losses of at least a temporary nature. The portfolios of the security affiliates indicate that the profits of years of operation can be wiped out through two or three unprofitable commitments of this kind.'[22] These statements deal with the underwriting risks that a securities affiliate faces. If a securities affiliate has one or more offerings go sour and as a result faces financial hardship, the commercial bank that it is affiliated with would not necessarily be faced with financial troubles as well. However, if the commercial bank was in some way directly exposed to the offering or offerings that went sour, it, as well as the securities affiliate, could be in trouble. A commercial bank is directly exposed to underwriting risk, when its funds are used to finance the underwriting process. This was one of the primary concerns of the framers of the Glass–Steagall Act as evidenced by the fact that Senator Glass himself said that thc purpose of the act was 'to provide against the use of the Federal Reserves facilities for stock speculation purposes'.[23] Today, a commercial bank itself can not underwrite a securities issue because the Gramm–Leach–Bliley Act did not repeal section 16 of the Glass–Steagall Act which prohibits commercial banks from purchasing securities for its own benefit.[24] Thus the only way that a commercial bank can finance the underwriting of securities is through loans to its securities affiliate or to its financial subsidiary . Such loans were a definitely a focal point of the Glass Subcommittee Hearings. In fact, the hearings focused almost entirely on banks lending to their securities affiliates.[25]

B. *The Risks of Stock Issues*

Securities firms primarily underwrite two different types of securities, stocks and bonds. Each type of security has its own unique risks, and securities firms value and market the two types of securities in different ways. In the case of an equity or stock offering, a securities affiliate or a financial subsidiary of a commercial bank can purchase the entire issue of the securities from the issuer and then attempt to market it to the investing public,

[22] Glass Subcommittee Hearings—Section IV of Part 7 (1931) (1057–8).
[23] Glass Subcommittee Hearings (1931) 272.
[24] 12 USC § 24.
[25] See Benston above n 5, at 217.

in what is known as a firm offer. The risk associated with the firm offer is that the underwriter will not be able to sell all of the securities to the investing public or that it will not be able to sell the securities at a price that will allow it recoup its initial investment. If either of these scenarios comes to fruition, the underwriter could face a large-scale financial loss, and if the money to finance the issue came from the securities firm's commercial banking affiliate, that bank could be facing a very large default. While the idea that a skilled, seasoned underwriter would not be able to sell the entirety of a stock issue, at a price that would allow it to recoup its investment, seems like a bit of a farce, it is a possibility given the inherent risks associated with a public stock offering. There are two types of public stock offerings. One of them is the initial public offering in which the issuer first makes its stock available to the public at large. Logic would dictate that the reason such an offering is risky is because potential buyers, including underwriters, have no idea how the market will value the stock once they have purchased it. While this is true, this is a simplified explanation. The actual reason is much more complex and has to do with the manner in which the market values the stock. When analysts value publicly-traded companies, they primarily use the discounted cash flow method which is considered by the finance industry to be the most accurate method of ascertaining a firm's value.[26] In using this method, analysts project the future yearly cash flows of the company for an infinite period and discount those cash flows back to their present value by the firm's cost of capital.[27] They then add the discounted cash flows up to arrive at the firm's market value. Because the cash flow of each year is discounted or divided by the cost of capital, this number is obviously a crucial factor in determining the value of a company. The higher the cost of capital is, the less valuable the company is and vice versa. The cost of capital of a firm is a measure of the firm's risk, and in order to quantify this risk and determine the cost of capital, the analyst must determine the equity beta of the firm.[28] Once the equity beta of the firm has been determined, the analyst plugs this number into an equation called the capital asset pricing model, which produces the firm's required return on equity.[29] This number is then plugged into another equation to determine the firm's cost of capital.[30] The equity beta of a firm is simply a measure of how the value of the firm's stock has moved with the market as a whole.[31] In the case of a firm seeking an initial public offering of its stock, it would not have an equity beta because its stock had not publicly traded before. The discounted

[26] Tom Copeland, Tim Koller, and Jack Murrin *Valuation: Measuring and Managing the Value of Companies* (John Wiley & Sons New York 2000) 73.

[27] ibid, at 63.

[28] ibid, at 214.

[29] ibid.

[30] ibid.

[31] Zvi Bodie, Alex Kane, and Alan Marcus *Investments* (McGraw-Hill Irwin Boston 2002) 978.

cash flow method cannot be used to value such firms, and less accurate valuation methods, must be used instead. In the IPO context, an analysis of the stock market's valuation of comparable companies is considered the most effective valuation tool for investment bankers.[32] The analysis involves composing a list of publicly traded companies that best match the business, profitability, risk structure, and growth potential of the company going public and then averaging them to arrive at a value.[33] The weakness of the valuation method is obvious in that it uses the market's valuation of other companies based on their numbers to determine the value of the firm being offered, rather than the numbers of that firm. Due to the fact that no two companies are the exactly the same, the comparables approach involves a great deal of uncertainty. In fact, so uncertain is this valuation technique that all IPO prospectuses include price spreads in which the underwriter sets out a broad price range at which the securities are expected to be offered.[34] Underwriters with a significant number of institutional customers often desire to price an IPO between $13.00 and $20.00 because a bias exists among some sophisticated investors against lower-priced offerings, despite the fact that their own valuation, utilizing the comparables method, may have yielded a different price.[35] These factors show that the securities industry as a whole does not place a great deal of faith in their preliminary evaluations of IPO's, based on this comparables method. In an environment ridden with this level of uncertainty, it is easy to see how an underwriter could inadvertently overvalue an offering and suffer serious financial consequences.

The other type of public offering is the secondary offering, which comes after the initial public offering. For a secondary offering, the investing public and the issuer does have some idea of how the market will value the stock because the existing stock of the company currently has a value at which it is trading. Analyst also will have the equity beta for the firm, which will help them arrive at much more accurate value, via the discounted cash flow valuation method, than the comparables method used for initial public offerings. One might assume that secondary offerings are less risky than IPO's, due to the fact that the value of such issues is more certain. While this might be true to a point, the security industry as a whole does not seem to buy into this philosophy. This is evidenced by the fact that the industry utilizes the exact same risk-reducing measures in secondary offerings as they do for initial public offerings. Underwriting syndicates are common

[32] Hambrecht and Quist *The Initial Public Offering Process* (1993) 817 PLI/Corp 397, 403.
[33] ibid.
[34] Samuel N Allen *A Lawyer's Guide to the Operation of Underwriting Syndicates* (1991) 26 NENGLR 315, 326.
[35] ibid, at 347.

both in IPO's and secondary offerings unless the issuer of the secondary offering is a seasoned firm.[36] An underwriting syndicate is formed to allocate total underwriting risk across multiple underwriting firms, so that no single firm bares all of the risk of overvaluation for a particular offering.[37] In secondary offerings and IPO's, underwriters often utilize Rule 430A of the 33 Securities Act which allows a registration statement to become effective without a set price as long as the price is set within five days of the effective date.[38] This allows the underwriter to get a better idea as to what price the issuer's securities will be trading at, before he purchases them, to mitigate the risk of overpayment.[39]

Another risk-reducing measure, common to both types of securities issues, is a stabilization agreement, which entitles the managing underwriters, in a syndicate, who will always have the largest stake in the issue, to purchase all of the securities issue, from the other underwriters, at a set price.[40] When the market price of the issued securities falls below the original issue price, the measure allows the managing underwriter to purchase the rest of the issue at the original price, thereby fixing the price at that level, so that other investors may not purchase it at a discount.[41] Though a stabilization agreement does allow the managing underwriter to fix the market price, it puts it in the unenviable position of having to purchase the securities at above what the market is willing to pay for it.[42] This will definitely lead to a short-term loss of profit to the underwriter, which it will not recover until the stock rebounds, assuming of course that it ever does. Depending on the size of the decrease in the post-issue price, the utilization of this risk-reducing measure, by the underwriter, could wipe out its profits or actually cause it to incur a loss.

Another risk-reducing measure involves what is known as overallotment, which allows an underwriter in a syndicate to sell more than its allotted share in the market, thereby creating a short position in the securities.[43] This method of risk mitigation demonstrates just how little confidence an underwriter has in his valuation and how concerned he is with the possibility of having to sell the securities at a price below what he paid for them. When an underwriter shorts securities, he is betting that the price of them will fall after he has purchased the securities from the issuer. In fact, the only way in which one can profit from a short sale, due to the transaction costs associated with it, is if the security does decrease in value. If the security increases in value, the underwriter will loose money covering the short, and if the increase is large enough, covering the short could cost the under-

[36] See Allen above n 34, at 333.
[37] ibid.
[38] ibid, at 348.
[39] ibid.
[40] ibid, at 349
[41] ibid.
[42] ibid.
[43] George W Bennet *The Underwriting Process, Commercial Law and Practice Course* Handbook Series A4-410 295, 305 (1984).

writer all of its profits and more, unless efforts are made to mitigate this risk.[44]

The fact that these extreme risk-reducing tactics are used in both initial public offerings and secondary offerings, demonstrates that underwriting risk is very real, and that, although secondary offerings may be as a whole less risky than IPOs, there is still a substantial amount of risk associated with them. While these measures can decrease the amount of risk that each underwriter faces, they cannot eliminate all underwriting risk. Furthermore, these measures are accompanied by transaction costs, and the underwriter must analyse each individual issue to determine whether they are necessary. If the underwriter guesses wrong, he could lose a great deal of money either from the security falling in value or from the risk-reducing measures themselves.

Those who work in the financial industry would inevitably counter this argument by pointing out that underwriters generally seek to undervalue issues in order to reduce the amount of underwriting risk that will face.[45] While this is true, their ability to do this is limited by the demands of the issuer, particularly when the issuer needs a certain amount of capital to finance a particular project.[46] In response to this, supporters of the Gramm–Leach–Bliley Act could argue that some stock offerings are obviously more risky than others, and that large commercial banks, which make up the vast majority of banks in the country that currently engage in securities underwriting,[47] would not allow their affiliates to deal with high-risk stock offerings out of fear of besmirching their reputations. This argument does seem to make a great deal of sense. There does not seem to be any logical reason for a large well-to-do commercial bank to associate itself with a securities firm that has a reputation for engaging in highly speculative stock offerings when such an association could potentially undermine the trust and confidence of its depositors. Unfortunately this argument has no basis in fact. By the end of 1999, several big banks had made substantial equity investments in high-tech firms.[48] High-tech firms are by nature inherently risky.[49] These risks did not stop banks from increasing their investment in tech stocks during the first half of 2000, and after the tech bubble burst, eight major banks reported combined losses of $4 billion dollars from losses on these investments.[50] These equity investments were venture capital deals, which are merchant banking activities rather than investment

[44] ibid.

[45] See Allen above n 34, at 346.

[46] ibid.

[47] Vincent DiLorenzo *Cost–Benefit Analysis, Deregulated Markets, And Consumer Benefits: A Study Of The Financial Services Modernization Experience* (2002) 6 NYUJLPP 321, 351.

[48] Arthur E Wilmarth *The Transformation of the* US *Financial Services Industry, 1975–2000: Competition, Consolidation, And Increased Risks* (2002) 215 UILLR 330.

[49] ibid at 331.

[50] ibid at 332.

banking activities. However, the fact that large commercial banks were willing to invest in the equity of tech firms, demonstrates that they are not opposed to dealing in high-risk equity.

C. *The Risks of Bond Issues*

Stocks are not the only securities that investment banks underwrite. They also underwrite bonds. As is the case with stock offerings, a securities affiliate or a financial subsidiary of a commercial bank can purchase the entire issue of the bonds from the issuer and then attempts to market it to the investing public, through a firm offer. Alternatively, the securities firm may lend the issuer what it believes will be the amount raised from the issue until it is able to locate purchasers of the bonds. This type of transaction is known as a bridge loan.[51] The risks associated with a firm offer of bonds are the same as those of a firm offer of stock. The underwriter may not be able to sell all of the securities to the investing public or it may not be able to sell the securities at a price that will allow it recoup its initial investment. As is the case with a stock offering, if either of these scenarios comes to fruition, the underwriter could face a large-scale financial loss. The risk of a bridge loan transaction is almost identical to that of the firm offer. If the underwriter cannot find enough investors to purchase all of the bonds or if it cannot sell the bonds at a price that will allow it to recoup the value of the loan, it could face a large financial loss. While it is true that the issuer could simply seek repayment of the loan that it made to the issuer to compensate for the loss, the issuer may not have adequate funds to pay back the entire amount of the loan, especially if it has already invested the majority of the funds from the loan into its operations.

The underwriting risks associated with bonds are identical to those associated with stocks, in that the underwriter might not be able to sell all of the securities or might not be able to sell them at a price that will allow it to recoup its investment in the issue. However, the reasons that an underwriter may not have success selling bonds to the investing public are very different from the reasons that it may not have success selling an equity issue. The value of a stock is based on the future cash flows of the firm that issued it, and consequently, its value changes based on perceived changes in the amount of those future cash flows.[52] The value of a bond is based on interest rates or effective yield and how far the coupon rate on the bond varies from the effective yield.[53] If interest rates remain the same from the time the bond is issued to the time that the bond matures, the value of the

[51] ibid, at 327.
[52] Above n 27.
[53] Frank Fabozzi *Bond Markets, Analysis and Strategies* (Prentice Hall New York 2000) 19.

bond at maturity will be its issue price or its par value. If interest rates rise, the value of the bond will fall and will have to be sold at a discount. The risk that any bondholder faces, including an underwriter, is that interest rates will rise while it is still holding the bonds, which would decrease their value.[54] If interest rates do decrease to the level that existed at the time of the issuance of the bonds, the underwriter may have to sell them at a discount and thus not be able to recoup its initial investment. Another risk that is unique to bonds has to do with the bond's coupon rate. The coupon rate or interest rate assigned to the bond reflects the default risk of the bond's issuer.[55] The market may believe that the coupon rate that the underwriter established for a particular bond issue is not high enough in that it does not adequately compensate the potential purchaser for the default risk of the issuer.[56] If this is the case, the underwriter may not be able to sell the bonds to the investing public. The final risk that is commonly associated with bonds, although it also applies to stocks, is default risk. If an issuer defaults on its coupon payments for a particular bond issue, and the issuer is still holding bonds from that issue, it is obviously going to be difficult if not impossible for the issuer to sell those bonds to the investing public, at least in the short term.[57]

Despite all of these risks, bonds are, for the most part, considered to be less risky investments than stocks. There is, however, one big exception, junk bonds. Junk bonds are high-yield bonds that are below investment grade. The reason that they are below investment grade is that the market believes there is a high probability that the firms that issue them may not have adequate cash flows to service the debt.[58] Events since 1989 have shown that underwriters in the junk bond market face significant liquidity, volatility, and default risks.[59] These risks became very evident to the investing public during the well-publicized junk bond debacle of the early 1990s. During this time period, there was a sudden rise in junk bond defaults, due in part to the recession of 1990–1.[60] Some of these defaults were quite large as evidenced by the fact that 10 of the 25 companies, that issued $1 billion or more in junk bonds during the period between 1985 and 1989, defaulted on their bonds.[61] These defaults triggered sharp declines in the market values of outstanding junk bonds, which in turn lead or contributed to the near insolvency of several leading securities firms and banks and the bankruptcy of the once mighty Wall Street powerhouse of Drexel, Burnham, and Lambert.[62]

Given the fact that junk bond issues have proven to be extremely risky, one might assume that these days, large commercial banks would seek to

[54] ibid, at 6. [55] ibid.. [56] ibid.
[57] ibid, at 7. [58] ibid, at 153.
[59] See Wilmarth above n 48, at 330.
[60] ibid, at 328. [61] ibid. [62] ibid.

avoid them at all costs, especially after the massive junk bond devaluation of the early 1990s put many large banks in financial jeopardy. Unfortunately, this is not the case. Leading banks now underwrite a major portion of domestic junk bonds and are aggressively expanding into oversees markets.[63] Even before the GLB Act was passed, commercial banks, through their Section 20 subsidiaries, underwrote one-third of all domestic junk bond issues in 1999, up from one fifth in 1996.[64] Now that the Glass–Steagall restrictions have been done away with, Citigroup, JP Morgan Chase, and Bank of America have become leading underwriters of junk bonds.[65] Chase has even gone so far as to direct much of its underwriting business to its non-investment grade customers.[66]

An argument could be made that junk bonds are really not that risky and that the massive junk bond devaluation of the early 90s was an anomaly, caused by the combination of a recession and the overheated LBO market of the late 1980s.[67] An LBO, or leveraged buyout, is an acquisition method that utilizes junk bonds financing.[68] This acquisition method became very popular in the late 80s. In fact, the largest acquisition in US history was the leverages buyout of RJR Nabisco by Kohlberg, Kravis, and Ross.[69] KKR ended up paying over $25 billion for the conglomerate, and most of those funds came from junk bonds underwritten by Drexel, Burnham, and Lambert.[70] This acquisition was one of many multi-billion dollar LBOs that were funded with junk bonds, during this time period.[71] Because it is unlikely that the LBO market will ever reach the overheated level that it did in the late 1980s and early 1990s and more unlikely that a recession would hit right in the middle of it, one could argue that junk bonds are simply not as risky as they were during that time period and might not ever be again. This assumption is invalid, though, as evidenced by the massive number of junk bond defaults that occurred between the years of 1998 and 2001. During this time period the junk bond default rate tripled, reaching its highest level in almost a decade, and as a result, yield rates on junk bonds reached their highest levels since 1991.[72] There was no recession in the time period between 1998 and 2001 and no LBO craze either. In fact, 'analysts blamed the sharp rise in defaults on the willingness of banks and securities firms to underwrite a record number of highly speculative junk bonds issues'.[73] The sheer magnitude of damage that junk bond defaults could inflict upon a firm became very evident during this time period. American Express lost over $1 billion from investing in junk bonds, and the Federal Reserve Board had to help organize rescues for Banker's Trust and LTCM,

[63] ibid, at 329.
[64] ibid, at 326.
[65] ibid.
[66] See Johnson above n 1, at 179.
[67] See Wilmarth above n 29, at 328.
[68] Above n 58.
[69] See Copeland above n 26, at 112.
[70] ibid.
[71] ibid.
[72] See Wilmarth above n 29, at 329.
[73] ibid.

two firms that had reached the point of insolvency due to their investment in junk bonds.[74] Junk bonds are therefore still very risky, but despite this risk, commercial banks are aggressively pursuing the underwriting of junk bond issues. Banks did not pursue junk bond underwriting until the very early 1990's, but now that they underwrite a major portion of domestic junk bonds, through their securities affiliates or financial subsidiaries, they are far more exposed to adverse developments in the market.[75]

D. The 'Double-Exposure Risks'

1. *Banks making loans to their securities affiliates to underwrite a firm's securities issue and then making loans to that firm*

Critics of Glass–Steagall charge that all the Act really does is prevent commercial banks from making loans to securities affiliates by not allowing commercial banks to affiliate with securities firms. The act does not prevent commercial banks from lending money to unaffiliated securities firms. This is a good point, but what the framers of Glass–Steagall were probably worried or, what they should have been worried about, was commercial banks engaging in transaction that would subject them to a two-tiered exposure to underwriting risk. This two-tiered or 'double exposure' risk could come about in two different ways. The first of the two would involve a situation in which a commercial bank lends money to its securities affiliate to underwrite an issue of securities for a particular firm and then lends money to that same firm. The framers of Glass–Steagall were concerned about commercial banks making loans to their securities affiliates to finance securities issues.[76] They also worried about banks making loans to firms that had contracted with the bank's securities affiliate to underwrite its securities. In fact, the Supreme Court, in interpreting the legislative history of Glass–Steagall, stated that one of the main problems with allowing banks to affiliate with securities firms, that Congress was concerned about, was that the bank might be tempted to loan money to a firm of which its securities affiliate had provided underwriting services.[77] The court here was commenting on a statement in the Glass Subcommittee Report, which said: 'The practice of lending to firms whose securities had been underwritten by the bank's affiliate clearly placed depositors funds in jeopardy.'[78] Whether Congress was worried about commercial banks being faced with double exposure to securities underwriting or if they were simply worried about commercial banks making unsound loans to firms, whose

[74] ibid, at 329–30.
[75] ibid, at 330.
[76] Above n 23.
[77] *Investment Company Institute v Camp*, 401 US 617, 631 (1971).
[78] Glass Subcommittee Report (1932, 8).

securities their affiliates had underwritten, is not clear from the legislative history. If Congress was concerned about the later, it is occurring today. Ever since the passage of the Gramm–Leach–Bliley Act in that 'commercial banks are offering customers inexpensive or barely profitable loans in order to land lucrative securities underwriting mandates'.[79] Low interest or barely profitable loans could definitely be unsound because the interest rate in a low interest rate or barely profitable loan may not adequately compensate the lender for the default risk of the borrower.

While there is no indication, in the legislative history of Glass–Steagall, that Congress contemplated the 'double exposure risk', they were concerned with commercial banks financing underwriting endeavors,[80] and they were concerned with commercial banks making loans to firms that their securities affiliate had underwritten securities for.[81] This 'double exposure risk' is simply a combination of these two risks and represents a greater danger to the safety and soundness of commercial banks than either of the aforementioned risks by themselves. The reason for this is that if the bank lends money to its securities affiliate to underwrite a securities issue for a particular firm and then loans that firm money, the bank could face two defaults if the securities affiliate is not able to sell the entire issue and defaults on its loan and if the firm itself defaults on its loan. The risk of these two defaults tied to one securities offering for one firm is the double exposure risk.

The risk that this 'double exposure risk' could come to fruition is much less likely if the issue involved was of stock rather than bonds. There is not necessarily a link between a firm defaulting on its loan and an underwriter not being able to unload that firm's stock on the open market. An underwriter not being able to sell all of a firm's stock at all or at a price that allows the underwriter to recoup its investment could be due to the initial overvaluation of the security or, in the case of a stock that has been public traded for a period of time, due to the fact that the market does not think that the firm's cash flows have grown at a fast enough rate to justify the initial offering price. While an underwriter not being able to unload a firm's stock at the price that it has set is not a good reflection on the financial position of the company, it does not necessarily mean that the company is in such bad condition that it will default on its loans. However, if the firm defaults on its loan, while the underwriter is still holding some of its securities, the underwriter will probably not be able to sell the securities to the public at the price that it has set for them. The reason for this is that an earnings disappointment, missed milestone or volatile operating perfor-

[79] See Johnson above n 1, at 161.
[80] Above n 23.
[81] Above n 70.

mance can cause a dramatic reaction in the market's valuation of the securities,[82] and all of these occurrences are consistent with a default.

The probability of a double default occurring is probably much higher if the securities involved are bonds. Bonds and loans are both forms of debt, and if a firm defaults on one, common sense would dictate that there is a high probability that it will default on the other. This is especially true today because many bond debentures and loan documents include cross-default clauses, which provide that if the borrower defaults on a loan or any other outstanding debt, the borrower has defaulted on the bonds. If this occurs, and the firm defaults on its commercial loans and then its bonds, it is doubtful that the firm's underwriter will be able to sell any remaining bonds, that it is still holding, at least in the short term. Even if the firm does not default on the bonds and only defaults on the loan, there is still a good chance that the underwriter of the bonds would not be able to sell any of those bonds that it is still holding. The reason for this is that the investing public may view the bonds as too risky, given the fact that the company has already defaulted on a portion of its debt. This double default risk would obviously be much more severe if junk bonds were involved. Junk bonds are, after all, are issued by companies, which have a high default risk.[83] Even though banks do not seem to be intimidated by the risks of underwriting junk bonds, one would assume that they would not make loans to the same non-investment grade company for whom their securities affiliate or financial subsidiary underwrote junk bonds. Once again, this is not the case. In recent years, leading banks have aggressively offered packages of loans and junk bonds to finance mergers and acquisitions by firms specializing in LBOs.[84] In these transactions banks provide loans to the LBO sponsor, who eventually becomes the owner of the acquired firm and is responsible for servicing the bonds that were used to finance the acquisition.[85]

2. *Banks making loans to their securities affiliate to underwrite a securities issue and then making rescue loans to that firm when it is in financial jeopardy*

The other type of 'double exposure risk' comes about in the following scenario. A commercial bank lends money to its securities affiliate for underwriting purposes, and later on the securities affiliate gets into financial trouble. The commercial bank then lends money to the securities affiliate to rescue it. If this is the case, the bank faces a double exposure to underwriting risk. The reason for this is that the initial loan for underwrit-

[82] See Allen above n 34, at 400.
[83] Above n 58.
[84] See Wilmarth above n 29, at 326.
[85] ibid.

ing obviously exposes it to underwriting risk and the second loan to the securities firm indirectly exposes it to underwriting risk because the securities firm itself is exposed to underwriting risk. This 'double exposure risk' was not mentioned in the legislative history of Glass–Steagall. However, Congress was concerned with banks making loans rescue loans to its affiliate. This is evidenced by a statement read before Congress which said 'Activities of a bank's securities affiliate as a holding or finance company or an investment trust are fraught with the danger of large losses during a deflation period. Bank affiliates of this kind show a much greater tendency to operate with borrowed funds than do organizations of this type which are independent of banks, the reason being that the identity of control and management which prevails between the bank and its affiliate tends to encourage reliance on the later'.[86] As mentioned earlier, Congress was also concerned with bank funds being used for underwriting.[87] Once again, this double exposure risk is a combination of two risks, contemplated by Congress, that is much more dangerous to the safety and soundness of a bank than either of the individual risks standing alone.

3. *Regulation W and its failure to mitigate the 'double-exposure risks'*

The concept of the 'double exposure risk' is based on the premise that a securities affiliate can get into financial trouble from not being able to sell security issues at the price that would allow it to recoup its investment in those securities. Once this occurs, the assumption made is that the affiliate will then default on its commercial loan. Whether or not a securities affiliate would default on its loans after a loss on a securities issue is debatable. While one bad securities offer might not be enough to put the firm in financial jeopardy, evidence presented at the Glass Subcommittee Hearings did demonstrate that two or three bad offerings could wipe out the profits of a securities firm. (Glass—1st paragraph) These profits would presumably be the source of the funds that the securities firm would use to service the debt. In light of this fact, the Federal reserve Board has enacted Regulation W in an attempt to insulate commercial banks from the risk of their securities affiliates defaulting on loans made by them.[88] Regulation W is a codification of Section 23 and 24 of the Federal Reserve Act, which requires that loans made by banks to their affiliates be collateralized at 100–130 per cent, depending on the nature of the transaction.[89] The regulation also requires commercial bank to set the interest rate on these loans at a market

[86] 1931 Hearings 20, 237, 1058.

[87] Above n 23.

[88] Eugene M Katz *Securities Activities, Merchant Banking and Functional Regulation Under the Gramm–Leach–Bliley Act,* (2002) 56 Consumer Fin LQ Rep 182, 183.

[89] ibid.

rate.[90] This requirement is in place, presumably to insure that the bank is adequately compensated for the risk of the loan. There are multiple problems with this regulation, both on its face and in its application. The first problem has to do with the market rate requirement. Commercial banks are already making barely profitable loans to firm that use their securities affiliates for underwriting services.[91] Wouldn't this be a market rate? There has been no litigation yet to determine this, but if the rate on these barely profitable loans is a market rate, the question is raised as to whether such a rate would adequately compensate a bank for the inherently high default risk of an underwriting firm. Another problem with the Regulation W is the collateralization requirement. Investment banks are not know for keeping large amounts of cash on hand for long periods of time because they invest most of the cash that they have in securities offerings. Thus the only thing that they could conceivably collateralize a large loan with would be securities. Regulation W does prevent securities firms from collateralizing loans from their commercial affiliates with securities that they issued[92], but securities in general are subject to value fluctuations and liquidity risks while cash is not. If the commercial bank is forced to seize these securities as collateral, it can't sell them to the public, because of Section 16 of Glass–Steagall.[93] It would have to sell them to another securities firm, but if the value of these securities depreciated, it may not be able to sell them at a price that would compensate it the amount of its loan or it might not be able to sell them at all.

The third and final problem with Regulation W is one of application. If the securities firm is in financial distress, there is a possibility that it may not be able to meet these collateralization requirements. If the securities firm is not able to find adequate rescue financing from another bank, its commercial banking affiliate may find itself in the position of having to standby idly while the firm goes under because Regulation W will not allow the commercial bank to make any loans to the firm that are not collateralized. This raises the question as to whether the FRSB would actually prevent a commercial bank from rescuing its affiliate in such a situation. The FRSB recently created a Too Big To Fail policy which was intended to assure the public that it would do everything in its power to prevent any large commercial bank from failing.[94] This doctrine was enacted to prevent depositors from panicking and seeking immediate withdrawal of their funds from a large bank if that bank entered a state of financial distress.[95] Large banks are generally the only banks that affiliate with securities firms.[96] The framers of the Glass–Steagall Act believed that if a securities affiliate was

[90] ibid.
[91] See Johnson above n 1, at 161.
[92] See Katz above n 56.
[93] Above n 9.
[94] See Wilmarth above n 29, at 225.
[95] ibid.
[96] Above n 28.

facing insolvency, depositors of the affiliated commercial bank might panic and try to withdraw all of their funds as they might if the bank itself was in trouble.[97] This has led many commentators to believe that, in the spirit of the Too Big to Fail Doctrine, the FRSB would not prevent a large commercial bank from rescuing a troubled securities affiliate in fear that the affiliate's insolvency would undermine the public's confidence in the bank.[98] If the FRSB did allow this rescue to happen, the commercial bank would face the double exposure risk, assuming that it had made loans to the securities affiliate to finance securities issues. Due to these three aforementioned problem with Regulation W, it is clear that the regulation does very little to insulate the firm from the 'double exposure risk'.

IV. ANTI-COMPETITIVE RISKS

The ability of banks to take on the double-exposure risk, in which they lend money to their securities affiliates to underwrite a firm's securities issue and then make loans to that same firms, has provided them with a competitive advantage over unaffiliated investment banking firms, the ability to exploit this advantage via anti-competitive activities, and the ability to become leaders in the underwriting industry. This trend, if allowed to continue, would result in a concentration of underwriting business within a small number of large banks that control the majority of deposits in this country, which could be detrimental to the safety and soundness of the banking industry as a whole.

A. *The Competitive Advantage of Banks*

The Congress of 1933 was concerned 'with the relationship between commercial banks and their subsidiaries that underwrote securities and the ability of the banks, through their subsidiaries, to dominate corporate underwriting'.[99] According to former Assistant Secretary of the Treasury for Domestic Finance, Roger Mehle, this ability stems from the fact that commercial banks have a significant competitive advantage over non-bank underwriters, including a lower cost of capital and the tax deductibility of carrying costs.[100] In regard to the lower cost of capital claim, Mehle points out that the majority of banks liabilities are low interest or interest-free deposits as opposed to investment banks, which borrow money from

[97] See Investment Company Institute above n 50, at 631. 'Pressures are created because the bank and the affiliate are closely associated in the public mind, and should the affiliate fare badly, public confidence in the bank might be impaired.'

[98] See Wilmarth above n 29, at 225.

[99] (1933) 75 Cong Rec 9887.

[100] Roger W Mehle *Bank Underwriting of Municipal Bonds* (1975) 26 SULR 1117, 1155.

commercial banks to finance their activities.[101] Another commentator pointed out that banks can also seek Federal Reserve discount window borrowing, while non-bank underwriters can not.[102] Because commercial banks have this ability to borrow at a lower interest rate than non-bank underwriters, underwriting would be a more profitable endeavor for them than for investment bankers. This profitability advantage is what creates the competitive advantage. Mehle also points that banks can deduct certain non-interest carrying costs that non-banks cannot.[103] For instance, banks can still the non-interest cost of deposits, which include salaries and other expenses incurred to process deposit accounts and serve customers.[104] Obviously, non-banking entities cannot utilize this tax subsidy because only a bank can accept deposits. The reason that this gives banks a competitive advantage is that they presumably pass on these non-interest deposit costs and other costs to their borrowers in the form of a one-time finance charge. Borrowers, including investment banks, cannot deduct this finance charge from their taxable income.[105] The non-interest cost of deposits for banks is the same thing as a finance charge, but they can deduct it. The basic effect of this subsidy, is that non-banks pay a finance charge when they borrow money, and banks do not. Because banks would not have to pay this finance charge, when they borrow money from their depositors, to finance securities underwriting, they would be in the position to make more profits than on underwriting deals than investment banks, which do pay a finance charge when they borrow money. Once again this advantage in profitability creates a competitive advantage in favor of the bank.

Because banks are no longer able to directly underwrite most securities, an argument could be made that they are no longer in the position to exploit this competitive advantage. However, the bank might be able to pass along this advantage to its securities affiliate, by loaning it money at an interest rate that is below that of what an unaffiliated investment bank would have to pay on a similar loan from a unaffiliated commercial bank. This would conceivably give the affiliated securities firm a profit advantage over unaffiliated securities firm, which would be a competitive advantage. Regulation W might prevent this from happening in that it requires a market rate of interest on loans between affiliates, but as discussed earlier, the question remains as to what a market rate is. The commercial bank might also choose to waive the finance charge to its affiliate. There is nothing in Regulation W that would prevent this from happening, and this would instill a profit advantage on the part of the affiliated securities firm, because unaffiliated securities firm would probably have to pay a finance charge on loans from commercial banks.

101 ibid.

102 See Benston above n 5, 165.

103 See Mehle above n 62.

104 ibid.

105 ibid.

Assuming that commercial banks are not able to make low-interest loans to their affiliates that would give them a competitive advantage over other underwriting firms, because of Regulation W restrictions, and that commercial banks are either unwilling to waive one-time finance charges to their affiliates or that such a waiver would constitute such a small amount of savings that it would be insignificant, securities firms, affiliated with commercial banks, still have one very substantial competitive advantage over unaffiliated securities firm. This advantage is the ability to secure low-interest, barely profitable loans, for the firms that they underwrite securities for, from their affiliated commercial banks. Because securities firms have to pay a higher interest rate on the money that they borrow than banks and because they have to pay finance charges, banks have a clear competitive advantage over securities firms in making loans. Large banks that are affiliated with securities firms are already exploiting this competitive advantage.

B. Banks as Leaders in the Underwriting Industry

As stated earlier, 'commercial banks are offering customers inexpensive loans in order to land lucrative securities underwriting mandates (for their affiliates)'.[106] There is a great deal of evidence that large banks are gaining substantial market share as a result of this competitive advantage. For instance, bank-affiliated investment banking firms topped the list of revenue producers in the industry in 2001.[107] Salomon Smith Barney, JP Morgan Chase, Bank of America Securities, and First Union Securities were all among the top 15 underwriters of US Debt and Equity Offerings in the United States.[108] In fact, Citicorp, the financial holding company of Citibank has become industry leader in underwriting revenues, and many believe that it risen to this position because it promises firms barely-profitable loans from Citibank if the firm allows its securities affiliate, Salomon, Smith, Barney, to provide underwriting services.[109] JP Morgan Chase also seeks to marry its lending and underwriting business together in efforts to further develop its investment banking activities.[110] More and more large corporations have become aware of the fact that commercial banks can offer these low-interest loans in tandem with underwriting services, and they have taken advantage of it, and though they have not necessarily stopped dealing with unaffiliated investment banking firms, but many have threatened to do so if their investment bank does not provide them with low-interest loans.[111] This strategy, known as pay to play, is becoming a

106 Above n 1.

107 See Schooner above n 12, at 349.

108 See Johnson above n 1, at 171.

109 See Schooner above n 12, at 389.

110 See Johnson above n 1, at 389.

111 ibid, at 176.

normal part of doing business, as evidenced by the fact that large corporations such as Ford, AT&T, Lucent, and Primedia have all disclosed that they are requiring underwriters to lend to them.[112] Premier securities underwriters, such as Merrill Lynch and Goldman Sachs, have found out the hard way that if they refuse such a request, many large firms are more than willing to take their business elsewhere, to a securities affiliate of a commercial bank that will provide the low-interest lending.[113] Many investment banks are not in the position to make the low-interest loans that commercial banks can offer.

C. *Tying Arrangements: Potential Anti-Competitive Activities*

Unaffiliated investment banks are understandably annoyed by the fact that banks are exploiting this competitive advantage and that they have the ability to do so in the first place, but many of these firms are crying fowl because they, like many industry analysts, believe that banks may be engaging in tying arrangements with some of their smaller, less influential, customers.[114] In this context, a tying arrangement could result if a commercial bank demanded that one of it's commercial clients contract with its securities affiliate for underwriting services or else the bank would cut off the firm's existing line of credit.[115] If this occurred, the firm could simply stop doing business with that bank and find another lender. The problem is that once a firm establishes a relationship with a commercial bank, over time the banks tend to provide the firm with more favorable terms for loans and other financial services as a reward for their loyalty. In addition to this, the credit market is tightening and it has become very difficult, even for large corporations, to retain important bank credit lines.[116] Thus it may be in the firm's best interest to allow the bank's securities affiliate to carry out its securities underwriting because it may not be able to find such favorable lending terms or any lending whatsoever from a different bank, that it has not done business with in the past. The ability of the bank to offer low-interest loans to entice large corporations to contract with their securities affiliates for underwriting services definitely provides them with a competitive advantage over non-affiliated investment banking firms. This competitive advantage is definitely a threat to non-affiliated investment banking firms. However, if these same commercial banks could use their existing relationships, with their smaller, less influential customers, as leverage to coerce them into contracting with their securities affiliate for underwriting services, such an arrangement would constitute a very potent, anti-competitive weapon, that if used on a large enough scale, could spell disaster for unaffiliated investment banks.

[112] ibid, at 177.
[113] ibid, at 176.
[114] ibid, at 161.
[115] ibid, at 172.
[116] ibid.

The good news for unaffiliated investment banking firms is that such coercive arrangements may be illegal under the Bank Holding Company Act. The anti-tying provision of the act states that a 'bank shall not in any manner extent credit on the condition or requirement that the customer shall obtain some additional credit, property, or service from the bank.[117] This provision also applies to products or services that might be offered by a bank's affiliate or subsidiary which is obviously important here because an underwriting/lending tying arrangement would involve the bank's affiliate or subsidiary.[118] This statute would seem to explicitly outlaw commercial banks from engaging in such tying arrangements, but it may not, for multiple reasons.

The first reason is that this provision of the BHCA was added in 1970 when the Glass–Steagall restrictions on affiliations between investment and commercial banks were still in effect. Thus it is questionable whether the BHCA's anti-tying provisions would apply to an underwriting/lending tie because Congress probably did not even contemplate the fact that such a tying arrangement was possible. Another reason that the BHCA may not apply to an underwriting/lending tie is that for a tie to exist, there must be two separate products, and a commercial bank could simply argue that lending and underwriting are both forms of corporate finance and not two separate products.[119] Whether or not this argument would prevail remains to be seen because there has been no litigation involving this matter.[120] Another problem with BHCA's applicability to such tying arrangement involves the burden of proof, required on the part of the plaintiff, to succeed in an anti-tying action. A tie is difficult to prove in the absence of a contractual provision that expressly establishes it, and there appear to be no examples of requirements in any loan document, thus far, that expressly condition the granting of the loan on the borrower utilizing the bank's securities affiliate for underwriting services.[121] This is probably because banks are well aware of the fact that the existence of such a clause would constitute clear and convincing evidence of a tying relationship.[122] The final and most important reason that the BHCA's anti-tying provisions may not apply to underwriting/lending ties has to do with the fact that banks are probably engaging in implied rather than express tying arrangements.[123] An express tying arrangement occurs, under the BHCA, when a bank states, either orally or in writing, that the customer cannot purchase one banking product if he does not purchase another. Assuming that the BHCA does apply to underwriting/lending ties, if a bank made demanded that a customer did business with its securities affiliate in order to obtain a loan from it, such

117 12 USC § 1972.
118 ibid.
119 See Johnson above n 1, at 187.
120 ibid.
121 ibid, at 183.
122 ibid.
123 ibid, at 185.

an action would constitute tying.[124] However, it is much more likely that banks are engaging in implied tying arrangements, in which the bank threatens to reduce or cut off credit unless the borrower agrees to use the banks securities affiliate for its underwriting needs.[125] Evidence of the existence of such implied tying arrangements stems from the fact that commercial banks have been very aggressive in publicizing that a customer should give the commercial bank other non-lending business if it wants the commercial bank to continue lending to them.[126] Some commercial banks have even gone so far as to limit their lending to customers that do not purchase additional services from them.[127] As counterintuitive as it may seem, such implied tying arrangements may not violate the BHCA's anti-tying provisions.[128] The statute says that a bank may not extend credit on the condition or requirement that the customer shall obtain some additional credit, property, or service from such bank. In defending its implied-tying practices, a bank could theoretically argue that it had already extended credit to it customer and was simply threatening to cut off the customer if it did not purchase underwriting services from the bank's securities affiliate. The bank would have a very plausible argument here because such an implied-tie would not seem to violate the statute, on its face. Whether such an argument would be successful in court is uncertain because there has not yet been any litigation dealing with implied ties under the BHCA. 184.

Despite the problems with the application of the BHCA to underwriting/lending ties, it does seem unlikely that courts would shy away from ruling that such arrangements violated the anti-tying provision of the BHCA. The wording of the anti-tying provision suggests that Congress passed the measure to prevent banks from blackmailing their customers into purchasing additional products. If banks are indeed conditioning the granting of credit on the purchase of underwriting services, such activity would seem to constitute the type of coercion that the statute was designed to prevent. While there is a compelling argument that the anti-tying provision may not apply to implied-ties, there is also a very strong argument that it does. When a bank threatens to cut off credit to an existing customer because the customer refused to purchase underwriting services, it is true that the bank did not make the purchase of such services a condition of the credit initially. However, it is conditioning the granting of additional credit, upon the purchase of underwriting services. Such action on the part of the bank would seem to violate the anti-tying provision on its face. Even if a court rules that the provision does not apply to implied ties, general anti-trust law, which does outlaw implied ties, might apply.[129] Congress, the

[124] ibid, at 183.
[125] ibid, at 185.
[126] ibid.
[127] ibid.
[128] ibid, at 184.
[129] ibid.

GAO, and banking regulators are currently investigating these alleged tying violations, on the part of commercial banks,[130] so there is also a possibility that new laws or regulations could come about that specifically bar banks from engaging in such activity.

D. The Potential Monopolization of the Underwriting Industry by Commercial Banks and the Resulting Threat to the Safety and Soundness of the Banking System

Assuming that commercial banks are not allowed to engage in underwriting/lending ties, they still have a substantial competitive advantage over unaffiliated investment banks, due to their ability to make low-interest loans to perspective underwriting clients. Large commercial banks have obviously exploited this advantage in that there is a growing concentration of securities activities within a small number of these large entities. If this trend continues, it is possible that these large commercial banks could one day dominate the industry. If this happens, these banks will be exposed to an enormous amount of underwriting risk. This in and of itself might not be a problem, if it were not for the fact that large banks, such as that have become revenue leaders in the underwriting industry, were not also the dominant firms in the lending industry. The ten largest banks in the country now control 49 per cent of the industry's assets, including over $1 trillion in deposits.[131] If these banks were to become the dominant firms in the underwriting industry, they would be exposed to substantial underwriting risks in addition to the substantial default risks that stem from their status as the dominant firms in the lending industry. It well known that the rate of loan defaults drastically rises during recessions. Securities also tend to suffer during a recession, in that the rate of junk bond defaults rises, and stocks tend to depreciate in value. With this fact in mind, one could conclude that large banks that have significant exposure to loans, junk bonds, and stocks could find themselves in a great deal of financial trouble during a recession, much more so than they would, if they were only involved in lending. This suspicion was recently confirmed by a study which found that large banks that engaged in capital market ventures faced higher risks and were more vulnerable to macroeconomic fluctuations than smaller banks that primarily engaged in lending.[132] As a result the growing concentration, of securities activities within a small number of large banks, greatly increases the likelihood that the failure of any of these institutions could result in a costly bailout by federal regulators.[133] More disturbing than this is the proposition that if more than two of these banks failed, there is a high probability

[130] ibid, at 179.
[131] See Wilmarth above at 252.
[132] ibid, at 250.
[133] ibid, at 224.

that the Bank Insurance Fund's current reserves would be insufficient to bail them out, according to the FRSB.[134] The implications of all of this are clear. If the concentration of securities underwriting and other securities activities, within a small number of large banks, continues to increase, the probability of this country facing a large-scale financial catastrophe also increases. The failure of one of these large banks would probably not lead to such a catastrophe, although a government bailout of the bank would probably cost the taxpayers a great deal of money, and such a failure could start another banking scare, at least in the short-term. However, if more than two of these banks failed, and federal regulators did not have adequate funds to bail them out, this could ignite a full-blown banking crisis.

V. INHERENT CONFLICTS OF INTERESTS

Besides the risks associated with securities underwriting and anti-competitive activities, Congress was also deeply concerned with conflicts of interest that could arise from the relationship between a commercial bank and a securities affiliate and more specifically, the detrimental effects that such conflicts could have upon overall public confidence in the bank.

A. The Role of Public Confidence in the Safety and Soundness of a Bank and the Entire Banking System

It is undisputed that what ultimately lead many banks to fail in the early 1930s were panics in which a bank's customers, upon hearing of its poor financial condition, sought the immediate withdrawal of their deposits. As a result Congress sought certain measures to restore and maintain public confidence in banks to prevent the likelihood of such 'runs' occurring in the future. One of these measures was the separation of commercial banks from their securities affiliates. While Congress was concerned about the possible negative perception of a bank, that could stem from its affiliation with a securities firm, in general, Congress was much more concerned with the conflicts of interest that could arise out of this relationship and their detrimental effects on the public confidence in that institution.

B. Banks Lending Money to their Financially-Distressed Securities Affiliate

One potential conflict of interest, which Congress addressed, involved situations in which the bank's securities affiliate fell on hard times, and in

[134] ibid, at 248.

response the bank made unsound loans to the affiliate in an attempt to rescue it from insolvency.[135] The reason that there is a conflict of interest inherent in such situations is because the commercial bank could be torn between its duty to protect its depositors' funds and its desire to rescue its troubled affiliate. The Supreme Court believed that the framers of Glass Steagall were indeed concerned that such loans made to a securities affiliate could jeopardize public confidence in the bank and that the very fact that the securities affiliate was in trouble, if widely known, could have the same effect[136]. A situation such as this may pose an even greater threat today than it did during the period in which Glass–Steagall was enacted. In the early 1930s, radio and newspapers were the primary media outlets. Now that there is the Internet, television, and even a cable station specifically dedicated to financial news, there is a much greater probability that a large majority of the public would be aware that a securities firm was in financial trouble, which bank that firm was affiliated with, and that the bank was making large-scale loans to that institution in hopes of rescuing it. However, an argument could be made that because only very large banks are currently affiliating with securities firms, if one of these firms was facing default and its affiliated bank lent it money in an attempt to rescue it, the public in general would not fear such a situation because it, as a whole, is well aware of the nearly unlimited capital resources of these institutions.

C. Banks Recommending Speculative Securities, which their Affiliates Underwrote, to their Depositors

Whether or not the aforementioned conflict of interest involving rescue loans, poses a threat to public confidence in commercial banks today is debatable. However one conflict of interest that Congress was particularly concerned about, could definitely pose such a threat. This conflict of interest involves situation in which commercial banks might provide biased investment advice to their depositors, in recommending that they purchase stocks that the bank's securities affiliate has underwritten. One Senator addressed this risk in a statement that he made during the Glass Subcommittee Hearings. In it he said 'Obviously the banker who has nothing to sell to his depositors is much better qualified to advise disinterestedly and to regard diligently the safety of depositors than the banker who uses the list of depositors in his savings department to distribute circulars concerning the advantages of this, that, or the other investment on which the bank is to receive an originating profit or an underwriting profit.'[137] In

[135] Above n 54.

[136] See Investment Company Institute above n 50, at 631.

[137] 75 Cong Rec 9912.

commenting on the possibility of a depositor losing money on an investment that the bank had recommended, the Senator said:

> although such a loss would possibly not result in any substantial impairment of the resources of the banking institution owning the affiliate, there can be no doubt that the whole transaction tends to discredit the bank and impair the confidence of its depositors.[138]

In these statements, Senator Bulkley, was basically saying that if a bank recommended the purchase of securities, underwritten by it or its securities affiliate, to its depositors, this constituted a conflict of interest, and that if depositors suffered a loss, as a result of investing in these securities, the confidence that they had in the bank would be impaired. In addition to the possible undermining of public confidence, Congress was also concerned with the detrimental effects that such conflicts of interests could have on the stock market. The reason that they had this concern is that they believed that these conflicts of interest contributed to the stock market crash of 1929, in that they believed that many banks were guilty of pushing the sale of speculative or in some cases worthless stocks, that they or their affiliates had underwritten, on the market.[139] Given these risks, the question arises as to whether such a scenario could come about today, now that banks are allowed to affiliate with securities firms. Interestingly enough, a very similar scenario not only came about, but became commonplace in the securities industry, prior to 2002, and did have a very detrimental effect on the stock market.

This scenario involved the treatment by securities analysts of stock issues that had been underwritten by their firm. In April of 2002, New York Attorney General Elliot Spitzer announced shocking findings that analysts at Merrill Lynch were consistently skewing reports and stock recommendations to generate business for their investment banking division.[140] Among the charges were that analysts strongly recommended the purchase of securities that their investment banking division issued, to the public, while privately referring to those same securities as 'dogs' or 'junk' in emails to each other. It was also revealed that Merrill's analysts hardly ever gave downgrade or sell recommendations on the securities that they covered.[141] In fact, such recommendations[142] were virtually non-existent. Perhaps more shocking than this, was the revelation that involved a memorandum, sent to analysts at Morgan Stanley, by the managing director of corporate finance of that firm. The memorandum said 'As we are all too aware, there

[138] 75 Cong Rec 9912.

[139] S Rep No 77, 73d Cong, 1st Sess, 6,8,10.

[140] Jill E Firsh and Hillary A Sale *The Securities Analyst as Agent: Rethinking The Regulation of Analysts* (2003) 60 IOLR 1035, 1037.

[141] ibid, at 1048.

[142] ibid.

have been too many instances where our Research Analysts have been the source of negative comments about (investment banking) clients of the Firm. Our objective is . . . to adopt a policy, fully understood by the entire Firm, including the Research Department, that we do not make negative or controversial comments about our (investment banking) clients as a matter of sound business practice.'[143] The implications of these two revelations are clear. Research analysts, who are supposed to provide independent and unbiased advice to their firm's brokerage clients, were skewing their recommendations in an effort to push securities that their firm had underwritten. This conflict of interest has been widely blamed for the equity crash in the technology sector and for contributing to well-publicized corporate scandals such as the Enron debacle.[144] The reasons that the senior management of such highly reputable securities firms, such as Morgan Stanley, authorized such activity are many. Positive coverage of companies that have used the securities firm for underwriting help to ensure that the securities firm will retain those companies as underwriting clients for future offerings.[145] In addition to this reason, a firm, whose analysts have a strong reputation for pushing the securities that their firm has underwritten, should be able to solicit new underwriting business with relative ease.[146]

Under section 16 of Glass–Steagall, commercial banks are allowed to purchase and sell securities at the direction of their customers,[147] and there is no law that prevents bank employees from recommending the purchase of securities that their affiliate has underwritten. Thus there is no legal barrier to such activities, and unfortunately, banks, much like securities firms that manage money and offer investment banking services, would have multiple motivations to encourage their employees to engage in them. For instance, if the bank has loaned its affiliate the funds to finance issue, the bank has a very strong interest in the success of that issue, so that the affiliate can pay back the loan. More importantly though, the Financial Holding Company, which controls the bank and the securities affiliate, has a very strong interest in the success of the issues of the securities affiliate because highly lucrative underwriting fees, which are deducted from the funds that the underwriter obtains from selling the securities to the public, greatly contribute to the overall profit of the FHC. One could argue that because there is no law that prevents banks from pushing securities that have been underwritten by unaffiliated securities firms that the bank has made loans to, there is no reason to enact a law or regulation that prevents banks from engaging in the same activity for the benefit of their own securities affiliate. While this is somewhat of a plausible argument, it does not recognize the fact that the two situations are very different, for two impor-

[143] ibid, at 1049.
[144] ibid, at 1035.
[145] ibid, at 1045.
[146] ibid.
[147] 12 USC § 24

tant reasons. The first one is obvious. Besides the ability of an unaffiliated securities firm to pay back the loan, a commercial bank has no stake in the fortunes of an unaffiliated securities firm of which it has provided financing. In contrast, a Financial Holding Company that has a securities affiliate does have a significant stake in the profits of that affiliate. The other reason has to do with the fact that the Gramm–Leach–Bliley Act repealed Section 32 of the Glass Steagall Act, which prevented banks and securities firms from having the same management.[148] Now than commercial banks and securities firms can come under common management, there is a much greater potential for the instatement of such a policy than in a scenario in which a commercial bank simply made a loan to an unaffiliated securities firm. If such a policy was adopted by a financial holding company and if depositors lost money on investments recommended to them by their commercial bank, public confidence in that bank could definitely be compromised. Such activities could also have extremely adverse effects on the stock market, as was the case the abuse of public trust by securities analyst, which lead to the stock market crisis of 2001. It does seem a bit pessimistic to assume that the management of Financial Holding Companies, which are often made up of large, prestigious financial institutions, would advise their employees to exploit their customers trust in such a manner, but the management of Morgan Stanley and other large prestigious financial institutions were doing just that.

VI. CONCLUSION: THREE NEW REGULATIONS THAT COULD SUBSTANTIALLY MITIGATE OR COMPLETELY ELIMINATE THESE RISKS

Despite the substantial risks that commercial banks face in affiliating with securities firms, the promulgation of three new federal regulations, by the relevant banking authorities, could mitigate or completely eliminate these risks. The Federal Reserve Board and the Office of the Comptroller Currency would have the ability to promulgate these regulations under their power to regulate the 'safety and soundness' of covered banking institutions.

A. *Regulation Forbidding Banks to Make Loans to Firms that have used their Securities Affiliates for Underwriting Services*

The first of these three regulations should forbid banks to make loans to companies that use their securities affiliate for underwriting services. This does seem a bit extreme, but it would completely eliminate a commercial bank's ability to engage in anti-competitive activities to the detriment of

[148] 12 USC § 78

unaffiliated investment banking firms. One of the primary motivations for the passage of the Gramm–Leach–Bliley Act was to stimulate competition in the financial industry by putting commercial banks on even footing with investment banks.[149] What it has ended up doing is giving commercial banks a huge competitive advantage over unaffiliated investment banking firms, which threaten their very existence. Thus in the spirit of competition, there is no reason why such a rule should not be enacted. Not only would it allow the unaffiliated investment banks to compete on even footing with the securities affiliates of commercial banks, it would help reduce the risk of future failures of commercial banks due to their excessive exposure to the securities market. It is no secrets that as these large banks continue to monopolize the underwriting industry, their exposure to the securities market increases exponentially. A bad securities market could definitely threaten the safety and soundness of these commercial banks particularly if they have committed substantial amounts of capital to underwriting endeavors. The Bank of the United States was thought to have failed because of its exposure to the securities market.[150] If one of these large banks fails for the same reason, a costly government bailout is sure to follow. The FRSB has already said that if more than two of these banks fail, it will not have sufficient funds to bail them out.[151] Thus a stagnant securities market could theoretically trigger another banking crisis. This regulation should definitely be passed to reduce the probability of this occurrence and to stimulate competition among unaffiliated and affiliated underwriters.

In addition to reducing the anti-competitive risks, this new regulation would do away with the first of the two double exposure risks, which is that banks will make loans to their affiliate to underwrite the securities of a particular firm and then make loans to that firm. While it is true that banks would still be allowed to make loans to their securities affiliates and to firms that's' securities were underwritten by other unaffiliated securities firms, bank do not face the two-tiered exposure to a single firm through such endeavors. This regulation will force banks, which wish to gain a strong presence in the securities markets, to diversify their efforts across different firms, rather than having underwriting commitments and commercial loans tied up within single firms. This diversification and the increased competition from unaffiliated investment banking firms, brought on by this regulation, would greatly contribute to the safety and soundness of these large commercial banks that have large stakes in the securities industry.

149 Above n 12.

150 Above n 7.

151 Above n 117.

B. Regulation Mandating that Commercial Banks Seek FRSB Approval before making Rescue Loans to their Securities Affiliate

Not allowing securities firms to collateralize loans from their commercial banking affiliates with securities might be too extreme of a measure, especially in light of the fact that securities firms do not generally keep a great deal of cash on hand. However, a regulation that requires securities, used as collateral, to be of a low-risk nature might be a good idea. Securities such as high-grade corporate bonds or municipal bonds are generally considered to be low-risk and highly liquid. If all loans between the bank and its securities affiliate were collateralized with securities such as these, the bank would probably have very little trouble selling these securities to another bank, or to the public, in the case of municipal bonds, if the affiliate defaulted on its loan. Even this requirement may be asking too much of securities firms though because they may prefer to hold higher risk securities, such as stocks and junk-debt because of the high profit margins that they can earn from their sale. However, if the loan in question is a rescue loan to be made by the bank to its affiliate, when the affiliate has yet to repay other loans made to it by the bank, a much more extreme rule should be required. This rule would be enacted to mitigate the possibility of a double default that stems from the second type of double exposure risk, in which the bank initially makes loans to its affiliate to engage in underwriting endeavors and than makes rescue loans to the affiliate, when it finds itself in financial hardship and has yet to pay back the initial loans. It would also help to mitigate the public perception risk that comes with the conflict of interest in which commercial banks might make unwise loans to their struggling securities affiliates to the detriment of their commercial depositors. This rule should not necessarily prevent securities firms from collateralizing rescue loans with securities, when it still has outstanding loans from its commercial banking affiliate.

Instead, it should not allow commercial banks to make rescue loans to their affiliate, when it is still owed money from that affiliate, without Federal Reserve Board Approval. In deciding whether to approve such a bailout, the FRSB's inquiry should include, but not necessarily be limited to, an analysis of the financial situation of the commercial bank. If the bank is financially sound to the point that it could handle a potential double default, on the part of its affiliate, there is probably no reason to prevent it from rescuing the affiliate, except for the fact that this might damage public confidence in the bank. As discussed earlier though, the banks that affiliate with securities firms are very large and have access to vast amounts of capital, so such a move probably would not scare the depositors to the point that a run would result. If the bank was not operating in a financially sound condition, the FRSB should definitely not allow it to rescue its affiliate. A double default on the part of a securities affiliate could definitely jeopardize the safety and soundness of a struggling bank, even if the loan were well-collateralized. The reason for this is that there is no guarantee that the bank would be able to cover its losses through the sale of the collateral securities because it may not be able to sell them at all or at a price that would cover the default. In addition to this risk, if the bank's depositors found out that their struggling institution was making very large loans to its struggling affiliate, this could incite a run on that bank, no matter how well-collateralized the loans were. This regulation would give the FRSB veto power over such rescue loans, rather than leaving the decision to the officers of the commercial bank, which is appropriate for two reasons. First, the FRSB is in the best position to decide whether such a loan is appropriate, in regard to safety and soundness concerns, because they have a long history of dealing with bank failures and are well aware of the warning signs the precede them. Secondly, it has a very strong interest in ensuring that such loans will not threaten the safety and soundness of a particular institution because if the institution was to fail, they are the ones who have to bail it out. While a commercial bank's officers may have some knowledge pertaining to bank failures and certainly have a strong interest in not allowing their bank to fail, the temptation to rescue a struggling securities affiliate may overcome their better judgment.

C. *Regulation that Forbids Commercial Banks from Recommending Securities, Underwritten by their Affiliates, to their Depositors*

The third regulation would address the conflict of interest that would result if bank employees engaged in pushing the securities that the bank's affiliate underwrote. Congress enacted section 501 of the Sarbanes Oxley Act to deal with the phenomenon of securities analysts pushing stocks that were underwritten by their firm.[152] This section basically requires the SEC and other SROs to promulgate regulations designed to curb the predominance of this phenomenon.[153] The potential conflict of interest, involving, banks, however, needs to be dealt with in a more stringent fashion. A regulation should be enacted that prevents banks from pushing any security, underwritten by its securities affiliate. Though there may be certain fiduciary duty obligations already in place, that might deal with this issue, the effectiveness of common law fiduciary duty rules, in preventing self-dealing, is indeed questionable. A regulation, that if violated could subject the perpetrator to jail time, would be a much more effective deterrent. This may seem a bit extreme, but overall public confidence in banks is much too important to be protected by just these fiduciary rules. There is definitely a potential

[152] See Firsh above n 140, at 1038. [153] ibid.

for self-dealing, given the fact that banks and securities firms can come under the same management if they are affiliated with each other under the umbrella of a financial holding company. In addition to this problem, banks deal with millions of depositors who could all be potential investors in the securities markets and the temptation to push these depositors into investing in securities, underwritten by their affiliates, may be very strong indeed given the fact that the overall profits of the financial holding company are derived in part from the profits of the securities affiliate. If banks were able to convince their depositors to invest in securities underwritten by their affiliates, and if a substantial number of those securities turned out to be 'dogs' or 'losers', not only could this scenario be very detrimental to the banking system, in terms of lost public confidence, but it could wreck havoc on the stock market as well. If enough of these securities did not perform well, the commercial bank's depositors may loose confidence in the bank and withdraw their funds from it. If enough depositors did in fact withdraw their funds, because of this loss in confidence, the resulting run could definitely cripple the bank and perhaps even cause it to fail. If the commercial banks were able to push a large number of depositors into speculative or sub-par securities, these could lead to an overvaluation of these securities and could possibly trigger a widespread overvaluation in the stock market as a whole. When the market realizes that its securities are overvalued, people will start dumping their stock as quickly as possible. If this trend continues for a significant time period, it could spell catastrophe for the market. This scenario may seem a bit far-fetched, but this is exactly what Senator Glass, a majority of congress, and a large number of banking regulators believed to have happened in 1929.[154] They believed that commercial banks had pushed their depositors into speculative stocks, and that this had been a substantial factor in bringing about the crash of 1929.[155] It is also useful to note that if the market does face a rapid decline, any firm with outstanding underwriting commitments is probably going to face some level of financial hardship, including affiliated securities firms and their commercial banking affiliates that lent the money to finance their underwriting endeavours. In light of all of these factors, there is simply too much risk involved in allowing commercial banks to attempt to entice their depositors to invest in securities underwritten by their affiliates.

[154] Above n 6. [155] ibid.

THE H SHARE EXPERIMENT: ITS MECHANISM, ACCOMPLISHMENTS, AND PROBLEMS

CHI KUEN SIMON WU*

CHAPTER OUTLINE

* LLB (First Class Honours), PCLL (award with credit) from The City University of Hong Kong and a Post-graduate Certificate in Education from The University of Hong Kong. He has worked as an associate at Baker & McKenzie (Hong Kong office) for four years in the Commercial and Securities Practice Group specializing in 'H' share listings.

I. INTRODUCTION

PRC[1] enterprises account for a significant share of funds raised through initial public offerings ('IPOs') on the Hong Kong stock exchange.[2] Of the HK$313.3 billion raised by a total of 431 IPOs during 1997–2002, HK$232.8 billion, accounting for 74.3 per cent of the total, was raised for 73 PRC enterprises. This included HK$113.9 billion raised for 50 H shares and HK$118.9 billion raised for 23 red chip companies.[3] The remaining HK$80.5 billion was raised by 358 non-PRC enterprises.[4] H shares are issued on the Hong Kong stock market to raise funds for PRC companies and the word 'H' stands for 'Hong Kong' while red chip shares are issued by Hong Kong incorporated companies with main business interest in the PRC or with substantial direct and indirect ownership by the PRC government.

On average PRC enterprises listed on the Hong Kong stock exchange from 1997–2002 raised three to four times more than the overall average listing on the Hong Kong stock exchange. The average PRC listing was able to raise HK$3.2 billion while the overall average raised only HK$0.73 billion.[5] If all PRC enterprises on the Hong Kong stock exchange were excluded from the calculation, the average fund raised by a non-PRC enterprise was even smaller. A non-PRC enterprise raised an average of HK$0.22 billion during the same period of time while most non-PRC enterprise raised even less with HK$0.1 billion.[6]

Of the top ten IPOs listed between 1997 to 2002 on the Hong Kong stock exchange, eight were PRC enterprises and the funds were mainly raised from international markets.[7] Hong Kong is therefore an important fund-raising centre and a preferred venue for overseas listings for PRC enterprises.[8] By the end of 2002, PRC enterprises had a total of 76 overseas

[1] For this chapter, the use of the word 'China' includes the PRC, Hong Kong Special Administrative Region ('Hong Kong') and Macao Special Administrative Region ('Macao') while the use of the words 'People's Republic of China ('PRC')' refers to Mainland China excluding Hong Kong and Macao.

[2] 'Hong Kong' is a short form of 'Hong Kong Special Administrative Zone'.

[3] Joseph Lee and Veronica Chang *IPO Activities in Hong Kong* (Securities and Futures Commission of Hong Kong research, Research Paper No 10, Oct 2003) at <http://www.sfc.hk/sfc/doc/EN/research/research/rs%20paper%2010.pdf> (Securities and Futures Commission: Research Papers & Statistics/ Research Papers/ RS Paper 10).

[4] ibid. [5] ibid. [6] ibid.

[7] Of the total amount of HK$188.6 billion raised on Hong Kong stock exchange, HK$21.2 billion (accounting for 11.2 per cent) was from Hong Kong while HK$167.5 billion (accounting for 88.8 per cent) was from international markets. *See Id.*

[8] Not only is Hong Kong the preferred venue, the trading of the PRC stocks in Hong Kong is more active than in the US or the UK. As of the end of June 2004, 18 PRC stocks were traded in both Hong Kong, and in the US and the UK. By the second half of 2003, the market shares of Hong Kong, the US and the UK in terms of the turnover of their PRC stocks were 73 per cent, 20 per cent and 6.9 per cent respectively. Joseph Lee and Joanna Poon, *The Listing*

listings of which 74 were listed in Hong Kong of which 60 were listed solely in Hong Kong, 11 were listed both in Hong Kong and the United States ('US'), two were listed both in Hong Kong and the United Kingdom ('UK') and one was listed in Hong Kong, the US and the UK).[9] Only two IPOs were listed outside Hong Kong during that period with one listed only in the US and the other one only in Singapore.[10]

Hong Kong is frequently chosen as the fund-raising venue for PRC companies[11] because it offers:

- access to foreign exchange;
- a broader investor base, international visibility;
- a sound legal and regulatory framework that meets international standards;
- a deep market with a wide product range and liquidity provided by institutional and retail as well as local and overseas investors;
- a critical mass of professionals and service-providers that adopt practices at international standard; and
- access to the rest of the world while geographically close to the PRC.[12]

This article sets out a critical examination of the role and function of H shares, examining their history and introducing the essential elements in the H share listing process. The extent to which the H share experiment has helped achieve a harmonization of laws and regulations between Hong Kong and the PRC will also be examined.

II. WHAT ARE H SHARES?

H shares refer to Renminbi-denominated ordinary shares issued by PRC incorporated companies, listed on the Hong Kong Stock Exchange[13]

of Mainland Companies on HKEx and the Implications for Hong Kong 4, 5 (Securities and Futures Commission of Hong Kong research, Research Paper No 17, Sept 2004) at <http://www.sfc.hk/sfc/doc/EN/research/research/rs%20paper%2017.pdf> (Securities and Futures Commission: Research Papers & Statistics/ Research Papers/ RS Paper 17).

[9] Lee and Chang, above n 3.

[10] ibid.

[11] See Appendix 1 for details of PRC companies listed on the Main Board and the GEM of the Hong Kong stock market up until 6 Feb 2004.

[12] Lee and Poon, above n 8.

[13] The full name is The Stock Exchange of Hong Kong Ltd. Hong Kong's Financial Secretary announced comprehensive market reform of the stock and futures in his 1999 Budget Speech. Under the reform, the HKSE and Hong Kong Futures Exchange Limited were demutualized and together with Hong Kong Securities Clearing Company Limited ('HKSCC'), they became wholly owned subsidiaries under a single holding company, Hong Kong Exchanges and Clearing Limited (HKEx). The merger was completed on 6 Mar 2000 and HKEx listed its shares by introduction on the Hong Kong stock exchange on 27 June 2000. After demutualization, the HKSE, HKFE and HKSCC become wholly-owned subsidiaries of

('HKSE'), subscribed and traded in Hong Kong dollars.[14]

H shares were created by the PRC companies to raise funds from foreign investors. PRC incorporated companies can raise funds from foreign investors by issuing shares to them in the Shanghai Stock Exchange ('SSE') and Shenzhen Stock Exchange ('SZE') in the form of B shares. They are registered shares, denominated in Renminbi ('RMB') but subscribed and traded in foreign currencies. They can also raise funds in designated foreign stock exchanges. Besides listing in Hong Kong as H shares, PRC incorporated companies also list on the New York Stock Exchange, NASDAQ, the London Stock Exchange and the Singapore Stock Exchange. However due to liquidity, valuation, regulatory and other reasons, most PRC incorporated companies seek either to list on the PRC or Hong Kong stock markets.

III. HISTORY OF H SHARES

In 1991 HKSE set up a China Study Group made up of key players in the PRC-Hong Kong financial field. Shortly after, in February 1992, the Group completed an Interim Report on the Way Forward (the 'Interim Report') for the PRC securities officials. The report sets out the general issues, including legal, accounting and regulatory issues that must be addressed before a PRC company can be listed in Hong Kong.[15] In July 1992, it set up the Sino-Hong Kong Securities Joint Liaison Group.[16] Following on from this vari-

HKEx. For a detailed history and general discussion of the demutualization, See Betty M Ho *Demutualization of Organized Securities Exchanges in Hong Kong: The Great Leap Forward* (2000) 33 Law & Pol'y Int'l Bus. 283 (2000) (the author argued the demutualization was initiated top down by the Hong Kong Government and rushed through the legislature without adequate consultation. The Hong Kong Government had hastily assumed that demutualization is a world wide trend and investor-ownership model is the most efficient model. The author seriously doubted whether there would be benefits conferred by such demutualization without creation of a competitive market environment.).

14 HKEx, H-Shares Index Futures and Options at <http://www.hkex.com.hk/prod/hhi/hshares_ product.htm> (last visited 2 Jan 2005).

15 Tse Wai Chun, Quesifer, PRC Enterprises Listing in the Hong Kong Stock Exchange 9 (1994) (unpublished MBA dissertation, the University of Hong Kong) (on file with the University of Hong Kong). The Interim Report has considered three different ways for PRC issuers to be listed on Hong Kong stock market. First, the listing of collective investment schemes which specialize in PRC companies. Second, listing of HK incorporated company with assets in the PRC. Third, direct listing of PRC enterprise. The PRC Government was interested in the direct listing. In terms of listing method, the PRC government has considered the establishment of a separate China board for the PRC enterprise but finally it settled for a special RMB denominated shares alongside with other Hong Kong companies by modifying the then Listing Rules, incorporating extra safeguard measures to protect H-share shareholders.

16 Gao Bao-ming and Fu Yan-mei 'Underwriting and Issuing H Shares and N shares Overseas' in *Securities Markets in China [Zhongguo Zhengquan Shichang Toushi]* 127 (Henry MK Mok and Leslie Young (eds) The Chinese University of Hong Kong, 1997).

ous legal, accounting and regulatory obstacles were overcome and various rules and regulations promulgated with the cooperation of the regulatory authorities, securities professionals, lawyers and accountants in both the PRC and Hong Kong.

In June 1993, the relevant Hong Kong and PRC regulatory authorities signed a cooperation memorandum of understanding, paving the way for the listing of the first H shares in July of the same year.[17]

IV. D. H SHARE STATISTICS

The H share experiment has seen a solid increase in listings of PRC companies on the Hong Kong stock exchange. The first listing took place in 1993 with nine PRC enterprises being listed.[18] The following year the second batch, consisting of 22 enterprises, were selected to be listed and in 1995 a further seven enterprises were also selected to be listed.[19] As at December 31, 2004, there were 72 listed H share companies on the main board and 37 listed H share companies on the Growth Enterprise Market ('GEM'), comprising approximately 8.1 per cent[20] and 18.1 per cent of the enterprises respectively listed in Hong Kong.[21]

V. COMPARTMENTALIZATION AND THE SEARCH FOR EQUIVALENCE

The drive and success of the H share experiment is in large part due to the mutual advantages it can bring to both Hong Kong and the PRC. Advantages for the Hong Kong stock market include increasing its liquidity and enhancing its competitiveness,[22] helping to establish Hong Kong as

[17] The cooperation, consultation, and technical assistance memorandum signed between the US and the PRC regulatory authorities in April 1994 also paved the way for the listing of N shares in the States.

[18] Gao and Fu, above n 16, at 127.

[19] See ibid.

[20] As at 31 Dec 2004, there were also 81 red chip companies listed on the main board of the HKSE and together with the H share companies, they comprised approximately 17.2 per cent of the companies listed on the main board. See Section G for more detail about the red chip companies. China Stock Markets Web, *Market Highlights* at <http://ww.hkex.com/csm/highlight.asp?LangCode=en> (HKEx: China Stock Markets Web/Market Highlights) (last visited 2 Jan 2005).

[21] *Id.*

[22] When Mr Charles Lee, as Chairman of SEHK Council from 1992 to 1994, started discussing H share issues with the Chinese side, he reasoned as follows: 'The Hong Kong stock market is now quite mature; and if we were just dependent on our own companies for new listings, the growth of the market would be very slow.' Mr. Lee hopes that 'Hong Kong will become as important to China as Manhattan is to the US.' *See* Niu Tiehang, *Regional Stock Market Integration in China and Hong Kong* (CAER II Discussion Paper No 16, Dec. 1996)

an international centre for bond trading[23] and invigorating its Growth Enterprise Market. While advantages for the PRC corporations include the ability to raise substantial funds on the Hong Kong market and attracting increased international investment in PRC listed enterprises due to confidence in the well-regulated Hong Kong stock exchange.

The Hong Kong stock exchange cannot afford to compromise its high standards and it has to ascertain that the PRC companies listed in Hong Kong will attain equivalent standards to other listed companies. However the HKSE does take into consideration the special characteristics of PRC companies and as a result, special laws and regulations have been passed in both the PRC and Hong Kong to accommodate these characteristics through the Listing Rules[24] specifically formulated for H share issuance. Hong Kong companies are not, however, allowed to be listed on PRC stock exchanges and so this set of rules and regulations is used only by PRC companies to facilitate their fund raising activities on the HKSE.

Despite this non-mutuality the search for equivalent standards can be seen as a process of harmonization. As the Listing Rules and the relevant provisions governing H share issuance do not allow for any addition and deletion, it can be seen as an attempt towards maximum 'harmonization'. However the word 'harmonization' may be misleading as it suggests that rules and regulations apply to both PRC and non-PRC companies. The fact is that there is a separate set of rules and regulations for the H share companies that have been created so that the H share companies can reach an equivalent standard in terms of corporate governance equal to other non-H share companies listed on the Hong Kong stock exchange. It is possible that at some future date, by applying the same principles, the same equivalence can be reached by a separate set of regulations allowing Hong Kong companies to be listed in the PRC.

at <http://www.cid.harvard.edu/caer2/htm/content/papers/paper16/paper16.htm> (last visited 2 Jan 2005).

[23] The Financial Secretary, The Hon Antony Leung, address moving the Second Reading of the Appropriation Bill 2003, para 39 at <http://www.budget.gov.hk/2003/eng/speech.htm>. *See also* the Financial Secretary, The Hon Donald Tsang *The 2000–1 Budget: Scaling New Heights*, address moving the Second Reading of the Appropriation Bill 2000, para 69 (8 Mar 2000) at <http://www.budget.gov.hk/ 2000/eindex.htm>. 'The Asian dollar bond market based in Hong Kong suffers the sized drawback, which in turn reinforces the liquidity drawback.' Quoted from Raul Fabella and Srinivasa Madhur *Bond Market Development in East Asia: Issues and Challenges* 13 (Asia Development Bank, ERD Working Paper Series No 35, 2003). On the other hand, PRC's bond market suffers in terms of regulatory framework, secondary market liquidity, and the government bond market yield curve. The small size of the private sector in the PRC also restricts the bond market development. *See* Raul Fabella and Srinivasa Madhur *Bond Market Development in East Asia: Issues and Challenges* 8 (Asia Development Bank, ERD Working Paper Series No 35, 2003). As a result, an integration of Hong Kong and PRC stock markets will greatly benefit both Hong Kong and the PRC.

[24] The full name is 'Listing Rules Governing the Listing of Securities on The Stock Exchange of Hong Kong Ltd'.

This article will refer to the principle and philosophy behind H shares as 'equivalent compartmentalization'. 'Compartmentalization' means that H shares are separate from other kinds of shares with their distinct listing requirements. 'Equivalent' means that H shares try to achieve equivalent listing standards comparable to non-PRC companies listing on the Hong Kong stock exchange.

H shares will now be examined in more detail to find out how such equivalence can be achieved.

VI. LAWS AND REGULATIONS RELATING TO H SHARES

The three-tier model of regulation as shown in Figure 1 below exists in most countries and is a standard model of the issue of securities and the subsequent trading of those securities among investors.

Company law represents the bottom tier as it applies generally to all companies, even though public companies may be subject to a different set of rules from private companies under company law. Different rules are also applicable to domestic and foreign companies. Mandatory rules may be found in company law that deals specifically with the issue of shares.

Securities law is represented in the second tier. This does not apply to all

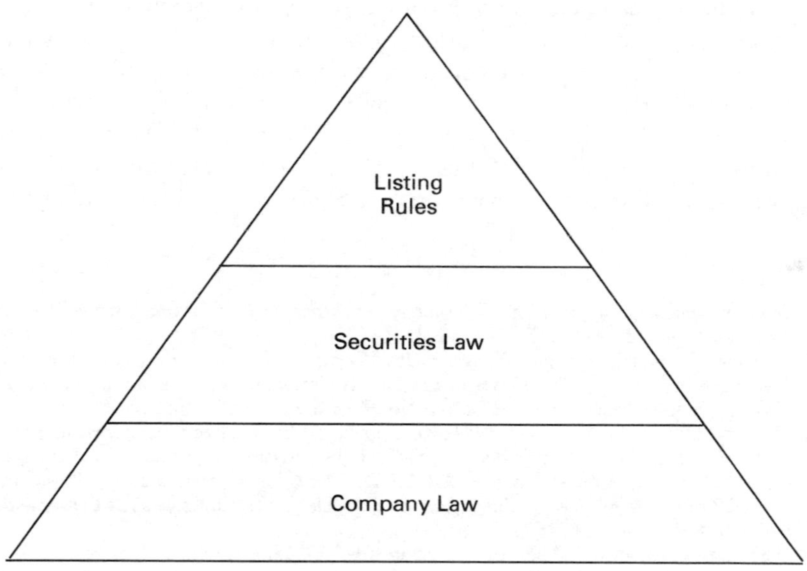

FIGURE 1

companies as only companies that make public issues of securities are affected. Unlike listing rules, it also covers unlisted public companies.

Listing rules are represented in the top tier as they only apply to companies which seek listing or whose securities are admitted to listing. Listing Rules are applied by the stock market and do not have the force of law. Listing rules lay down the conditions under which public companies can gain access to capital markets. Within a single jurisdiction, the three tiers of regulation should be carefully coordinated so that conflict and overlapping can be avoided.[25]

The law governing the listing of PRC shares in Hong Kong is Hong Kong law only because the listing of shares is governed by the place where they are listed. However the actual listing is the last stage of a long and complex process. The first stage of this process involves setting up a shareholding company from the State-owned enterprise ('SOE') in accordance with the Company Law[26] in the PRC. Therefore before looking at Hong Kong law, Company Law should be taken into consideration as it is particularly relevant for the listing candidate in the restructuring process.

As far as securities laws are concerned, in July 1994 the State Council promulgated the Special Regulations Concerning Overseas Offering and Listing of Shares by Joint Stock Limited Companies (the 'Special Regulations') to prepare for H share listing.[27] The Special Regulations govern foreign invested shares that are listed overseas and cover areas such as share issuance, share management, protection of shareholders' interests etc. In addition, the operation of a company depends heavily on its articles of association, being the constitution of an enterprise. To ensure that the PRC companies operate in accordance with international standards, the State Council Securities Committee ('SCSC') and State Commission for Restructuring the Economic System ('SCREC') jointly issued the Mandatory Provisions in the Articles of Association for Companies Listing Overseas (the 'Mandatory Provisions') on 27 August 1994[28] to specify

[25] See Iain MacNeil and Alex Lau *International Corporate Regulation: Listing Rules and Overseas Companies*, 50(4) ICLQ 787, 787–8.

[26] *Zonghua Renmin Gongheguo Gongsi Fa* [the Company Law of the PRC] adopted at the Fifth Session of the Standing Committee of the Eighth National People's Congress on 29 Dec 1993, promulgated as the Presidential Decree No 16 of the People's Republic of China on the same day and effective as of 1 July 1994. Revised based on the decision of revision of the Company Law of the People's Republic of China at 13th Session of the Standing Committee of the Ninth National People's Congress on 25 Dec 1999 and effective as the Presidential Decree No 29 of the People's Republic of China on 25 Dec 1999, effective as of the same day.

[27] Gao and Fu, above n 16, at 129.

[28] Dao JingwaiI Shangshi Gongsi Zhangcheng Bibei Tiaokuanin Zheng Wei Fa (1994) No 21 on 27 Aug 1994 promulgated by the State Council Securities Policy Committee and the State Commission for Restructuring the Economic System (hereinafter 'Mandatory Provisions').

minimum standards and model requirements.[29] The Mandatory Provisions cover registered capital, reduction of capital, share repurchase, financial assistance, share and shareholder registers, shareholders' rights and obligations, procedures regarding annual general meetings and board of directors' meetings, qualifications and obligations of directors, company secretary, supervisors, general managers and senior management personnel, accounting systems, profit allocation, mergers and spin-off, liquidation procedures, dispute settlement, amendments of articles of association, etc. The Mandatory Provision was amended by the Letter Concerning Opinion on Supplementary Revision of the Articles of Association of Companies to be Listed on the Hong Kong Stock Exchange promulgated by the China Securities Regulatory Commission ('CSRC') and SCREC on 3 April 1995 in response to the then new Appendix 3 and Appendix 13 Part D Section 1 of the Listing Rules.

For PRC listed companies to be listed abroad, the Notice on Several Issues Concerning Regulating Overseas Initial Public Offerings of the Enterprise Affiliated to the Domestic Listed Companies is also applicable.[30] The Notice is intended to keep profitable assets of Chinese companies in domestic markets and avoid dissipation of state assets. The Securities Law[31] promulgated on 29 December 1998 and effective from 1 July 1999 only governs companies which seek to be listed in the PRC.

As the PRC legal system is based mainly on the civil law system and not the common law system, the legal protection rendered to investors under PRC law is not well-developed and extra safeguard mechanisms are required for the listing of PRC companies in Hong Kong.

As the listing vehicles are incorporated in the PRC, the main relevance of the company law in Hong Kong is Part XII of, and the Third Schedule to, the Companies Ordinance which stipulates certain mandatory disclosures in the prospectus for companies seeking to be listed on the HKSE.[32] The Securities and Futures Ordinance ('SFO') which consolidated ten previous ordinances[33] was enacted on 13 March 2002 and finally became effective

[29] See ibid.

[30] *Guanyu Guifan Jingnei Shangshi Gongsi Suoshu Qiye Dao Jingwai Shangshi Youguan Wenti de Tongzhi* issued by the CSRC on 10 Aug 2004. Para 8 of the Notice states that this Notice does not apply to PRC incorporated companies which seek to list domestically and abroad at the same time.

[31] *Zhonghua Renmin Gongheguo Zhengquan Fa* adopted by the Sixth Session of the Standing Committee of the Ninth National People's Congress of the PRC promulgated as Presidential Decree No 12.

[32] Under schedule 1 of the Companies (Amendment) Ordinance, Ord No 30 of 2004 A1777, which came into force on December 3, 2004, the newly added Seventeenth, Eighteenth, Twentieth and Twenty-first Schedules are also relevant as they clarify the definition of 'prospectus' and envisage 'programme' prospectuses which are particularly useful for debt offerings. However such changes will have little impact on H share offerings.

[33] The following 10 ordinances have been consolidated into the SFO and were repealed accordingly: 'Securities and Futures Commission Ordinance (Cap 24) (enacted 1989)

on 1 April 2003.[34] It governs the licensing requirements of the financial intermediaries, disclosure of interests, market misconduct, the extent of power of the SFC and remedies of aggrieved investors.

As far as the listing requirements in Hong Kong are concerned, the governing rules were laid down in the Rules Governing the Listing of Securities on The Stock Exchange of Hong Kong Ltd (the 'Listing Rules') published by the HKSE. In addition to Chapters 3 and 8 of the Listing Rules, special provisions in Chapter 19A and Appendix 13 Part D have been added to modify the listing requirements for the PRC companies tailor-made specifically for such companies. Chapter 13 and Appendix 16 of the Listing Rules contains the listing agreement between the HKSE and the PRC issuer which stipulates further listing requirements and post-listing continuing obligations for the PRC issuer.

To facilitate mutual assistance, exchange of information, regular liaison and exchange of personnel to pave the way for an H share listing, the HKSE entered into a non-binding, five-sided Memorandum of Regulatory Cooperation with the Securities and Futures Commission ('SFC') on the one side, and the CSRC and SZSE and SSE on the other in June 1993 (the 'MRC'). The MRC indicates a willingness on the part of the signatories to cooperate with each other in the regulation of their respective markets and articulates all the basic principles of securities market regulation important to any international market.[35]

Commodities Trading Ordinance (Cap. 250) (enacted 1976)
Securities Ordinance (Cap. 333) (enacted 1974)
Protection of Investors Ordinance (Cap. 335) (enacted 1974)
Stock Exchanges Unification Ordinance (Cap. 361) (enacted 1980)
Securities (Insider Dealing) Ordinance (Cap. 395) (enacted 1990)
Securities (Disclosure of Interests) Ordinance (Cap. 396) (enacted 1988)
Securities and Futures (Clearing Houses) Ordinance (Cap. 420) (enacted 1992)
Leveraged Foreign Exchange Trading Ordinance (Cap. 451) (enacted 1994)
Exchanges and Clearing Houses (Merger) Ordinance (Cap. 555) (enacted 2000)
See Legislative Council Brief, *Regulatory Reform for the Securities and Futures Market—The Securities and Futures Bill* (SU B38/31, 2000) and §406 of the SFO.'

[34] *Securities and Futures Ordinance expected to commence on April 1, 2003*, Press release, 13 Dec 2002 available at <http://www.fstb.gov.hk/fsb/ppr/press/c_release2002.htm> (last visited 2 Jan 2005) and also Hong Kong Economic and Trade Office USA, *Hong Kong To Implement Securities & Futures Ordinance on April 1*, press release, 31 Mar 2003 at <http://www.hongkong.org/press/ny_033103.htm> (last visited 2 Jan 2005).

[35] See also The Stock Exchange of Hong Kong, *Listing Chinese Companies in Hong Kong* 70 (The Stock Exchange of Hong Kong, 1998).

VII. PRE-LISTING PREPARATION AND CONSIDERATION

A. Reorganization and its Considerations

Reorganization is usually the first step towards listing overseas. In the PRC, a number of problems have to be taken into consideration before reorganization which include addressing the issue of the non-productive elements of the issuers, their pension funds, government approvals and their accounting systems.

In the 1950s under the central planning system, SOEs were required to provide schools, hospitals and dormitories for their employees and their relatives. Some of the enterprises even needed to fulfil social and government functions. Now, in order to list such SOEs, the non-productive elements of the enterprise may have to be separated from the productive sectors.[36]

Under the centrally planned system in the past, the state would take care of the welfare of the retired employees—often an impressively large number. It is important that restructuring takes into account liability relating to the retirement of employees.[37]

The SOEs are also governed by a complex matrix of government departments either at the same or at different levels of government. The restructuring plan will therefore have to be approved by all these relevant government departments, which may take considerable time. Valuation of the state-owned assets has to be carried out by the State Administration Bureau of State-owned Asset to ensure no under-evaluation or dissipation of State assets.[38]

The accounting system in China was designed for the communist operating environment and the finances of the SOEs were not usually independently audited. The restructuring plan has to take into consideration of the difference between the Chinese accounting standards and the international standards especially their difference over asset depreciation and provision of bad debts.[39]

Assuming that the enterprise is not a shareholding company, the restructuring plan will usually include the following:

- Asset valuation;
- Auditing the enterprise's accounts;
- Ascertaining the number of shares to be owned by the state and the shareholding structure after listing;
- Restructuring the company (determining which assets to be kept or disposed and packaging for listing);

[36] Gao and Fu, above n 16, at 130.
[37] ibid, at 129.
[38] ibid, at 130.
[39] ibid.

- Obtaining necessary government approvals;
- Drafting various legal documents including the articles of association, the prospectus, underwriting agreements etc.
- Proposal dealing with land issues.

There are three considerations in restructuring:[40]

- Listing requirements of the HKSE be met;
- Approvals from all relevant government authorities in the PRC be obtained;
- Appealing to investors.

1. *Listing Requirements of the HKSE*

The listing requirements of the HKSE are governed by the Listing Rules which in 2004 have been significantly amended. Under the amended Listing Rules, to ensure an open market for the listed securities, the minimum percentage of H shares which must be in the hands of the public is 15 per cent of the total issued share capital. This is the case if there are existing issued securities of the PRC issuer held by the public and the aggregate amount of H shares and such other securities held by the public must be not less than 25 per cent of the total issued share capital of the issuer.[41]

If there are no existing issued securities of the PRC issuer other than H shares, then H shares held by the public must constitute not less than 25 per cent of the total existing issued share capital of the issuer. [42]

There must also be an adequate spread of holders of the securities to be listed and as a general guideline, there must be a minimum of 300 shareholders[43] and not more than 50 per cent of the securities in public hands at the time of listing can be beneficially owned by the three largest public shareholders.[44]

Expected market capitalization of at least HK$200,000,000 must be offered including listed or unlisted securities on other regulated market(s).[45] A PRC issuer must have such securities held by the public which have an expected market value of not less than HK$50,000,000.[46]

Among all other listing requirements, the listed company must have sufficient management presence in Hong Kong. As a result, normally at least two of the new applicant's executive directors must be originally resi-

[40] ibid, at 131.

[41] The Listing Rules, R. 8.08(1).

[42] See ibid.

[43] This does not apply to companies sought to be listed under the market capitalization/revenue test. R. 8.08(2) of the Listing Rules.

[44] The Listing Rules, R. 8.08(3).

[45] The Listing Rules, R. 8.09(2).

[46] The Listing Rules, R. 8.08(1)(b) & R. 8.09(1).

dent in Hong Kong[47] and at least one of the independent non-executive directors must be ordinarily resident in Hong Kong.[48] The PRC issuer has to have a sponsor,[49] usually a merchant banker, to communicate with the HKSE regarding the issuing matter.[50] Under the new amended rule which came into effect on 1 January 2005[51], instead of retaining a sponsor, it shall retain a compliance adviser which is any corporation or authorized financial institution acceptable to the HKSE, licensed or registered under applicable laws to advise on corporate finance and compliance matters. This should commence on the date of initial listing of the listed issuer's equity securities and ending on the date on which the listed issuer's publication of its financial results for the first financial year commencing after the date of its initial listing (the 'Fixed Period').[52] Among all its duties, the Compliance Adviser must act as the PRC issuer's principal channel of communication with the HKSE in Hong Kong.[53] During the Fixed Period, a listed issuer must consult and, if necessary, seek advice from its compliance adviser on a timely basis regarding the following: matters concerning public announcements, possible notifiable or connected transactions, change of use of listing proceeds, change of business activities or new development of the business which are different from the forecast, estimate or other information in the prospectus etc.[54] The PRC issuer must also appoint one process agent to accept process and notices on its behalf in Hong Kong.[55] The issuer also needs to have two authorized representatives to be the principal channel of communication with the HKSE.[56]

Like other issuers, a new applicant must satisfy one of the three following tests: the profit test, the market capitalization/revenue/cash flow test or the market capitalization/revenue test. These three tests give more flexibility to large enterprises that seek to be listed on the HKSE. In the past, the only test available is a profit test similar to the amended profit test. Under the profit test, a company seeking to be listed on the HKSE must have an

[47] The Listing Rules, R. 19A.15.

[48] The Listing Rules, R. 19A.18(1).

[49] The sponsor must agree to observe the guidelines set out in the model code for sponsors issued by the HKSE (a copy of which is set out in App 9 of the Listing Rules) and it has to carry out due diligence in respect of initial listing application in accordance with Practice Note 21 of the Listing Rules.

[50] The Listing Rules, R. 3A.02.

[51] HKEx, *Consultation Conclusions and Amendments to the Listing Rules Relating to the Regulation of Sponsors and Independent Financial Advisers* (press release, 19 Oct 2004) at <http://www.hkex.com.hk/ news/hkexnews/041019news.htm>.

[52] The Listing Rules, R. 19A.05(2).

[53] The Listing Rules, R. 19A.06(4).

[54] The Listing Rules, R. 3A.23.

[55] The Listing Rules, R. 19A.13(2).

[56] They can be two directors or one director and one company secretary. *See* R. 3.05 and R. 19A.05(1) of the Listing Rules.

adequate trading record under substantially the same management and ownership. The issuer must have a trading record of not less than three financial years during which the profit attributable to shareholders must, in the most recent year, be not less than HK$20 million and in respect of the two preceding years, be in aggregate not less than HK$30 million. There should also be management continuity for at least three preceding financial years and ownership continuity and control for at least the most recent audited financial year.[57] By introducing two more tests, the HKSE relaxes the profit requirement regarding larger corporations and allows more flexibility. Under the other two tests, requirements for management and ownership continuity and control are the same as the profit test. For companies with market capitalization of not less than HK$2 billion at the time of listing, they should have revenue of at least HK$500 million for the most recent audited financial year and a positive cash flow from operating activities of at least HK$100 million in aggregate for the three preceding financial years.[58] It is called the market capitalization/revenue/cash flow test. If the business of the company sought to be listed is even bigger with a market capitalization of at least HK$4 billion, they can seek to be listed under the market capitalization/revenue test. Like the market capitalization/revenue/ cash flow test, there should be revenue of at least HK$500 million for the most recent audited financial year. However, for such companies, no positive cash flow is required and they only need to show that there are at least 1,000 shareholders at the time of listing.[59]

The PRC issuer must also include a working capital statement in the prospectus to show that it has available sufficient working capital for the group's present requirements for at least 12 months from the date of publication of the prospectus and the sponsor of the PRC issuer also needs to confirm to the HKSE in writing that this is the case and the issuer has confirmed it after due and careful enquiry and the person or institutions providing finance have stated in writing that the relevant facilities exist.[60]

The GEM board in Hong Kong is a capital raising vehicle for high growth enterprises with good potentials which cannot fulfill all the stringent requirements of listing on the Main Board. The listing requirements for such enterprises regarding past profit trading record are looser than the Main Board but in order to protect investors, extra safeguard measures have to be placed on them instead. As a result, the GEM in Hong Kong is governed by a separate set of rules.[61]

[57] The Listing Rules, R. 8.05(1).

[58] The Listing Rules, R. 8.05(2).

[59] The Listing Rules, R. 8.05(3).

[60] The Listing Rules, R.8.21A(1).

[61] A comparison of main differences between listing and post-listing requirements of the GEM and the Main Board is set out in the Growth Enterprise Market website at <http://www.hkgem.com/investor/ e_default.htm?ref=32> (GEM: Investor Education/ Listing in Hong Kong/ Salient Features of the Main Board Listing Rules and the GEM Listing Rules).

2. *PRC Government Approvals*

The securities industry and the stock markets in the PRC are governed by a matrix of ministries and government departments under the State Council. While some government bodies regulate the securities industry without issuing approvals, approvals for listing and listing-related matters have to be obtained from the others. Over the years, the PRC Government had taken measures to rationalize the government structure and streamline the approval process for securities issuance.

Under the Notice promulgated by State Council Concerning Further Strengthening Macro-Administration of the Securities Markets[62] in 1992 (the 'Notice'), the SCSC is the authority responsible for the unified overall administration of the national securities market and the CSRC is its executive arm.[63] The other government bodies under the State Council and the local or provincial governments responsible for the macro-administration of the PRC securities markets as stated in the Notice include the State Planning Commission ('SPC'), the SCRES, the People's Bank of China ('PBOC'), Ministry of Finance ('MOF') and the two exchanges in the PRC.[64] Since then, many changes have taken place to the organizations above and they are listed as follows:

- In 1998, SCSC was abolished while the CSRC was elevated to ministry level under the State Council and became the prime regulatory body of the securities industry.[65]

62 The Notice, para 1.1.

63 ibid para 1.2.

64 ibid para 1.3.

65 In the early stage, the People's Bank of China ('PBOC') and its local branches oversaw the securities market. As the national stock exchanges are located in Shanghai and Shenzhen, the respective local governments in these two municipals also participate in the regulation of the stock exchanges in conjunction with the local branches of the PBOC in Shanghai and Shenzhen. To complicate the bureaucratic structure, different aspects of securities activities are also regulated by various government bodies including the SPC, the SCREC, and the Ministry of Finance ('MOF'). Widespread fraud and government corruption in the stock markets involving the PBOC resulted in a riot in Shenzhen in 1992. In its place, the SCSC was established as an independent body to coordinate various ministries, formulate polices and draft laws and regulations for the securities market. The SCSC was made up of various government ministries and commissions including the PBOC, the SPC, the SCREC, the MOF, the State Bureau for the Administration of State Assets, the State Administration of Industry and Commerce, the State Tax Bureau, the Supreme Court and the State Administration for Foreign Currency Control. The CSRC was established as the executive arm of the SCSC to implement the administrative measures of the SCSC. As CSRC was a quasi-government vice-ministerial body, it could not communicate with ministry-level departments unless through the SCSC. Bearing in mind the composition of SCSC, any action taken by CSRC in China might need the approval and cooperation of a galaxy of bureaucratic ministries. The CSRC therefore devoted most of its time to explore listing mainland companies in Hong Kong. *See* Zhu Sanzhu, *Securities Regulation in China* 8–14 (Transnational Publishers & Simmonds & Hill Publishing, 2001); Carl E Walter et al *To Get Rich is Glorious—China's Stock Markets in the*

- Under the Notice,[66] SPC is to prepare a development plan for the securities industry after considering the plans and proposals made by the SCSC. The SPC has been renamed the State Development and Planning Commission ('SDPC'). One of the functions of the SDPC is to develop securities markets by recommending enlarging the scope of direct financing, helping enterprises to restructure and list, setting up a high-tech board with its own listing requirements and better regulating securities markets.[67] In the 2003 government restructuring, it was renamed the National Development and Reform Commission ('NDRC').[68]
- The SCRES was responsible for drafting regulations for trial shareholding enterprises as well as organizing and coordinating related matters.[69] The SCRES lost its primary patron along with many of its policy-making functions when Zhao Ziyang, its founder, lost his power after sympathizing with the protestors at Tiananmen Square.[70] In 1998, its power to issue orders to enterprises and oversee enterprise reform was transferred to the State Economic and Trade Commission ('SETC'). It was demoted to an office and renamed as Economic Restructuring Office of the State Council.[71] It was abolished in the 2003 restructuring and its functions were taken over by the NDRC.
- The SETC is not mentioned in the Notice but since then it has taken up some of the functions of the SPC and the SCRES. The SETC was formerly known as the State Economic Commission and served as a counterweight to the SPC by concerning less with long term plans and goals and more with coordinating with day-to-day enterprise operations and advocating for their interests.[72] The SETC has been amalgamated with the SPC and was later separated under different names.[73] In the early 1990s it was called the Production Office, a name which was changed in the latter part of that decade into SETC.[74] It also has taken up some functions from the SCRES. In the 2003 reorganization, it was

'80s and '90s 10–11 (Palgrave 2001) and; Jay Zhe Zhang *Securities Markets and Securities Regulation in China* (1997) 22 NC J Int'l L & Com Reg 557.

66 The Notice, para 1.3.

67 *Ministry Profile: State Development Planning Commission (SDPC)* at <http://www. chinaonline.com/refer/ ministry_profiles/SDPCb3.asp> (last visited 2 Jan 2005).

68 See its official websites at <http://www.sdpc.gov.cn or http://www.ndrc.gov.cn> (last visited 2 Jan 2005).

69 The Notice, para1.3.

70 *Ministry Profile: Economic Restructuring Office of the State Council (SERO)* at <http://www. chinaonline.com/refer/ministry_profile/c00121168.asp> (last visited 2 Jan 2005).

71 See ibid.

72 Barry Naughton, *The State Asset Commission: A Powerful New Government Body* (2003) 8 China Leadership Monitor 1 available at <http://www.chinaleadershipmonitor. org/20034/default.htm> (last visited 2 Jan 2005).

73 See ibid.

74 See ibid.

abolished and its function was divided between the newly created State-owned Asset Supervision and Administration Commission ('SASAC') and the super-ministry, the Ministry of Commerce.[75]

- The objective of the SASAC is to fully realize the Government's role as investor and owner by separating government's functions as investor and owner of state assets from its function as public manager of society as a whole.[76] The SASAC only has authority over a specific list of enterprises which to date includes 196 firms, comprising all the big, central government-controlled firms.[77] The main responsibilities of the SASAC are to monitor such enterprise operations financially and operationally. Among other things, they will approve major decisions of these enterprise operations, eg the issuance of new securities and enterprise restructuring.[78]
- The PBOC, which reported directly to the SCSC,[79] was once in charge of the examination and approval of securities. It also had the power to oversee their overall administration. However, such powers have since been taken away. With the creation of the China Banking Regulatory Commission in the 2003 restructuring, the PBOC was stripped of most, if not all, of its financial regulatory functions. Now the PBOC mainly concentrates on its role and functions as the central bank in the PRC with responsibility for the issue of treasury bonds.[80]
- The MOF will be in charge of the overall administration of registered accountants and accounting firms although it is the responsibility of the CRSC to decide whether an auditing firm may engage in the securities-related business.[81]
- The Shanghai and Shenzhen Securities Exchanges are to be administrated by the local governments but supervised by the CSRC.[82] They undertake the normal functions performed by most other stock exchanges, such as regulating the activities of their members and approving securities for listing.[83]
- Local enterprises require examination and approval at provincial level or by departments authorized by the Municipal People's Government listed on the plan, together with the enterprise's department-in-charge.[84]

[75] See ibid.
[76] See ibid.
[77] See ibid.
[78] See ibid.
[79] The Notice, para 1.3.
[80] The (Amended) Law of the People's Bank of China of the PRC promulgated by the Sixth Session of the Standing Committee of the NPC on December 27, 2003. See its official website at <http://www.pbc.gov.cn> (last visited 2 Jan 2005).
[81] The Notice, para 1.3.
[82] See ibid.
[83] Robert Nottle *The Development of Securities Markets in China in the 1990s* in Securities and Futures Commission, Securities Regulation in Hong Kong 116 (Securities and Futures Commission (ed) 2002).
[84] See ibid.

Although the Notice emphasizes the role of self-regulation by the securities industry in establishing securities system with Chinese characteristics[85] this role is small when it comes to enterprises seeking listing abroad.

An enterprise which is seeking to issue H shares has to apply to the main regulatory bodies that is, the SFC and HKSE in Hong Kong, and the enterprise has to fulfill the requirements set out in the Listing Rules or the GEM Listing Rules depending on where the enterprise prefers to be listed. In the PRC, CSRC is the main regulatory body and the listing of an enterprise aboard requires its approval.[86] The restructuring of the PRC enterprise may need approval from NDRC. The registration of the restructured Chinese enterprise may require the approval of the State Administration of Industry and Commerce ('SAIC') which is also responsible for issuing business certificates, evidencing that a company has a legal person status.[87] The enterprise-in-charge has to be given its approval. For instance, when the China Eastern Airlines and China Southern Airlines applied for listing, approvals were obtained from the Civil Aviation Administration of China

[85] The Notice, para 1.4. Self-regulatory bodies include China Securities Association (CSA) and the Stock Exchange Executive Council (SEEC). Founded in August 1991 and licensed by both the PBOC and the CSRC, the CSA strengthens the professional management and co-ordination of its members, conducts research and training, establishes trading rules, lobbies the PRC government on behalf of its members, and liaises among various government bodies, issuers, traders and investors. The SEEC was set up in March 1989 as a private organization to advise the CSRC and to create a nationwide treasury bond trading system, STAQ, which was established on 5 Dec 1990. See Peng and Gauthier, *China's Financial Markets: One Country, Two Systems* 57, 58 (*Financial Times*, 1998) and Nottle, above n 83, at 101–2. The SEEC has only participated in the planning and establishment of the Shanghai and Shenzhen stock exchanges and taken an active part in the drafting of many laws such as the Securities Law and the Company Law. The SEEC has developed into a holding company, integrating financial investment, media, consultation, training and high-tech matters.

[86] See Special Regulations, Art 2. Red chip companies also need to seek the approval of the CSRC or they may need to file relevant information to the CSRC for registration. According to Notice promulgated by State Council Concerning Further Strengthening Administration of Share Offering and Listing Overseas (20 June 1997 *Guofa* [1997] No 21, effective as of the same day) (commonly known as 'Red Chip Guidelines'), any PRC invested but foreign registered enterprise which owns assets in the PRC shall require the approval from provincial government or the relevant supervising authorities under the State Council and for those which own assets in the PRC less than 3 years, listing abroad is not allowed unless they are examined and approved by the CSRC and after listing, the shares owned by the PRC entities shall be filed to the CSRC for registration (the Red Chip Guideline, para 2). Any restructuring of PRC invested and foreign registered enterprises shall also be approved by the provincial government or any supervising authorities under the State Council and examined by the CSRC and other state planning authorities (the Red Chip Guideline, para 3). Backdoor listing of such enterprises is not allowed (the Red Chip Guideline, para 4).

[87] Administrative Regulation on Company Registration of the PRC promulgated by the State Council as Decree No 156 on 24 June 1994 and effective on 1 July 1994, Art 3. Also *See* Nottle, above n 83, at 117 and Ministry Profile, *State Administration for Industry and Commerce (SAIC)* at <http://www. chinaonline.com/refer/ministry_profiles/c01040363.asp>. The SAIC also co-handles the licensing of commodities brokerage firms, as well as the supervision of commodity trading, along with the CSRC. It also approves project financing deals and registers currency traders. See Peng and Gauthier, above n 85, at 57.

and when the People's Insurance Company of China and China Insurance Co. Ltd. sought H share listing in Hong Kong, approvals were required from China Insurance Regulatory Commission. If the concerned enterprise falls into the list of enterprises under the responsibility of the SASAC, approval from the SASAC is also required.[88]

Enterprises relating to foreign trade and economic cooperation may need to obtain various approvals from the Ministry of Commerce. Any tax relief or tax exemption enjoyed by the H share companies may need approval from the State Administration of Taxation.[89] If the listing application involves foreign exchange matters, approval from State Administration of Foreign Exchange may be required.[90]

If the listing involves transfer of state assets, Measures for the Administration of State-owned Asset Valuation[91] requires that asset valuation must be conducted. The state asset regime is governed by the State Asset Administration Bureau which has been taken over by the Ministry of Finance.[92] Valuation is also required when the enterprise that seeks listing has properties in the PRC. Practice Note 12 of the Listing Rules governs the establishment of title in the PRC and it requires a valuation report to mention whether the relevant party has vested legal title to the relevant property. For land-related issues, approval may be required from the Ministry of Land and Resources[93], formerly the State Land Bureau.

Due to the number of approvals possibly required for listing, the HKSE has published Guidelines for the Legal Opinion on PRC Approval Issues in connection with New Listing Applications. Under these Guidelines, the HKSE may ask the issuer or its sponsor for a legal opinion from a law firm registered in the PRC and certified by the Ministry of Justice and the CSRC as being qualified to engage in securities matters.

The issuer or its sponsor also needs to produce a legal opinion that no governmental or regulatory authority is required for the listing of the issuer's shares on the HKSE or if approval is required, such approval has been obtained.[94]

[88] Civil Aviation Administration of China is a State Council ministry responsible for national civil aviation affairs and the China Insurance Regulatory Commission is an institution directly under the State Council to formulate insurance-related laws and regulations, oversee insurance business operation and promote insurance industry reforms and restructuring. *See* their official websites at <http://www.caac.gov.cn and http://www.circ.gov.cn>.

[89] See its official website at <http://www.chinatax.gov.cn>.

[90] See its official website at <http://www.safe.gov.cn>.

[91] The Measure was promulgated by the State Council as Decree No 91 on 16 Nov 1991, Art 3.

[92] Paul Brown and Brett Shadbolt *Revolution in China Valuations* at <http://www.asialaw.com/bookstore/ china2000/chapter08.htm> (last visited 2 Jan 2005).

[93] See its official website at <http://www.mlr.gov.cn>.

[94] According to R. 25.16(5) of the GEM Listing Rules, PRC companies which apply to be listed on the GEM also need to submit legal opinions to the HKSE by PRC lawyers authorized

After restructuring and before listing, the issuer also needs to register as overseas company under Part XI of the Companies Ordinance in Hong Kong.

3. *Appealing to Investors*

When subscribing for shares in a company investors are mainly looking for financial returns. A few investors may also be dictated by their political or religious beliefs. In general, a potential investor will look carefully at the following factors:

- past trading records and the profitability of the issuer;
- nature of the business and its prospect (including all the risk factors);
- the competence of its directors and secretary;
- the issuer's corporate governance; and
- current economic climate and the market situation (alternatives other than investing in shares).

4. *Non-Competition*

In accordance with the HKSE Listing Rule 8.10 and Rule 19A.14, where a new applicant is a controlling shareholder[95] with an interest in a business apart from the applicant's own business which competes with or is likely to compete with that business either directly or indirectly, the HKSE may regard such an applicant as unsuitable for listing. In the past state-run enterprises were all owned by the State[96] but after the institution of the

by the relevant authority in the PRC to advise on securities laws, confirming the due incorporation and legal person status of the PRC issuer as a joint stock limited company under the PRC law and the obtaining of all relevant regulatory approvals in the PRC required for the issue and listing contemplated by the PRC issuer's listing application. The CSRC also issued the Guidelines on Approval and Supervision of Domestic Enterprises Applying for Listing on the Growth Enterprise Market in Hong Kong on 21 Sept 1999. Under the Guideline, CSRC's approval for listing on the GEM in Hong Kong requires, among other things, a legal opinion issued by a PRC law firm qualified to practice securities law on whether the listing candidate has complied with relevant laws and policies and whether the listing candidate has committed any significant breach of the law during the previous two years for CSRC's approval.

[95] 'Controlling Shareholder' means any shareholder or other person or group of persons together entitled to exercise, or control the exercise of 30 per cent (or such other amount as may from time to time be specified in the applicable PRC law as being the level for triggering a mandatory general offer or for otherwise establishing legal or management control over a business enterprise) or more of the voting power at general meetings of the issuer or who is in a position to control the composition of a majority of the board of directors of the issuer. *See* Listing Rules, R. 19A.14.

[96] HKSE will normally not consider a PRC Government Body as a controlling shareholder of a PRC issuer and PRC Government Body is defined in the Listing Rules of HKSE as the PRC Central Government, PRC Provincial-level Governments and PRC local government immediately under the PRC Provincial-level Government. See Listing Rules, R. 19A.14. However enti-

open door policy and the restructuring of SOEs, many such enterprises became more independent and commercially oriented and therefore more competitive. For competitive commercial businesses within the same government department, non-competition agreement may be signed to show that such businesses are not competing with each other either because their target customers or the products provided are different. Moreover in terms of provision of raw materials, production or sales assistance, the controlling shareholder will treat the listed company as fairly and reasonably as its other subsidiaries which are not included in the listed company.

B. Connected Transactions

Improper connected transactions will significantly diminish the shareholders' value. A typical way of restructuring a SOE for listing would be by demerger.[97] In a typical demerger a SOE would transfer its operating business to a joint stock company, wholly owned by the State-owned enterprise, in exchange for shares of the joint stock company.[98] Non-operating sectors like schools, hospitals, canteens etc. would usually be left out from the listed company. If such sectors were included in the listed company, it would increase the net asset of the listed company and decrease the profit per share of the company. Such sectors usually stay with the parent company of the listed company.

Although in terms of accounting purpose such sectors were separated from the listed company, in reality, the operation of such sectors might remain unchanged and would remain an integrated part of the listed company through connected transactions. The listing requirements of the HKSE require such connected transactions to be approved by the independent shareholders and/or to make adequate disclosure. However it was difficult for the listed company to be completely separated from such non-operating sectors which catered for the welfare of the listed company and it was equally difficult to obtain independent shareholders' approval whenever the listed company entered into transactions with such sectors. With the help of the financial advisor and the lawyers, the issuer would apply for a waiver from obtaining independent shareholders' approval for such connected transactions. In order for such a waiver to be granted, the issuer

ties under the PRC Government that are engaging in commercial business or operating another commercial entity will be excluded from this definition.

[97] Examples of such restructuring are China Southern Airlines Company Limited and China Eastern Airlines Company Limited. The formation by merger method was also adopted by many PRC listed companies like the Tsingtao Brewery Company Limited and Shanghai Worldbest Co Ltd. Where enterprise are merged and then corporatized to establish one new single joint stock company. *See* Jenny SC Chung *Chinese Law: Tax Benefit Enjoyed by H Share Companies: A Legal Analysis*, 29 Hong Kong LJ 294.

[98] See ibid.

had to show that the transactions were conducted in the normal course of the business and at arm's length. The HKSE might also require the sponsor to conduct due diligence to ensure that the transactions were fair and reasonable on normal commercial terms. The HKSE would also require the issuer to conduct such connected transactions within the monetary cap agreed by the HKSE and the issuer. A PRC government body[99] will not usually be considered by the HKSE as a connected person of a PRC issuer.[100]

C. *Independent Directors*

Every board of directors of a listed issuer must include at least three independent non-executive directors and at least one of the independent non-executive directors must have appropriate professional qualifications or accounting or related financial management expertise.[101] Each director must satisfy the HKSE that he has the character, integrity, experience and independence to fulfil his role effectively.[102]

To assess the independence of a non-executive director, the HKSE has set up some guidelines for reference although none of them is necessarily conclusive. The guidelines takes into consideration both the director's possible direct[103] or indirect financial interests in the concerned company, past or present direct or indirect connections with the company, its subsidiaries, its directors, substantial or controlling shareholders and the interests such a director represents.[104] An independent non-executive director needs to submit to the HKSE a written confirmation in respect of Rule 3.13 of the Listing Rules concerning his independence showing that there are no other factors that may affect his independence. Such confirmation has to be provided annually.[105]

Every listed issuer must establish an audit committee comprising non-executive directors only.[106] The audit committee must comprise a minimum

[99] PRC Government Body is defined in the Listing Rules of HKSE as the PRC Central Government, PRC Provincial-level Governments and PRC local government immediately under the PRC Provincial-level Government. *See* Listing Rules, R. 19A.04.

[100] See The Listing Rules, R. 19A.19.

[101] The Listing Rules, R. 3.10(1) & R. 3.10(2).

[102] The Listing Rules, R. 3.09.

[103] Independent non-executive director usually cannot hold more than 1 per cent of the total issued share capital. If the non-executive director is given shares equivalent to 1 per cent or less of the total issued share capital as a gift or by means of financial assistance from a connected person, such non-executive director will still be regarded as not independent unless those shares were received from the listed issuer or its subsidiaries as part of his director's fee or pursuant to share option schemes established in accordance with the Listing Rules. *See* Listing Rules, R. 3.13(2).

[104] See the Listing Rules, R. 3.13 (1–8).

[105] The Listing Rules, R. 3.13.

[106] The Listing Rules, R. 3.21.

of three members; at least one of them is an independent non-executive director with appropriate professional qualifications or accounting or related financial management expertise as required under the Listing Rules.[107] The majority of the audit committee members must be independent non-executive directors of the listed issuer and the audit committee must be chaired by an independent non-executive director.[108] Listed issuers may refer to 'A Guide for Effective Audit Committees' published by the Hong Kong Society of Accountants in February 2002.[109]

D. Financial and Commercial Issues

A number of financial and commercial issues have to be taken into consideration. PRC issuers are expected to present their annual accounts in accordance with Hong Kong or international accounting standards. Normally if an issuer chooses the International Financial Reporting Standards ('IFRS')[110] instead of the Hong Kong Financial Reporting Standards ('HKFRS'),[111] they have to disclose and explain differences of accounting practice between the HKFRS and IFRS which have a significant effect on its financial statements and such an issuer is also required to compile a statement of the financial effect of any such material differences.[112] However if the PRC issuer chooses the IFRS as their accounting standards, the above explanation is not required.[113] In reality, the PRC issuer will prepare report of financial information conforming to applicable PRC accounting rules and regulations alongside the financial report in accordance with IFRS and they will contain a statement of the financial effect of the material differences from IFRS.[114] In order to accomplish this task, the PRC issuer is required to retain accountants firm from both Hong Kong and the PRC. The change of accounting standards may have a significant impact on the trading and profit record of the issuer.

A company cannot survive on its own unless it has entered into contractual relationship with other companies or individuals in the form of suppliers' agreement, service agreement, tenancy agreement, facility letter and so on, depending on the nature of the business. To prepare for listing after the

[107] See ibid. [108] See ibid. [109] See ibid.

[110] It is defined in the Listing Rules as the financial reporting standards and interpretations approved by the International Accounting Standard Board, and include all International Accounting Standards and interpretations issued under the former International Accounting Standards Committee from time to time.

[111] It is defined in the Listing Rules as financial reporting standards approved by the Council of the Hong Kong Society of Accountants ('HKSA'), and includes all Statements of Standard Accounting Practice and interpretation of HKFRS approved by the HKSA from time to time.

[112] The Listing Rules, R. 4.11(b).

[113] The Listing Rules, R. 19A.10.

[114] The Listing Rules, R. 19A.10 (Note).

necessary restructuring the issuer may need to enter into new agreements with its bank, supplier, service provider and with its customers. Some of the above may become connected parties and hence the agreement with them may become part of the connected transactions. The issuer may reconsider the terms of the old agreement and make some amendments accordingly if such commercial relationship is to be kept.

E. Prospectus Drafting

The public disclosure of the initial public offering ('IPO') is in the form of a prospectus. Any listing requires the publication of a prospectus to be drafted by the issuer's and underwriter's legal counsel and/or its sponsor with the assistance from the issuer. The prospectus will set out the subscription procedures, the share and offering structure, the business of the issuer and risk factors relating to this initial public offering. It also offers important financial information like the accountants' report and valuation report.[115] The prospectus will also summarize the articles of association of the issuer, the restructuring process and details of the connected transactions.

For H shares, the prospectus has to warn the would-be shareholders of the following: (a) the PRC laws and regulations relevant to the business of the PRC issuer; (b) the political structure and economic environment of the PRC; (c) foreign exchange controls in the PRC and the exchange rate risk of the RMB; (d) the different regulatory framework for PRC issuers listing outside the mainland of the PRC; (e) specific risk factors relating to the business of the PRC issuer and/or its products; and (f) the law(s) governing the resolution of disputes arising from the PRC issuer's articles of association and the transfer of the PRC issuer's shares.[116]

Such a prospectus will be vetted meticulously by the HKSE and SFC. Both the legal counsel and the underwriter will have to carry out legal and financial due diligence respectively to ensure that every statement is true, accurate and complete, that no statement is misleading and that there are no significant omissions. Each of the directors, including proposed directors named in the prospectus, is required to accept responsibility for the information which the prospectus contains and a statement to that effect is required to be incorporated into the prospectus.[117] Written consents from any experts involved[118] need to be included in the prospectus. An inclusion of any recommendation by such experts in relation to acceptance or rejec-

[115] Gao and Fu, above n 16, at 134.

[116] The Listing Rules, App 1: Part A, para 64 and Part B, para 49. See also the GEM Listing Rules, App 1: Part A, para 67 and Part B, para 49.

[117] The Listing Rules, R. 11.12 and R. 19A.26(1) and the GEM Listing Rules, R. 14.23.

[118] 'Expert' is defined in the Listing Rules to include engineer, valuer, accountant and any other person whose profession gives authority to a statement made by him.

tion of an offer in the prospectus should also require written consents from them. [119]

Directors, supervisors and sponsors are all required to declare that the Listing Rules have been complied with.[120] Directors also need to declare that the prospectus has complied with all the legal requirements and no amendments have been made to the prospectus after the HKSE has approved the prospectus.[121]

F. Enforcement

As Hong Kong and the PRC are under different legal systems with their own separate courts, any dispute may result in a conflict of laws and problems with the enforceability of a judgment from either court. Under the MOU between the SFC, the HKSE, the CSRC, the SZSE and SSE, a mechanism has been established to resolve disputes. Any H share dispute will be resolved by arbitration in accordance with PRC law ie the Company Law and all relevant laws and regulations.[122] In terms of venue, arbitration may take place either at the China International Economic and Trade Arbitration Centre ('CIETAC') or the Hong Kong International Arbitration Centre ('HKIAC'), at the election of the claimant.[123] As both CIETAC and HKIAC are parties to the New York Convention on the Recognition and Enforcement of Foreign Arbitral Awards, arbitral awards from either one of the centres will be enforceable in both jurisdictions.[124]

A PRC issuer is required to enter into a written contract with every director, officer and supervisor an undertaking that any disputes or claim arising from the company's articles of association or any rights or obligations conferred by the Company Law or other relevant laws and administrative regulations concerning the affairs of the company will be referred to arbitration[125] and the award of the arbitral body is final and binding on the parties involved[126] and the hearing shall be open and the award be published.[127]

119 The Listing Rules, R. 9.14 (3). See also Companies Ordinance, s 38C.

120 The Listing Rules, App 5, Form E (Sponsor's Declaration), Form H (Declaration and Undertaking with regard to Directors of an Issuer incorporated in the People's Republic of China ('PRC')) and Form I (Declaration and Undertaking with regard to Supervisors of an Issuer incorporated in the People's Republic of China ('PRC')). Similar declarations have to be made for issuers applying to be listed on GEM. *See* The GEM Listing Rules, Apps 6B and 6C and App 7 (As the sponsor takes on a more important role in GEM to protect the investors, their declarations are more detailed than the Main Board).

121 The Listing Rules, App. 5, Form F (Declaration), paras 1 and 10.

122 The Listing Rules, R. 19A.54(3)(f) and the GEM Listing Rules, R.25.41(3)(f).

123 The Listing Rules, R.19A.54(3)(d) and the GEM Listing Rules, R.25.41(3)(d).

124 Nottle, above n 83, at 124–5.

125 The Listing Rules, R.19A.54(3)(b) and the GEM Listing Rules, R. 25.41(3)(b).

126 The Listing Rules, R.19A.54(3)(g) and the GEM Listing Rules, R. 25.41(3)(g).

127 The Listing Rules, R.19A.54(3)(i) and the GEM Listing Rules, R. 25.41(3)(i).

VIII. ALTERNATIVE METHODS FOR PRC COMPANIES TO BE LISTED ON THE HONG KONG STOCK EXCHANGE

Other than being listed as an H share company incorporated in the PRC, a PRC company can be listed on the Hong Kong Stock Exchange through a Hong Kong incorporated vehicle with controlling shareholders from the PRC entities.[128]

In the early stage of the H share experiment a number of PRC companies bypassed the official listing channels through reverse take-over, commonly known as 'backdoor listing'.[129] Backdoor listing is the acquisition of a listed company or the shell company by an unlisted company to gain a listing on the securities exchange. It may happen where a listed company acquires a non-listed company's assets or shares, and the value of the acquired assets, based on the criteria set by each Exchange, is larger than the acquirer's original assets, resulting in a change in the control of the listed company to major shareholders of the non-listed company. As a result, it allows companies that may not be able to meet the listing requirements of the Hong Kong Stock Exchange to be listed on it and it will also enable private companies to be listed on the Stock Exchange much faster than companies which have to go through the listing procedures formally.

Red chip companies are predominately diversified conglomerates which have grown rapidly due to the asset injection from the parent companies in the PRC.[130] They include China Telecom, Beijing Enterprises Holdings, China Everbright, Shanghai Industrial Holdings, China Resources Enterprises and the 'window-companies' or 'International Trust and Investment Corporations (ITICs)' of provincial governments.[131]

Strictly speaking, red chip companies did not originally fall within the jurisdiction of the PRC authorities. However in June 1997, the CSRC in conjunction with the State Council introduced the Notice Concerning Further Strengthening Administration of Share Offering and Listing Overseas (commonly known as 'Red Chip Guidelines')[132] to prevent the dissipation of state assets. The PRC Government was worried that state assets would be injected into the red chip companies and they might be sold off indirectly to overseas investors at a discount. The Red Chip Guidelines

[128] DongweiI Su, *Chinese Stock Markets—A Research Handbook* 54 (World Scientific, 2003).

[129] See HKEx Listing Rules, R. 14.06(6) for a detailed definition of 'reverse takeover'.

[130] SU, above n 128, at 54.

[131] ibid.

[132] *Guanyu Jinyibu Jiajiang zai Jingwai Faxing Gupiao he Shengshi Guanli de Tongzhi* [Notice promulgated by State Council Concerning Further Strengthening Administration of Share Offering and Listing Overseas] (20 June 1997 *Guofa* [1997], effective as of the same day).

provides more stringent requirement for reporting to, and obtaining approval from, the Chinese authorities. Under the 1997 guidelines Chinese shareholders who controlled foreign listed companies or Chinese shareholders who intended to inject assets to red chip companies were either required to report to the CSRC or alternatively required to obtain consent from the local provincial government or relevant department of the State Council depending on their circumstances.[133]

On 30 January 2004, the HKEx announced a number of changes to the Listing rules which came into effect on 31 March 2004. Among them, reverse takeovers were added as a new category of notifiable transactions, making it more difficult to achieve back door listings.[134] Such notifiable transactions require notification and approval from the HKEx, approval from the shareholders, an accountant's report on the preceding three financial years of the business or companies acquired, publication on the newspaper and circular to the shareholders.[135] With the new amendments, the HKSE was determined to stop companies from circumventing the Listing Rules by using reverse takeovers.

IX. STRENGTHS AND SHORTCOMINGS OF H SHARE COMPANIES

A. Accounting Systems

Accountants are generally regarded as the guard dog for investors and for them to be effective, they have to raise the alarm in times of danger. The Listing Rules applicable to PRC companies ensure that the accounting standards employed by PRC companies seeking to be listed on the Hong Kong stock exchange should be the same as those for other companies listed there. PRC issuers can choose to adopt the Hong Kong Financial Reporting Standards ('HKFRS') or International Financial Reporting Standards ('IFRS'). PRC issuers that adopt IFRS are exempt from disclosing differences of accounting practice between IFRS and HKFRS and compiling a statement of the financial effect of any such differences.[136] A PRC issuer may, in addition, report separately financial information confirming with applicable PRC accounting rules and regulations provided that the report contains a statement of the financial effect of the material differences (if any) from HKFRS or IFRS, as the case may be.[137]

[133] Red Chip Guidelines, paras 1, 2, and 3.
[134] HKEx, *Note to Subscribers for the Amendments to the Rules Governing the Listing of Securities—Update No 80* (31 Mar 2004).
[135] HKEx Listing Rules, R. 14.33.
[136] Listing Rules, R.19A.10.
[137] Listing Rules, R. 19A.10 (note).

H share companies tend to have better governance than the other PRC companies not only because of adopting international accounting standards but also because of other professional requirements that support the accounting profession in Hong Kong. H share companies require the use of professional accountants who are qualified under the Professional Accountants Ordinance[138] and they must be independent both of the issuer and of any other company in accordance with the Companies Ordinance and the requirements on independence issued by the Hong Kong Society of Accountants.[139]

Although the scale of accounting fraud in China cannot be compared with the Enron case,[140] commentators often remark that accounting fraud in China is more blatant than in the West.[141] The Shanghai Stock Exchange found problems in 1999 annual reports of 38.06 per cent of companies listed at that time, while the Shenzhen stock Exchange discovered problems with 25.67 per cent.[142] The frequency of accounting fraud in China can be illustrated with reference to the National Audit Office carried out in December 2001 as a random check of 32 audit reports prepared by 16 accounting firms licensed to audit PRC listed companies.[143] Of these, 23 audit reports prepared by 14 accounting firms were described as 'gravely inaccurate'.[144] Such errors amounted to a combined RMB7.14 billion.[145] The long list of offences included forging sales revenue and bank deposits as well as dishonestly altering debt, profit and losses data.[146] In 2001, Chinese Institute of Certified Public Accountants has disciplined more than 100 accounting firms and 120 certified public accountants in more than 220 cases of irregularity since 2000.[147]

The 2002 litigated Macat case is a telling example. Macat Optics and Electronics Company, Limited obtained approval from the CSRC and launched an IPO on the Shenzhen Stock Market in August 2000.[148] At the

[138] Listing Rules, R. 19A.08 and R. 4.03.
[139] ibid.
[140] Biochemical firm Gangxia (Yinchuan) Industry, the Shenzhen-listed A-share company whose deception caught the most public attention in 2001, declared total assets of about RMB3.15billion at the end of 2000. It was exposed by Beijing's influential *Caijing* magazine to have inflated it profits. This was only a small fraction of Enron's total assets of US$61.78 billion at the end of September 2001. SCMP, *Chinese Cookery Books*, Mar. 26, 2002 at <http://archive.scmp.com>.
[141] Ernst and Young's head of China and Hong Kong, Anthony Wu Ting-yuk pointed out that Chinese accounting fraud cases are more blatant fraud while Enron, whose account massaging with off-balance-sheet activities and off-shore vehicle took advantage of a very grey area of accounting principles. See SCMP, above n 140.
[142] ibid.
[143] ibid.
[144] ibid.
[145] ibid.
[146] ibid.
[147] ibid.
[148] See Huawei Ling et al, *Maikete E'Meng—Yitiao Kongqian Wanzheng de Zhengquan Shichang Zaojia Liushuixian de Wanzheng Baoguang* [Macat's Nightmare—A Whole Production Line Making Falsified Reports in the Securities Market is Exposed], in Caijing Mag, 20 Mar 2002, available at <http://bsuiness.sohu.com/39/60article200406039.shtml> (last visited 15 Oct 2004) (hereinafter 'Macat's Nightmare').

beginning of November 2000, the CSRC identified that Macat had falsified hundreds of millions of dollars of profit and revenue in its financial statements.[149] According to both the CSRC report and court judgment of the case, 'not only did the company, a small entity without any substantial assets, purposely defraud the public, but all the intermediaries, including an accounting firm, an asset valuation institution, a law firm, and a securities company also helped Macat to fabricate the false statements'.[150] The case was therefore characterized as involving a 'sophisticated production line for producing false accounting reports and numbers in the securities market'.[151]

Although some commented that China's endemic accounting fraud is no different from early days of the US securities market[152], the root causes of China's accounting fraud plague are believed to be structural and historical.[153]

Structurally, unless the accounting firms are financially strong and have a broad audit and accounting business, it is very difficult for them to remain independent.[154] However, the Chinese accounting profession is still dominated by numerous small firms. The Chinese accounting market was estimated to be worth Renminbi seven to eight billion in 2000 with 4,446 accounting firms and 52,000 practising certified public accountants sharing the pie.[155] Of them, only a few dozen firms employed more than 100 CPAs.[156] Small accounting firms, especially those outside of the major cities, are dependent on the particular industry or business in that particular locality.[157] They may risk losing a client if they issue qualified opinions which may result in a customer's failure to gain a listing or suspension from trading.

Historically, China's accounting fraud is also believed to be a legacy of its planned economy.[158] Under the planned economy, accounting was viewed more as a paper game to meet official targets.[159] More than 40 per cent of Chinese accountants are older than 50 and they were trained under the planned economic system.[160] Until 1998, most Chinese accounting firms were operated by government agencies and as such, the accounting practice was prone to government interference.[161] A number of issuers were

[149] Steven Shi and Drake Weisert, Commentary *Corporate Governance with Chinese Characteristics*, 29 China Bus Rev. (Sept–Oct 2002), available at <http://www.chinabusiness-review.com/public/0209/ shi.html> (last visited 17 Oct 2004).

[150] Jiangyu Wang *Dancing with Wolves: Regulation and Deregulation of Foreign Investment in China's Stock Market* (2004) 5 Asian-Pacific L & Pol'y J 1, 40.

[151] *See* Ling, above n 148.

[152] One professional who held this view is Ernst and Young's China executive partner Alfred Shum. *See* SCMP, above n 140.

[153] ibid. [154] ibid. [155] ibid.

[156] ibid. [157] ibid. [158] ibid.

[159] ibid. [160] ibid. [161] ibid.

appointed by the Chinese Government or State-owned enterprises not to 'restructure into modern enterprises', but simply to raise capital to alleviate financial difficulties. Accountants tended to act according to their instructions.[162] During an interview, Fung Liufang stated that:

> When a SOE obtains a quota for IPO, even though it has suffered loss in the past three years [which hence cannot meet the initial legal requirement for IPO], it can immediately have profit earnings in the past three consecutive years simply by requesting those 'securities accountants' to cook accounting statements for them, of course with extra high pay to those accountants . . . The issuers 'make-up' fee is eventually absorbed by the 'issuance cost', which shall be deducted from the capital contribution paid by investors purchasing the shares. SOE's made-up—intermediaries provide make-up service—investors pay the bill: this is the entire process of the game.[163]

H share companies are comparatively less susceptible to accounting fraud not only because of the international accounting standards that they have had to adopt but also because they are monitored by large, international accounting firms. This does not necessarily guarantee that they are fraud free as even Arthur Anderson failed to whistle blow in the case of Enron, but it does mean that it is more difficult for blatant accounting fraud to succeed. However accountants may only examine figures and, unlike forensic accountants, they may not examine what are behind those figures. To stamp out accounting fraud, internal accounting control should be in place alongside good corporate governance.

B. *Connected Transactions*

A connected transaction is, among other things, a transaction between a listed issuer and a connected person. A connected person is broadly defined as a director, chief executive, substantial shareholders, or the associate of the listed issuer. In the case of a PRC issuer, it will include its promoter, supervisor or associate of its promoter or its supervisors. However, a connected person does not include any wholly-owned subsidiary of the listed issuer. Such connected transactions need to be announced publicly and a circular must be sent to shareholders giving information about the transaction. The approval of the shareholders given at a general meeting is

[162] Qinglian He, Xiandaihua De Xianjing—Zhongguo Zhi Wenti [*The Trap of Modernization—China's Problems*] 24 (Jinri Zhongguo Chubanshe [Today China Publishing House], 1998).

[163] Yingbo Shao 'Guodu Gauanzhi Daozhi de Cuoche—Fang Liufang Jiexi Zhongguo Zhengquan Shichang' [Frustration Caused by Over-Regulation—Fang Liufang on China's Securities Market], in JingiI Guangcha Bao [Econ Watch Daily], 6 Dec 2001, available at <http://news.sohu.com/17/39/news147363917.shtml> (last visited 28 Mar 2004) quoted by Wang, above n 150, at 39.

required before the transaction can proceed. Some categories of connected transactions are exempt from disclosure and independent shareholders' approval requirements and certain transactions are subject only to disclosure requirements. Connected transactions can be one-off or continuing. The reason for imposing such requirements is to protect the interests of shareholders and provide certain safeguards against listed issuer's directors, chief executives or substantial shareholders (or their associates) from taking advantage of their positions as a listed issuer.

As discussed earlier, the H share companies are all SOEs before the quota system was scrapped. Although the PRC Governmental Body as defined by the Listing Rules is not regarded as a connected person, entities under the PRC Government that are engaging in commercial business or operating another commercial entity are excluded from the definition of PRC Governmental Body. SOEs also carry out political and social functions and through restructuring, such functions have to be transferred to the parent companies so as to boost the profit of the proposed listed SOEs. The parent company will become a non-productive, loss-making entity which is burdened with pensions and various administrative expenses. To close down the parent company will create massive unemployment and hence social unrest. To cope with the situation, the issuer will provide sweeteners to the parent company through connected transactions. The Hong Kong stock exchange will ensure that such connected transactions are conducted properly without adversely affecting the shareholders' interests. For the sale of consumer goods or consumer services, the Hong Kong stock exchange will ensure, among other things, that the sale or purchase is conducted in the ordinary and usual course of business and it must be on normal commercial terms. It can pose a problem in the early days of market economy as most SOEs are monopolies with no alternative market and a market mechanism is not available in the planned economy. Payment is then usually set on reasonable assumption and estimation.

In addition, the separation of the listed issuer and its parent company is more legal than factual. The management of the listed company and its parent company originally belonged to one team and their previous relationship and their political hierarchy in the Government will enable the continued influence of the parent company over the listed company. As a result, some decisions taken by the listed issuer are believed to benefit the parent company rather than investors as a whole.

C. *Accountability*

Under the Listing Rules which incorporate the Mandatory Provisions for Companies Listing Overseas,[164] the articles of association of the listed

[164] Listing Rules, App. 13 Part D s 1(a).

issuers provide that there are three tiers of control over a company's operations: the shareholders' general meeting, the board of directors and supervisors, and the management. The shareholders' general meeting is the highest authority in the listed company and has the final say over key issues of the listed company.[165] The board of directors makes investment decisions[166] and the board of supervisor overseas the decision making process and performance of the directors and senior management.[167] The management is responsible for the day-to-day management of the listed company and implements the decisions made by the board of directors.[168] The division of labour is to ensure the accountability of directors, supervisors and managers.[169] With checks and balances in place, it is difficult for any parties to abuse their positions.

However the PRC Government remains the largest shareholders for all SOEs which have listed on the Hong Kong stock exchange. The state is, after all, an abstract owner and typically, the PRC Government does not exercise its rights as a shareholder to influence management effectively.[170] In practice, key managers can sometimes gain control over the shareholders' meeting so it functions like a rubber stamp approving everything decided by the management.[171] When everything belongs to the State, it belongs to no one and creates a moral hazard. Most directors on the board are the same management personnel for the pre-listed company. They tend to manage the company in the old ways. The prevalent mindset among SOEs managers is that capital raised in the stock market is free, an attitude rooted in the era of the planned economy when SOE managers would receive loans from State-owned banks with no obligation to repay them.[172] Such a mindset does not encourage responsibility and accountability and proceeds raised in such a way are not always allocated to their best use.

In addition, most Chinese investors are retail investors who focus more on the names of the company's key institutional investors and its relation-

[165] Mandatory Provisions, Arts 49 and 50.

[166] Mandatory Provisions, Art 88.

[167] Mandatory Provisions, Art 108.

[168] Mandatory Provisions, Arts 97 (for company secretary) and 100 (for managers).

[169] According to the Mandatory Provisions, the board of directors and the board of supervisors are both accountable to the shareholders in general meeting and the managers are accountable to the board of directors. *See* Mandatory Provisions, Arts 88, 100, 108.

[170] Steven Shi and Drake Weisert, Commentary *Corporate Governance with Chinese Characteristics*, 29 China Bus Rev. (Sept–Oct 2002), available at <http://www.chinabusinessreview.com/public/ 0209/shi.html> (last visited 17 Oct 2004). 'With so many administrative entities still able to claim ownership rights over SOEs, including state-asset management companies, affiliated companies belonging to local administrations and supervisory councils and managers, no party can be held responsible for any losses they incur and for the risk of investing in them.' *See* John Child 'Management and Organizations in China: Key Trends and Issues' in *Management and Organizations in the Chinese Context* 44(JT Li et al (eds) Macmillan Press 2000).

[171] ibid.

[172] ibid.

ship with the PRC Government than on a company's basic performance.[173] There is also a lack of incentive mechanisms that is linked to their performance.[174] As a result, with a lack of accountability and incentive and a poor salary package, managers and directors alike are more prone to use their positions to divert money to their personal accounts.[175] This situation is more commonly found in companies listed in the PRC than in Hong Kong. One possible reason is that the H share companies are more high profile and the Chinese Government will keep a closer eye on such companies. The lack of profitability of H share companies is still a major concern and it reflects on the efficiency and accountability of the management level of such companies.

D. *Executive and Managerial Competence*

Other than accountability, the other problem in the PRC is the competence of directors and company secretaries in discharging their duties. The Listing Rules have tried to ensure that the directors and company secretaries have the necessary experience and competence to deal with the listed companies through the use of a sponsor and detailed qualification requirements.

In the past, the appointment of a sponsor was required to assist the issuer regarding listing application and after the listing, it had the responsibilities of educating the senior management level about all relevant laws. For non-PRC issuers, the Hong Kong stock exchange recommends retaining the services of its sponsor for at least one year following the listing.[176] However for PRC issuers this is not a recommendation but a requirement.[177] A sponsor must be any corporation or authorized financial institution licensed or registered to advise on corporate finance matters and appointed as a sponsor by the issuer.[178] In practice, the sponsor is usually the lead underwriter of the IPO. Under the new rule effective on 1 January 2005, the sponsor's responsibilities are limited to preparing the issuer for listing, for lodging the formal listing application and all supporting documents and for dealing with the Hong Kong stock exchange on all matters arising in connection with the application.[179] It also needs to carry out due diligence inquiries and ensure that the information submitted to the Hong Kong stock

173 ibid.

174 ibid.

175 Since the beginning of 2001, there were a series of scandals for companies listed on the stock exchanges in the PRC, namely, Guanxia (Yinchuan) Industry Co Ltd, Lantian Co Ltd, Zhenzhou Baiwen Co Ltd, Sanjiu Pharmaceutical Co and Macat Optics and Electronics Co, Ltd. For details, See ibid.

176 The Listing Rules, R. 3.02 (now repealed).

177 Listing Rules, R. 19A.05 (1) (now repealed).

178 The Listing Rules, Ch 1.

179 The Listing Rules, R. 3A.11 (1).

exchange be true in all material aspects with no material omission.[180] For PRC issuers, they have to ensure that the PRC issuers are suitable to be listed and the directors and supervisors understand their responsibilities and can be expected to honor their obligations.[181] A sponsor must perform its duties with impartiality[182]and at least one sponsor must be independent from the issuer under the test set out under the Listing Rules.[183] Their work will come to an end immediately upon the listing of the issuer.[184]

Compliance advisers are any corporation or authorized financial institution licensed or registered to advise on corporate finance matters and appointed as a compliance adviser by the issuer. They are appointed during the Fixed Period to assist the issuers on all compliance issues and they have to perform their duties with impartiality.[185] Compliance advisers must inform the PRC issuers on a timely basis of any amendment or supplement to the Listing Rules and any new or amended law, regulation or code in Hong Kong applicable to such issuers.[186] In other words, the compliance advisers have the responsibilities of educating the senior management level about all relevant laws. They also have to provide advice on the continuing requirements under the above laws.[187] In addition, they have to be the channel of communication with the Hong Kong stock exchange if the authorized representatives of the issuers are not in Hong Kong.[188] The new Listing Rules requires both the sponsors and compliance advisers to ensure corporate governance of the issuer instead of relying on the sponsors alone. By separating the role of the sponsors and compliance advisors, the independence of sponsors from the issuers can be better facilitated.

The duties of directors are also spelt out in the Listing Rules. Each director has to satisfy the Hong Kong stock exchange that he has the necessary character, experience and integrity and to demonstrate that he has a standard of competence commensurate with his position as a director of a listed issuer.[189] Every board of directors of a listed issuer has recently been increased to include at least three independent non-executive directors[190] and for the first time, it states that at least one of the independent non-executive directors must have appropriate professional qualifications or accounting or related financial management expertise.[191] For PRC issuers, one of the independent non-executive directors must also demonstrate an acceptable standard of competence and adequate commercial or professional experience to ensure that the interests of the general body of share-

180 The Listing Rules, R. 3A.11 (2) and Practice Note 21.
181 The Listing Rules, R. 19A.06 (1).
182 The Listing Rules, R. 3A.06.
183 The Listing Rules, R. 3A.07.
184 The Listing Rules, R. 3A.02.
185 The Listing Rules, R. 3A.25.
186 The Listing Rules, R. 19A.06 (3).
187 ibid.
188 The Listing Rules, R. 19A.06 (4).
189 Listing Rules, R. 3.08 and R. 3.09.
190 Listing Rules, R. 3.10(1).
191 The Listing Rules, R. 3.10(2).

holders will be adequately represented.[192] Furthermore, at least two of the executive directors[193] and one of the independent non-executive directors must be ordinarily resident in Hong Kong.[194] Supervisors also need to demonstrate a standard of competence commensurate with their position as supervisors.[195]

The company secretary of a PRC issuer need not be ordinarily resident in Hong Kong[196] but has to have the requisite knowledge and experience to discharge the functions of a secretary. Such a person has to be a member of The Hong Kong Institute of Company Secretaries, a solicitor or barrister as defined in the Legal Practitioners Ordinance or a professional accountant.[197] If not the holder of this position has to have suitable academic or professional qualifications or relevant experience in discharging the functions of this position. For an issuer listed before 1 December 1989, a candidate for the post could meet the requirement if he or she held the office of secretary of the issuer before that date.[198] Such strict requirements are important as a number of listed companies in the PRC have had members of the senior management or accountants who have been incompetent in discharging their duties.[199]

In the early day of H share issue, all the issuers were SOEs. They are large monopolistic organizations with expertise in certain areas such as energy, airlines, highways etc. The senior management of such companies had acquired invaluable specialized knowledge of such industry that was very difficult to be replaced. When the SOEs were listed, understandably they retained the senior management especially when more often than not, the listing was initiated by them. The management level might have expertise in their areas but they started their management when the PRC was still

192 The Listing Rules, R. 19A.18(1).
193 The Listing Rules, R. 19A.15.
194 ibid.
195 The Listing Rules, R. 19A.18(2).
196 The Listing Rules, R. 19A.16.
197 When the PRC company secretaries do not possess either one of these qualifications, they may make a submission to the Hong Kong stock exchange that they can discharge the function of company secretaries by pleading that they have the relevant experience. Among other things, the Hong Kong stock exchange will take into consideration the period of their employment with the PRC issuers and their familiarity with the Listing Rules. *See* Listing Rules, R. 19A.16 (note).
198 The Listing Rules, R. 8.17.
199 One of the examples is Anhui Gujing Distillery Company Limited which was set up in 1959. In 1996, the stocks of Gujing Gong B and A were issued on the Shenzhen Stock Market. The company admitted in its board of directors' resolutions that accounting methods were adopted improperly due to the negligence and insufficiency of relevant financial personnel's understanding of relevant rules and regulations and the company has organized relevant personnel to further study Accounting Rules for Stock Limited Companies and Enterprise Accounting Rules. *See* Bulletin on Resolutions of the 10th Session of the 3rd Board of Directors of Anhui Guijing Distillery Company Limited, Bulletin No 2004-02 Para. III, 4, 5, and 6, 23 Feb 2004 at <http://www.wenweipo.com/special/anhui-gujing/anhui-gujing.html>.

a planned economy and they were government officials and party members. The management method under a planned economy is very different from the way a company should be operated under a market economy, especially when it is publicly listed. After listing new management methods need to be learned and senior management needs to change their mindset as they are no longer government officials but directors who should protect the interests of shareholders. Such a transition may take time but the Listing Rules are paving the way for such transition with the use of sponsors and independent non-executive directors.

E. Full Disclosure

There are many differences between a PRC company and a Hong Kong company which an investor may not be aware of. The investors should have an adequate understanding of the risks involved in subscribing for H shares. Based on similar principle as the US securities law, the HKSE Listing Rules demand full disclosure as the best way to deal with such potential problems.

Under the Listing Rules, a PRC issuer has to disclose in its prospectus risk factors that will include, among other things, a brief summary of:[200]

- the relevant PRC laws and regulations;
- the political structure and economic environment of the PRC;
- foreign exchange controls in the PRC and the exchange rate risk of the Renminbi;
- the different regulatory framework for PRC issuers listing outside the mainland of the PRC;
- specific risk factors related to the business of the PRC issuer and/or its products; and
- the law(s) governing the resolution of disputes arising from the PRC issuer's article of association and the transfer of the PRC issuer's shares.

There will also be a description of applicable company law matters including material differences between the requirements of the PRC and of Hong Kong. Such description should include the following:[201]

- the quorum and voting requirements for general meetings of shareholders and for separate meetings of holders of domestic shares, foreign shares and H shares;
- the PRC issuer's ability, by way of a special resolution in a general meeting, to issue, allot or grant up to 20 per cent of its existing share capital in domestic shares, foreign shares and H shares once every 12 months, without a separate vote by holder of foreign shares;

[200] The Listing Rules, R. 19A.42 (para 64).
[201] ibid (para 65).

- the PRC issuer's ability to issue domestic shares, foreign shares and H shares pursuant to a share issue plan adopted at the inaugural meeting of the PRC issuer without a separate vote by holders of foreign shares;
- any right of action a shareholder may have against director of the PRC issuer;
- the special features of arbitration; and
- the standard of shareholder protection, which is different from that generally available in Hong Kong.

Such disclosure is to allow the investors to have a full picture of the H share company and if they are well-informed and understand the risks investors can make an informed decision about whether to apply for the shares of such companies.

X. CONCLUSION

The legal regime governing H shares is to facilitate the listing of PRC enterprises on the Hong Kong stock exchange. The philosophy behind such a regime is to ensure that PRC companies will meet the international standards required by the Hong Kong stock exchange.[202] Listing on the HKSE enables the PRC companies to access foreign funds from the Hong Kong capital market while affording investors proper protection.

As shown by the statistics quoted earlier, H shares were very popular when they were first launched as such share companies were handpicked by the Chinese Government and therefore most investors assumed that they would have the backing of the PRC Government even though the profitability of some such enterprises was of a dubious nature. Prices of the H shares were easily affected by the policies adopted by the PRC Government or the relevant ministries and corruption was also allegedly widespread among concerned communist officials.

Evidence from different countries seems to suggest that both the legal protection of investors and some form of concentrated ownership are essential to ensure managerial accountability.[203] The Listing Rules and the relevant Securities and Futures Ordinance aim to protect investors by equipping them with some legal recourse. However the concentrated ownership is in the hands of the PRC Government and the resulting moral hazard from such an 'abstract' owner is not helpful in ensuring the accountability of directors and managers.

Despite all these problems, the SOEs have undergone a rapid transfor-

202 Nottle above n 83, at 119.

203 Andrei Shleifer and Robert W. Vishny 'A Survey of Corporate Governance', Journal of Finance, 52, 737–83.

mation showing improved performance and a separation of enterprises from government intervention. The enterprise reform programmes in the PRC have come a long way since adoption of the open door policy in 1979. Considering that the PRC was still a planned economy less than three decades ago, the improvement in corporate governance and the protection of shareholders' interests has been remarkable.

To put such progress in context, it is important to trace its development. Dramatic changes in the PRC's reform policies began between 1984 and 1988 when enterprises became the focus of the reform and decentralization was formally adopted on a national scale.[204] The decentralization programme aimed at two goals—to separate the Government from enterprise operations and remove the Party from direct enterprise management, with the director as the main decision-maker supported by the Party.[205] In 1989 the reforms were put on hold with the political upheavals and the fall of Zhao Ziyang, who favoured the market economy.[206] The market economy was still largely labeled as capitalism and the opposite of socialism.[207] Many reform projects were in limbo until 1992 when Deng Xiaoping toured southern China and restarted the reform momentum.[208] The partial market programme was replaced by comprehensive markets.[209] The reform effort after 1992 was aimed at clarifying the ownership structure and introducing a new enterprise governance based on market economy.[210]

Developments since 1992 showed that the market economy had progressed at full speed. In his report to the 15th Communist Party Progress held in September 1997 President Jiang Zemin in his 'Report to the

[204] Yuan Lu, *Management Decision-Making in Chinese Enterprises* 18 (Macmillan Press, 1996). On 10 May 1984, the State Council published *Guanyu Jinyibu Kuoda Guoying Gongye Qiye Zizuquan De Zhanxing Guiding* [Temporary regulations on further expansion of autonomy in large and medium-sized state enterprises] by granting enterprises autonomy in 10 areas including production planning, product sales, pricing, supplies, the use of capital retained from profits, disposal of unnecessary assets, management of labour and personnel, organizational design, rewards and salary and the formation of industrial groups among enterprises. In the same month, the SCRES circulated *Guanyu Chengshi Jingji Tizhi Gaige Shidian Gongzuo Zuotan Hui De Jiyao* [Key Points of the Working Conference on an Experiment of Economic Institutional Reform in Urban Cities] to simplify government administrative systems and create a context to ensure enterprise autonomy.

[205] ibid 19.

[206] ibid 22.

[207] ibid 23.

[208] ibid.

[209] 'Party Congress Introduces Market Economy', 42 Beijing Review, 5–6; Fang Sheng 'Opening Up and Making Use of Capitalism', 12 Beijing Review, 17–19. In July 1992, the State Council published *Guanyu Zhuanhuan Guoying Qiye Jingying Jizhi De Guiding* [Regulation on the Changes in the Operating Mechanisms of State-Owned Enterprises] which delegate 14 decision-making powers, namely, production planning, pricing, purchasing, foreign trade, investment, use of retained profits, disposal of fixed assets, formation of alliances with other firms, employment recruitment and selection, personnel management, labour management, allocation of wages and bonuses, organizational design and change and the rights to reuse funds, materials and services allocated by government agencies. LU, above n 204, at 158–9.

[210] LU, above n 204, at 159.

Congress' stated that the PRC favoured a joint stock system which separated ownership and management, this helped raise the efficiency of the operation of enterprises and capital.[211] In 1993, the first batch of H share companies were listed on the Hong Kong stock exchanges. The number of domestic joint stock companies in the PRC is reported to have risen from 3600 in 1995 to 9000 by the end of 1997.[212] At the same time the managements of the SOEs had been granted a considerable degree of decision-making autonomy.[213] As a result, their accountability and governance constitute the natural next step in the PRC's economic reform.[214]

Listing of H shares helps PRC companies to raise funds from international investors. However with the stringent listing requirements imposed by the Hong Kong stock exchange, it also helps to restructure the proposed PRC companies by making full use of a ready pool of international financial and legal intermediaries existing in Hong Kong. The listing rules stress the importance of full disclosure and so the listing of H shares and the introduction of foreign capital have required a significant increase in the transparency of the SOEs concerned, and it is thus a force for the reform of their corporate governance.[215] The Listing Rules and the relevant SFO also formalize the relationship between the Hong Kong stock exchange and the SOEs and provide more structural support. As a result, it can minimize the impact of the guanxi network[216] and ensure a level playing field based on competence and market mechanism.[217]

The listing of H shares may not solve all, or even most of, the problems of the SOEs regarding corporate governance but it is the right move in the right direction. The relevant rules in the Listing Rules and the SFO take into consideration the international standard required by the Hong Kong stock exchange and also the particular characteristics of PRC companies. Although such rules and laws were not created to harmonize the laws

211 Full text of report delivered at the 15th National Congress of the Communist Party of China (12 Sept 1997), *Beijing Review*, 6 Oct 1997, at 10–33.

212 Child, above n 170, at 42.

213 ibid 41 and App.

214 ibid 41.

215 Child, above n 170, at 18.

216 *Guanxi* refers to a special relationship due to the existence of particularistic ties. It involves some sort of family or achieved relationship between two parties. Examples of *guanxi* bases include individuals' having worked together previously, having studied together, having been labours, having been teacher or student to each other, or being members of the same family (immediate or extended). Native origin is also a common basis of *guanxi* in the PRC by coming from the same home town or having the same ancestral roots. Through identification, friendship and felt obligations, *guanxi* promotes interpersonal trust, interpersonal liking, loyalty and favouritism that affect the operation of a company. *See* Anne S Tsui et al *Guanxi in the Chinese Context*, in LU, above n 204, at 225–8 and fig. 8.1.

217 It has been proposed that guanxi is a substitute for formal institutional support and a guanxi network takes on more importance for private sector firms because of the lack of a reliable rule of law.

between Hong Kong and the PRC, they indirectly paved the way for such harmonization. If the same 'equivalent compartmentalization' can be devised by the PRC companies for Hong Kong or foreign companies, it will draw the legal requirements between the PRC and Hong Kong even closer and harmonization may eventually be achieved.

APPENDIX 1

Source:

- Stock Exchange Fact Books ('Fact Books') are available from 1994 to 2003;
- Fact Books dating back to 1999 can be viewed online at the HKEX official website (last visited 3 January 2005) (formerly the 1998 Fact Book was also included on the site);
- Information regarding the number of shares offered is not given in the 1997 Fact Book or in any other books prior to that date;
- Business Sector is not given in the 1996 Fact Book or any other books prior to that date;
- Information in the table below regarding the number of shares before 1998 is taken from the prospectuses of the listed companies;
- Please note that as some information comes from different sources, the figures may not tally with each other but the differences are generally slight. Business sector information is not given for companies listed before 1997 in this table.

*Note: (a) Hong Kong offer price
(b) International offer price
(a)Main Board

Listing Date (DD/MM/YY	Company	Listing Method/ Business Sector	No of Shares Offered	Offer Price* (HK$)	Funds Raised (HK$)
15/07/93	Tsingtao Brewery Co Ltd	Offer for subscription	317,600,000	2.8	889,280,000
26/07/93	Shanghai Petrochemical	Offer for subscription	1,680,000,000	1.74	2,654,400,000
06/08/93	Guangzhou Shipyard International Co Ltd	Offer for subscription	145,000,000	2.08	301,600,000
06/08/93	Beiren Printing Machinery Holdings Ltd	Offer for subscription	100,000,000	2.08	208,000,000

LISTING DATE (DD/MM/YY	COMPANY	LISTING METHOD/ BUSINESS SECTOR	NO OF SHARES OFFERED	OFFER PRICE* (HK$)	FUNDS RAISED (HK$)
03/11/93	Maanshan Iron & Steel Co Ltd	Offer for subscription	1,732,930,000	2.27	3,933,750,000
07/12/93	Kuming Machine Tool Co Ltd	Offer for subscription	65,000,000	1.98	128,700,000
29/03/94	Yizheng Chemical Fibre Co Ltd	Offer for subscription	1,000,000,000	2.38	2,380,000,000
17/05/94	Tianjin Bohai Chemical Industry (Group) Co Ltd	Offer for subscription	340,000,000	1.20	408,000,000
06/06/94	Dongfeng Electrical Machinery Co Ltd	Offer for subscription	170,000,000	2.83	481,100,000
08/07/94	Luoyang Glass Co Ltd	Offer for subsription	250,000,000	3.65	912,500,000
17/08/94	Qingling Motors Co Ltd	Offer for subscription	500,000,000	2.07	1,035,000,000
11/11/94	Shanghai Hai Xing Shipping Co Ltd	Offer for subscription	1,080,000,000	1.46	1,576,800,000
02/12/94	Zhenhai Refining & Chemcial Co Ltd	Offer for subscription	600,000,000	2.38	1,428,000,000
13/12/94	Chengdu Tele Cable Co Ltd	Offer for subscription	160,000,000	2.80	448,000,000
16/12/94	Harbin Power Equipment Co Ltd	Offer for subscription	435,000,000	2.58	1,122,300,000
23/05/95	Jilin Chemical Industrial Co Ltd	Offer for subscription/ Offer for placing	893,027,000	1.589 (a) 1.605 (b)	1,431,880,000
06/07/95	Northeast Elec T&T Machinery Mfg Co Ltd	Offer for subscription/ Offer for placing	247,950,000	1.80	446,310,000
02/02/96	Jiangwei Textile Machinery Co Ltd	Offer for subscription/ Offer for placing	160,000,000	1.29	233,230,000
02/05/96	Nanjing Panda Electronics Co Ltd	Offer for subscription/ Offer for placing	242,000,000	2.13	515,460,000
14/05/96	Guangshen Railway Co Ltd	Offer for subscription/ Offer for placing	1,244,650,000	2.91 (a) 2.9395 (b)	633,832,920 3,567,047,976

Listing Date (DD/MM/YY	Company	Listing Method/ Business Sector	No of Shares Offered	Offer Price* (HK$)	Funds Raised (HK$)
23/07/96	Guangdong Kelon Electrical Holdings Co Ltd	Offer for subscription/ Offer for placing	201,352,000	3.67	738,961,840
13/11/96	Anhui Expressway Co Ltd	Offer for subscription/ Offer for placing	483,010,000	1.77	872,627,700
31/12/96	Shangdong Xinhua Pharm Co Ltd	Offer for subscription/ Offer for placing	140,000,000	1.82	273,000,000
05/02/97	China Eastern Airlines Corp Ltd	Offer for subscription/ Offer for placing/ Consolidated enterprises	483,000,000 1,083,950,000	1.38 (a) 1.39 (b)	666,540,000 1,506,960,500
12/03/97	Shenzhen Expressway Co Ltd	Offer for subscription/ Offer for placing/ Industrials	747,500,000	2.20	1,644,500,000
14/05/97	Beijing North Star Co Ltd	Offer for subscription/ Offer for placing/ Properties	707,020,000	2.40	1,696,848,000
15/05/97	Zhejiang Expressway Co Ltd	Offer for subscription/ Offer for placing/ Industrials	1,433,854,500	2.38	3,412,573,710
21/03/97	Beijing Datang Power Generation Co Ltd	Offer for subscription/ Offer for placing/ Public utilities	1,430,669,000	2.52	3,605,285,880
12/06/97	Jiangxi Copper Co Ltd	Offer for subscription/ Offer for placing/ Industrials	656,482,000	2.55	1,674,029,100
23/06/97	First Tractor Co Ltd	Offer for subscription/ Offer for placing/ Industrials	335,000,000	4.50	1,507,500,000
25/06/97	Beijing Yanhua Petrochemical Co Ltd	Offer for subscription/ Offer for placing/ Industrials	144,210,000 867,790,000	1.76 (a) 1.78 (b)	253,809,600 1,544,666,200
27/06/97	Jiangsu Expressway Co Ltd	Offer for subscription/ Offer for placing/ Industrials	1,222,000,000	3.11	3,800,420,000
24/07/97	Angang New Steel Co Ltd	Offer for subscription/ Offer for placing/ Industrials	890,000,000	1.63	1,450,700,000

Listing Date (DD/MM/YY	Company	Listing Method/ Business Sector	No of Shares Offered	Offer Price* (HK$)	Funds Raised (HK$)
31/07/97	China Southern Airlines Co Ltd	Offer for subscription/ Offer for placing/ Consolidated Enterprises	71,000,000 1,103,178,000	4.70 (a) 4.75 (b)	333,700,000 5,240,095,500
29/09/97	CATIC Shenzhen Holdings Ltd	Offer for subscription/ Offer for placing/ Industrials	242,000,000	1.73	418,660,000
07/10/97	Sichuan Expressway Co Ltd	Offer for subscription/ Offer for placing/ Industrials	895,320,000	1.55	1,387,746,000
17/10/97	Chongqing Iron & Steel Co Ltd	Offer for subscription/ Offer for placing/ Industrials	413,944,000	1.71	707,844,240
21/10/97	Anhui Conch Cement Co Ltd	Offer for subscription/ Offer for placing/ Industrials	361,000,000	2.28	823,080,000
30/10/97	Guangzhou Pharmaceutical Co Ltd	Offer for subscription/ Offer for placing/ Industrials	219,900,000	1.65	362,835,000
21/01/98	Huaneng	Introduction/	–	–	–
01/04/98	Yanzhou Coal Mining Co Ltd	Offer for subscription/ Industrials	82,000,000 768,000,00	2.42 (a) 2.44 (b)	198,440,000 2,072,360,000
30/06/99	Shangdong Int'l Power Development Co Ltd (1071)	Offer for subscription/ Offer for placing/	64, 678,000 1,366,350,000	1.58 (a) 1.58 (b)	102,191,240 2,158,833,000
05/08/99	Great Wall Technology Co Ltd (0074)	Offer for subscription/ Offer for placing/ Industrials	142,222,000 266,662,000	3.15 (a) 3.15 (b)	447,999,300 839,985,300
16/12/99	Shenyang Public Utility Holdings Co Ltd (0747)	Offer for subscription/ Offer for placing/ Utilities	90,300,000 330,100,000	1.70 (a) 1.70 (b)	153,510,000 561,170,000
01/02/00	Beijing Capital International Airport Co Ltd (0694)	Offer for subscription/ Offer for placing/	26,470,000 935,450,000 384,230,000	1.87 (a) 1.87 (b) 2.4497 (b)	49,498,900 1,749,291,500 941,248,231
07/04/00	PetroChina Co Ltd (0857)	Offer for subscrition/ Offer for placing/ Miscellaneous	879,122,000 16,703,296,000 0	1.27 (a) 1.27 (b)	1,116,484,940 1,213,185,920

LISTING DATE (DD/MM/YY	COMPANY	LISTING METHOD/ BUSINESS SECTOR	NO OF SHARES OFFERED	OFFER PRICE* (HK$)	FUNDS RAISED (HK$)
19/10/00	China Petroleum & Chemical Corporation (0386)	Offer for subscription/ Offer for placing/ Industrials	839,024,000 15,941,464,000 0	1.59 (a) 1.59 (b)	1,334,048,160 25,346,927,760
07/02/01	Travelsky Technology Ltd (0696)	Offer for subscription/ Offer for placing/ Consolidated enterprises	19,765,000 291,089,000	4.10 (a) 4.10 (b)	81,036,500 1,193,464,900
10/12/01	Zhekiang Glass Co Ltd (0739)	Offer for subscription/ Offer for placing/ Industrials	85,000,000 93,713,000	2.96 (a) 2.96 (b)	251,600,000 277,390,480
12/12/01	Aluminium Corporation of China Ltd (2600)	Offer for subscription/ Offer for sale/ Offer for placing/ Industrials	235,294,000 249,989,815 2,264,605,553	1.37 (a) 1.37 (b)	354,588,880 3,191,294,440
31/07/02	BYD Co Ltd (1211)	Offer for subscription/ Offer for placing/ Industrials	13,000,000 136,500,000	10.95	1,637,025,000
15/11/02	China Telecom Corporation (0728)	Offer for subscription/ Offer for sale/ Offer for placing Consolidated enterprises	377,820,000 730,494,300 6,919,095,700	1.47 (a) 1.47 (b)	555,395,400 10,552,512,600
18/11/02	Hainan Meilon Airport Co Ltd (0357)	Offer for subscription/ Offer for sale/ Offer for placing/ Consolidated enterprises	16,470,000 3,700,000 206,743,000	3.78 (a) 3.78 (b)	76,242,600 686,183,400
20/11/02	China Oilfield Services Ltd Co (2883)	Offer for subscription/ Offer for sale/ Offer for placing/ Industrials	400,396,000 139,532,000 994,924,000	1.68 (a) 1.68 (b)	672,665,280 1,905,886,080
13/02/03	Sinotrans Ltd. (0698)	Offer for subscription/ Offer for sale/ Offer for placing/ Consoldidated enterprises	466,280,000 1,158,835,000	2.19 162,461,000 (a) 2.19 (b)	1,021,153,200
19/06/03	Beijing Capital Land Ltd (2868)	Offer for subscription Offer for sale/ Offer for placing/ Properties	56,464,000 51,330,000 456,836,000	1.66 (a) 1.66 (b)	93,730,240 843,555,560

LISTING DATE (DD/MM/YY	COMPANY	LISTING METHOD/ BUSINESS SECTOR	NO OF SHARES OFFERED	OFFER PRICE* (HK$)	FUNDS RAISED (HK$)
27/06/03	Lianhua Supermarket Holding Co Ltd (0980)	Offer for Offer for placing/ Consolidated enterprises	60,000,000 112,500,000	3.875	668,437,500
30/06/03	Baoye Group Co Ltd (2355)	Offer for subscription/ Offer for placing/ Industrials	18,072,000 162,612,000	1.43 (a) 1.43 (b)	25,842,960 232,535,160
24/09/03	Weiqiao Textile Co Ltd (2698)	Offer for subscription/ Offer for placing/ Industrials	124,886,000 162,350,500	8.50 (a) 8.50 (b)	1,061,522,500
30/10/03	AviChina Industry & Technology Co Ltd (2357)	Offer for subscription/ Offer for sale/ Offer for placing/ Industrials	799,920,000 152,710,500 727,170,000	1.21 (a) 1.21 (b)	967,903,200 1,064,655,405
06/11/03	PICC Property and Casualty Co Ltd (2328)	Offer for subscription/ Offer for sale/ Offer for placing/ Finance	1,502,600,000 764,180,000 1,189,200,000	1.80 (a) 1.80 (b)	2,704,680,000 3,516,084,000
15/12/03	Great Wall Automobile Holding Co Ltd (2333)	Offer for subscription/ Offer for placing/ Industrials	57,000,000 74,100,000	13.30	1,743,630,000
18/12/03	China Life Insurance Company Ltd (2628)	Offer for subscription/ Offer for sale/ Offer for placing/ Finance	1,294,118,000 676,470,000 676,470,000	3.59 (a) 3.59 (b)	4,645,883,620 22,067,934,630
23/12/03	Fujian Zijin Mining Industry Co Ltd (2899)	Offer for subscription/ Offer for sale/ Offer for placing/ Miscellaneous	174,150,000 36,413,090 189,960,910	3.3	1,321,800,000
06/02/04	Shanghai Forte Land Co Ltd			2.35 (a) 2.35 (b)	749,969,600

Remarks: (a) Hong Kong Offers
(b) International Offers
(b) GEM

Listing Date (dd/mm/yy	Company	Listing Method/ Business Sector	No of Shares Offered	Offer Price (HK$)	Funds Raised (HK$)
27/07/00	Beijing Beida Jade Bird Universal Sci-Tech Co Ltd	Offer for placing/ IC software design	26,400,000	11.00	290.40
04/08/00	Shanghai Fudan Micro-electronics Co Ltd	Offer for placing/ IC software design	143,750,000	0.80	115.00
31/10/00	Tong Ran Tang Technologies Co Ltd	Offer for placing/ Pharmaceutical	72,800,000	3.28	238.78
30/03/01	Changdu Top Sci-Tech Co Ltd	Offer for placing/ Enterprise software	169,000,000	0.72	121.68
24/04/01	Jiangsu Nandasoft Co Ltd	Offer for placing/ Enterprise software	234,000,000	0.36	84.24
24/05/01	Jilin Province Huinan Changlong Bio-pharmacy Co Ltd	Offer for placing/ Pharmaceutical	172,500,000	0.50	86.25
18/12/01	Mudan Automobile Shares Co Ltd Automobile	Offer for subscription/ Offer for placing/	7,700,000 80,850,000	1.13	100.06
21/12/01	Capinfo Co Ltd	Offer for sale/ Offer for placing/ Internet solution	70,408,909 704,089,091	0.48	371.76
28/02/02	Northeast Tiger Pharmaceutical Co Ltd	Offer for placing/ Pharmaceutical	207,000,000	0.26	53.82
03/05/02	Zheda Lande Scitech Ltd	Offer for placing/ Telecom solutions	112,125,000	0.83	93.06
18/06/02	Tianjin TEDA Biomedical Engineering Co Ltd	Offer for placing/ Medical & health	100,000,000	0.98	98.00
28/06/02	Changchun Da Xing Pharmaceutical Co Ltd	Offer for placing/ Pharmaceutical	161,000,000	0.45	72.45
28/06/02	Changmao Biochemical Engineering Co Ltd	Offer for placing/ Chemical product	183,700,000	0.55	101.04

Listing Date (DD/MM/YY	Company	Listing Method/ Business Sector	No of Shares Offered	Offer Price (HK$)	Funds Raised (HK$)
31/07/02	Shanghai Jiaoda Withub Information Industrial Co Ltd	Offer for sale/ Offer for placing/ System developer	12,000,000 120,000,000	0.66	87.12
13/08/02	Shanghai Fudan-Zhangjiang Bio-Pharmaceutical Co Ltd	Offer for sale/ Offer for placing/ Pharmaceutical	18,000,000 180,000,000	0.80	158.40
07/10/02	Launch Tech Co Ltd	Offer for placing/ Automobile related service	110,000,000	0.72	79.20
29/10/02	Zhengzhou Gas Co Ltd	Offer for sale/ Offer for placing/ Energy	50,060,000 500,600,000	0.25	137.67
08/11/02	Zhejiang Yonglong Enterprises Co Ltd	Offer for placing/ Textile	250,000,000	0.26	65.00
12/12/02	CCID Consulting Co Ltd	Offer for sale/ Offer for placing/ Consulting services for IT industry	19,000,000 190,000,000	0.25	52.25
12/12/02	Powerleader Science & Technology Co Ltd	Offer for placing/ Server solution provider	220,000,000	0.28	61.60
29/01/03	Shenzhen Dongjiang Environmental Co Ltd	Offer for sale/ Offer for placing/ Environmental protection	177,900.000	0.34	60.13
22/04/03	Yantai North Andre Juice Co Ltd	Offer for placing/ Production and sale of juice	38,000,000	3.70	140.60
03/0703	Shaanxi Northwest New Technology Industry Co Ltd	Offer for placing/ Energy Products	230,000,000	0.25	57.50
10/10/03	Shenzhen EVOC Intelligent Technology Co Ltd	Offer for placing/ EIP Provider	116,800,000	0.90	105.12
05/11/2003	Xi'an Haitian Antenna Technologies Co Ltd	Offer for sale/ Offer for placing/ Antenna provider	161,764,706	0.68	110.00

Listing Date (dd/mm/yy	Company	Listing Method/ Business Sector	No of Shares Offered	Offer Price (HK$)	Funds Raised (HK$)
13/11/03	Nanjing Dahe Outdoor Media Co Ltd	Offer for subscription/ Offer for placing/ Advertising	250,000,000	0.53	132.50
14/11/03	Ningbo Yidong Electronic Co Ltd	Offer for subscription/ Offer for placing/ Controller systems	130,000,000	0.50	65.00
21/11/03	Wumart Stores, Inc	Offer for subscription/ Offer for placing/ Retail chain store	87,952,000	6.22	547.06
09/01/04	Tianjin Tianlian Public Utilities Co Ltd	Offer for placing/ Energy	330,000,000	0.25	82.50
18/02/04	Zhejiang Prospect Co Ltd	Offer for placing/ Automotive parts & components	23,000,000	1.33	30.59
27/02/04	Shangdong Weigao Group Medical Polymer Co Ltd	Offer for placing/ Medical equipment	264,500,000	0.62	163.99

COMMENTS

THE OIL MARKET POSTWAR IRAQ

WALEED AL-NUWAISER*

The war in Iraq will have a great impact on the international oil market and on the stability of the Middle East. To rebuild Iraq, the occupying powers or the new government will need to increase Iraqi oil production. That, however, is likely to affect the stability of the oil market by disrupting the quota system organized by members of OPEC. This article will not discuss the legality of the invasion of Iraq by the United States, but it will discuss the scenarios that may occur when Iraq increases its oil production, bearing in mind that OPEC, when setting its quota, did not provide for an increase for oil production in Iraq. Furthermore, a leading contender for the Iraqi presidency has stated that he plans to have Iraq withdraw from OPEC, an act which would redraw the map of the oil industry.

Iraq produced, in 1979 and before the First Gulf War with Iran, 3.5 million barrels per day (b/d). This level of production was disrupted by the war something which forced the Iraqi Government to decline its production sharply at the beginning of 1980–1. Since then, it has never reached the 3.5million b/d level. During the First Gulf War, to finance its budget Iraq had to borrow money from neighboring countries, such as Saudi Arabia and Kuwait.[1] The disruption continued during the Second Gulf War in 1990 and was maintained further still by the imposition of sanctions, which were first imposed on Iraq in 1991 and which continue to exist until the time of writing. Had it not been involved in these conflicts—which lasted for more than two decades, Iraq would have reached the 6 million b/d mark by 2003. Iraq has 112 billion barrels of oil in reserve, coming second after Saudi Arabia which has 296 billion barrels of oil in reserve. Iraq produced 2.4 million b/d before the current war started and that makes it possible for the new Iraqi government to restart production at that level.[2]

It will take Iraq 2 years at a cost of $5 billion to $7 billion to reach the pre-1979 production of 3.5 million b/d. Another study showed that Iraq will be able to produce 4 million to 4.5 million b/d by the end of this

* SJD (PHD) at SMU School of Law, focusing on International, and the Economic Development of International Joint Ventures in the Oil Industry LLM Harvard Law School, 2001

[1] Iraq borrowed $1Billion monthly from Saudi Arabia from 1980 to 1985

[2] Although Iraq, according to OPEC, had the capacity to produce 2.850 million b/d, see *The Oil Daily*, 23 Sept 2002.

decade. [3] Iraq will need 9–10 years to produce 6 million b/d, but will the market be able to support that level of increase? Is it going to be possible for Iraq to produce 6 million b/d without disrupting the oil market? Also, what will happen to OPEC's quota and what will happen if Iraq withdraws from OPEC? If the market collapses, is it going to be profitable for the oil companies to invest in Iraq? In this paper, I will describe the likely consequences that may result if Iraq increases its oil production without complying with OPEC's quota.

The oil market is dominated by giant producing countries and international oil companies, one of which is Saudi Arabia, presented by ARAMCO, the biggest oil company in the world. ARAMCO produces 7.8 million b/d making it the biggest oil producing company in the world and is capable of reaching 10.5 million b/d in three months.[4] In addition, other key OPEC producers-Iran, with the capacity of producing 4.050 million b/d, Venezuela 2.800 million b/d, Kuwait 2.400 million b/d, and the UAE 2.450 million b/d-play an important role in the oil market.[5] These countries are paying close attention to the war in Iraq and have been trying to foresee its outcome and the effect that it will have on the international oil market. While these countries play a role in the oil market, however Saudi Arabia is the only country which has the ability to vary rates of oil production from a low of about 5 million to 6 million b/d to a maximum of over 10 million b/d. Market conditions are a primary determinant of the output that the Saudis will choose within this range. Therefore, Saudi Arabia derives its influence in the world energy market by using its oil production as an instrument to stabilize the oil market and the oil price by meeting the world demand for oil.

While more investment and resources are needed to improve the oil infrastructure in Iraq, many of the oil fields and reservoirs having been damaged through overwork, lack of fresh investment and spare parts, Iraq will face serious difficulties that might slow or prevent it from increasing its oil production. The main obstacle will be trying to compete with other producing countries to get a bigger share in the market. Not only has Iraq been off the oil market for more than two decades, but most OPEC members are not happy with their shares in the market. The quota system designed by OPEC to set the oil price from $22–$28 requires members of OPEC to cut their production to a level where they can achieve their target price. Countries—such as Nigeria with the capacity of producing 2.4b/d and a quota of 1.8 b/d, Algeria with the capacity of producing 900 b/d and

[3] *The Oil Daily*, 4 Oct 2003

[4] During a US visit in April 2002, Saudi Oil Minster Ali Naimi said his country could put 9 million b/d on the market within two weeks and an additional 1 million b/d within 90 days. It produces 7.8, complying with its quota.

[5] *The Oil Daily*, 23 Sept 2002.

a quota of 690 b/d—are not really happy with this level of production. Therefore, Saudi Arabia—with capacity of producing 10 million b/d and quota of 7.8—is the candidate for the Iraqis to ask for a larger share in the market. Thus, if Iraq wants to increase its share in the market, it will have to be from Saudi Arabia.

Since Saudi Arabia has the biggest share in the market, the Iraqis will be demanding that the Saudis give up some of their share. This may cause conflict since Saudi Arabia has already been complaining about loosing a significant portion of its share in the market because of OPEC's quotas and because of the non-OPEC producers.[6] Saudi Arabia will no doubt be willing to give up a small portion of its share in the market in order to provide assistance to the Iraqis, but this will not be enough to rebuild Iraq.

Several observers suggest that the new Iraqi Government may consider withdrawing from OPEC. First, some of the opposition parties have indicated that they would have Iraq withdraw from OPEC because of the restriction that OPEC's quota might impose on Iraq's production.[7] Secondly, with no restriction on production, Iraq would be very attractive to international oil companies, especially with its potential massive oil reserve. Thirdly, increasing the oil production may lead the new Government to take a new political approach supportive of the West. Most legal scholars think of OPEC as instrument of the producing countries to control the market and restrain trade.[8] They may want to create a new relationship with the Arabic States that opposed the war by keeping a political and economic distance thinking that might help create a new Iraq without any religious or social complication. Most of the Arabic States are socially and religiously complex. If the new Iraqi Government decides to withdraw from OPEC then the situation will be complex. In that case, the Saudis will be competing with a non-OPEC producer which means that they will be less likely to give up part of their OPEC share in the market. If Iraq remains a member of OPEC, then the members will be able to negotiate a settlement, but the situation will continue to be difficult to resolve. The scenarios will be as follows

If Iraq does not withdraw from OPEC, the first scenario is that Saudi Arabia and Iraq may not reach an agreement as to how respective quotas should be altered. Over the next few years, Iraq increases its production and gains a larger share of the market Saudi Arabia will consider such behavior as a threat to the Saudi national interest, which would be better served by

[6] Although Iraq has been producing oil for the past two decades, but still not included in OPEC's quota, The non-OPEC producers are: Russia, Norway, Mexico, Oman, and Angola.

[7] The Iraqis have requested from OPEC to be exempted from complying with the quota' system until Iraq reaches the 3.5 million b/d mark.

[8] Professor Adelman, The World Petroleum Market, thinks that the market will take care of its self and opec is a restraint of trade.

maintaining the same level of production. Therefore, Saudi Arabia will resort to increasing its production which would bring about a crash in the market and make it difficult for both international oil companies and the Iraqi government to invest profitably in Iraq's oil fields. By increasing its production, Saudi Arabia will be able to destroy its competitors, buy them out and then regain control of the oil market. Such a tactic might be difficult to carry out in practice because of the impact it would have on the Saudi economy, which is dependent on oil revenue. In addition, pressure from the United States might also prevent the Saudis from crashing the market; considering that most of the international oil companies that are going to invest in Iraq are American companies, it is likely that such pressure will be applied.[9] But Saudi Arabia needs to fulfill its duty to OPEC's quota by keeping the price between $22 and $28 p/b and needs to address the increasing demand from the growing Saudi population for more revenue. Thus, in order to not lose its share in the market, Saudi Arabia will be force to crash the market. Otherwise, it will not have the same power as it has now in the world energy market in the next coming years, and the social, economic, and political system in Saudi Arabia will be severely disrupted. That also may destabilize Saudi Arabia and the whole Middle East.

A second scenario, even if Iraq and Saudi Arabia do not agree on the way to handle the need for Iraq to produce more oil and even if Saudi Arabia does not increase its oil production, is that oil prices will be disrupted by the increase in the supply of oil to the market. That may drive other OPEC and non-OPEC producers to defend their market shares by pumping more oil to the market. In any event, an agreement should be reached between major producing counties to help Iraq to rebuild the county and to keep the oil market from crashing.

Another possibility has been raised by Professor John Lowe.[10] He thinks that the occupying powers have a duty under international law to use Iraq resources to rebuild the country. He suggests that a crash in oil markets would be in the best interest of developed countries. Indeed, if the oil price were at $10 per/b, or less the international economy would be greatly strengthened. According to Professor Lowe, international oil companies may lay off employees because of the loss in revenue that they will suffer under this possibility, but because of the increased activity in the economy other companies such as Delta and American Airlines will probably

[9] Last month, Halliburton unit Kellogg, Brown, and Root (KBR) was awarded a contract estimated to near $900 million to contain oil well fires and restore oil facilities and infrastructure in Iraq. The Defense Department said that (KBR) would: 'Perform engineering design and repair and reconstruction of damaged infrastructure, operate facilities, and distribute products, if required', *see The Oil Daily*, 26 Mar 2003. KBR was awarded this contract without a competitive bidding process.

[10] Professor John Lowe, George W Hutchison, Professor of Energy Law, Southern Methodist University, School of Law.

increase their hiring. Developed countries will need 2–3 years to strength their economy and could profit from a decrease in the price of oil, but such a loss of revenue will inevitably affect the Middle East economy. Professor Lowe believes that in these circumstances the United States economy 'will prosper and either let the Iraqi rot or rebuild Iraq with American Airlines saving in the cost of fuel'.'

It is the opinion of the author of this article, however, that an important decrease in the price of oil could destabilize the entire Middle East to the extent that the supply of oil to the industrialized countries may be disrupted. Many people believe that the main reason that the United States has gone to war in Iraq is to stabilize the area and to guarantee that oil will continue flowing. However, a crash in the market will cause the area to be vulnerable to major political, economic and social changes. All of the Gulf Countries depend on oil revenues to finance their budgets and to provide economic assistance to other countries in the region, such as Syria and Lebanon. They take control of the economic structure by injecting the market with money and jobs. A country, such as Saudi Arabia, as the leading producing oil country in the world, will be destabilized by the shortage of revenue coming from oil since the Saudi population depends on the Saudi Government to provide it with jobs and money. The oil revenue is the main resource that Saudi Arabia depends on to finance its budget and to provide development to the country. Bad economy might initiate dissatisfaction with the Saudi government and therefore might lead to a change of regime to something which may not necessarily be in favour of the West. In the long run, however, any such change may severely affect oil supply to the oil market especially if an anti-western regime comes to power in Saudi Arabia. The Middle East is highly important to the whole world because of its rich oil fields; any destabilization would therefore not be in the world's best interest. A study shows that the last barrel of oil will be lifted from that area which indicates the importance of it to the world energy market.

Since Saudi Arabia is likely to be the one oil producing nation to lose part of its share in the market, it may use the 'Red Line Agreement' which would lead to the third possible scenario. The Red Line Agreement provided that the participants in The Iraqi Petroleum Company (IPC) could not operate independently anywhere inside the red line. Gulbenkian, a former adviser to the Ottoman Empire, took a thick red line and drew a line along the boundaries of the now-defunct Turkish Empire, within which were to be found all the major oil-producing oil fields of the Middle East except those of Persia and Kuwait.[11] It precluded all the companies from

[11] Gulbenkian was an Armenian millionaire who put the entire Turkish Petroleum Company deal together which made him a 15 per cent owner of the company. He was also a financial adviser to the Turkish Government itself, and to its Paris and London embassies.

operating independently in any area within the confines of the lines specified on the map. Therefore, Saudi Arabia can invite international oil companies, such as Exxon Mobil, Chevron Texaco, BP, etc to invest in the country while signing an agreement similar to the 'Red Line Agreement' which would prevent the major oil companies from investing independently in the Middle East, especially in Iraq. This plan might be difficult to carry out for various reasons. First, it will not be easy for the Saudis to attract the major players in the oil industry to invest in Saudi Arabia. The potential opportunities in Iraq are very attractive that Saudi Arabia will probably not prove as attractive as investment prospect. Secondly, the major oil companies, most of them American, would be better off dealing with Iraq under the supervision of the United States than dealing with Saudi Arabia under the strict supervision of the Saudis. Furthermore, this agreement might be struck down by the threat of an antitrust case against the majors for the violation of the Sherman Act, since Saudi Arabia will be protected by its sovereignty as a State.

The 'Red Line' agreement may work wonderfully and overcome the difficulties that we have described, however. Saudi Arabia can be attractively irresistible to the majors, since oil in Saudi Arabia is cheap to produce and is accessible to the oil market. The majors will not face as many technical difficulties in Saudi Arabia as they may face in Iraq. In addition, Saudi Arabia has more oil reserves than any other country in the world, which makes it attractive for long term investments. The Saudi government and the majors can agree on a deal that might be beneficial for both parties. In addition, the antitrust problem might be avoided. The Justice Department did not oppose the merger of four oil companies in 1948 to create ARAMCO. Socal (Chevron) and Texaco invited Standard of Oil New Jersey (Exxon) and Socony-Vacuum (Mobil) to buy a 40 per cent share of ARAMCO. The four companies, beside their massive marketing system, owned ARAMCO with its massive oil reserves. The Justice Department allowed the merger to go through, even though it would have made a prefect antitrust case. The merger was allowed to go through because it was viewed as being vital for the national interest of the United States. The new agreement could be also viewed as being important for the national interests of the United States, something which is certainly arguable considering that it will secure the flow of oil to that country for a long period of time.

Another possibility is that, the Saudis may have the majors invest in Saudi Arabia while having ARAMCO invest in Iraq. Thus, Iraq will develop its oil fields and be able to rebuild the country, the oil market will not be disrupted by the increase of oil production, Saudi Arabia will maintain its share in the market and its revenue, and the majors will obtain a great opportunity to invest in a rich country. This deal will allow Iraq to use its oil production to rebuild the country without interfering with the Saudis' share. It will also allow the Saudis to maintain their revenue, if they do not get more from investing in Iraq and from the investment in Saudi by the majors. But the problem with this scenario is that ARAMCO never invests outside Saudi Arabia and that ARAMCO is the only company that has the right to deal in oil within Saudi Arabia. Oil is a matter of a national interest for the Saudis. It will therefore be difficult to convince them to share their cheap oil with their competitors and to ask them to invest in an unstable country, such as Iraq. The majors will also demand a fair deal with the Saudis as a compromise for leaving Iraq to ARAMCO. Furthermore, the new Iraqi government may not accept the Saudi national company, since they have their own national oil company and need sophisticated oil companies with a well-developed marketing system.

The last scenario will be that Saudi Arabia is given the opportunity to compete with other international oil companies in the concession in Iraq. This will have a great political and economic impact on the Middle East and the international oil market. Politically, it will show the Arab States that the United States does not intend to occupy Iraq or control its oil fields through its military or its oil companies. It will also increase the credibility of the United States towards resolving the Palestine-Israeli conflict neutrally. Economically, it will force Saudi Arabia to cut its production down to be able to invest in Iraq and cover this cut by increasing the Iraqi oil production. It will also create a new era in the oil industry where for the first time ARAMCO will be conducting exploration outside the borders of Saudi Arabia something which—by allowing oil companies to invest in the oil sector in Saudi Arabia and giving ARAMCO the chance to invest outside Arabia Saudi—may change the Saudis' way of dealing with their oil.

It is in the best long economic interest for Saudi Arabia to open its doors up to International Oil Companies and to spread out beyond its border. In order to do so, the Saudis should revise their current laws and polices regarding investing in oil nationally and internationally. Nationally, they should relinquish part of their interest in Aramco by enacting appropriate national regulations through which the Saudi Government could permit some level of ownership on one hand and certain level of administrative control over Aramco on the other hand. The creation of a joint venture on the Saudi soil should be legally formed under strict rules to protect the Saudi interest and to achieve the desired mutual benefit. Internationally, the rules of the International Joint Venture (IJV) have been constantly developed by International Oil Companies' engagements in several transactions in the oil industry. Therefore, the Saudis should properly evaluate them and compromise the differences between their interest and these rules to be able to engage in drilling and exploring oil with national players who know better the local market. Also, the internationalization of Aramco could be viewed as a diversification of Aramco's economic interests. Therefore, Iraq will be the best place for Aramco to start investing outside Saudi Arabia. Similar to Saudi Arabia, Iraq has a cheap cost of oil production and is accessible to the international oil market. Investing in Iraq could be viewed as a test for Aramco to evaluate its capability of conducting business outside Saudi Arabia.

However, this approach might be interrupted by the way the Saudis are used to conducting business in the oil sector.[12] Furthermore, international oil companies may oppose this approach since Saudi Arabia is the leading producing country in the world and with this concession, it will increase its stocks in the oil market. The new Iraqi Government may also oppose it, fearing that the Saudis will not develop the Iraqi oil fields as sufficient as the international oil companies.

In conclusion, Saudi Arabia remains the most important player in the oil market and without a deal with the Saudis, the market will not be in good shape. Iraq ought not to withdraw from OPEC; especially because of the fact that it is not in a strong position to compete against members of OPEC. Otherwise development in Iraq will take longer than what has been predicted, or it may even stop. Since Iraq needs 2–3 years to reach 3.5 million b/d, members of OPEC will be willing to assist Iraq as a vital member in their organization. Also, the demand for more oil is increasing rapidly and that might give room for OPEC to reorganize its quota and distribute a fair share to Iraq. The worst case scenario is the situation where Iraq withdraws from OPEC without enough oil production to compete in the oil market; if this is done, a weak market or low oil price will have a negative effect on the development that Iraq urgently needs to rebuild the country after the hostilities end.

[12] The Saudis think that it is not economically beneficial to invest in a place where the cost of one barrel of oil exceeds the cost of a barrel of oil in Saudi Arabia. A barrel of oil costs $1.5–$2 to produce in Saudi Arabia. Beside that, Saudi Arabia is the leading producing oil country and it has the biggest oil reserve in the world.

THE DEVELOPMENT OF FINANCIAL HOLDING COMPANIES IN SOUTH KOREA: A COMMENT

JW BAIK*

CHAPTER OUTLINE

I. INTRODUCTION

Since the era of soaring interest rates in 1998, South Korean banks have been competing more closely with securities firms and insurance companies. The decreased interest margins, the shrinking of banks' source of income and the competition with financial institutions for direct financing, have driven the banks to look for alternate business opportunities in developing new products and forming strategic alliances.

* PhD Candidate (Kyungpook National University (KNU) School of Law, Korea); LLM (KNU); LLB (KNU); Member & Editor of Korea Commercial Cases Association (KCCA), Korea; Research Fellow, KNU Legal Institute, KNU School of Law, Taegu, Korea; LLM (Southern Methodist University (SMU) School of Law); Research Fellow, SMU Institute of International Financial, Commercial and Technology Law, SMU Dedman School of Law, Dallas, Texas.

Further, the globalization of financial markets has also prompted the introduction of the 'financial conglomerate', which takes the legal form of the 'financial holding company group'. A recent example of the legal system covering to respond to this marketplace phenomenon is the passage of Gramm–Leach–Bliley Act[1] in 1999 in the United States; and similar movements in other industrialized countries has prompted South Korea to begin to deregulate in domestic banks in order to keep them globally competitive and also to enact financial holding company legislation.

The need for banks to meet the challenges of rising costs of technological advancements such as the computerized risk management system and the modernized infrastructure as well as employing innovative management structure also has contributed to the adoption of a financial holding company group as a new alternative through which banks can enhance their credibility and reduce costs. The introduction of the financial holding company in South Korea is expected to open up a many prospective business opportunities for the South Korean banks.

The 'Financial Holding Company Act of Korea' (FHCA) was enacted in November 2000 and revised in April 2002 to strengthen the South Korean economy in the global market. It is too early to predict whether the FHCA has had a positive impact on the South Korean economy. However, South Korea has seen the transformation of the large financial institutions into financial holding companies, with further prospective companies lining up to do the same. This Comment generally considers the current Korean financial holding companies and emerging financial holding company. In addition, this Comment reviews generally several key legal aspects related to the FHCA: (1) the Korean Government's determination under the FHCA

[1] The purpose of the Gramm-Leach-Bliley Act is to facilitate affiliations among banks, securities firms, and insurance companies. Some of its provisions include: (1) Creating a new 'financial holding company' under s 4 of the 'Bank Holding Company Act' (BHCA). Such holding company can engage in a statutorily provided list of financial activities, including insurance and securities underwriting and agency activities, merchant banking and insurance company portfolio investment activities. Activities that are 'complementary' to financial activities also are authorized. The nonfinancial activities of firms predominantly engaged in financial activities (at least 85 per cent financial) are grandfathered for at least ten years, with a possibility for a five-year extension; (2) Provides for State regulation of insurance, subject to a standard that no State may discriminate against persons affiliated with a bank; (3) If any insured depository institution or insured depository institution affiliate of a financial holding company received less than a satisfactory rating in its most recent 'Community Reinvestment Act' (CRA) exam, the appropriate Federal banking agency may not approve any additional new activities or acquisitions under the authorities granted under the Act; and (4) Streamlines bank holding company supervision by clarifying the regulatory roles of the Federal Reserve as the umbrella holding company supervisor, and the State and other Federal financial regulators, which 'functionally' regulate various affiliates. *See, eg,* US Senate Committee on Banking, Housing, and Urban Affairs, *Gramm-Leach-Bliley: Summary of Provisions: Title I—Facilitating Affiliation Among Banks, Securities Firms, and Insurance Companies* (Nov. 1, 1999), *available* on the Internet *at* <http://banking.senate.gov/conf/grmleach.htm> (last visited 22 Apr 2004).

to prevent commerce (ie non-financial industry)[2] from controlling banking abusively;[3] and (2) the FHCA's function to regulate or supervise primarily holding company's relationship to the bank subsidiary and not also to the securities, insurance and other subsidiaries.

II. FACTUAL BACKGROUND

A. In General

There are currently a total of four financial holding companies in South Korea, three of which were created under the current FHCA.[4] There currently are also several companies that are seeking to convert into financial holding companies under the FHCA.

B. Sejong

Unlike the other three, the Sejong Financial Holding Company (Sejong) was established on 1 April 2000 under the 'Monopoly Regulation and Fair Trade Act' (MRFTA) before the FHCA became in forced. However, despite its time frame, Sejong still had to comply with the FHCA. On 22 February 2002, the Financial Supervisory Commission (FSC) dissolved Sejong on counts of bribery committed by its former CEO under the FHCA.[5] In other words, Sejong had violated Article 38 of the FHCA, which provides that persons who have been convicted of major crimes shall not be principal officers in the financial holding company.[6]

[2] It is so called 'chaebol' in Korea.

[3] Korea has experienced the financial crisis since 1997 due to the abuse of 'chaebols' (ie Samsung, Hyundai, LG, etc) so-called commerce in the Korean financial market.

[4] The three financial holding companies are 'Woori Financial Group' (Establishment: 27 Mar 2001), 'Shinhan Financial Group' (Establishment: 1 Sept 2001), and 'Dongwon Financial Holding' (Establishment: 30 May 2003).

[5] See, eg Moon-Soon Kang, *Cancellation of Authorization of the Sejong Financial Holding Company Acknowledged by the Court*, THE FINANCIAL NEWS (Korean daily newspaper) (15 July 2004), *available at* <http://www.fnnews.com/html/fnview/2004/0715/ 0919926517 18111400.html> (last visited 4 Aug 2004).

[6] See, eg Arts 38 and 3 of the FHCA (2002); see also, Articles 5(2) and 5(3) the Enforcement Decree of the FHCA (2002). Under Art 38 of the FHCA, any person who falls under any of the following cases is prohibited from operating as a principal officer in the financial holding company: (1) a minor or a person who is incompetent or quasi-incompetent; (2) a bankrupt who has not been reinstated; (3) a person who has been sentenced to imprisonment without prison labor or more severe punishment and for whom five years have not elapsed since he completed the sentence or was exempted from the sentence (which includes where he is deemed to have completed the sentence); (4) a person who has been sentenced to a fine or more severe punishment under the FHCA or finance-related Acts and subordinate statutes (which include the Bank of Korea Act, the General Banking Act of Korea, the Act of on the Establishment, etc., of Financial Supervisory Organizations, the Act on the Structural

C. Woori Financial Group

The Woori Financial Group was established on 2 April 2001, as the first Korean financial holding company created under the FHCA.[7] However, the Woori Financial Group did not establish itself through private capital, but through public (ie government) funds[8] and exchange and transfer of stock.[9] Subsidiaries of the Woori Financial Group were primarily its banking subsidiaries:[10] Hanvit, Peace, Kwangju, Kyongnam, and Hanaro.[11]

At the time of the incorporation into the Woori Financial Group, the economic indicators of these four bank subsidiaries before they become a financial holding company were as shown in Table 1.

After the establishment of the Woori Financial Group as a financial holding company group under the FHCA, the financial situations of Hanvit Bank and Kyongnam Bank, the leading bank subsidiaries under the Woori Financial Group, were as follows.[12]

As shown in Tables 1 and 2, financial assets of Kwanju Bank and Kyongnam Bank of the Woori Financial Group fared better after the Woori Financial Group established itself and incorporated its bank subsidiaries into a financial holding company group.

Improvement of the Financial Industry, or any foreign country's finance-related Acts and subordinated statutes. See, eg, Art 17 of the Enforcement Decree of the FHCA) as determined by a Presidential Decree and for whom five years have not elapsed since he completed the sentence (which includes where he is deemed to have completed the sentence) or was exempted from the sentence; (5) a person who has been granted a suspended sentence of a sentence to imprisonment without prison labor or more severe punishment and who is under a stay of execution; (6) a person who has been dismissed or removed from office by disciplinary punishment under the FHCA or finance-related Acts and subordinate statutes (See, eg, Art 17 of the Enforcement Decree of the FHCA) as determined by a Presidential Decree, and for whom five years have not elapsed since he was dismissed or removed by disciplinary punishment; or (7) a person (who is limited to any person directly or likewise responsible for the occurrence of the cancellation cases involved, and any person who is determined by a Presidential Decree) who is or was an officer or employee of a legal entity or company whose permission or authorization for operation has been cancelled by the FHCA or finance-related Acts and subordinate statutes as determined by a Presidential Decree, and for whom five years have not passed since the date when such cancellation was made against the legal entity or company involved.

[7] See, eg Byung-Tae Kim, Korea's Banking Law Reform: Post Asian Crisis 52 (2003).

[8] See, eg Jung-Yol Kim, Risk of Financial Holding Company and Management (Korea Deposit Insurance Corporation Survey 2003–2) 18 (June 2003).

[9] See, eg, Art 62–2 of the FHCA (2002). The previous provisions of the FHCA were incorporated in the 'Korea Commercial Code' (KCC) (2001). See, eg, Arts 360–2 through 360–23 of the KCC (2001).

[10] See Kim, above n 8, at 7.

[11] See, eg, Ho-Kyung Park, *The Woori Financial Group*, CIO Korea (1 May 2001), available at <http://www.ciokorea.com/2000/2001/010501/c86.htm> (last visited 27 Jan 2004).

[12] The Woori Financial Group renamed Hanvit Bank to Woori Bank. In fact, before Hanvit Bank was renamed as Woori Bank, it merged with Peace Bank in December 2001. As a result, Peace Bank went out of the Korean financial markets. See, eg, Bank of Korea, Annual Report 106–7 (2003); see also, the Financial News, *Death of Peace Bank*, The Financial News (Korean daily newspaper) (29 Sept 2003), available at <http://www.fnnews.com/html/fnview/2003/0929/091949008329501200.html> (last visited 11 Mar 2004).

TABLE 1 Five Banks Before Financial Holding Company Group of 2000 (Unit: Trillion Won)[13]

Bank			*Hanvit*	*Peace*
Kwangju	*Kyongnam*			
Total assets (Ranking)	80.9 (113)	8.5 (N.A)	6.8 (N.A)	8.2 (528)
Total deposits	58.0	6.7	5.4	5.9
Employees	10,933	1,223	1,392	1,661
Branches	702	87	134	146
Return on assets (ROA) (%)	0.26	0.54	3.46	0.79
Heavy stockholder (%)	KDIC[14] (74.7) Daeshin Securities (2.9)	KDIC (38.5) Hankook Steal *4.2	Kumho (9.2) Hanhwa Securities (2.9)	Hyosung (6.2)

Source: Press Release of the Financial Supervisory Commission of Korea (FSC), *The Progress of the Establishment of Financial Holding Companies*, 1 Dec 2000, *available* on the Internet *at* <http://www.fsc.go.kr>.

Table 3 shows that the main financial indicators of the Woori Financial Group fared better as a financial holding company in 2002 than the previous year 2001 before the Woori Financial Group became a financial holding company. The financial indicators of the Woori Financial Group, as an entire group, were as follows:

TABLE 2 Three Financial Subsidiaries of the Woori Financial Group (Unit: Trillion Won)

Year 2002	*Woori Bank*	*Kwangu Bank*	*Kyongnam Bank*
Total assets	101.1	8.7	9.4
Total deposits	76.2	6.5	6.7
Total loans	64.4	5.3	5.1

Source: Investor Relations of the Woori Financial Group, *Financial Data*, *available at* <http://www.woorifg.com/index.html>.

13 The rate of exchange is approximately 1200 Korean Won per 1 Dollar.
14 The KDIC stands for the Korea Development Insurance Corporation.

TABLE 3 Financial Indicators of the Woori Financial Group (Unit: Trillion Won)

Year	*2003*	*2002*	*2001*
Total assets	2Q 122.6/ 1Q 120.7	114.8	98.8
Total deposits	2Q 85.6/ 1Q 82.2	78.9	69.3
Total loans	2Q 81.6/ 1Q 78.0	73.6	58.6
Capital stock	2Q 6.1/ 1Q 5.5	5.3	4.4

Source: Financial Information of the Woori Financial Group, *Balance Sheet*, Jun. 30, 2003, *available* on the Internet *at* <http://www.woorifg.com/index.html>.
*The year Woori became incorporated as a financial holding company.

Currently, the Woori Financial Group has eight subsidiaries and five second-tier subsidiaries:[15]

- Subsidiaries (8): Woori Bank, Kyongnam Bank, Kwangju Bank, Woori Card, Woori Investment Trust Management, Woori Finance Information System, Woori F & I, and Woori Securities;
- Second-tier subsidiaries (5): Woori Credit Information, Korea Finance Security, BC Card, Nexbitec, and Woori CA Asset Management.

D. *Shinhan Financial Group*

The Shinhan Financial Group was established through pure private capital[16] in September 1, 2001 and became the second Korean financial holding company under the FHCA.[17] Currently, the Shinhan Financial Group is the largest financial holding company in Korea.[18]

The Shinhan Financial Group was also incorporated through the exchange and transfer of stocks between the financial holding company[19]

[15] See Woori Financial Group, *Line of Group Companies*, available on the Internet at <http://www.woorifg.com/index.html> (last visited 3 Feb 2004); see also, Korea Information Service, *Report: Woori Finance Holdings*, 30 Sept 2003, available on the Internet at <http://www.kisinfo.com/sangjang/html/053000_2.htm> (last visited 3 Feb 2004).

[16] See, eg, the Mindan Times, *The Best Shinhan Bank*, THE MINDAN TIMES (Korean and Japanese online daily newspaper) (No 2427) (16 Apr 2003), available on the Internet at <http://www.mindan.org/kr/newspaper/read_artcl.php?newsid=78> (last visited 29 Jan 2004).

[17] See, eg, Seung-Ho Han, *Shinhan Financial Group Launched*, CHOSUN ILBO (Korean daily newspaper) (1 Sept 2001), available at <http://www.chosun.com/w21data/html/news/200109/200109010061.html> (last visited 3 February 2004); see also, KIM, above n 8, at 18–19.

[18] See, eg, Citigroup, *Citibank Depositary Receipt Issuer*, available on the Internet at <http://www.buyside.com/archives/2003/0312/pdf/fs_c.pdf>. (last visited 3 Feb 2004).

[19] See, eg, Art 62-2 of the FHCA (2002); see also, Arts 360-2-360-23 of the KCC (2001).

TABLE 4 Shinhan Bank of Before & After Financial Holding Company Group (Unit: Trillion Won)

Year	*3Q 2003*	*2002*	*2001*
Total assets	80.6	69.7	62.0
Total deposits	49.7	45.9	42.5
Total loans	48.1	40.9	34.4
Capital stock	3.3	2.9	3.2

Source: Investor Relations of the Shinhan Financial Group, *Financial Statements*, 30 Sept 2004, *available* on the Internet *at* <http://www.shinhangroup.com/ir/04_02.html>.

and its subsidiary and the financial holding company focused primarily business on banking institutions.[20] When the Shinhan Financial Group was established, it comprised six financial institutions: Shinhan Bank, Shinhan Securities, Shinhan Capital, Shinhan Investment Trust Management, Shinhan Macquarie Financial Advisory, and *e*-Shinhan.[21] Out of all its financial institutions, Shinhan Bank is a leading company in the Shinhan Financial Group. According to Table 4, Shinhan Bank performed far better in terms of its total assets, deposits and loans after it became a financial holding company in late 2001.

As shown in Table 5, the major financial indicators of the Shinhan Financial Group, which comprise assets, deposits and capital stock increased after its establishment as a financial holding company group:

As indicated in Tables 4 and 5, the conversion into a financial holding company group benefits the financial holding company group because the

TABLE 5 Financial Indicators of Shinhan Financial Group (Unit: Trillion Won)

Year	*3Q 2003*	*4Q 2002*
Total assets	140.6	66.8
Total deposits	87.3	38.7
Total loans	97.0	45.2
Capital stock	2.0	1.5

Source: Investor Relationship of the Shinhan Financial Group, *Financial Statements (Consolidated) of Financial Status*, 30 Sept 2003, available on the Internet *at* <http://www.shinhangroup.com/kor/ir/finance_data/SFG_Cons0309_kor.xls>.

[20] The Shinhan Financial Group has three non-bank subsidiaries and one non-bank second-tier subsidiary. See, eg, KIM, above n 8, at 19–20.

[21] See, eg, Han, above n 17.

financial holding company is able to derive economic advantages from its diversified subsidiaries. Such effects are attracting other companies to convert into a financial holding company group under the FHCA.

Currently, the Shinhan Financial Group has eleven subsidiaries and one second-tier subsidiary company:[22]

Subsidiaries (11): Shinhan Bank, Chohung Bank, Goodmorning Shinhan Securities, Shinhan Card, Shinhan Capital, Shinhan BNP Paribas ITMC, Jeju Bank, *e*-Shinhan, Shinhan Macquarie Financial Advisory, SH & C Life Insurance, and Shinhan Credit Information;

Second-tier Subsidiary (1): The Shinhan Institute.

E. Dongwon Financial Holding

On 30 May 2003, the Dongwon Financial Holding became established as the third financial holding company under the FHCA in Korea.[23]

The Dongwon Financial Holding, unlike the Woori Financial Group and the Shinhan Financial Group, incorporated itself through pure private capital under provision of the 'Korea Commercial Code' (KCC) on division[24] of a company[25] and through the exchange and transfer of stocks of financial

[22] See, eg, Shinhan Financial Group, *Business Line of About Us*, available on the Internet at <http://www.shinhangroup.com/english/introduce/07_01.html> (last visited 6 Feb 2004).

[23] See, eg, Dong-Hoon Song, *Dongwon Financial Holding*, CHOSUN ILBO (Korean daily newspaper) (Jun. 4, 2003), available at <http://www.chosun.com/w21data/html/news/200306/200306040013.html> (last visited 7 Feb 2004); see also, KIM, above n 8, at 22.

[24] See, eg, Jun-Hyun Kim, *Dongwon Financial Holding Launched*, JOONGANG ILBO (Korean daily newspaper) (30 May 2003), available on the Internet at <http://news.joins.com/money/200305/30/200305301801369731500054005420.html> (last visited 9 Feb 2004); see, eg, Arts 530-2 through 530-12 of the KCC (2001). Art 530-12 of the KCC regarding 'Real Division' is one of the primary provisions of the division of company under the KCC: Section 11 of the KCC including Arts 530-2 through 530-12 shall apply *mutatis mutandis* where a company to be divided acquires the total number of shares of a company to be incorporated due to a division or a merger through division.

[25] The KCC stands for the Korea Commercial Code. The major characteristics of the KCC are as follows: (1) the KCC is a law that regulates the existence and the relationships of the enterprises that have the purpose of profit-making, is composed of five parts, such as General Provisions, Commercial Activities, Companies, Insurance, and Maritime Commerce, was enacted on 20 Jan 1962 as Act No. 1000, and entered into force on 1 Jan 1963. Furthermore, the KCC has arrived at its present form as the result of being amended eleven times, and the latest amendment was on 29 Dec 2001; (2) the companies under the KCC are divided into four categories: *Hapmyong-hwesa* (Partnership Companies), *Hapja-hwesa* (Limited Partnership Companies), *Joosik-hwesa* (Stock Companies) and *Yuhan-hwesa* (Limited Liability Companies). The general information of these four companies under the KCC are as follows:
a. A *Hapmyong-hwesa* (Partnership Company) shall be incorporated jointly by at least two members, and no member of a *Hapmyong-hwesa* may, without the consent of the other members, transfer his shares to other persons, effect any transaction which falls within the class of business carried by the company, or become a member with unlimited liability at, or a director of, another company whose business purpose is the same kind of business as the company. If no managing member is designated, each member shall represent the company, and if the assets of the company are insufficient to fully satisfy all its obligations, each member

holding company[26] and the primary focus was on the securities business.[27] The incorporation of the Dongwon Financial Holding group comprises five financial institutions and one non-finance institution: Dongwon Securities, The Dongwon Institute, Dongwon Mutual Savings, Dongwon Venture Investment, Dongwon Capital, and Dongwon Investment & Trust Management.[28] As shown in Table 6, the major financial indicators of Dongwon Securities after the Dongwon Financial Holding Group became a financial holding company have not increased compared to the figures of Dongwon Securities before the Dongwon Financial Holding Group became a financial holding company. However, because less than a year has passed since the establishment of the Dongwon Financial Holding Group as a financial holding company, fiscal year balance sheet of the Dongwon

shall be jointly and severally liable to discharge the obligations. With the consent of all of the members the company may be transformed into a *Hapja-hwesa* (Limited Partnership Company);

b. A *Hapja-hwesa* (Limited Partnership Company) shall be composed of members with limited liability and members with unlimited liability. Members with limited liability may not provide personal services or credits as a form of contributions, and every member with unlimited liability shall have the responsibility and duty to manage the affairs of the company unless otherwise provided in the articles of incorporation. A member with limited liability may, without the consent of the other members, effect a transaction that falls within the class of business carried on by the company and, with the consent of all of the members with unlimited liability, transfer shares to other persons. With the consent of all of the members the company may be transformed into a *Hapmyong-hwesa* (Partnership Company);

c. A *Joosik-hwesa* (Stock Company) shall be incorporated jointly by at least one person, and the total number of shares authorized to be issued, the par value per share, and the total number of shares to be issued at the time of incorporation shall be determined. The number of shares to be issued at the time of incorporation shall be no less than one fourth of the total number of shares authorized to be issued by the company, and the capital shall be no less than fifty million won. The par value per share shall be at least one hundred won, and shares may be transferred. A *Joosik-hwesa* shall have a general shareholders' meeting, directors and the board of directors, auditors and an audit committee. The general shareholders' meeting shall be the highest organ, and the minority shareholders (shareholders who hold no less than three hundredths of the total issued and outstanding shares) may propose certain matters as issues to be resolved at the general shareholders' meeting. Directors and the board of directors shall manage the affairs of the company; and

d. A *Yuhan-hwesa* (Limited Liability Company) shall be incorporated jointly by at least one member, the total number of members of which shall not exceed fifty, total amount of capital of which shall be at least ten million won, and the amount of each unit of contribution to which shall be no less than five thousand won and shall be equal. The liability of a member shall be limited to the amount of his contribution to the company. A member may transfer his shares pursuant to the resolution of a general members' meeting, and the company shall have one or more directors who shall represent the company.

[26] See, eg, Art 62-2 of the FHCA (2002); see also, Arts 360-2-360-23 of the KCC (2001).

[27] See, eg, Sang-Yon Lim *Dongwon Financial Holding focused on Securities* THE SEOUL FINANCE (Korean weekly newspaper) (4 Jan 2003), available on the Internet at <http://www.seoulfn.com/Newsview.asp?NC_Index=680> (last visited 28 Jan 2004); see also, KIM, above n 8, at 21.

[28] See, eg, Kim, above n 24; see also, Press Release of the Fair Trade Commission of Korea (FTC), *The Current Holding Companies of 2003* (15 Aug 2003), available on the Internet at <http://www.ftc.go.kr> (last visited 29 Jan 2004).

TABLE 6 Financial Indicators of Dongwon Securities (Unit: Trillion Won)

Year	*3Q 2003*	*1Q 2003*	*4Q 2002*
Total assets	2.6	1.6	1.5
Total liabilities	1.5	0.7	0.5
Capital stock	0.4	0.4	0.4

Source: Korea Information Service, *Report: Dongwon Financial Holding*, Mar. 31, 2003, *available* on the Internet *at* <http://www.bookook.co.kr/home/kis/html/05890_4.htm>; IR of Dongwon Securities, *Balance Sheet*, Sep. 30, 2003, *available* on the Internet *at* <http://www.choiceup.com/index.asp>.
*Year Dongwon incorporated as a financial holding company.

Financial Holding Group for the year 2004 has yet to be released. Of all these institutions comprising the Dongwon Financial Holding Group, the main financial indicators of Dongwon Securities merits examination because it is a leading company under the Dongwon Financial Holding Group:

Currently, the Dongwon Financial Holding Group has one financial subsidiary and five second-tier financial subsidiaries as follows:[29]

- Subsidiary (1): Dongwon Securities;
- Second-tier Subsidiaries (5): The Dongwon Institute, Dongwon Mutual Savings, Dongwon Venture Investment, Dongwon Capital, and Dongwon Investment & Trust Management.

F. Emerging and Potential Financial Holding Companies

1. Hana Bank

The chief executive officer (CEO) of Hana Bank announced the company's attempt to convert itself into a financial holding company group in 2005.[30] If Hana Bank becomes established as a financial holding company group in 2005 as planned, it will be one of the largest Korean financial holding company under the FHCA.[31] As shown in Table 7, the major financial indi-

[29] See, eg, Dongwon Financial Holding, *Group Companies*, available on the Internet at <http://www.dongwonfh.com/group/sub02.htm> (last visited 12 Feb 2004); see also, Press Release of the Fair Trade Commission of Korea (FTC), above n 28.

[30] See, eg, Hee-Jung Kim, *Synergy of Hana Bank*, SEOUL ECONOMIC DAILY (Korean daily newspaper) (28 Sept 2003), available at <http://economy.hankooki.com/lpage/economy/200309/e2003092817524918390.htm> (last visited 20 Nov 2003).

[31] ibid.

Table 7 Financial Indicators of Hana Bank (Unit: Trillion Won)

Year	*4Q 2003*	*4Q 2002*	*4Q 2001*
Total assets	91.8	87.6	54.4
Total deposits	68.8	67.9	43.0
Total loans	53.8	50.9	31.1

Source: Hana Bank, *Financial Highlights*, 31 Dec 2003, *available* on the Internet *at* <http://www.hanabank.com/info/ir/finance/fin_index.jsp#3>.

cators of Hana Bank demonstrate its financial stability. How it will financially function as a financial holding company remains to be seen. The main financial indicators of Hana Bank are as follows:

2 *Heon-Jae Lee's Fund*

Since the 1997 Korean financial crisis, Korea has opened its financial market to overseas investors. As a result, foreign investors have invested in the Korean domestic financial markets. As set forth in Table 8, the ratios of market shares of foreign investors are very substantial as compared with other industrialized countries: the United States of America (19 per cent), Japan (7 per cent) and Germany (4 per cent).[32] That is, the ratio of market shares of overseas investors in the Korean financial markets is almost double as compared with the other industrialized countries. Foreign investors currently have increased their market shares of Korean financial markets from 1998 to 2003 as follows:

TABLE 8 Korean Financial Markets Shares of Overseas Investors (Unit: %)

Year	*2003*	*1998*
Securities	30.7	15.0
Banks	26.7	7.0
Insurances	12.5	1.5

Source: Kwang-Ki Kim, *Private Equity Fund For Domestic Financial Markets*, *Joongang Ilbo* (Korean daily newspaper), 23 Dec 2003, *available* on the Internet *at* <http://news.joins.com/money/200312/23/200312231728200771500052005240.html>.

[32] See, eg, Hyung-Dong Kim, *Foreign Capital Versus Domestic Capital*, EDAILY (Korean news agency) (2 Jan 2004), available on the Internet at <http://search.edaily.co.kr/SearchArticle.asp> (last visited 5 Jan 2004).

Recently, in order to limit foreign investors purchasing stock in Hana Bank, and to the Woori Financial Group,[33] the Heon-Jae Lee's Fund (Fund) was launched. However, because the leader of the Fund, Heon-Jae Lee, was appointed as new Deputy Prime Minister of the Ministry of Finance and Economy and accepted the position in February 2004, the launching of Heon-Jae Lee's Fund has been temporarily stopped.[34] Most probably, Hana Bank and the Woori Financial Group will come to welcome foreign investors. The situation with the Fund, however, shows the tension existing in Korean society as to opening up the FHCs to foreign investors.

III. LEGAL BACKGROUND

A. *In General*

The FHCA has the following two main characteristics: (1) the Korean government has a strong public policy for the FHCA to prevent commerce[35] from abusively controlling banking;[36]and (2) the FHCA was enacted in order to regulate or supervise primarily the banking business of the 'bank' holding company. Such two characteristics need to be briefly reviewed because they permeated the whole FHCA.

B. *Purposes of the FHCA*

The purposes of the South Korean FHCA are to facilitate the establishment of a financial holding company system, to encourage efficient management between a financial holding company and its subsidiaries, and to improve the competitiveness of the South Korean economy.[37]

[33] See, eg, Byung-Yul Yoo *Enhancement of Korean Domestic Capital against Foreign Investors*, HANKOOK ILBO (Korean daily newspaper) (7 Dec 2003), available on the Internet at <http://news.hankooki.com/lpage/economy/200312/h2003120718345221520.htm> (last visited 21 Dec 2003).

[34] See, eg, Jong-Shik Gong, *New Deputy Prime Minister of the Ministry of Finance and Economy*, DONGA ILBO (Korean daily newspaper) (11 Feb 2004), available on the Internet at <http://www.donga.com/view_t.news?f=a_s&n=200402110402> (last visited 13 Feb 2004); See, eg, Eung-Yol Kim, *Future of Private Equity Fund Without Captain*, THE DIGITAL TIMES (Korean daily newspaper) (16 Mar 2004), available on the Internet at <http://www.dt.co.kr/content/2004031602012166618002.html> (last visited 5 Aug 2004). The same topic is found in the English version. See, eg, Chi-Dong Lee, *Woori Privatization Program Hits Snag*, THE KOREA TIMES (13 Feb 2004), available on the Internet at <http://search.hankooki.com/times/times_view.php?terms=Woori+Privatization+Program+Hits+Snag.+code%3A+kt&path=hankooki3%2Ftimes%2Flpage%2Fbiz%2F200402%2Fkt2004021318513811860.htm> (last visited 16 Feb 2004).

[35] It is so-called 'chaebol' in Korea.

[36] Korea has experienced the financial crisis since 1997 due to the abuse of 'chaebols' (ie Samsung, Hyundai, LG, etc) so called commerce in the Korean financial market.

[37] See, eg, Art 1 of the 'Financial Holding Company Act of Korea' (FHCA) (2002).

The main objective of the FHCA is not only to facilitate the establishment of a financial holding company group and to recover the South Korean banking industry from the financial crisis of late 1997, but also to promote the expansion of its financial institutions to become globally competitive.

The exchange and transfer of stock between a financial holding company and its subsidiaries under the FHCA and the 'Korean Commercial Code' (KCC) create a financial holding company group. Since the process of establishing a financial holding company group is not complex, most of the current South Korean financial holding companies establish themselves through exchange and transfer of stock under the FHCA and the KCC.[38]

When the FHCA was revised in 2002, the financial holding company and its subsidiaries were able to share customer information under one financial holding company group. Such sharing of information is another incentive to establishing a financial holding company group because the financial institutions are able to have access to customers' portfolios and sell them other financial products, such as securities, insurance and bonds.

C. *Key Legal Concepts in the FHCA*

1. *Financial Holding Company*

A financial holding company, under the FHCA, is a company that controls, or is closely related to the financial activities of the company by its ownership of that company.[39] Under the FHCA, such financial holding company can control more than one financial institution by obtaining authorization from the Financial Supervisory Commission (FSC).[40]

[38] The KCC stands for the Korea Commercial Code. The major characteristics of the KCC are as follows: (1) the KCC regulates the existence and the relationships of the enterprises that have the purpose of profit-making, composed of five parts: General Provisions, Commercial Activities, Companies, Insurance, and Maritime Commerce, enacted on 20 Jan 1962 as Act No. 1000, and entered into force on 1 Jan 1963. Furthermore, the KCC has arrived at its present form as the result of being amended eleven times, and the latest amendment was on 29 Dece 2001; (2) The companies that are the most important part under the KCC are divided into four categories: (i) *Hapmyong-hwesa* as compared with partnership companies, (ii) *Hapja-hwesa* as compared with limited partnership companies, (iii) *Joosik-hwesaa* as compared with stock companies; and (iv) *Yuhan-hwesa* as compared with limited liability companies. For more detailed information, see above n 25.

[39] See, eg, Art 2 (1) of the FHCA (2002).

[40] This legal definition of FHC under the Korean Law is broader than that under the US GLBA, as it would cover all holding company/ subsidiaries involving financial and financial-related subsidiaries (though, for practical purposes, the FHCA is concerned with 'bank holding companies'). Under the US GLBA, an FHC is, in fact, a bank holding company with special authorization and whose non-bank subsidiaries would become have broader financial-related powers than would those of a regular authorized bank holding company under the US Bank Holding Company Act (BHCA). Under the BHCA, the non-bank subsidiaries can only engage

2. *Qualifications of a Financial Holding Company*

In order to qualify as a financial holding company under the FHCA: (1) The company must hold de jure shares[41] of a secondary company;[42] (2) The company being supervised by a financial holding company must be a financial institution or a company and its business purpose and engagements must be 'closely related to financial activities.'[43] Under the FHCA, financial activities constitute financial and insurance activities as classified by the Korean Standard Industrial Classification (KSIC).[44] The term 'closely related to financial activities' describes a company that provides services such as electronic data processing (EDP) for a financial institution, manages the assets of the financial institution such as properties, studies and examines the project related to financial activities, or operates other activities directly related to inherent activities of other financial institutions;[45] (3) The financial holding company must have control over its subsidiaries by having a special relationship[46] solely with its subsidiaries and must be the largest investors of its subsidiaries;[47] and (4) The ratio of ownership of a financial holding company over its subsidiaries has to exceed that of the ownership of a person in a special relationship with a financial holding company over subsidiaries of a financial holding company.[48] Specifically,

in activities 'closely related to banking,' but, if the BHC is authorized as an FHC under the GLBA, such subsidiaries would have expanded 'financial-related' powers. Under the Korean FHCA, a BHC through its non-bank subsidiaries has always expanded 'financial-related' powers under that Act.

[41] The prescribed *de facto* means to be in effect even if not formally or legally recognized. See generally BRYAN A GARNER, *Black's Law Dictionary* 183 (2 d Pocket edn 2001). *De jure* describes to exist by right or according to law. See ibid at 190. Shares discussed also include shares in related to value of distribution to its subsidiaries: Partnership Companies or *Hapmyong-Hwesa* in Korean language, Limited Partnership Companies or *Hapja-Hwesa* in Korean language, and Limited Liability Companies or *Yuhan-Hwesa* in Korean language. Even if these three companies mentioned have stocks, their stocks are not generally listed for the public. Therefore, we may regard these three companies as companies that did not issue their stock when they were incorporated. In addition, under the 'Korea Commercial Code' (KCC), Stock Companies or *Joosik-Hwesa* in Korean language that generally list their stocks for the public is added. Totally, there are four company types under the KCC. See, eg, Art 178 through 267 of the KCC (2001) for Partnership Companies, Art 268 through 287 of the KCC (2001) for Limited Partnership Companies, Art 288 through 542 of the KCC (2001) for Stock Companies, and Articles 543 through 613 of the KCC (2001) for Limited Liability Companies. For more detailed information, see above n 25.

[42] See, eg, Art 2(1)a of the FHCA (2002).

[43] See, eg, Art 2(1)a of the FHCA (2002).

[44] See, eg, Art 2(1) of the Enforcement Decree of the FHCA (2002).

[45] See, eg, Art 2(2) of the Enforcement Decree of the FHCA (2002).

[46] See, eg, Art 11(1) of the Enforcement Decree of the 'Monopoly Regulation and Fair Trade Act' (MRFTA) (2002).

[47] See, eg, Art 2(3) of the Enforcement Decree of the FHCA (2002); see also, Art 2(3) of the MRFTA (2002).

[48] See, eg, Art 2(3) of the Enforcement Decree of the FHCA (2002). A person in a special relationship with a financial holding company is so called a specially related person. For more

the amount that a financial holding company holds or owns over its subsidiary must be more than 50 per cent of total assets of the financial holding company concerned.[49]

Finally, in order to be a financial holding company under the FHCA, an applicant of the financial holding company involved must receive the authorization from the Financial Supervisory Commission (FSC).[50] In the United States, in order to qualify as a financial holding company under the 'Gramm-Leach-Bliley Act' (GLBA),[51] applicants of a financial holding company in the United States of America must be an authorized under the BHCA and now must receive approval from the US Federal Reserve Board of Governor (FRB) to operate as an FHC.[52] In this regard, the South Korean system is similar to the US system where applicants for a financial holding company must also receive 'approval' from the banking authority: in the case of South Korea, this would be the approval of the FSC, while in the United States this would be that of the FRB.[53]

3. *Subsidiary*

Subsidiary is a company controlled by a financial holding company.[54] Even if a financial holding company does not own more than 50 per cent and owns 20–30 per cent of the total number of the issued voting stocks of its

detailed information on a specially related person, see, eg, Art 3 of the Enforcement Decree of the FHCA (2002); *see also,* Art 1–4 of the Enforcement Decree of the 'General Banking Act of Korea' (GBA) (2002).

[49] See, eg, Art 2(4) of the Enforcement Decree of the FHCA (2002). On the other hand, any of the followings triggers the 'US Bank Holding Company Act' (BHCA): (1) share ownership over than 25 per cent of any class of voting shares issued by a bank or a bank holding company; (2) ability to elect a board majority; or (3) effective control of management. *See generally* JJ Norton an SC Whitley, *Banking Law Manual* 4-23-24 (Patricia A McCoy 2nd edn 2004). *Cf* 12 USCA § 1841(a)(2) (2001).

[50] See, eg, Arts 2(1) and 3-5 of the FHCA (2002); see also, Arts 4 and 5 of the Enforcement Decree of the FHCA (2002).

[51] Prior to enactment of the Gramm–Leach–Bliley Act, bank holding companies under the Bank Holding Company Act could not operate securities business and insurance business while many European banks could operate securities business and insurance business at the same time. As a result, the US banks could not catch up with the European banks. Due to this situation, the US Congress enacted the GLBA in 1999 in order to enhance its bank competitiveness against that of the European banks. The GLBA permitted the U.S. banks to operate securities business and insurance business simultaneously. Ho1wever, if bank holding companies do not satisfy the requirements of the GLBA, bank holding companies are still subject to the Bank Holding Company Act. See, eg, Joeng-Woong Baik, *Critical Study of Sarbanes-Oxley Act*, 15 KOREA COMMERCIAL CASES L Rev 743, 758 n 59 (2003) (in Korean language).

[52] See, eg, Joseph J Norton et al, *A By-product of the Globalization Process: The Rise of Cross-Border Bank Mergers and Acquisitions—The US.Regulatory Framework*, 56(2) BUS LAW 591, 623–2 (Feb 2001).

[53] In this sense, South Korea has a mega-unitary regulatory system. See, eg, Art 3 of the FHCA (2002); see also, Art 4 of the Enforcement Decree of the FHCA (2002); see also, Art 8 of the 'Regulation on Supervision of Financial Holding Companies' (RSFHC) (2004).

[54] See, eg, Art 2(1)b of the FHCA (2002).

subsidiary under the FHCA, the financial holding company will still have control over its subsidiaries.[55]

4. *Second-Tier Subsidiary*

Subsidiaries of subsidiaries are companies controlled by the first-tier subsidiaries.[56] Generally, the subsidiary of a subsidiary is not permitted under the FHCA.[57] However, there are some exceptions to this rule, where the activities of a subsidiary are related or so related to those of its subsidiary, that second-tier subsidiaries are permitted:[58] (1) where subsidiaries are banks, the second-tier subsidiaries include credit information companies, credit card companies, investment advisory companies, trust companies, trustee companies, futures business companies and asset management companies; (2) where subsidiaries are securities companies, the second-tier subsidiaries include trustee companies, investment advisory companies, asset management companies and futures business companies; and (3) where subsidiaries are insurance companies, the second-tier subsidiaries include trustee companies and companies operating activities incidental to insurance business.[59]

5. *Wholly Owned Financial Holding Company & Wholly-Owned Subsidiary*

Where a financial holding company holds the total number of the issued voting stocks of its subsidiary, the financial holding company concerned is a wholly-owned financial holding company, and its subsidiary is also a wholly owned subsidiary over the financial holding company.[60]

In a 100 per cent ownership subsidiary, conflict of interest between a financial holding company and its subsidiaries or between bank subsidiaries and non-bank subsidiaries do not occur: in the wholly owned context, a

[55] See, eg, Art 2(1)a and 2(1)b of the FHCA (2002).

[56] See, eg, Art 2(1)c of the FHCA (2002).

[57] See, eg, Art 19 of the FHCA (2002); see also, Dong-Hoon Kim *Regulation toward and Responsibility of Financial Services Holding Companies* 20(4) KOREAN COM L REV 319, 337 (2002); see also, Moon-Jae Kim *Review of the Korean Financial Holding Company Act and Some Suggestions*, 8(1) KOREAN COMP PRIVATE L REV 789, 796–7 (June 2001).

[58] See, eg, Art 19 of the FHCA (2002). A Presidential Decree determines the range of second-tier subsidiaries. *See* Arti 15 of the Enforcement Decree of the FHCA. However, the 'Monopoly Regulation and Fair Trade Act of Korea' (MRFTA) unlike the FHCA prohibits subsidiaries from controlling second-tier subsidiaries. Cf. Art 8-2(2) of the MRFTA (2002).

[59] See, eg, Article 15(1)c of the Enforcement Decree of the FHCA (2002). Where subsidiaries are banks, the scope of second-tier subsidiaries is more extensive than any other non-bank financial institutions, such as securities companies and insurance companies.

[60] See, eg, Art 2(1)d of the FHCA (2002).

financial holding company and subsidiaries are safe and sound under 'one roof' of a financial holding company group.[61] In this regard, the current FHCA and its Enforcement Decree of the FHCA require a subsidiary (which is so called an 'intermediary financial holding company') to hold the total number of the shares issued by its subsidiary (which is so called a 'second-tier subsidiary').[62]

6. *Bank Holding Company*

Under the FHCA, a bank holding company is a financial holding company that controls the company as follows: (1) a financial institution established under the 'General Banking Act of Korea' (GBA);[63] (2) a long-term credit bank established under the Long-Term Credit Bank Act of Korea; (3) a financial institution, prescribed by a Presidential Decree, which runs the banking business under Article 2(1)a of the GBA;[64] or (4) a financial holding company that controls financial institutions referred to (1) through (3).[65]

7. *Local Bank Holding Company*

Under the FHCA, a local bank holding company is a financial holding company that controls only local banks or local bank holding companies.[66] However, Korea, as a unitary governmental system and not a federal system, does not expect the practical adoption of a local bank holding company for a financial holding company group under the FHCA.

8. *Same Person*

Same person under the FHCA means a person himself and other person in a special relationship, determined by a Presidential Decree, with the former so called a specially related person.[67] A specially related person under the

[61] See, eg, KIM, above n 7, at 56; see also, DONG-WON LEE, HOLDING COMPANY 199–202 (1998); see also, HYUN-SEOK YOON, LEGAL ASPECTS OF HOLDING COMPANY 22 (1998).

[62] See, eg, Art 7 of the FHCA (2002); see also, Art 6 of the Enforcement Decree of the FHCA (2002).

[63] A financial institution established under the General Banking Act is so called a bank. See, eg, Art 2(1)e of the FHCA (2002).

[64] However, to date, any regulation in order to enforce Art 2(1)e of the FHCA on financial institution that runs the banking business under Art 2(1)a of the GBA has not been provided in a Presidential Decree.

[65] See, eg, Art 2(1)e of the FHCA (2002).

[66] See, eg, Art 2(1)f of the FHCA (2002).

[67] See, eg, Art 2(1)g of the FHCA (2002); see also, Art 3 of the Enforcement Decree of the FHCA (2002).

FHCA and the Enforcement Decree of the FHCA is described in the Enforcement Decree of the General Banking Act of Korea.[68]

9. *Non-Financial Business Operator or Non-Financial Devotee*

Non-financial business operator or non-financial devotee was introduced into the FHCA in order to explain the separation between banking and commerce (ie non-banking industry). In general, South Korea, like many countries, has separated banking from commerce.

In cases where anyone falls under one of the following categories, he or she becomes a non-financial business operator or non-financial devotee[69] under the FHCA: The same person with respect to which the total amount

[68] See, eg, Art 3 of the Enforcement Decree of the FHCA (2002); see also, Art 1-4 of the Enforcement Decree of the 'General Banking Act' (GBA) (2002). A specially related person under the FHCA is any person who has a special relationship with a principal. Under Art 1-4 of the Enforcement Decree of the GBA, the specially related person means a person who is in the relationship falling under any of the following cases: (1) Spouse, blood relatives within a third cousinship, and relative within a cousinship: *Provided*, that the same shall not apply to an independent manager under Art 3-2(1)b of the Enforcement Decree of the 'Monopoly Regulation and Fair Trade Act of Korea' (MRFTA), and a person for whom the Fair Trade Commission (FTC) recognizes to be excluded from the scope of the same person relationship under the Articles of the same item; (2) Non-profit juristic person, association or organization in which the principal and the persons under subparagraph (1) or (4) occupy a majority of executives, or the said persons together with those under subparagraph (3) or (5) have invested not less than 50 per cent, or one of these persons is the founder; (3) A company in which the principal and the persons under subparagraphs (1), (2), and (4) own not less than 30 per cent of the gross number of the issued voting stocks, or they take part in the management as the largest shareholders; (4) Persons employed by the principal and the persons under subparagraph (2) or (3) referring to executives, in case where the employer is a juristic person, association or organization; the commercial employer, the employees under an employment contract, or the persons who maintain their livelihood by money or property of such individual, in the case of an individual; (5) A company in which the principal and the persons under subparagraphs (1) through (4) own not less than 30 per cent of the gross number of the issued voting stocks, or they take part in the management as the largest shareholders; (6) In case where the principal is a person who controls (hereinafter referred to as the 'affiliated holder') the enterprise group under Art 2b of the MRFTA (hereinafter referred to as the 'enterprise group'), a company which belongs to the enterprise group controlled by him including the foreign juristic person in which the affiliated holder corresponds to the requirement of the text of subparagraphs a and b of Art 3 of the Enforcement Decree of the MRFTA, independently or jointly with the persons who are in the relationship corresponding to any of the items of subparagraphs a and b of the same Art, and the executives of such company; (7) In case where the principal is a person in the relationship under the provisions of subparagraph (1) or (2) with the affiliated holder, or is an executive of the company belonging to the enterprise group controlled by the affiliated holder, a company which belongs to the enterprise group controlled by him and the executives of such company; (8) In case where the principal is a company belonging to the enterprise group, a company which belongs to the enterprise group identical with that of said company, and the executives of such company; and (9) Persons who jointly exercise the voting rights including such rights as entitled to direct an exercise of voting rights pursuant to an agreement or contract with the principal or the persons under subparagraphs (1) through (8).

[69] See, eg, Art 2(1)h of the FHCA (2002).

of gross capital (referring to the gross amount of assets less the gross amount of debts, on the balance sheet; hereinafter the same shall apply) of persons who are non-financial companies (referring to companies that run such non-financial businesses as determined by a Presidential Decree; hereinafter the same shall apply) is not less than 25 per cent of the total amount of gross capital of persons who are companies; The same person with respect to which the total amount of gross capital of persons who are non-financial companies is not less than such an amount as prescribed by a Presidential Decree, which is not less than two billion won; and A securities investment company under the Securities Investment Company Act (hereinafter referred to as the 'securities investment company') with respect to which a person as referred to in item orholds more than 4 per cent of the total number of the issued stocks (referring to the case that the same person owns stocks under his or another person's name or has voting rights to them through a contract; hereinafter the same shall apply).

Non-financial companies of Article 2(1)h of the FHCA are companies that do not operate financial and insurance activities determined by the Korean Standard Industrial Classification (KSIC).[70] Under the FHCA, the same person may hold shares of a bank holding company in excess of 4 per cent of the total number of the issued voting shares of the bank company in question.[71] On the other hand, non-financial business operator like industrial capital cannot hold stocks of a bank holding company in excess of 4 per cent of the total number of the issued voting stocks of the bank holding company in question in order to prevent industrial capital from controlling the Korean financial market.[72]

However, a 'securities' investment company of Article 2(1)h of the FHCA has to be readjusted into just an 'investment' company because the Securities Investment Company Act was converted into the 'Indirect Investment Assets Management Business Act of Korea' on 4 October 2003 and the Indirect Investment Management Act provided an 'investment' company of the Indirect Investment Management Act instead of a 'securities' investment company of the Securities Investment Company Act referred to the other Acts.[73] Consequently, the range of the Indirect Investment Management Act is wider than that of the Securities Investment Company Act.

[70] See, eg, Art 3-2(1) of the Enforcement Decree of the FHCA (2002).

[71] See, eg, Art 8 of the FHCA (2002).

[72] See, eg, Art 8-2 of the FHCA (2002). In fact, where a non-financial business operator exceeds the ratio of four percent of holding stocks of the total number of the issued voting stocks of the bank holding company involved, he cannot exercise voting rights to stocks held in excess. See, eg, Art 10(1) of the FHCA (2002).

[73] See, eg, Art 20(3) of the Addenda of the Indirect Investment Assets Management Business Act (Addenda No 6987, 4 Oct 2003); see also, Yoo-Sok Kim *Brief Study on the Indirect Investment Assets Management Business Act* 73 MONTHLY FUTURES MARKET 36, 38 (Nov 2003).

10. Large Shareholder

Under the FHCA, a 'large shareholder' is a definition used for only a bank holding company. Prior to its revision, the FHCA provided that a large shareholder could not hold more than 4 per cent of the total number of the issued voting shares of the bank holding company. However, when the FHCA was amended in 2002, a large shareholder could own more than 4 per cent of the total number of the issued voting shares of the bank holding company in question.[74] A large shareholder means a person falling under any of the following items: (1) One shareholder of a bank holding company in case that the same person including such shareholder holds more than 10 per cent [15 per cent (in case of a bank holding company which does not operate nationwide (hereinafter referred to as the 'local bank holding company')] of the total number of voting shares issued by the bank holding company; and (2) One shareholder of a bank holding company in case that the same person including such shareholder holds more than 4 per cent of the total number of voting shares (excluding nonvoting shares under Art 8–2(2)) issued by the bank holding company (excluding a local bank holding company) and the same person is the largest shareholder of the bank holding company or exercises a substantial influence over the major managerial matters of the bank holding company in a manner of appointing or dismissing its officers as prescribed by a Presidential Decree.

Even if the voting rights of a non-financial business operator or non-financial devotee over a bank holding company are limited within the 4 per cent restriction of the total number of the issued voting shares of the bank holding company concerned, he can also become a large shareholder over the bank holding company concerned because the nonvoting shares of the non-financial business operator or non-financial devotee of the bank holding company concerned are excluded from the total number of the issued voting shares of the bank holding company.[75]

IV. CONCLUSION

This Comment has reviewed the four current Korean financial holding companies (ie Sejong, Woori, Shinhan, and Dongwon) and the two emerging financial holding companies (ie Hana Bank and Heon-Jae Lee's Fund). In particular, under the FHCA, the three current financial holding companies (ie Woori, Shinhan, and Dongwon) have derived greater financial

[74] See, eg, Art 8 of the FHCA (2002). Art 8 of the FHCA provides a ceiling on stock holdings in which a large shareholder can hold 10 per cent, 25 per cent or 33 per cent of the bank holding company in question. Ibid.

[75] See, eg, Arts 2(1) and 8-2(2) of the FHCA (2002).

benefits compared to its previous status.[76] This forecast has been encouraging to many prospective companies hoping to transform into financial holding companies.

As noted above, the two characteristics of the current FHCA are (1) prevention of commerce's control over banking and (2) the Act's focus primarily on a 'bank' holding company. However, because of the FHCA's excessive prevention for commerce's control over banking, the ratios of the Korean financial market shares of foreign investors are very substantial as compared with other industrialized countries, such as the United States of America (19 per cent), Japan (7 per cent) and Germany (4 per cent).[77] In addition, because the current FHCA was enacted as an Act based primarily on a 'bank' holding company, several financial groups, such as Woori and Shinhan,[78] that own a 'bank' are expected to select financial holding companies as their new business organizations.

The FHCA enacted in 2000 is expected to be appropriately applied to the Korean financial market. However, the new financial holding company under the FHCA has just emerged and there has not been any decision of the Korean courts regarding the new financial holding company. Furthermore, because many of the FHCA's provisions are not clear, their exact meanings are expected to be decided by future Korean judicial proceedings.

[76] Sejong is not formed under the FHCA, but under the antitrust legal regime (ie the 'Monopoly Regulation and Fair Trade Act of Korea' (MRFTA)). For practical, operational purposes, Sejong is effectively defunct.

[77] See, eg, Kim, above n 32.

[78] As mentioned above, there are three current financial holding companies, such as Woori, Shinhan and Dongwon, in Korea. Woori and Shinhan are 'bank' holding companies while Dongwon is a 'securities' holding company.